FRENCH CULTURAL STUDIES

CRITICISM AT THE CROSSROADS

Marie-Pierre Le Hir

Dana Strand

editors

STATE UNIVERSITY OF NEW YORK PRESS

The reproduction of the cover art, *Débarcadère de Saint-Denis* is courtesy of Propriétaire-Conseil général. Archives départementales de La Réunion.

Published by
STATE UNIVERSITY OF NEW YORK PRESS, ALBANY

©2000 State University of New York

No part of this book may be used or reproduced in any manner whatsoever without written permission. No part of this book may be stored in a retrieval system or transmitted in any form or by any means including electronic, electrostatic, magnetic tape, mechanical, photocopying, recording, or otherwise without the prior permission in writing of the publisher.

For information, address
State University of New York Press,
State University Plaza, Albany, NY 12246

Production and book design, Laurie Searl
Marketing, Patrick Durocher

Library of Congress Cataloging-in-Publication Data

French cultural studies : criticism at the crossroads / edited by Marie-Pierre
  Le Hir and Dana Strand.
    p. cm.
  Includes bibliographical references and index.
  ISBN 0-7914-4585-2 (alk. paper) — ISBN 0-7914-4586-0 (pb : alk.
paper)
    1. France—Civilization—1945–. 2. France—Cultural policy—Social
aspects. 3. Culture—Study and teaching. 4. France—Relations—French
speaking countries. 5. French-speaking countries—Relations—France.
6. Civilization, Modern—French influences. I. Le Hir, Marie-Pierre.
II. Strand, Dana. III. Title.

DC33.9.F76 2000
306'.0944—dc21
                                                              99-089485

10 9 8 7 6 5 4 3 2 1

FRENCH CULTURAL STUDIES

Contents

Illustrations

Acknowledgments

The papers collected in this volume grew out of a 1995 NEH Summer Institute, "French Cultural Studies: Identities, Communities, and Cultural Practices." The editors of this volume would like to thank the National Endowment for the Humanities for its financial support of that Institute; Françoise Lionnet, Nelly Furman, and Lawrence Kritzman, its director and co-directors; the guest faculty and participants for their enthusiasm, warmth, and the quality of the intellectual exchange; and finally those among them who agreed to prolong the NEH Summer Institute experience by contributing to this volume.

We also wish to express our gratitude to the following journals and publishers for granting us permission to reprint the following essays: Lawrence D. Kritzman. "Identity Crises: France, Culture and the Idea of the Nation," *SubStance* 76/77 24, no. 1 & 2 (1995); Timothy Scheie, "Performativity, Agency, and Césaire's *A Tempest*," *College Literature* 25: 2 (Spring 1998): 17–29; Françoise Lionnet, "Reframing Baudelaire: Literary History, Biography, Postcolonial Theory, and Vernacular Language," *Diacritics* 28, no. 3 (Fall 1998); Réda Bensmaïa's "Political Geography of Literature: On Khatibi's 'Professional Traveler,'" First appeared in 1996 *La Traversée du Français dans les Signes Littéraires Marocains,* edited by Y. Bénayoun-Szmidt, H. Bourzoui, and N. Redouane, under the title "Géographie politique de la littérature: à propos de la notion de voyageur professionnel' chez Abdelkébir Khatibi." Thank you to the Editions La Source in Toronto for allowing us to print this English translation.

The editors gratefully acknowledge the support they received from their respective institutions, Case Western Reserve University and Carleton College, while completing this project. Special thanks to the Elizabeth M. and William C. Treuhaft Foundation for its continuous and generous support of the Humanities. Finally, we would like to express our deep appreciation for Mary Tatge's professional skill and unfailing equanimity, without which this volume would no doubt never have made it to the printed page.

PART I

Rethinking the Discipline

From French Studies to French Cultural Studies

INTRODUCTION

The present volume, *French Cultural Studies: Criticism at the Cross-roads* grew out of intensive discussions on the theory and practice of French cultural studies during a 1995 NEH Summer Institute at Northwestern University entitled "French Cultural Studies: Identities, Communities, Practices." Touching upon topics that ranged from the place of French cultural studies in the academy to the ethical questions raised by certain approaches or lines of inquiry within the field, our conversations were richly nuanced by the diversity of the participants' perspectives and experience. In deciding to put together a collection of essays that would reflect the provocative intellectual exchanges in which we engaged, we therefore have sought to preserve that multiplicity of perspectives, while at the same time highlighting the spirit of critical self-awareness underlying our discussions.

We realize that there are risks involved in assembling a collection of essays that spans the entire field of cultural studies in French. Diversity may easily be perceived as a lack of focus, particularly by readers used to working within narrower disciplinary constraints. The organization of the volume in two, seemingly unrelated parts, one devoted to an explicit rethinking of the discipline of French, the other to the negotiation of postcolonial identities, might create a similar impression of eclecticism. From our vantage point, however, the benefits of accepting this challenge are numerous. If we cannot, nor wish to, impose an artificial homogeneity on a disciplinary spectrum where heterogeneity is the rule, we do hope to encourage dialog among its various branches by presenting, in the same volume, contributions that would typically find their own, separate roads to publication. As for the two-pronged organization of this book, it has the merit, in our mind, of exemplifying the cultural studies approach theorized and illustrated in its pages: by illuminating the varying degrees to which various sectors of the field have responded to the cultural studies challenge, it lays bare the forces at work in it today, registering the state of the power relations that currently shape the field of French in American colleges and universities. Relating the relative interest in cultural studies displayed by the contributors to the areas of French studies they represent offers a way to verify the validity of this assertion. Contributors to Part I, those who engage most directly with the issue of French cultural studies, tend to come from the traditional sectors of the field: French language, literature, culture, and theory; contributors to Part II, those who are less inclined to address that issue directly, from the fields of gender studies, ethnic studies, Francophone, and postcolonial studies. To point to this imbalance is not merely to acknowledge that our field is structured by relations of power and prestige, that the newer, interdisciplinary fields are, currently, the dominant ones. It is also to recall that, in spite of its much-rumored decline, the field at large has never stopped making ground-breaking advances. With this volume, we hope to demonstrate that Charles Stivale is right when he claims that "French/Francophone critical models still have much to offer to CS for developing transdisciplinary and counter-disciplinary critiques" (82).[1]

As mentioned above, the first part of the volume "Rethinking the Discipline: From French Studies to French Cultural Studies" provides a theoretical framework for reconsidering the domain of knowledge and expertise traditionally associated with the discipline of French. As investigations of the relations between "French" and cultural studies, most of the essays included here deal with the theoretical and pedagogical implications of redefining "French" as an inter-, multi- disciplinary field of French cultural Studies that would identify, refine, and challenge notions that have typically informed the commonsense understanding of the discipline. It therefore seemed appropriate to begin with a reflection on the "French" in our title, or more specifically with a discussion of the concept of national identity that has given the discipline its name, a task taken up here by Lawrence D. Kritzman and Jean E. Pedersen.

One of the merits of Kritzman's essay "Identity Crisis: France, Culture, and the Idea of the Nation" is to provide an overview of arguments and assumptions that have served historically to justify the singularity of the French nation, and by extension also, to ground the discipline of French in the United States. The universalist discourse that constructs "the reified object known as *la France*," he points out, has always been achieved at the cost of erasures, the myth of national unity always implying violence, "brutality" even, as Renan already recognized but considered legitimate. For Kritzman, by contrast, overlooking that the "aesthetic of civilization is often the result of forced consent" is at the same time unethical, unscientific, and pedagogically unsound. The new French cultural studies he envisions leaves behind all approaches to culture that fail to "uncover a multiplicity of discrete and singular truths": the "Big C" Civilization courses, and the "small c" culture courses of the 1960s developed in reaction to them, of course, but also all brands of French Studies rooted in the notion of the singularity of France. No longer conceived as an object-based discipline devoted to the acquisition of "factual"—that is, mythical—knowledge, French cultural studies becomes a critical field of inquiry, an intellectual training ground for "cultural competence" open to a variety of hermeneutic approaches. Four such possible models are sketched out here: the semiotic, based on the work of cultural theorists such as Roland Barthes or Clifford Geertz; the socio-epistemic approach, represented here by Pierre Bourdieu; the memorialist approach practiced by Pierre Nora; and the ethno-cultural approach characteristic of postcolonial studies— illustrated here by Tahar Ben Jelloun. Although comparative studies are granted a central role in Kritzman's version of French cultural studies his definition corresponds overall to the one proposed by Simon During in his *Cultural Studies Reader* whereby "French" is no longer a term referring to an object (France), but rather to the national origin of the theorical approaches it draws from.

Originally published in *Substance* in 1995, Kritzman's contribution is also interesting to read as a document on the recent history of the field, and more specifically as a reminder of the often hostile, Francophobe academic environment in which the French cultural studies project was launched. In a more subtle way, his essay betrays the sense of threat, or challenge, the new field of Anglo-American cultural studies represented for French studies at the time. If this academic context helps explain how cultural studies may have been overlooked as a possible model for French cultural studies, Jean E. Pedersen's article, "Nana and the Nation: French Cultural Studies and Interdisciplinary

Work," represents a first attempt, in this volume, to situate French cultural studies in relation to cultural studies. Singling out interdisciplinarity as the most widely accepted characteristic of cultural studies projects, Pedersen begins by discussing the limitations (and the artificial character) of a disciplinary division of knowledge that typically pits historians and literary critics against each other—"each claiming privileged access to the creation and analysis of their own and other people's stories." Centered on the examination of a highly canonical text, Emile Zola's *Nana*, in relation to its many interpretative contexts, her essay exemplifies Cary Nelson's contention that if "cultural studies does not mean that we have to abandon the study of what have been historically identified as the domains of high culture . . . it does challenge us to study them in radically new ways" (279). Foremost among them here, is the relational approach adopted in this study of the novel's "production, reception, and varied uses" (Nelson, 280), from its origin as a popular, commercial product in the nineteenth century, to, among other things, the key role it has come to play for "scholars of gender, sexuality, and private life." Pedersen, who is keenly aware of the gendered nature of the critical "uses" made of *Nana*—the focus on the private (women, sexuality, gender) functioning as an exclusion of the public (war, politics, the nation)—sets out to overcome this dichotomy, reading the novel both as a tale of sexual politics, imperial decadence, and military defeat, and as an allegory of the nation, or more specifically, of "the dying France of the second Empire." In that respect, her essay provides a sophisticated and solidly documented analysis of particular ways in which "France" has been constructed, and thereby also, a concrete illustration of some of the points made in the preceding article.

If not all of the contributors to this volume agree with Cary Nelson that "people who comment on or claim to be 'doing' cultural studies ought at least to familiarize themselves with the British cultural studies tradition" (273), Ross Chambers certainly does. In his early critical forays into the relation between French and cultural studies, he has tended, for that very reason, to question the willingness and the ability of French studies—particularly, as he puts it here, of its "literary and civilizational wings"—to take cultural studies seriously.[2] This mistrust resurfaces in this essay in the perhaps unexpected choice of language pedagogy as the potentially most fertile ground for French cultural studies. The conviction that French is, and has always been, a language-based discipline makes him consider reconceptualizing the "language-culture nexus" as one of French cultural studies' most pressing tasks.

Numerous difficulties stand in the way of such a project, however, as much on the "French" side (the implicit understanding of culture as unproblematic "background material" that typically informs foreign language pedagogy), as on the cultural studies side (an obvious lack of interest in the relation between culture and language). Against the convenient, but, for Chambers, erroneous notion that to "one" language corresponds "one" culture, against the reductive assumptions on which this notion is based—the "unity" of national cultures and the model of the ideal native speaker—Chambers proposes his own theory of the "language-culture nexus." At its core is the recognition of the primacy of language use, and therefore also of the "indissoluble solidarity between language and cultural circumstances." By redefining the language-culture nexus in terms of relations between language use and local, sociocultural contexts, Chambers seeks to ensure its resistance to generalizations, its ability to take differences of all kinds into account. Thus conceived as a pragmatics of language use, his "language-culture nexus" provides the ground on which to develop a new foreign language pedagogy geared toward pragmatic proficiency. Such a project, he concludes, might conceivably position French studies at the forefront of new and important developments in cultural studies.

Alawa Toumi's "Creolized North Africa: What Do They Really Speak in the Maghreb" exemplifies the relevance of Chambers's preoccupation with the "language-culture nexus": not only does Toumi's essay vividly illustrates the impossibility of maintaining the myth of a one-to-one correspondence between a language and a "national culture," it also provides a political perspective on this issue by highlighting how high the stakes can be of maintaining that artificial unity. In today's Algeria, Toumi reminds us, which language one speaks or writes is not a trivial issue, but often a matter of life and death. While Chambers indirectly demonstrates that the notion of linguistic and cultural homogeneity is hardly sustainable in a country such as France, in spite of centuries of efforts to impose it, Toumi shows that it is even more so in a region with a short history of nationalism and a long tradition of colonization—long at least from the Berber perspective adopted here. Against the all-too-common vision of a unified Algerian people speaking Arabic,[3] or even of an Algeria linguistically polarized between Francophones and Arabophones, Toumi characterizes the linguistic situation of the Maghreb as one of diglossia, "the co-existence within the same geographic region of a wide variety of linguistic practices." Ironically, he points out, the languages that are usually overlooked are the vernaculars, *Farabé* (or creole Arabic) and Berber, "the two spoken languages of Algerians, Moroccans and Tunisians." In addition to its overall informative value, Toumi's article provides a useful introduction to the dilemmas of Maghrebian writers—as described in more length by Réda Bensmaïa in Part Two—and to the distinction between "rai" and "rap" made by Mireille Rosello in the next essay.

"Rap Music and French Cultural Studies: For an Ethics of the Ephemeral" is arguably the most distinct representative of cultural studies in this volume. Rosello's contribution centers on the project of inventing an "ethics of the ephemeral"—which is not to be confused with an ephemeral ethics. Her conception of French cultural studies is that of the "strange attractor," a model that may, in practice, take different forms (course design, research unit, etc.), but that ideally involves a rethinking of "how time should be theorized as part of our conception of knowledge and culture." In this essay, rap music serves as this strange attractor, the catalyst for a reconsideration of the traditional organization of knowledge, and the instigator of all sorts of disciplinary transgressions, from "illicit" intertextual readings (Rap/ Rimbaud/medieval poetry) that challenge established historical and generic boundaries, to investigations in an unchartered, cross-disciplinary territory that spans music, literature, law, politics, current events, and everyday life in contemporary France and beyond. Rosello's focus on rap is unlikely to be the result of a coincidence, since contemporary popular music was one of the targets of Sandy Petrey's critique of French cultural studies.[4] In what looks like a response to Petrey, Rosello demonstrates that the preoccupation with ephemeral cultural artifacts need not lead to intellectual bankruptcy, but rather to the discovery of new knowledge. As for the pedagogical implications of her project, there is no compelling reason to dismiss it as the basis for the development of serious undergraduate courses. At a time when research institutions are under fire for allegedly neglecting the "research component" in undergraduate education,[5] Rosello's model could very well be emulated for that very purpose.

Part I of the volume concludes with two essays that may appear more critical of cultural studies insofar as they point to some of its theoretical weaknesses, but that we would see as exemplifying the type of contributions French theory can make to Cultural Studies. In her essay, "In Search of a Postmodern Ethics of Knowledge: The Cultural Critic's Dilemma," Michèle Druon adopts a philosophical—Derridean— approach to describe the dilemma of contemporary cultural criticism in general, and of cultural studies in particular. Caught in a postmodern aporia that is at once epistemological—since it raises the issue of the legitimacy of any group to speak about others—and ethical—given cultural critics' tendency to view speaking for others on moral and political grounds as legitimate—cultural criticism oscillates between two corresponding "cognitive postures," she argues: that of the impartial, disinterested observer who speaks about the Other; and that of the interested partial participant who speaks for the Other. Druon devotes precious little time to the first—the theoretical credentials associated with that posture have lost their currency value in the postmodern age. But it ironically reappears in the second, when ethico-political reasons are advanced to legitimatize a politics of representation that comes loaded with its own epistemological premises—the "de-neutralization" of knowledge, the critic's ideological situatedness—but also corresponds to a "democratic" model of representational justice ("equality in representation"). The paradox is of course that an egalitarian ethics implies impartiality, a disinterested standpoint that cannot be reconciled with "the situatedness of all cognitive positions postulated by the postmodern perspective." Druon illustrates her argument through a reading of representative essays in cultural studies—Lata Mani's article on the practice of *sati* [widow burning] in India and Douglas Crimp's essay on representations of PWA [people with AIDS], thereby pointing to cultural studies' inability to escape the postmodern aporias.

While Druon and Marie-Pierre Le Hir, in "The 'Popular' in Cultural Studies," raise essentially the same epistemological and ethical questions,[6] their responses vary a great deal. Druon accepts deconstruction's philosophical pessimism—aporias cannot be resolved, the impossible "figure of impartiality . . . can only exist as a shadow of itself, nostalgically, or as the ghost of an impossible neutrality." Le Hir, adopting Pierre Bourdieu's more optimistic mode of thinking, ascribes the deconstructive posture to the cultural critic's reluctance to subject her practice to her own deconstructive test, and discusses the difference self-reflexivity can make in solving the cultural critic's dilemma. For Le Hir, cultural studies and Bourdieu share common, epistemological, political, and ethical goals and what sets them apart from other theories of "culture" is their insistence on the necessity to account for and understand "the popular" for cultural studies, "practice" for Bourdieu. For cultural studies is not "about" popular culture, as is often assumed. The concept of "the popular" does play a significant role in cultural studies, Le Hir argues, but as a term of reference to the realm of "lived experience," of "practice"—as opposed to that of reified, commodified culture (cultural studies), or objectified knowledge (Bourdieu). But if both agree that disciplinary approaches "reify the popular" (cultural studies), or distort practice by submitting it to the process of objectification (Bourdieu), they disagree on how to revolve that problem. From a cultural studies perspective disciplines are the problem and their nega- tive effects can be avoided by adopting anti-, counter-, inter- disciplin- ary practices. This is an insufficient remedy for Bourdieu, who points out that these practices too are the product of the academic universe, a world that radically differs from the world of practice. A general economy of sociocultural practices has to account for the realm of lived experience, but the way to develop it is not to abandon objectivist approaches entirely—since the subjectivist alternative is just as danger- ous[7]—but rather, to overcome this antinomy. Concretely, this means accepting both—Kritzman's (objectivist) model of "cultural competence" and Chambers's (subjectivist) model of "pragmatic proficiency"—while taking into account the fact that these models are the products of the scholarly point of view. Self-reflexivity thus conceived and practiced offers the advantage of making it easier to distinguish between prob- lems that are truly epistemological in nature and those that are primarily driven by the logic of the academic field. If it is obvious that the interest of the discipline of French in cultural studies must be ascribed to a number of forces at work in the American academic field (and that we don't need Bourdieu to see that), an exclusive focus on "obvious" issues can also be detrimental to the resolution of more important ones. Is it legitimate or illegitimate for French to appropriate cultural studies? Does Bourdieu truly represent the French cultural‧ studies tradition? With hindsight such issues appear rather futile. What matters in the end are the concrete contributions the field of French cultural studies will make (or fail to make) to the advancement of knowledge.

Notes

1. Stivale's article is published in a special issue of *Contemporary French Civilization,* "Cultural Studies/Culture Wars" which very much deserves to be read along with the work presented in the first part of this book.

2. See Chambers, "Cultural Studies as a Challenge to French Studies."

3. An example will suffice to illustrate how prevalent this stereotype is, not only in France, but in the United States as well. In a well-intentioned article devoted to Tahar Ben Jelloun's efforts to explain racism to children ("The Mystery of Racism: A Tale for the Young"), *New York Times* journalist Marlise Simons describes the growing racial mix of French schools in the following way: "More than ever before, schools that were used to mostly white, Christian students now have children of legal and clandestine immigrants—*Arabic-speak- ing Muslims from Morocco, Algeria and Tunisia, and French-speaking blacks from France's former West African colonies*" (4) (My italics).

4. Petrey's critique is aimed at a very watered-down version of "cultural studies"—which simply consists in using "a video cassette demonstrating the multicultural credentials of the French language and those who sing it, King Daddy Yod, Bashung, and au P'tit Bonheur, among others" (386) to encourage students to learn French. This type of critique is slippery: on the one hand, one can only agree with Petrey (this is not CS, the whole concept is naive), but on the other hand, agreeing with the critique normally entails accepting the insignificance thereby conferred on popular music and therefore also its exclusion from significant scholarship—a notion Rosello rightly contests.

5. We're referring here to the Boyer Commission on Educating Undergraduates in the Research University. The report it produced a few years ago is entitled *Reinventing Undergraduate Education: A Blueprint for America's Research Universities*. No publication place or date are indicated.

6. For Druon: "If knowledge is relative to 'local' conceptual frameworks, how is it possible to step 'outside' these frameworks to make any kind of legitimate epistemological assertion?"; for Le Hir: "How it is possible to reconcile the project of understanding subjective, lived experience from an academic standpoint that cannot but construct the world as object?"

7. For a critique of both models, see *Theory of Practice* and *Language and Symbolic Power*.

Works Cited

Bourdieu, Pierre. *Language and Symbolic Power*. Harvard, Harvard UP, 1991.

————. *The Logic of Practice*. Stanford: Stanford UP, 1990.

Chambers, Ross. "Cultural Studies as a Challenge to French Studies." *Australian Journal of French Studies* 33, 2 (1996): 137–156.

During, Simon. "Introduction." *The Cultural Studies Reader*. Ed. Simon During. London: Routledge, 1993.

Nelson, Cary. "Always already cultural studies: academic conferences and a manifesto." *What is Cultural Studies?* Ed. John Storey. London, New York, Sidney: Arnold, 1997, 273–286.

Petrey, Sandy. "French Studies/Cultural Studies: Reciprocal Invigoration or Mutual Destruction?" *French Review* 68, 3 (1995): 381–392.

Pfister, Joel. "The Americanization of Cultural Studies." *What Is Cultural Studies?* Ed. John Storey. London, New York, Sidney: Arnold, 1997, 287–299.

Simons, Marlise. "The Mystery of Racism as a Tale for the Young." *The New York Times,* July 27, 1998: A4.

Schehr, Lawrence, and Jean-Francois Fourny. "Introduction." *Contemporary French Civilization* 21, 2 [Special issue "Cultural Studies, Culture Wars"] (Summer/Fall 1997): 1–4.

Stivale, Charles J. "On Cultural Lessons." *Contemporary French Civilization* 21, 2 [Special issue "Cultural Studies, Culture Wars"] (Summer/Fall 1997): 65–86.

1

Identity Crises

France, Culture, and the Idea of the Nation

Lawrence D. Kritzman

*An American who comes to understand France is so profoundly stirred
that he finds himself forced to stay there always.*

—Paul Morand

*If a little day-dreaming is dangerous, the cure for it is not to dream less
but to dream more, to dream all the time.*

—Marcel Proust

THE IDEA OF THE NATION

Much has changed in France over the last twenty years. We hear
amongst those lugubrious Gallic harbingers of doom that France is
undergoing an identity crisis that is symptomatic of a feeling of decline.
The French are experiencing what Stanley Hoffmann has termed "a
new disillusionment resulting from a series of blows to French pride
and hopes in our own time."[1] But this is only a recent phenomenon
in the postwar period, perhaps a delayed but final act of mourning for
the loss of the last great architect of the French nation-state, Charles de
Gaulle. The defeated nation of World War II had emerged in the
postwar period, thanks to the Gaullist politics of the 1960s, as a major

11

industrial power that once again played an important—albeit sometimes mythical—role on the international scene. To a certain extent, de
Gaulle's masterful statesmanship helped reinforce the image that France
was still a great power, one whose cultural mission and idea of "the
nation" was associated with a universalism based on the exigencies of
centralized power and the transmission of an imperative with which all
were meant to identify. De Gaulle's vision that French nationhood
represents universal values was certainly not a new phenomenon. Already in Ernst Robert Curtius's 1932 *Essai sur la France*, the author
opposes the French concept of the nation to that of Germany, and
thereby establishes France's paradoxical particularity amongst the nations of the world:

> If we compare the development of France and Germany we see that
> in Germany the idea of nationality and the idea of the universal are
> constantly opposed to each other, whereas in France they are con-
> stantly united (27–28).[2]

More recently, in his 1987 polemic against what he calls *"la défaite de
la pensée,"* Alain Finkielkraut takes up Curtius' s proclamation and
makes a useful distinction between the national community as the
product of a nodal contract, versus one that functions as the sociological expression of a preexisting *Volksgeist*. According to Finkielkraut, the
French Enlightenment's privileging of human freedom is revealed in the
very idea of a social contract, with its vision of a community created
by the prior, rational consent of its future citizens.

France's difference from other European powers (such as Germany) thus derives from the tradition of thought that produced the
Declaration of the Rights of Man. For if the great line of demarcation
for French cultural identity is the divide between monarchical and
republican France, it is because, as Marcel Gauchet suggests, the "one
and invisible will" of the absolute monarch was replaced by the absolute will associated with national sovereignty.[3] The distinctly French
concept of *fraternité* was used to ensure the creation of the universal
in terms of cultural and political issues; it established France's place in
the community of nations as a country capable of realizing the legitimate representation of the "general will." Endowed with a mission
similar to that of ancient Rome, France's role was, as Curtius suggests,
to affirm everywhere the essential traits of its national tradition as one
based on the desire for assimilation:

> All the claims for universalism were transferred to the national idea,
> and it is in serving its national idea that France claims to achieve

a universal value. In the course of its historical formation we see it engender a new universalism whose ambitions are pitted against those of other powers. In annexing the ideas of universality potentially contained in the Roman heritage, the French nation annexed the Roman idea itself; and in so doing it carried over in its own name the totality of the claims of Rome (28–29).

The traditions associated with the French Revolution put their stamp on the concept of the nation, which created a civic religion joining freedom with equality, as they were to be lived in an ideal community of citizens. What Etienne Balibar has termed in another context "the proposition of equaliberty" sees man as citizen defending his common interests as the constituting force of this shared universality (47).

The "truth" contained in the text of the *Déclaration* of 1789 opens the right to politics to humankind, producing the illusion of universalism.[4] With this concept came a series of assumptions associated with such Enlightenment values as progress, rationalism, justice, and tolerance. Later, a number of theoretical meditations were added to this, such as Ernest Renan's "What is a Nation?" (1882) in which the author describes in quasi-religious terms how universality is transformed into a kind of national superiority. In Renan's discourse, France is represented as having founded "nationhood," having invented it with the French Revolution; all other models of the nation are described as mere imitations, and somewhat inferior. He writes:

> France can claim the glory for having, through the French Revolution, proclaimed that a nation exists of itself. We should not be displeased if others imitate us in this. It was we who founded the principle of nationality. (12)

French culture was thus seen as the mediator of the values of the nation and the French language, as Gustave Lanson put it during the prime of the Third Republic, would be "the language of culture, the language that can liberate the civilized man of today" (203).

The teaching of French in the United States (by this I mean literature, language, and culture) from the end of the nineteenth century to the mid-1970s was dominated by *une certaine idée de la France*, and the impact of its culture. The study of French was not just that of its national literature in an American setting; it was based on the Platonic ideal of a cultural model whose universal imperative was derived from a discrete chauvinism, disguised as a form of public virtue. Thus, the teaching of French culture was based on a highly aestheticized model of the nation, one that balanced heart and intellect, particular and universal, and seemed to emanate from a kind of instinctive conscience.

Today we find ourselves in a predicament that requires a pedagogical rethinking of the teaching of French culture. We have finally recognized (in this our own *fin de siècle*) how models such as Renan's were constructed in the image of a harmonious equilibrium for which Renan and *la France* have composed the "text" and established an idealized history by ignoring "dissonance" and forgetting violence. Renan writes:

> Forgetting—I would even go so far as to say historical error—is a crucial factor in the creation of a nation. The essence of a nation is that all individuals have many things in common, and also that they have forgotten many things. No French citizen knows whether he is a Burgundian, an Alan, a Taifale, or a Visigoth, yet every French citizen has to have forgotten the massacre of Saint Bartholomew, or the massacres that took place in the Midi in the thirteenth century. (11)

For Renan, the conflicts and struggles associated with the founding of the nation became invisible in the seamless rhetoric of the accomplished, reified object known as *la France*. In our own times, both in France and here at home we have witnessed, to a certain extent, the undoing of the nineteenth-century idea of the nation: for the past decade, it has been undercut throughout Europe by phenomena as diverse as the creation of the European community, the growth of a transnational global economy, and the influx of immigrants from former colonies who have failed to assimilate easily, paradoxically engendering new forms of xenophobic nationalism. Particularly because of the latter situation, we have finally come to realize that the irrational and the violent cannot be forgotten, and indeed must be taken seriously into account. In studying culture and the idea of the nation we must recognize that the aesthetic of civilization is often the result of forced consent, and that the "national contract" has an unpleasant side that forces an insidious means of cohesion on the nation. As Renan put it, "unity is always effected by means of brutality"(11). The questions are indeed now obvious: how do we displace the orthodoxy of the universal in order to uncover a multiplicity of discrete and singular truths? Can we still adhere to the concept of "equaliberty" within the parameters of a disunified totality? How do the conflicts amongst the various networks of power, and the dynamics of multiculturalism undo the quintessentially French ideal of the nation and affect the transmission of French culture? Let us now reflect briefly on the history of what we today term the study of culture within the discipline of French in the American university.

handwritten margin note: globalization lessens image of 'high cultural' France

FRENCH STUDIES IN THE UNITED STATES

In the 1920s, when French became a major discipline in leading American universities, culture was linked to the study of this foreign culture in particular. The study of French was regarded primarily as *belles lettres* or fine arts (high culture). Dartmouth College, for example, was somewhat in the avant-garde in this respect; the 1876 Dartmouth catalogue reveals that the study of French began in the sophomore year with Knapp's *Grammar* and a text entitled *La France littéraire*. Nevertheless, from the 1920s on the study of French had a special function in the American university. First, because it signified a certain elitism due to its supposed cosmopolitanism and to the elegance of its culture (this being a mark of distinction, upward mobility, or the habitus of culture—as Pierre Bourdieu might describe it), and second, because of this very association, it was widely regarded as superior to the other European languages. To be sure, the study of French was then, as it still is today in many universities, founded on the assumption that high culture and literary studies are interrelated. Beyond that, teaching French meant introducing students to the *belle lettriste* context of literature and deducing from the study of those texts a somewhat instrumentalist ethic that identified its theoretical humanism with the cultural patrimony. The study of French was thought to represent something beyond itself, for engaging in it meant glowing with the torch of civilization.

In the postwar years, the function of the French department in the American university became somewhat ambiguous. On the one hand, its role was to represent the "target culture" in a nondomestic context so that its "consumers" or students could become part of an "imaginary aristocracy." The study of French was first a mark of class status (the unfortunate syndrome of associating French with finishing school); later it became a sign of intellectual difference. Here one can think of the prestige associated with figures such as Sartre and Camus, Beauvoir, Barthes, and Lévi-Strauss, and, since the 1970s, the more "boutique"-oriented theories such as deconstruction, Lacanian psychoanalysis, and feminism. On the one hand, the role of the French department became far more pragmatic after World War II, when the American university became democratized through the GI Bill, and emphasis shifted away from *les grandes étapes de la civilisation française* to the more mundane practices of language acquisition.

In the 1960s, much of the approach to foreign language teaching was based on sociological and anthropological models that studied people's daily lives and value systems, as a way of displacing the contextual historicism that dominated conceptions of the nation as a cultural force. (Here I am thinking of the work of Jean Carduner, Michel Benamou, and Jacques Ehrmann). Some of this work was quite important, since it helped us to see that there were indeed many languages within a particular "target culture." This study of daily life authenticated a social tradition based on the "real" experiences of a so-called collective body, functioning in the name of the nation. Yet the idea of living the locality of culture was more mythological than ideological. Accordingly, the complex strategy of cultural identification was seen as an attempt to conflate meaning and community in a totalized whole, secured through the undisputed authority of a projected, sublime Ideal.

This intuitive approach to the study of French culture was not welcomed by the more parochial traditionalists. But sometimes their critiques of the more vulgarized versions of this method were highly justified, since the latter often degenerated into "wine and cheese"—*son et lumière*, preparing crêpes, or the more archaic practices of learning to buy a telephone *jeton* or how to use a *pissoir*. In reaction to this anecdotal study of French culture, which overemphasized individual freedom and autonomy, there developed another approach based on factual knowledge (the kind of historical and geographical information found in the green *Guide Michelin* or the patterns of behavior reduced to sometimes meaningless formulations in the omnipresent *Guide de France*). Often these courses squeezed into a single semester selective information about history from the Middle Ages to the twentieth century, French art (cathedrals and slide shows), and a smattering of sociological data. In fact, the troubling presupposition underlying this kind of curriculum was that integration would somehow become automatic, the result of some magical thinking. This kind of course was conceived mostly as a passive activity that degenerated into transforming the target culture into a series of "facts" and cultural stereotypes.

The first person to really challenge these approaches in a serious way was Lawrence Wylie of Harvard. He developed what could be termed a comparative, intuitive approach to teaching French culture based on a secularized anthropological model that displaced the sclerotic demands of purified historicism. Wylie asked questions such as: how do French and Americans differ in their conception of the past and their physical environment? How do these differences explain certain differences in the behavior of the French nation? Wylie helped develop French cultural studies in a significant manner by moving it away from cultural stereotypes, to more clearly measured generalizations. In his own department at Harvard, where the study of *belles lettres* was still the order of the day, Wylie was forced to pursue his unconventional

approach in exile, in the general education program of social sciences
at that university. But, however innovative Wylie was in his approach,
he nevertheless focused his attention on the *singularity* of France—a
national characteristic that has since been addressed by Fernand Braudel,
Theodore Zeldin, and Eugen Weber, to name but a few.[5] Without a
doubt this method had its implicit dangers: for the nation to be itself,
it has to be culturally *singular.* The imperative to create the object
known as *la France* meant that exogenous elements had to be isolated
and perhaps even obliterated from view.

Yet, in most French departments throughout the 1970s and beyond,
the stereotypical approach to the teaching of French culture still dominated. It tended to be anecdotal, by presenting everyday life situations—often dehistoricized—through the study of current events found
in magazines, newspapers, and, more recently, video clips. Students
reified already existing clichés, and the result was disastrous. In many
French departments, the weaker students were attracted to this brand
of cultural studies, so often lacking in analytic rigor.

How could and should we begin to remedy this? How can we get
beyond the old civilization studies derived from the ideology of (or
perhaps the nostalgia for) the civilizing mission of the nation, and the
more mundane "wine and cheese" approach? To transcend the universal and uncritical (albeit empirical) approaches, we need to emphasize
the students' ability to explain and understand cultural information and
patterns—beyond nineteenth-century French nationalism and the belief
that there existed a seamless consubstantiality between national unity
and the unity of culture. This form of thinking was not only essentialist
in tone; it was based on a conception of national character derived
from the republican tyranny of conformity. Our students need to gain
cultural competence—the ability to comprehend cultural patterns in
terms of their multiple meanings, their syntax and their interrelation-
ships within a global context. We need to train our students to read the
signs of culture in its many manifestations, so that they can account for
the strangeness and the perceived incoherence they may encounter in
certain cultural representations (French or other). At the very least, the
interpretation of culture must be practiced by those who are cognizant
of the cultural field and have assimilated it so that they can bring it into
contact with various models of intelligibility. In our attempt to engage
in cultural hermeneutics concerning the identity of France, can't we get
beyond our overdetermined ideology of what France *should* be and
what Gérard Noiriel has termed "the [French] construction of the 'sense
of belonging'"? (320).

The professor of French should prepare students to become more culturally competent by drawing on various analytic models and critical conceptions that focus on the following hypothetical areas: 1. *the semiotic*; 2. *the socio-epistemic* (the examination of social fields and the problematics of power); 3. *the memorialist* (the relationship between history and memory); and 4. *the ethno-cultural*. What I am urging, at the very least, is the creation within French departments of an undergraduate course such as "Approaches to the Study of French and Francophone Cultures," which would be methodological, and would make students more attentive to how and why they read the signs of culture.

The Semiotic

As analysts of culture, we must be trained and we must train our students to decode what Clifford Geertz calls "catalogued expressions of social experience." These are essentially our constructions of other people's constructions of what they believe they are doing. Cultural analysis in a semiotic vein is the sorting out of structures of signification—how meaning is made within a particular social context. As Philip Schlesinger has suggested, "national cultures are not simple repositories of shared symbols to which the entire population stands in identical relation" (260–261).[6]

Let us therefore begin with the hypothesis that culture is a socially symbolic activity with forces and purposes of its own. It is played out over definitions of symbolic value. For cultural theorists such as Clifford Geertz and Roland Barthes, culture must be viewed as a public phenomenon because the production of meaning is observed from that perspective. As Geertz puts it in *The Interpretation of Cultures*:

> Man is an animal suspended in webs of significance he himself has spun. I take culture to be those webs, and the analysis of it to be therefore not an experimental science in search of law but an interpretative one in search of meaning (5).

Following this line of thought, our students must become more attentive to the flow of behavior within French culture; they must learn how to specify how cultural forms find articulation in a heterogeneous social space. In examining the representational modes that constitute the substance of culture, we should become more aware, as Barthes suggests in *Mythologies* (1957), of how the generation and reification of a particular world view is far from innocent, and how contemporary mass culture presents homogenized bourgeois values as natural and universal.

The Socio-Epistemic

Highly different from the Anglo-American school of cultural studies (Hogarth, E. P. Thompson, Stuart Mill) based on empirical data and the phenomenological experience of subordinate groups, "the socio-epistemic" enables students to gain cultural competence by teaching them to decode the signs of culture and the symbolic capital they incarnate as mediators of power. To do this, we must start with the premise that all social systems owe their existence to relations of power, and that they embody the inclination of various sectors of society to dominate and exclude other sectors. If the idea of the modern nation seeks to represent itself according to certain aspects of Enlightenment thought, one must never forget that its universal ideal necessitates the exclusion of any excess (the nonhomogeneous) so that the autonomy of the universal may be affirmed. Accordingly, the sovereignty of political rationality sustains the status of those who are included, to the detriment of those who are destined to remain on the fringes of the social order.

For example, in drawing upon some of the theoretical material articulated by Pierre Bourdieu in *La misère du monde* (1993), one may examine how the issue of domination is inextricably linked to that of cultural power and legitimacy. Here we may wish to have our students see how symbolic capital functions within French society and acts as a mark of distinction. The act of making distinctions and the cultural competence acquired by the student in elucidating this process enables him or her to see how dominant sections of society reinforce institutionalized fields of power. As Homi Bhabha has observed in *The Location of Culture*, if we start with the premise that culture is not a holistic entity, it is because the modern French nation can no longer be observed from the perspective of a "horizontal gaze" that overdetermines the existence of an undifferentiated social conglomeration. Instead of conceiving of French culture in the Hegelian tradition, as a monolithic entity of synthesized contradictions, we must regard it as an ongoing series of agonistic relationships founded on the competition for symbolic values—symptomatic of the war over competing cultural entities.

The Memorialist

Perhaps more than anyone else, Pierre Nora has directed our attention to the identity crisis France is currently undergoing in terms of the traditional idea of the nation and its relationship to the past. In his

monumental seven-volume *Les Lieux de mémoire* (1984–1992), Nora and
his 130 colleagues, drawing on the epistemological models put forth by
Maurice Halbwachs and Frances Yates, seek to locate the "memory
places" of French identity that have been elaborated since the Middle
Ages.[7] Starting with the classical rhetorical assumption that the art of
memory functions as an inventory of *loci memoriae*, Nora represents the
concept of the *locus* in a rather broad perspective. He extends it to
specific geographical places (Vézelay and Paris), monuments and build-
ings (Versailles, the cathedral of Strasbourg, the Eiffel Tower), historical
figures (Charlemagne, Jeanne d'Arc), national institutions (the educational system), literary and artistic objects (Proust's *Remembrance of
Things Past*), rituals (the coronation of the kings at Reims), emblems,
commemorations, and symbols (the French flag, "La Marseillaise," the
Republican calendar) and ideas signifying Frenchness (conversation,
gallantry, gastronomy), all of which are the result of an imaginary process that codifies and condenses a national consciousness of the past.

According to Nora, modern French history derived from the tradition of Comtean positivism, of definable causes and effects—and the
idea that the progressive movement of time produces positive knowledge—is no longer possible. Furthermore, adherence to the belief that
an organic relationship exists between internalized national values and
the places of their external commemoration has been relegated to a
distant past. The already somewhat anachronistic idea of the European
union has pushed national sentiment to the fore, but this time expressing itself as a form of cultural melancholia. "It is no longer genesis that
we seek," Nora suggests, "but, rather, the deciphering of who we are
in light of who we are no longer" (I, xxxii). As a postmodern historian
of sorts, Nora is keenly aware of the discontinuities that exist today
between the present and the past. Memory has been dislocated; in the
places where historical continuity with national identity might once
have existed, memory's very embodiment is problematic. If, as Nora
claims, there are no longer any spontaneous memories, it is because
memory can now only be evoked artificially, through the rituals of a
society without memory. In recognizing that the ties with the past have
been broken, Nora affirms that history can no longer be a simple
mnemonic reconstruction. "One looks for *lieux de mémoire*, sites of
memory," claims Nora, because "there are no longer *milieux* of memory,
real environments of memory" (I, xxv). Actually, the idea of nationhood
is engendered by a nostalgic reflection, articulated through the disjunc-
tive remembrance of things past. The quest for memory is therefore an
attempt to master the perceived loss of one's history.

What are the pedagogical implications of this outlook? In more
classical historical analyses, the student's attention was focused on the
continuity of traditions and on the absolute relationship between past
and present (French "exceptionalism"), and not on the discontinuous
thread of the past remembered. Nora's method may serve to introduce
students to the history of the present or "the ephemeral film of current
events." By focusing on how history is revealed through the representations of France's commemorative record, Nora's method engages us
in a kind of genealogical approach, through which we are able to
retrospectively "unlayer" traditions, and see how they were once constructed. The attraction of Nora's method is that it rejects the artificial
determinism that once dominated the historiography of the *Annales*
school. It veers away from the linearity of simple historical narrative, to
engage us with a variety of cultural objects of "quintessential France"
that are imbued with memories. For example, Mona Ozouf's remarkable
study of the Pantheon as cultural object is rich in possibilities for what
we might do in our own pedagogical experiments, especially in terms
of interpreting staged and spectacular commemorative events. Reading
the Pantheon teleologically, in a somewhat literalist way, one might say
that it is an expression of national consensus, since it is supposed to
represent the unity and continuity of the country: "*aux grands hommes,
la patrie reconnaissante.*" However, Ozouf's reading of Mitterrand's May
1981 presidential inauguration demonstrates how a monument, a memory
place intended to embody the shared patriotic emotions of pride, was
used by the new President for political purposes—in this case, to
transform a memory site into the *locus* of the ideologically correct. The
archeological approach of *Les Lieux de mémoire*, similar in some ways
to Foucault's genealogical method, enables us to move away from
history as mere fact grounded in evidence, or as a continuous determinist enterprise. By reading culture through the lens of memory we
are able to go beyond mere recollection, for memory is more a matter
of associations and symbolic representations, and also includes forgetting. If history is regarded as a reconstruction of what no longer exists,
then memory is the symbolically differential reenactment of it in a
sacred or ritualistic manner. In order for a *lieu de mémoire* to exist, it
must have a capacity for metamorphosis—for a recycling of knowledge
that can proliferate cultural material in a discontinuous manner. To
teach our students to decipher the traces of memory in various cultural
representations is to enable them to read the signs of culture in places,
objects, and images that are marked by vestiges of the past, and remembered in the vicissitudes of contemporary consciousness.

The Ethno-Cultural

We have learned in recent years that the concept of the modern nation can no longer be viewed from a monocultural perspective. To begin with, the idea of unity or social cohesion underlying the discourse of the nation must be interrogated and displaced. Starting in the mid-nineteenth century, Western nations—and France in particular—experienced, on the one hand, mass migration from other European countries, and, on the other, colonial expansion in Africa and Asia. While these changes took place more than one hundred years ago, paradoxically, in the name of republican patriotic ideals, many of us working in French cultural studies in the United States were still entranced by the horizontal development of the modern nation-state, or the so-called homogeneity of its identity. Forgotten were the voices from the other spaces of Francophone culture, from Senegal to Hanoi and from Algiers to the Caribbean (those colonial and postcolonial identities), not to mention the voices of migration within France itself (immigrants from Europe or the Third World). Our students need to ask who were and are "we the French" in their diversity, but also "who are *they*"—their supposed cultural others. But the imperative to recognize the *étranger* can lead to idealizing such constructions in the pieties of a naive multiculturalism, tending toward an unreflected Stalinist humanism. The case of Tahar Ben Jelloun, the francophone Moroccan writer, is a good case in point, and may be used for a variety of pedagogical goals, including the deconstruction of ethnic and national stereotypes.

In *Hospitalité française* (1984), Ben Jelloun presents a quasi-journalistic account of racism in contemporary France, through a dazzling juxtaposition of the anecdotal and the historical in a multiplicity of individual testimonies.[8] Curiously, Ben Jelloun demystifies the idealized space known as the country of origin, and underscores the impossibility of a return to a place ("la patrie") that perhaps only exists within the confines of the imagination. By citing the countries of origin and inscribing some of them in the paradigm of oppressor state, Ben Jelloun ironically refuses to reduce France to the evil colonizer—the unique instigator of social and political malaise. The author represents cultural diversity through many individual narratives, drawn from the *fait divers*, to illustrate the process of "othering" of North Africans living in France. The North African voices in the text are sometimes those of ordinary French citizens; others have never been to North Africa, or even travelled outside of France; some, as Ben Jelloun claims, have been alienated from Islam; some do not speak any Arabic language, while others do not speak French at all. Consequently, there is a great deal of indecision concerning what constitutes the idea of the homeland, the native language, or the immigrant—who we discover is sometimes required to become one in spite of being a French citizen and "never having made the journey" (144). Nevertheless, Ben Jelloun suggests that the category of "immigrant" is an essentialized trope of difference, representing everything resisting assimilation to a national consciousness that it perceives as lacking in subjectivity. Racism becomes "blind, reactive and instinctive" (36). In a way, Ben Jelloun's text uncovers an archeology of buried stories so as to avoid condensing the immigrant subject and entrapping it in a discursive network where one always speaks anonymously in the name of the Other. As antidote to the universalizing gesture of racism, Ben Jelloun engages in a rhetoric of nomination that essentially becomes a political act of differentiation. By naming a murder victim, seventeen-year old Algerian Ahmed Binkhidi, Ben Jelloun chooses to represent in his text an individual whose death embodies anti-Arab sentiment and whose story is yet to be told.

Through texts such as Ben Jelloun's, we need to teach our students to be more critical in their ethno-cultural analyses, and less judgmental—however correct those judgments may be. As Homi Bhabha suggests, the study of difference "must not be read as the reflection of pre-given ethnic or cultural traits set in the fixed tablet of tradition" (2). The danger of the naive differentialism practiced by many today stems from classificatory activities derived from "anthropological universals" that prioritize certain concepts of authenticity. By reverting to this cultural practice we reify, however unconsciously, the ideology of homogenization and the artificial notions of authenticity that limit the very parameters of true diversity. We need to be able to analyze the multiple spaces of culture within and external to the nation so as to provoke a crisis in the representation of a unified national subject. We must get beyond the delusions of a totalized identity and the oversimplifications produced by the practitioners of a born-again, politically correct humanism. Here the study of ethno-cultural issues from the perspective of the politics of commemoration might uncover how history may have oppressed differences within national identity. Oral histories by deportees concerning the memory of the 1942 *Rafle du Vel d'hiver* might be contrasted with French secondary school "official" textbook renditions of Vichy, to demonstrate how the ethnography of the past might be remembered in counternarratives that deprive the nation of the unity of its historically "imagined community."[9]

FRENCH CULTURE UNDER SIEGE

At the end of the twentieth century, French Studies in the United States finds itself challenged by momentous changes, such as the emergence of Spanish as our second language (perhaps no longer classified as "foreign" at all), and debates within the university on the nature of culture itself. Until very recently France has held a special distinction among nations (equivalent to the prestige associated with the stereotypes of American "fair play" and Japanese "know-how") concerning the civilizing mission of its culture, the humanistic ideals of the French Revolution, and the secular imperatives of the Third Republic. *Hélas*, French is no longer the preeminent language of culture. However, the simple memory of that myth has left French Studies open to attacks from those who see it as a mere symptom of European elitism. Some have unjustifiably targeted it and sought refuge in the construction of a reductive image representing France as the exemplar of European culture's desire for political hegemony and social malice. Others, representing either the Reagan Right or the traditional humanist Left, have engaged in personal and sometimes xenophobic attacks against the French in general and the major French intellectuals of the past quarter-century in particular: Bourdieu, Derrida, and Foucault. Witness the sheer stupidity of Camille Paglia's writing, which intermittently graces the pages of the *New York Times* with news that is unfit to print. On May 5, 1991, the *Times Book Review* gave us a preview of Paglia's forthcoming *magnum opus, Sex, Art, and American Culture*, in a front-page article entitled "Ninnies, Pedants, Tyrants and Other Academics." In this so-called essay, Paglia displays a xenophobic violence that suggests a problematic relationship between French and European cultures, and a lack of understanding of the difference between popular culture and genuine intellectual endeavor. Paglia naively asks us to choose between Deneuve and Derrida, Foucault and Dylan, French theorists and black Gospel choirs. She refers to "Warhol and Oldenburg . . . *killing* the European avant-garde forever," "the French . . . *crushed* by Germany," and France *"lying flat on her face* under the Nazi boot" [my emphasis]. But the violence does not end here. In her book she states:

> Lacan, Derrida, and Foucault are termites compared to the art, culture and archaic topography of India. One remedy for today's educational impasse: more India and less France. The followers of Derrida are pathetic, snuffling in French pockets for bits and pieces of a deconstructive method. . . . Our French acolytes, making them-

selves the lackeys of a foreign fascism, have advertised their intellectual emptiness to the world . . . . The American Sixties already
contained every revolutionary insight. We didn't need Derrida: we
had Jimi Hendrix. . . . The French theorists are eros-killers. The smoldering eroticism of great European actresses like Jeanne Moreau [is]
completely missing from the totalitarian world-view of the misogynist Foucault. For me, the big French D is not Derrida but Deneuve.
(215–218)

Critiques such as these characterize France (and French Studies) as
politically retrograde, opposed to the discourse of empowerment and
liberation, and therefore ironically align themselves with some of the
concerns that have dominated much of American and British cultural
studies. Certain unreflective critics have vehemently adapted this stance,
seeing French culture as quintessentially elitist and the epitome of
"boutique" theoretical abstraction—culture with a capital C—a luxury
item from Saks, easily disposable. Without a doubt some French figures
and teachers of French have continued to perpetuate an anachronistic
narrative of high culture, which can be seen as derived from an impe-
tus to create an imaginary aristocracy. But what some have failed to see
is that while France is perhaps waning in its universal aspirations, it is
nevertheless rich in diversity, and multiple in its signs of identity. It is
a culture that must be studied as an ongoing social process, located on
the precipice of the present, and situated in the timelessness of a new
postmodern global context. Can French Studies survive the death of the
traditional idea of the nation, and the teleology of its progress? Does
France's own identity crisis—the loss of its exceptional status, its role
as an imperial messianic nation, its integration into the European community—endanger our own discipline of French Studies? By enabling
our students to gain cultural competence through new hermeneutic
paradigms for the study of a multiplicity of cultural representations
(literary or otherwise), we can begin to get beyond the stereotypical
quagmire we now face, and to explore the imaginary sites where the
nation was once conceived, and the sites where we have invested the
energy of our own desires. There is, indeed, a bright future for French,
but we must work diligently to reflect on what we are doing, and on
how the climate we once worked in has changed.

Notes

1. See Hoffmann, "France: Keeping the Demons at Bay;" "French Dilemmas and Strategies after the Cold War."

2. All translations from French to English are my own.

3. See Gauchet, *La Révolution des droits de l'homme*. Also consult Schnapper, *La Communauté des Citoyens*.

4. See Schor on the concept of the "universal" in French thought in "Lanson's Library."

5. Zeldin, *The French*; Braudel, *L'Identité de la France*; Weber, *My France*.

6. On this issue, see Lebovics, *True France*.

7. See Halbwachs, *Les Cadres sociaux de la mémoire*; Yates, *The Art of Memory*.

8. On this subject see Taguieff, *La Force du Préjugé*.

9. See Anderson, *Imagined Communities*.

Works Cited

Anderson, Benedict. *Imagined Communities*. London: Verso, 1983.

Balibar, Etienne. " 'Rights of Man' and 'Rights of the Citizen.' " *Masses, Classes, Ideas*. New York: Routledge, 1994.

Barthes, Roland. *Mythologies*. Paris: Seuil, 1957. [*Mythologies*. Trans. Richard Howard. New York: Mill and Wang, 1971.]

Ben Jelloun, Tahar. *Hospitalité française. Racisme et immigration maghrébine*. Paris: Seuil, 1984.

Bhabba, Homi. *The Location of Culture*. New York: Routledge, 1994.

Bourdieu, Pierre. *La Misère du monde*. Paris: Seuil, 1993.

Braudel, Fernand. *L'Identité de la France*. 3 Vols. Paris: Arthaud-Flammarion, 1986.

Curtius, Ernst. *Essai sur la France*. Trans. J. Benoist-Mechin. Paris: L'Aube, 1990.

Finkielkraut, Alain. *La Défaite de la pensée*. Paris: Gallimard, 1987. (*The Defeat of the Mind*. Trans. Judith Friedlander. New York: Columbia UP, 1995.)

Gauchet, Marcel. *La Révolution des droits de l'homme*. Paris: Gallimard, 1989.

Geertz, Clifford. *The Interpretation of Cultures*. New York: Basic Books, 1973.

Halbwachs, Maurice. *Les Cadres sociaux de la mémoire*. Paris, 1915; New York: Arno Press, 1975.

Hoffmann, Stanley. "France: Keeping the Demons at Bay." *New York Review of Books* LXI, no. 5 (March 3, 1994): 10.

———. "French Dilemmas and Strategies after the Cold War." In Robert Keohane, Joseph Nye, and Stanley Hoffmann, eds. *After the Cold War*. Cambridge: Harvard UP, 1993.

Lanson, Gustave. *Trois mois d'enseignement aux Etats-Unis. Notes et impressions d'un professeur français*. Paris: Hachette, 1912.

Lebovics, Herman. *True France: The Wars Over Cultural Identity, 1900–1945*. Ithaca: Cornell UP, 1992.

Nora, Pierre. *Les Lieux de mémoire*. 7 vols. Paris: Gallimard, 1984–1992. (*Realms of Memory: Rethinking the French Past*. Edited and with a foreword by Lawrence D. Kritzman. Trans. Arthur Goldhammer. New York: Columbia UP, 1996–).

Noirel, Gérard. *Tyrannie du national: Le Droit d' asile en Europe, 1793–1993*. Paris: Calmann-Lévy, 1991.

Ozouf, Mona. "Le Panthéon." In Nora, *La République* (Vol. 1), 139–166.

Paglia, Camille. "Ninnies, Pedants, Tyrants and Other Academics." *New York Times*, May 5, 1991:1.

———. *Sex, Art, and American Culture*. New York: Vintage, 1992.

Renan, Ernest. "What Is a Nation?" Trans. and annotated by Martin Thorn. *Nation and Narration*. Ed. Homi K. Bhabha. New York: Routledge, 1990.

Schlesinger, Philip. "On National Identity: Some Conceptions and Misconceptions Criticized." *Social Science Information* 16 (1987).

Schnapper, Dominique. *La Communauté des Citoyens*. Paris: Gallimard, 1994.

Schor, Naomi. "Lanson's Library." *FLS* (22) 1995: 1–10.

Taguieff, Pierre-André. *La Force du Préjugé. Essai sur le racisme et ses doubles*. Paris: Gallimard, 1987.

Weber, Eugen. *My France: Politics, Culture, Myth*. Cambridge: Harvard UP, 1991.

Yates, Frances. *The Art of Memory*. Chicago: U of Chicago P, 1966.

Zeldin, Theodore. *The French*. New York: Pantheon, 1982.

2

Nana and the Nation

French Cultural Studies and Interdisciplinary Work

Jean E. Pedersen

"French cultural studies" is a phrase that means different things to different people. For the editors of one recent book by that name, Jill Forbes and Michael Kelly, its object is "French culture" (v), seen as a mediating force "to negotiate the insertion of the individual into society . . . by exploring a multiplicity of identities . . . which people can recognize and relate themselves to" (1). By contrast, Simon During, editor of a cultural studies anthology, suggests that "the French model" is defined, not by its object, but by the national origin of its inspirational theorists, "Pierre Bourdieu, Michel de Certeau, and Michel Foucault" (10–12). The current range of possibilities is so large that one of Vera Mark's central "questions for French cultural studies" is how to define it.[1] Amidst the many conflicting definitions,[2] there seems to be agreement on only one point: French cultural studies should be interdisciplinary.

In that spirit, this essay combines approaches from history and literary criticism to examine the relationship between a literary text and its many interpretive contexts. The text is Emile Zola's *Nana*, a novel that explores the links between sexual behavior and national identity by paralleling the life of the prostitute Nana with the life of the Second Empire, ending in Nana's death of smallpox on the first day of the

Franco-Prussian War. The nineteenth-century context includes Zola's public and private writing, not only on the novel itself, but also on the epochs and events that surrounded its creation, particularly the Second Empire, the Franco-Prussian War, the Paris Commune, and the Third Republic. Reading *Nana* in the light of Zola's other representations of imperial war and republican peace reveals the extent to which *Nana* presents not only a moralistic commentary on the decadent sexual behavior of the Second Empire, but also a republican nationalist criticism of bellicose imperial politics.

History and literary criticism are two disciplines whose relationship has become particularly rich, but also particularly vexed, perhaps because each field claims privileged access to the creation and analysis of its own and other people's stories.[3] While literary scholars argue over the merits and demerits of "literary history" or "the new historicism," historians debate the possibilities and pitfalls of "the linguistic turn." Although conventional wisdom might decree that literary critics are interested in the text and historians in its context, such clear distinctions are difficult to maintain. For example, recent approaches to *Nana* include the work, not only of literary critics, but also of historians and art historians, all interested in analyzing the novel, the social structures and sexual practices it represents, and the historical situation to which it responds.[4]

Surveying the multidisciplinary literature on *Nana* suggests that there are no easy distinctions between disciplines. Indeed, the differences among scholars in the same field can be as significant as the differences between scholars in contrasting ones. For example, while some literary critics have focused on the literary work itself, others reject the distinction between a privileged literary text and other documents that only "explain" it.[5] A similar tension can be observed among historians: some read a novel as a reflection of the culture of which its author was a part; others are not so sure that they can treat a literary text simply as confirmation of a "real" historical record.[6] In such circumstances, it makes less sense to seek to isolate different disciplinary approaches than it does to explore the benefits and drawbacks of different critical perspectives, different methods of reading texts, and different ways of handling evidence.[7]

SEXUAL POLITICS IN *NANA*

French intellectual Emile Zola, whose work has been canonized from his mention in the first edition of Gustave Lanson's *Histoire de la littérature française* to the recent appearance of *Les Rougon-Macquart* in a Pléiade edition, might seem like an odd subject for an essay in a volume on cultural studies, a field that began as the study of working-class culture in England.[8] However, it is important to remember that many of what we now think of as Zola's classic novels, *Nana* included, began as *feuilletons* in the popular press before appearing as books. Although Zola eventually made his mark in French intellectual life not only as a novelist, but also as a literary critic, a theatre reviewer, and a political commentator, most notably in the Dreyfus Affair, he began his writing life as a free-lance journalist for any paper that would have him. Zola not only enjoyed, but actively sought, both a popular and an elite audience. Even after the beginnings of his success as a novelist, he took advantage of his earlier experience as advertising director for Librairie Hachette to advise his editors and publishers on how to market his work to the widest possible audience.[9]

While Zola's *Nana* has become a key text for scholars of gender, sexuality, and private life, especially those working on prostitution, his novel has rarely been discussed by scholars of nationalism in general, or the Franco-Prussian War in particular. Although this is symptomatic of the way in which studies of "private" sexuality and "public" nationality have often developed in isolation from each other, the editors of a volume of essays on "nationalisms and sexualities" have called for more extensive studies of the ways in which "these categories interact with, constitute, or otherwise illuminate each other."[10] Nana's death functions as part of a larger republican discourse, which requires sexual purity to guarantee national identity, but Zola's own ambiguities and later readers' persistent interest in his heroine's complex character suggest that such a pure national identity can never be achieved.

Zola's novel, controversial when it first appeared, has remained controversial to the present day. Published in serial installments in the radical republican daily *Le Voltaire* from October 1879 to February 1880, it appeared simultaneously with Zola's literary manifesto *Le roman naturaliste*, an extended essay in which Zola argued that naturalist novels should be both scientifically accurate and dispassionately moral. Ironically, however, although writers such as Flaubert and Huysmans acclaimed *Nana* as a daring work of genius, reviewers in the Paris press complained that Zola's portrayal of prostitution was both inaccurate and obscene. These accusations came not only from the conservative Right, offended by Zola's detailed descriptions of sexual excess, but also from the republican Left, offended by Zola's portrayal of a working class that was too degraded to be heroic.[11]

Contemporary scholars have continued to argue over how to read *Nana*, especially over whether to interpret Nana herself as a dangerous threat to French society or as a valiant warrior against sex and class oppression.[12] Nana, a chorus girl from a working-class background, makes her name and her fortune by driving a never-ending succession of wealthy and aristocratic lovers to poverty, dishonor, despair, and death by suicide. She sleeps indiscriminately with both men and women; there are even suggestions that she sleeps with her dog. It is easy to see her frightful death of smallpox as a moralistic authorial comment on her dangerous life. Charles Bernheimer argues that Zola's focus on Nana's voracious sexuality functions as part of a "conservative patriarchal ideology" that scapegoats the working class as the source of "libidinal sexuality, primitive instinct, and excremental release" (217). He characterizes the novel as part of a literary tradition whose "sexual and political implications" are "reactionary" and "misogynist," part of a "repressive cultural scenario" (119).

However, while Nana's lesbian love affairs serve as titillating evidence of her perverse sexuality, her relationship with one woman, Satin, contains the seeds of a powerful female solidarity which Zola portrays with some sympathy. Satin shelters Nana both from her lover Fontan's beatings and from the clutches of the police, while Nana rescues Satin from the gutter after her arrest. The two women share memories of childhood poverty which their wealthy male clients can never understand. Similarly, when Nana is dying of smallpox, her former rivals leave jealousy aside to come to her aid. The bravery of the women around her deathbed, who risk their health, their beauty, and with it, their livelihood, to tend to her last needs, compares favorably with the cowardice of the men in the street, former lovers who do not rely on their looks professionally, yet are afraid to go upstairs.[13] Feminist critic Bernice Chitnis argues: "Zola's thesis is that what Nana accomplishes single-handedly . . . is the rout of patriarchy" (3). She concludes: "What I think Zola is working towards is a statement about true humanity which means revealing the essential androgyny of all biological males and females, and breaking down the barriers of gender" (86).

These conflicting readings rely on divergent interpretations of Zola's intentions, especially at the scene of Nana's death, a scene whose significance Zola heightens by combining it with the outbreak of the Franco-Prussian War. Zola worked particularly hard to make the ending horrific, reporting triumphantly on its completion that he had frightened even himself: "I do not believe I could ever surpass this horror of massacre and dissolution."[14] His commitment to the shock value of the ending overrode even his commitment to the scientific accuracy of the naturalist novel. Although he had created Nana's deathmask without seeing an actual corpse, he told his friend Henri Céard to stop looking for one: "My position is taken, and I am sure that I would not correct it even from exact documents."[15] Reflecting on the novel's symbolism almost ten years after its publication, he explained: "It is perhaps helping the symbol too much to say that the rotten corpse of Nana is the dying France of the Second Empire. But, obviously, I must have meant something close."[16]

Zola's intentions, ambiguous in his preliminary sketches for the novel,[17] become clearer if one explores his development of the parallels between Nana and the nation more extensively. Reading the novel in the light of his other writing on imperial war and republican peace clarifies the political opinions that informed his description of Nana's death. Analyzing the process by which Zola identified his heroine as a threat to his country in earlier sections of the novel clarifies the necessity of her death at the end. Nevertheless, reviewing contemporary readers' responses suggests that Zola's popular novel may always escape his original purposes.

IMPERIAL DECADENCE, MILITARY DEFEAT,
AND REPUBLICAN RENEWAL

The Franco-Prussian War, predicted in the second chapter of the novel and erupting in the last, produced not only a political shift from the Second Empire to the Third Republic, but also a profound shift in national self-consciousness from the assurance of France as a world power to the anxiety of France as a defeated country. Remembering the French reaction to news of the first Prussian victory at Froeschwiller, Zola recalled: "All of Paris was in a stupor. [The victory] not only struck at our patriotism, but destroyed in us a faith."[18] After going to the National Assembly to hear the final terms of the Prussian peace, he reported that the crowd outside reacted like "a people in mourning who had just conducted a funeral ceremony for their country."[19] Even after the final French surrender to the Germans, the bloody civil war between the Versailles government and the Paris Commune produced new challenges to any simple national self-understanding.[20]

Although republican authors, artists, and politicians could present the emergence of the Third Republic in triumphant cultural terms as the victory of restrained bourgeois virtue over aristocratic sexual excess, they had a harder time coming to terms with the military defeat and civil war that had accompanied the transition from one regime to another.[21] Zola himself returned to the linked topics of war and civil war repeatedly throughout his life, not only in *Nana*, but also in essays, in short stories, and, most notably, in *La débâcle*, a painstakingly re-searched novel on the Franco-Prussian War and the Paris Commune, which attracted international attention when it appeared twenty years after the original events of 1870–1871.[22]

When Zola juxtaposed Nana's licentious life with that of the em-pire, he was clearly criticizing both decadent imperial society and the political elite that enjoyed it. Many scholars have pointed out the ways in which Zola's early newspaper essays prefigured the themes and images of *Nana* when they presented corrupt politicians, powerful courtesans, adulterous wives, effeminate bachelors, and lesbian women as emblems of imperial decadence.[23] Rarely discussed, but equally important for understanding Zola's imagery in the novel, is the way in which he associated the Empire with the unnecessary suffering pro-voked by imperial war. Although the government of the Second Empire was French, Zola consistently portrayed it as foreign.

In the tense days leading up to the outbreak of Franco-Prussian War, Zola's republican opposition to the Empire initially made him into a pacifist. For example, "La guerre" warned against any impulse to fight by counting the cost of Louis-Napoleon's previous imperial campaigns. In a series of vivid anecdotes, Zola contrasted Parisians shouting songs of joy with dead bodies weeping blood in Italy and Russia; schoolboys hoping for a holiday to celebrate the Battle of Magenta with an old man grieving the loss of two sons on that foreign field; and the public applause for polished troops on their way to the Crimea with the public disinterest in the reappearance of the same troops when they returned "in the opposite direction, crippled, bleeding, [and] dragging themselves down the streets."[24]

Zola reconciled his political opposition to the Empire with a strong French national identity by blaming both the eventual war and the subsequent defeat on imperial politics, which he characterized as anti-French. He linked his initial pacifism, not to a cosmopolitan disinterest in the special fate of France, but to a patriotic republican desire to spare French lives by opposing foreign campaigns. Unified French forces from "the north and . . . the *midi*," should fight, not against another country, but against the imperial government, which consti-tuted the true threat to their nation. "We will fight no more," he concluded, "we will no longer espouse the quarrels of royal families; and so that they have no more armies, we will disband the armies; and so that they no longer contest each other for thrones, we will burn the thrones!"[25]

Only when Prussian advances into France made the conflict into a war of self-defense did Zola's opposition turn to support. He now argued that, instead of refusing to fight, as he had recommended earlier, republican soldiers should defeat the invading Prussians as the necessary prerequisite to overthrowing the imperial government and ending war forever. In this context, a death for France became a vote for the Republic, "a new devotion to the country, a new ballot for liberty in the national urn."[26] To mobilize republican support for the war but against the Empire, Zola combined republican symbols with patriotic fervor, proclaiming that "the *Marseillaise* belongs to us," comparing the Prussian invaders to criminals who deserved execution, and looking forward to "the dawn of tomorrow, [with] the tricolor flags which [will] wave in the open sky."[27]

Zola dramatized both the violent destruction and the occasional necessity of war by portraying military force in sexualized terms as the rape of an innocent woman. For example, in "*Le petit village*," written less than a week after the Franco-Prussian War began, he maximized the horror of war not only by contrasting the fertile farms and happy workers of peacetime with the desolate battlefields and dead bodies of wartime, but also by figuring the conflict itself as the story of a "virgin land which the war is going to violate."[28] In a fictional memoir which he published in 1872, shortly after the Franco-Prussian War had ended, he summed up the impact of the war by comparing the physical destruction of a friend's country home with the symbolic rape of his friend's dead wife. Describing his arrival at their house, he talked about the way in which this woman's "modest bedroom" had been "brutally opened by Prussian gun-fire." The privacy of the conjugal bedroom had been turned into the publicity of a "loving alcove which could now be seen across the entire valley." When Zola concluded by imagining his friend's death in defense of his wife's grave, the man's fighting behavior seemed completely justified.[29]

Once the Third Republic replaced the Second Empire, Zola's identification with republican France led him to two positions that were in tension with each other. As early as 1872, he accepted the war as a "heroic remedy" for imperial decadence, claiming: "It is in this bath of blood that the country was washed clean of the decrepitude of the Empire, and that it rediscovered its radiant republican youth."[30] He would expand on this position twenty years later in *La débâcle*, where he compared the new France to a man who had suffered the amputation of a gangrenous limb for the sake of his future health.

However, from 1878 to 1880, when Zola was composing and publishing *Nana*, his writing on the war tended to be less resigned to its necessity and more concerned with its gratuitous horror. His most famous short story on this topic, *"L'attaque du moulin,"* was so popular that it was reprinted four times, most notably in *Soirées de Médan* in 1880. This collection of short stories on the Franco-Prussian War, like *Nana*, combined examples of naturalist writing with criticisms of the war. Contributor Guy de Maupassant explained the political orientation of the volume: "We wanted above all to try to give to our stories an accurate note on the war, to strip them of the chauvinism of a Déroulède, of the false enthusiasm which is judged necessary in every story with red trousers and a rifle." He promised the reader that the book would not be "anti-patriotic," but, rather, "simply true."[31]

Zola's contribution contrasted the peace of a French country village on the eve of war with its destruction after a battle. By the time French armies had conclusively retaken the spot from the Prussians, the only person left alive in the now-ruined mill of the title was the heroine, Françoise, driven to insanity by the death of her father and her *fiançé* on what should have been her wedding day. Although Françoise was physically unharmed, Zola repeated his motif of war as rape by summing up the destruction of the windmill in the way "one saw, through a breach, the bedroom of Françoise, with its bed, whose white curtains were carefully drawn." He heightened the horror of the situation by contrasting Françoise's pain with the pleasure of the French captain, who interpreted the tragic scene as a triumph: "And seeing Françoise an imbecile between the corpses of her husband and her father, in the midst of the smoking ruins of the windmill, he saluted her gallantly with his sword crying, 'Victory! victory!' "[32]

A similar critical attitude toward war is clear in *Nana* when Zola describes the crowd that punctuates the conversations of the main characters at Nana's death with the repeated refrain, "To Berlin! To Berlin! To Berlin!"[33] Far from presenting the war as a source of national renewal, he describes a crowd whose "gazes shone out of pale faces, while a great breath of anguish and spreading stupor transported all of them" (2: 1473). When the first group of pro-war agitators arrives, the crowd watches with "*une morne défiance,*" a gloomy suspicion (2: 1474). Although they quickly rouse their enthusiasm for war to a fever pitch, Zola describes their cries in uninspiring terms as "*hurlant,*" howling (1475); "*saccadé,*" irrregular (1477); "*entêté,*" obstinate (1477); "*enroué,*" hoarse (1484); "*déchiré,*" torn (1484); and finally "*désespéré,*" desperate or disconsolate (1485).

Zola further signals his criticism of blind imperial patriotism by putting the most explicitly military words in the mouth of one of his most grotesque working-class characters, the actor Fontan, who "took a pose like Bonaparte at Austerlitz" (2: 1474) to defend the necessity of war. As new men arrive on the scene, they gather around Fontan to hear him explain "his campaign plan to take Berlin in five days"(2: 1480). Zola's image of Fontan as Bonaparte implicitly links support for the war with support for France as an empire.

Unlike Fontan and the men on the street, the prostitutes around Nana's deathbed have no politics of their own. Léa de Horn, who criticizes the war, is only echoing her clients, supporters of the Orleanist prince Louis-Philippe, while Lucy, who defends it, does so out of loyalty to an imperial prince who was once her lover. Similarly, Blanche de Sivry defends the Prussians because her new lover is a Prussian, while Simonne, Tatan Néné and Louise Violaine accept the war because they expect to find new customers among the French soldiers. The prostitutes' opinions ultimately coalesce around support for the emperor, for whom even Blanche confesses that she has burned candles. As Zola describes the scene: "the others broke out in furious words against the republicans, spoke of exterminating them at the frontier, so that Napoleon III, having defeated the enemy, could reign peacefully amidst universal delight" (2: 1483). When Léa de Horn persists in her prediction of defeat, the others accuse her of being *"une mauvaise Française,"* a bad Frenchwoman (2: 1483).

Although Léa de Horn criticizes the emperor's advisors as "crazy" (2: 1482) and Blanche defends Bismarck as a man who "adores women" (1483), neither woman criticizes the war from Zola's preferred republican point of view. Zola's alignment of the prostitutes with monarchist or imperial politics suggests that they would be as much of a threat to a republican France as they are to France under the Empire. Nana's sexual exploitation of the aristocracy can bring the Empire down, but her potential as a national heroine is limited by the fact that she cannot put a new Republic in its place. When the Empire dies, Nana must die with it.

NANA AS THE NATION

Nana's death at the end of the novel actually represents the third time that her fate is linked to that of the nation. Nana makes her opening appearance at the Théâtre des Variétés in 1867, the same year as the International Exposition that would bring Bismarck on a peaceful visit to Paris. She reaches the height of her public power at a hugely attended race at Longchamps when she becomes the toast of Paris after a filly bearing her name races to an unexpected French victory over a favorite from an English stable. Although Nana clearly represents imperial France when she dies at the end of the novel, her earlier connections to the nation are ambiguous, as Zola associates her not only with France, but also with foreigners. To the extent that Zola identified imperial aspirations as a threat to the French nation, Nana's association with the Empire makes her national status uncertain even at her death.

When Zola described the causes of the Franco-Prussian War twenty years later, he explained: "In my eyes, Germany was only the fatal accident, and her triumph was due only to the internal illness from which we were in the process of dying."[34] Similarly, in an essay on prostitution, which Zola wrote shortly after publishing the novel, he stressed that although there were foreign and provincial prostitutes in Paris, the real problem in 1881 was "girls born in Paris, raised in Paris, corrupted by the soil of Paris itself for the debauchery of Paris."[35] He was furious when a German edition of La débâcle featured a cover that figured Bismarck's victory as a result of superior German strength instead of temporary French weakness.[36]

The high and low society conversations after Nana's début underestimate both the power of Bismarck, who will become the external threat to France, and that of Nana, who is already a potent internal threat. At Comtesse Sabine's party, the society women who dislike Bismarck object, not to his political power, but to his bad manners. Madame de Joncquoy, remembering a dinner meeting characterizes him as "brutal and badly raised . . . [and] stupid" (2: 1147). The aristocratic men who disagree defend Bismarck's breeding, but show no greater awareness of his threat. Comte de Vandeuvres calls him "a good drinker and a good gamer . . . very witty." (2: 1147–48) When Madame Chantereau reports that she has heard rumors in Alsace that Bismarck will defeat France, her audience laughs and Madame du Joncquoy replies: "What! What! . . . You think that Monsieur de Bismarck will make war on us and beat us. . . . Oh! That beats everything!" (2: 1164). Comte de Muffat concludes more seriously, but with equal ignorance of the future: "Fortunately, the emperor is there" (2:1164).

The prostitutes at Nana's dinner party the following night are no more concerned about Bismarck's political power and military might than their aristocratic counterparts. Simonne, who claims to have slept with him, characterizes him as "a charming man" (2: 1178). Although Labordette, one of Nana's male guests, jokingly paints Bismarck as a monster who eats raw meat and takes women by force, the prostitutes are more interested in the number of his illegitimate children than in what these frightening details might say about his foreign policy.

Although Nana's power at the outset of the novel is even more pervasive than Bismarck's, the imperial elite is no more concerned about her than about him. Most of the men at Comtesse Sabine's society party are planning to go to Nana's theatre party the following night. Comte de Vandeuvres has the audacity to invite Comte de Muffat to the prostitute's dinner while standing in Muffat's own wife's *salon*. In a parallel violation of good manners, the young journalist Fauchery spends the evening speculating on the virtue of his married hostess, who has a black mole in the same place as Nana's blonde one. Although none of the guests notice, the incipient collapse of the Muffats' imperial world is apparent even in their furniture. The Muffat home has remained the same for over a century, but its solid Empire furnishings are now being challenged by Comtesse Sabine's new chair, a "modern piece of furniture" upholstered like a "corner of fantasy" in padded red silk (2: 1144–1145).

Although Zola stressed that Nana was native to France, born and bred in a working-class quarter in the heart of Paris, he heightened both her attraction and her threat by associating her with exotic foreigners. Her first house on the boulevard Haussman is funded by an anonymous "rich merchant from Moscow" (2: 1122). Her triumphal *début* in *Blonde Venus* corresponds with the International Exposition of 1867, which brought record numbers of foreigners to Paris.[37] When Muffat sets her up in style at the height of her career, Nana furnishes her vestibule with "Chinese bronzes and *cloisonnés* filled with flowers, divans recovered with old Persian rugs, [and] armchairs covered with old tapestries" (2: 1347). The foreign influence is even more pronounced in her intimate salon filled with "a world of objects from every country and in every style, Italian cabinets, Spanish and Portuguese chests, Chinese pagodas, a Japanese folding screen" (2: 1348). Her last theatrical appearance in Paris is in the Orientalist drama *Mélusine*, and the rumors after her departure for Cairo are even more exotic, associating her alternately with an Egyptian viceroy, a "*grand nègre*" (2:1471), or a Russian prince.

The destructive effects of Nana's power and her ambiguous position as simultaneously French and foreign are both visible in her moment of greatest triumph, when she wins the hearts of the crowd at the prestigious Grand Prix at Longchamps in the eleventh of the novel's fourteen chapters. Zola did extensive research on the world of the track, and foreshadowed this section of the novel with several essays on the crowds at Longchamps.[38] Covering the Grand Prix of 1872, Zola criticized the blind patriotism that led French spectators to support a supposedly French horse, Berryer, over a more obviously English horse, Cremorne. He pointed out: "*Berryer* is as English as *Cremorne*, raised in England, and ridden by an English jockey." The only things that made Berryer French were his French name and his ownership by a French stable. Zola concluded: "I would hesitate to place my chauvinism in the legs of a horse of such dubious nationality."[39] In a later piece on the Grand Prix of 1876, he alluded to the confused national identity of Longchamps again when he characterized it as a place where the crowd spoke an almost-incomprehensible French language that was *"toute hérissée de mots anglais,"* bristling all over with English words (2: 1659).

Zola described the fictional Grand Prix in his novel as a similar contest between the French and the English. True to his observations of the mixed world of the track, he described the scene in a French language that is remarkably punctuated by English words. The crowd arrives not only in French *"landaus," "fiacres"* (2: 1379),*"calèche[s]"* (1381), and *"coupés"* (1388), but also in British "dog carts," "victorias," "four-in- hand[s]," "mailcoaches," and "tandems" (1379). Even the French spectators use English terms as they discuss "jockeys," "tipsters," "book-makers"(1380), "stepper[s]" (1382), and the "starter" (1399). In the middle of the day, they break for "lunch[e]s"(1382). The British visitors, proud of their victory the previous year, walk among the crowd, "as if they were at home, faces inflamed and already triumphant," while in the general buzz of conversation, "the lively phrases of the Parisians" contrast with the "guttural exclamations of the English" (2: 1384).

In his essays about the early Third Republic, Zola had criticized the false patriotism of republican officials, ignorant crowds, and aristocratic women. In his novel about the late Second Empire, Zola initially associated such patriotism only with the prostitutes in Nana's circle, commenting: "all these women became passionately interested out of national pride" (2: 1384). Nana refuses to bet on any English horses, remarking: "I am a patriot" (2: 1380). When Hector La Faloise goes to bet on the English anyway because their horses look better, Nana is "scandalized" (2: 1383).

Nana's influence extends to the crowd when the unexpected winner of the race is a French filly who is also named Nana. Women wave their umbrellas, men turn somersaults and throw their hats in the air, and even the empress applauds. The winning horse is almost interchangeable with the acclaimed courtesan: her gleaming hide is the color of Nana's own glorious hair; she runs for the stable of one of

Nana's lovers, Comte de Vandeuvres; and her jockey's colors match those of Nana's provocative equestrian dress and the outfits of her entourage. As Nana the horse races, Nana the woman loses her breath and beats her thighs in sympathy. When Nana the horse wins, the crowd erupts in patriotic cries of "Long live Nana! Long live France! Down with England!" (2: 1404) and Nana the woman becomes "the queen of Paris" (1405). By this time, Nana and the filly are so closely associated in the crowd's mind that "no one knew any longer if it was the animal or the woman who filled their hearts" (2: 1405). As in Zola's essay on the Grand Prix of 1872, so in the novel, the victory of the French stable is accepted by the spectators as a victory for France despite the fact that the winning horse is ridden by an English jockey and associated with a dangerous woman.

Nana's victory only seems like a victory for France; her triumphant gain brings tragic loss in its wake. While Nana and her followers dance the night away under the complacent eyes of the municipal police, Comte de Vandeuvres, barred from the track for cheating at the races, loses his fortune, burns his stables, destroys his horses, and, in conflicting reports, either kills himself or disappears dishonored forever. Nana's breathtakingly inadequate responses are to blame Vandeuvres for not sharing his money-making betting scheme with her, to refuse responsibility for the risks he took to make money for her support, and to exhibit a grizzly fascination with the story of the fire.

Zola's most memorable equation of Nana and the nation comes at the end of the novel, when her decaying body represents, in Zola's words, the decaying society of the "France of the Second Empire."[40] In this final chapter, Zola reintroduces the links between Nana's life and Bismarck's career, which he had used in the opening chapters. As her former lovers arrive outside her hotel they discuss prostitution and politics in the same breath, "exclaim[ing] over the death of this poor girl; then discussing politics and strategy" (2: 1480). Similarly, as her former rivals congregate in the room around her bed, they alternate stories of Nana's life and death with speculations about their own place in a country that is going to war.

To the extent that the same men and women who are ready to fight Bismarck have now come to pity Nana, the parallel between the Prussian enemy without and the prostitute enemy within seems to break down temporarily. In the face of a foreign threat, Nana, her rivals, and her surviving customers all become French together. However, it is significant that when Zola looked back, he identified Nana, not simply with France, but with what he called "the dying France of

the Second Empire." Zola, himself a republican critic of imperial politics
and society, might regret the temporary defeat of his nation in the
Franco-Prussian War, but could only rejoice at the permanent defeat of
the Second Empire as a result. Nana's aristocratic lovers and prostitute
rivals regret her loss, but they themselves are symptomatic of a social
system that Zola's republican politics forbade him to admire. Although
Nana can be an object of pity in death, she could never become a
model of republican virtue in life.

Andrew Parker, Mary Russo, Coris Summer, and Patricia Yeager
have pointed out that the "trope of the nation as woman . . . depends
for its representational efficiency on a particular image of woman as
chaste, dutiful, daughterly, or maternal" (6). When Nana stands for the
nation throughout the novel, she violates all of these rules. Far from
being "chaste, dutiful, daughterly, or maternal," she makes her living
with her body, rebels against every authority, and has no living parents.
Although she catches her lethal illness at her son's deathbed, she
usually exhibits no more interest in the boy than she does in her
admittedly pampered dog. This contradiction suggests that although
Nana clearly represents the decadent Empire, she can never represent
the ideal French nation.

Indeed, where Zola associated the Second Empire with prostitution
and sexual excess, he represented republican France as a virginal bride,
a faithful wife, or a tender mother. For example, in an 1872 article, he
praised the new Republic for providing such beautiful weather that the
Tuileries were overflowing with orange blossoms for her "*couronne de
mariée*," her bridal crown. "Under the Empire," he pointed out, "the
orange trees did not flower with this brightness, no doubt because they
did not know on which heads to let their chaste blossoms fall."[41] The
"virginal flowers" that could find no home in the Second Empire would
be loved and cherished by the Third Republic. In Zola's extended
allegory, the Republic walked down the aisle with Prime Minister Thiers,
accompanied by an honor guard of equally important republican politicians. Zola certified the legitimacy of their union not only by imagining it as a wedding, but also by promising that the republican couple
would enjoy a fertile union with "many children" (93).

In the races at Longchamps, Nana had become the toast of Paris.
However, Nana could only symbolize imperial France, never true France,
which in Zola's view had to be a republican nation, symbolized in
peace by a virgin girl, a retiring bride, or a tender mother. In Zola's
idealized view, a sexually active prostitute with a single sickly son
should have no place in a virtuous French republic or a strong and
populous republican France.

CULTURAL STUDIES AND A CANONICAL TEXT

Despite Zola's best moralizing intentions, the attraction of Nana's character remains more powerful than the lesson of her painful death. Naomi Schor has characterized Nana as "the enigmatic, which is to say, hermeneutic object par excellence" (*Breaking the Chain*, 47), and the hundreds of books and articles on the novel suggest that this is true even for those who do not share Schor's critical approach. Literary critics have reinterpreted Zola's novel through the frameworks of theorists from Karl Marx and Georgy Lukacs to Michel Foucault and Judith Butler. Art historians have debated the relationship between Zola's Nana and Manet's painting of the same name, and historians have sought to place Zola in the nineteenth-century debate over prostitution. Zola may have imagined his novel as an indictment of Nana and her society, but readers have not necessarily come to the same conclusions. For example, critic Terry Castle has recently valorized Nana as the erotic lesbian intertext to Henry James' *Bostonians,* while Bernice Chitnis has appropriated Nana for Monique Wittig's tradition of feminist heroines, proclaiming: "Nana has not been a *femme fatale,* Nana has been . . . a *guérillère*" (86). Many readers are clearly fascinated by Nana in spite of, rather than because of, her death at the end of the novel.

Interest in the novel has not been confined to the academy. The novel was playing in pirated theatrical versions throughout Italy before it even finished its run in *Le Voltaire*. Zola's own dramatic version ran for more than one hundred performances in Paris before going on the road to Turin. Zola expected the novel to make both his fortune and his reputation, and this proved to be the case. The initial printing of 55,000 was sold out before it even appeared, and when a complete edition of the Rougon-Macquart series was issued from 1927 to 1928 *Nana* was still his best-selling novel. By the time of the Livre de Poche edition in 1972, it had dropped to sixth place, but its appeal had spread to other genres, inspiring six movie versions in Europe, the United States, and Mexico, including one directed in France by Jean Renoir. More recently, it has become the basis for a ballet at the Opéra de Paris and a fourteen-part television series.[42]

Scholars working in contemporary cultural studies can interview readers to discover how they respond to the books they buy or the performances they see. It is harder to imagine how to get similar information about those who read Zola in late nineteenth-century France. Although Zola did not want for reviewers, his critics were more likely to talk about their individual reactions than to seek the secret of his broad appeal.[43] However, there is no reason to think that popular readers a century ago were more unified in their responses to Zola's work than critics then or now.

French historians of popular culture in other periods have stressed the ways in which people can turn cultural scripts and literary texts to their own purposes. For example, in her classic essay "Women on Top," Natalie Zemon Davis showed that the same carnivalesque role reversals that were supposed to preserve the early modern social order by offering a periodic pressure valve for accumulated tensions could also facilitate the political expression of those very same tensions. Writing more recently on a more recent revolution, print historian Roger Chartier has argued that in the relationship between Enlightenment writing and the French Revolution that followed, what was said mattered less than how it was read. After outlining the results of a critical "reading revolution" in the eighteenth century, he asks: "Why not think, then, that the key factor was less in the subversive content of 'philosophical' books, . . . than in an original mode of reading which, even when the texts which it used were entirely in conformity with the political and religious order, developed a critical attitude, detached from the dependency and obediency which founded the old representations?" (115).

Responding to Chartier's question could be one project for French cultural studies. Such an investigation of the significance of Zola's popularity would not only stress the ways in which texts have plural and contested meanings, but also seek to understand the meanings they hold in particular times and places. Talking about the relationship between Zola and his readers would mean looking at the whole field of French culture, neither simply the canonized text of high culture nor the sociologized response of popular culture, but the interaction between the two. Having analyzed the links between Zola's political project and his popular novel, we still need to seek the secret of *Nana*'s enormous appeal.

Notes

1. Mark's approaches to a definition include: identifying the field's core concepts or "keywords"; writing an "intellectual history of how France has been studied, taught [and] written about"; and producing a "sociology of knowledge" that not only analyzes what appears on the syllabi of cultural studies courses in French departments but also explains why French departments are now interested in cultural studies at all (433).

2. For one particularly complete set, see Peer, who suggests that French cultural studies could be not only "a cognate for civilization" but also any one of the following: "interdisciplinary scholarship using social science methodol-

ogy and historical analysis"; "applying methods of textual analysis and cultural criticism to non-canonical forms"; "studying the interrelationship of literary texts and historical context in the new historical mode"; and "working on questions of class, race, gender, sexuality or post-colonialism [in France] from whatever approach" (416).

3. For histories of history, see Novick; Hunt et al.; Smith. For a history of "academic literary studies," see Graff. On the relation between history and historical fiction, see Tax.

4. See, for example, Adler; Bernheimer; Chitnis; Clayson; Corbin; Thompson; Schor, *Breaking the Chain.*

5. See, for example, Bernheimer, who asserts that "there is no necessary break between the texts we recognize as 'literary' and those we designate officially as social, political, historical, or legal" (2–3).

6. Compare, for example, Corbin's and Adler's contributions to the historical literature on French prostitution. Corbin, who characterizes *Nana* as "the daughter of post-Commune regulationist obsessions" (28–29), uses examples from Zola's novel only when they correspond to the image of the past that he has reconstructed from police records and other, implicitly more accurate, archival sources. By contrast, Adler, who also reads the novel in combination with archival sources, warns her readers not to expect "impartiality"; qualifies the conclusive objectivity of her account, "itself the result of a weave of multiple accounts which have constructed the object prostitution"; and confesses, "the more I advanced in research, the more truth stole away" (21–22).

7. See, for example, La Capra's discussion of five "protocols of reading" for historians.

8. For brief histories of the various schools of cultural studies, see During; Hall.

9. See, for example, Emile Zola, letter to Jules Lafitte, 15 September 1879, in Bakker's edition of Zola's *Correspondance,* 3: 374. On the advance publicity and subsequent demand for *Nana,* see Auriant.

10. Parker et al., 2. See also Walby; Mosse; Higonnet et al.

11. See Auriant; Becker's "Introduction" to *Nana,* lxvii–lxxiii; Rey's "Preface" to *Nana,* 16–17.

12. See, for instance, Clive Thompson's "Introduction" to "Emile Zola: Lectures au féminin."

13. For a compelling structural analysis of the novel's opposition between men and women, see Schor, *Zola's Crowds,* chapter 3.

14. Zola, letter to Henri Céard, 25 December 1879, in *Correspondance,* 3, 424.

15. Zola, letter to Henri Céard, 7 January 1880, in *Correspondance,* 3, 432.

16. Zola, letter to Jacques van Santen-Kolff, 5 March 1888, in *Correspondance,* 6, 258.

17. For Zola's working notes, see Zola, "Dossier préparatoire," and "Fiches-personnages," in Zola, *Nana,* ed. Becker. For *Nana's* advance publicity, see *"La mouche d'or,"* which not only ran in *Le Voltaire* as a teaser for the serialized novel to follow, but also played a key role in the final book.

18. Zola, "Mes souvenirs de guerre," *Le messager de l'Europe*, June 1877, reprinted as "Les trois guerres" in *Oeuvres complètes*, 9, 1028.

19. Zola for *La cloche*, 1871, quoted in Mitterand, *Zola journaliste*, 134.

20. See further Boime; Gullickson.

21. See Boime; Gullickson; Leith.

22. On the reception of *La débâcle*, see Rufener, chapters 4–5.

23. See Kanes, *Atelier*; Mitterand, *Zola journaliste*.

24. Zola, "La guerre," *La cloche*, 14 July 1870, in Kanes, *Atelier*, 239.

25. Zola, "La guerre," in Kanes, *Atelier*, 239.

26. Zola, "Vive la France!" *La cloche*, 5 August 1870, in Kanes, *Atelier*, 244.

27. Zola, "Vive la France!" and "Les Nerfs de la France," *La cloche*, 17 August 1870, in Kanes, *Atelier*, 243, 248.

28. Zola, "Le petit village," *La cloche*, 25 July 1870, in Kanes, *Atelier*, 242.

29. Zola, untitled essay in *La cloche*, 11 May 1872, in *Nouveaux contes à Ninon*, in *Oeuvres complètes*, 9, 445.

30. Zola, "Le rajeunissement républicain," *La cloche*, 25 October 1872, in *Oeuvres complètes*, 14, 196.

31. Maupassant, letter to Gustave Flaubert, 5 January 1880, in Zola, *Oeuvres complètes*, 9, 1176.

32. Zola, "L'attaque du moulin," in *Oeuvres complètes*, 9, 1058.

33. In the Pléiade edition, the refrain "A Berlin! A Berlin! A Berlin!" appears eight times in only fourteen pages (2: 1474, 1475, 1477, 1479, 1481, 1482, 1484, 1485).

34. Zola, letter to A. Loewenstein, 11 March 1900, in *Correspondance*, 10, 148.

35. Zola, "Comment ils poussent," *Le Figaro*, 21 February 1881, in *Oeuvres complètes*, 14, 525.

36. See Zola's letters to A. Loewenstein, 22 March 1900, 29 March 1900, 9 April 1900, 4 May 1900, in *Correspondance* 10, 140, 145–146, 148–149, 152.

37. See Greenhalgh and Çelik.

38. See Auriant, 77–84; Mitterand's "Notes et choix de variantes," in Zola, *Les Rougon- Macquart*, 2, 1723–1724; Zola, "Notes parisiennes," 14 June 1876, reprinted in Mitterand, "Etude," in Zola, *Les Rougon-Macquart*, 2, 1658–1660; Zola, "Lettres parisiennes [Les courses de Longchamps]," *La cloche*, 13 June 1872, in *Oeuvres complètes*, 14, 83.

39. Zola, "Lettres parisiennes [Les courses de Longchamps]," *La cloche*, 13 June 1872, in *Oeuvres complètes*, 14, 83.

40. See Zola's letter to van Santen-Kolff, 5 March 1888, in *Correspondance*, 6, 258.

41. Zola, "Les miracles," *La cloche*, 22 June 1872, in *Oeuvres complètes*, 14, 93.

42. See Becker's "Introduction" to her edition of Zola, *Nana*, lxxvii–lxxix.

43. See, for example, Rod; Doumic; Brunetière.

Works Cited

Adler, Laura. *La vie quotidienne des maisons closes*. Paris: Hachette, 1990.

Auriant. *La véritable histoire de Nana*. Paris: Mercure de France, n.d.

Bernheimer, Charles. *Figures of Ill Repute: Representing Prostitution in Nineteenth-Century France*. Cambridge: Harvard UP, 1989.

Boime, Albert. *Art and the French Commune: Imagining Paris after War and Revolution*. Princeton: Princeton UP, 1995.

Brunetière, Fernand. *Le roman naturaliste*. Paris: Calmann Lévy, 1893.

Castle, Terry. *The Apparitional Lesbian: Female Homosexuality and Modern Culture*. New York: Columbia UP, 1993.

Çelik, Zeynep. *Displaying the Orient: Architecture of Islam at Nineteenth-Century World's Fairs*. Berkeley: U of California P, 1992.

Chartier, Roger. *Les origines culturelles de la révolution francaise*. Paris: Seuil. 1990.

Chitnis, Bernice. *Reflecting on Nana*. London: Routledge, 1991.

Clayson, Hollis. *Painted Love: French Art of the Impressionist Era*. New Haven: Yale UP, 1991.

Corbin, Alain. *Women for Hire: Prostitution and Sexuality in France after 1850*. Trans. Alan Sheridan. Cambridge: Harvard UP, 1990.

Davis, Natalie Zemon. *Society and Culture in Early Modern France*. Stanford: Stanford UP, 1965.

Doumic, René. *Portraits d'écrivains*. Paris: Perrin, 1902.

During, Simon. "Introduction." *The Cultural Studies Reader*. Ed. Simon During. London: Routledge, 1993.

Forbes, Jill, and Michael Kelly, eds. *French Cultural Studies: An Introduction*. Oxford: Oxford UP, 1995.

Graff, Gerald, *Professing Literature: An Institutional History*. Chicago: Chicago UP, 1987.

Greenhalgh, Paul. *Ephemeral Vistas: The Expositions universelles. Great Exhibitions and World's Fairs, 1851-1939*. Manchester: Manchester UP, 1988.

Gullickson, Gay. *Unruly Women of Paris: Images of the Paris Commune*. Ithaca: Cornell UP, 1996.

Hall, Stuart. "Cultural Studies and Its Theoretical Legacies." *Cultural Studies*. Eds. Lawrence Grossberg, Cary Nelson, and Paula Treichler. New York: Routledge, 1992.

Higonnet, Margaret Randolph, Jane Jenson, Sonya Michel, and Margaret Collins Weitz, eds. *Behind the Lines: Gender and the Two World Wars*. New Haven: Yale UP 1987.

Hunt, Lynn, Margaret Jacob, and Joyce Appleby. *Telling the Truth about History*. New York: Norton, 1994.

Kanes, Martin. *L'atelier de Zola: Textes de journaux, 1865-1870*. Genève: Droz, 1963.

La Capra, Dominick. "History, Language, and Reading: Waiting for Crillon." *American Historical Review* 100, 3 (June 1995): 799–828.

Leith, James A., ed. *Images of the Commune*. Montreal: McGill-Queens UP, 1978.

Lanson, Gustave. *Histoire de la littérature française*. Paris: Hachette, 1895.

Mark, Vera. "Questions for French Cultural Studies." *French Historical Studies* 19, 2 (Fall 1995): 433–449.

Mitterand, Henri. *Zola journaliste de l'affaire Manet à l'affaire Dreyfus*. Paris: Armand Colin, 1962.

Mosse, George. *Nationalism and Sexuality: Middle-Class Morality and Sexual Norms in Modern Europe*. Madison: U of Wisconsin P, 1985.

Novick, Peter. *That Noble Dream: The "Objectivity Question" and the American Historical Profession*. Cambridge: Cambridge UP, 1988.

Parker, Andrew, Mary Russo, Coris Sommer, and Patricia Yaeger, eds. *Nationalisms and Sexualities*. New York: Routledge, 1992.

Peer, Shanny. "French Civilization and Its Discontents." *French Historical Studies* 19, 2 (Fall 1995): 415–432.

Rod, Edouard. *Les idées morales du temps présent*. Paris: Perrin, 1897.

Rufener, Helen. *Biography of a War Novel: Zola's* La débâcle. New York: King's Crown Press, 1946.

Schor, Naomi. *Breaking the Chain: Women, Theory, and French Realist Fiction*. New York: Columbia UP, 1985.

———. *Zola's Crowds*. Baltimore: Johns Hopkins UP, 1978.

Smith, Bonnie. "Historiography, Objectivity, and the Case of the Abusive Widow." *Feminists ReVision History*. Ed. Ann-Louise Shapiro. New Brunswick: Rutgers UP, 1994.

Tax, Meredith. "I Had Been Hungry All the Years." *Unequal Sisters: A Multicultural Reader in U.S. Women's History*. Ed. Ellen Carol Dubois and Vicki L. Ruiz. New York: Routledge, 1990.

Thompson, Clive, ed. "Emile Zola: Lectures au féminin." *Les Cahiers naturalistes*, 69, 1995.

Walby, Sylvia. "Woman and Nation." *International Journal of Comparative Sociology* 33, 1–2 (1992): 81–100.

Zola, Emile. *Correspondance*. 10 Vols. Ed. Bard. H. Bakker. Montreal: PU de Montréal, Paris: CNRS, 1978–1995.

———. *Nana*. Ed. Colette Becker. Classiques Garnier. Paris: Dunod, 1994.

———. *Nana*. Ed. Pierre Louis Rey. Paris: Presses Pocket, 1991.

———. *Oeuvres complètes*. 15 Vols. Ed. Henri Mitterand. Paris: Cercle du livre précieux, 1966–1970.

———. *Les Rougon-Macquart: Histoire naturelle et sociale d'une famille sous le Second Empire*. Ed. Armand Lanoux and Henri Mitterand. Paris: Pléiade, 1960.

3

On the Language-Culture Nexus

Ross Chambers

COMMUNICATING IN A VACUUM

We've all met their ilk, in books with snappy titles that take the form of cheery exhortations (*Allons-y!*) or dubious puns (*Tu parles!*). Here they are, Courtney and Jason: American college students, white and middle class of course, presumed straight, and native speakers of English (not Spanish or Korean). They're in France on a summer visit, and they've taken a trip on a Parisian *bateau-mouche*, let's say. They are wholeheartedly admiring the monuments on both sides of the Seine, and conscientiously ignoring the sweaty crowd of tourists surrounding them (the tourist industry isn't part of the "France" they've come to "see"). And here are Jean-Pierre and Sylvie—Parisian students, also white and middle class, also presumed straight, but French speakers— who just happen somehow to be on the boat too. The foursome gets on famously: it goes without saying that they will speak French, they compare notes about, oh, their respective schools, teachers, and programs of study, and part with cheery farewells after agreeing to meet again (for a bike ride, perhaps, or a visit to the musée d'Orsay).

What is wrong with this picture? (Yes, I know it's a caricature, and like all caricatures "unfair"). Well, for one thing, no one seems to have any particular agenda. Courtney never seems moved to ask in a puzzled tone: "Was that guy coming on to me? Or are French boys like that all the time?" Jean-Pierre is never recorded acting blasé (*"Ces Américains, quand-même, ils sont bien gentils, mais qu'est-ce qu'ils sont sérieux! Y'*

a vraiment pas de plaisir à les faire marcher!") [*These Americans are
pretty nice, but are they ever serious! It's really fun to lead them on."*]
As a result, there never seem to be any miscommunications or
misunderstandings, gaffes or social hitches. In these pedagogical encounters, everyone quite preternaturally means exactly what they say
and says exactly what they mean; no moves and countermoves take
place—just pleasant chat and the exchange of bits of information (*"Mon
prof de français est bien gentil"* or *"Regarde! c'est le dôme de l'Institut!"*)
[*"my French prof is really nice. . . . Look, it's the dome of the Institute!"*].
Everything is transparent, straightforward, immediately interpretable,
bland. Everyone gets to practice their French but, discursively speaking,
nothing happens, because nothing in particular is ever at stake.

Culture, for example, never gets in the way of things, never has to
be negotiated. That's because either it has the status of *décor* (like the
banks of the Seine—forget the tourist industry that brings Courtney and
Jason there) or it figures in conversation as a topic of *information*,
about what goes on in French classrooms, for example. For communication to occur in this somewhat eerie world of pedagogical dialogue,
it's enough—necessary but also sufficient—that the participants have a
common language (French) and know how to string words together
into grammatically well-formed sentences. On that single condition,
communication is always perfect. In short, there is language on the one
hand, and culture on the other, the latter being something one might
talk *about* but never something that enters actively into social interactions, mediating them and shaping their dynamics. There is no acknowledgment that the language-culture relation might form a "nexus" (that
they might be distinguishable from each other while being indissolubly
bound together, such that the one cannot occur without the other).

What, then, would a language education look like that was attentive to the language-culture nexus? What might a "French cultural studies" that would understand culture as something other than "background material" have to say about how we, in United States schools
and colleges, go about the business of teaching students to "speak
French"?

LEARNING TO NEGOTIATE CULTURAL DIFFERENCE

There's a reason why I raise this question. Because French studies has
heretofore been a language-based discipline, the presumption is that
any "French cultural studies" we might invent will have to relate to
language and the teaching of language. Yet that is not otherwise a self-

evident proposition. Cultural studies "proper," for instance, has shown no more interest in the relation between culture and language than our linguistic pedagogy has acknowledged the nexus. Furthermore, and as the existence of world languages (of which French is one) clearly demonstrates, there is no one-on-one tie between "a" language and "a" (or "the") culture that might correspond to it. Any given language, it seems, can be appropriated for purposes of communication, including cross-cultural communication, between people of many and widely different cultures, so how can language and culture form a "nexus"?

Well, cultures themselves aren't unitary "things," in the way that nationalisms of all stripes (and other forms of cultural essentialism) would have us believe. The concept of a "national" culture (e.g., that of France) is imaginary, for example, in the same sense as the unitary national community itself is, as Benedict Anderson famously put it, imagined; in other words, it is an ideological construct. (And the same is true, incidentally, of supposedly unitary "national" languages). The widespread belief in France that there *is* such a thing as a national French culture, and that it is tied to the French language (so that foreign or non-native speakers of French are expected to conform to it) has everything to do with the history of French republicanism (*"la République, une et indivisible"*) and a long-standing politics of central-ization; it is in particular a tribute to the power of what Althusser calls the "state ideological apparatuses." So, in the event, the famous "Frenchness" that is held to be part and parcel of speaking French will normally turn out to be defined as a function of the class, gender, race, education, politics, regional affiliation, and social status of the persons concerned—it differs widely, not only from milieu to milieu but from interaction to interaction. There is thus nothing to be learned from this essentially empty concept, either about the putative content of such an allegedly unitary culture or about its relation to a French language that experience shows can be used effectively in many different cultural environments, including "cross-cultural" ones.

So the peculiarity of "French cultural studies," if it should ever get off the ground, will be that it will have to define its object as a study of the *many* cultures of French-speaking people in the world, in the knowledge that French-speakingness does not, of itself, define anything like a unitary cultural field capable of designating "national" groups of French-speakers (*"les Francais," "les Québecois"*), let alone the total population of French-speakers-in-general. The ability to speak French (whether acquired from birth or as a second/foreign language) gives one a means of linguistic communication by means of which social interaction becomes possible with so wide a range of other, culturally diverse or culturally similar, French speakers, "native" and otherwise, that the only possible hypothesis is that these speakers have nothing more in common, and nothing less, than any other population of globally assembled humans of similar size but speaking different languages. And yet (forgive the military metaphor) I stick to my guns, there *is* a nexus of language and culture such that linguistic relations are inevitably culturally mediated and cultural relations are, equally inevitably, enacted in linguistic interchanges. What, then, does it mean to speak of such a nexus? And how should we conceive French-language pedagogy in the United States (i.e., as the acquisition of a "foreign" language), in light of the hypothesis that culture is neither an autonomous "background" to linguistic exchanges (which may but need not refer to it) nor a homogeneous formation of, for example, a "national" kind, but is nevertheless an indissoluble factor, as the concept of a nexus implies, in supposedly "linguistic" exchanges?

These are the questions I want to raise. They amount to asking what a culturally oriented language education might look like when it is understood that there is no "target" culture, or set of "target" cultures, that can be identified, isolated, described, and drilled, and that there is no realistic prospect, therefore, of teaching non-native French speakers to become (or to simulate), for the purposes of speaking French, culturally "French" subjects in any sense (or, if it comes to that, any other kind of "foreign" cultural subject).

Taking up a banner first raised by Anne Freadman, I'll propose that, under such circumstances, we should be teaching learners of French as a foreign language (and indeed any other foreign or second language) that, to the extent that they are learning the language for purposes of social interaction, they will need (in addition to grammatical and morphological competence, a decent lexicon and a degree of phonetic skill in the target language) certain kinds of *pragmatic* know-how—forms of sensitivity and flexibility—amounting to an ability to recognize and accommodate to a multiplicity of variable cultural differences. Such pragmatic skills would amount to a necessary *rhetorical* competence, not "in the language" (and any supposedly corresponding culture) but *as* non-native users of a particular language, who will find themselves engaging with other (non-native and native) users of the language in interactions regulated by a large and somewhat unpredictable diversity of cultural circumstances. Using a language such as French, North American learners will often find themselves, of course, in readily recognized and relatively familiar cultural circumstances. But they will also encounter more unexpected and unfamiliar situations (worldwide as well as in France); and, indeed, the stronger their specifically linguistic skills become, the more likely they are to discover the extent to which supposedly familiar circumstances are themselves the product of misrecognition, so that an illusion of cultural similarity with respect to the interlocutor may always mask so-called "subtle" but actually crucial divergences, which are tricky precisely because they may go so readily undetected. In other words, cultural diversity should always be the primary expectation of the non-native speaker of French, who should therefore be in possession of well-honed skills of adaptability and flexibility.

For it is scarcely feasible, pedagogically speaking, to prepare such learners *specifically* for every familiar, and falsely familiar, as well as obviously or subtly different, cultural situation they're likely to find themselves in. In the past we've tended to solve this problem by ignoring it: we've tried to teach a supposedly neutral or all-purpose version of "the" language, leaving the issue of what happens in actual situations of language use for our language learners to work out on their own. Whence the odd linguistic exercises I parodied a moment ago. I'm arguing instead that we might want to put correspondingly less emphasis on "proficiency" in pedagogically defined and predetermined language skills (on the assumption that they will prove universally applicable), and more emphasis on pragmatic (rhetorical) adaptability in making suitable use of linguistic knowledge in circumstances that can't themselves be foreseen, let alone taught. The theoretical axioms on which my case rests are thus the following: (a) language occurs only as a use of language; (b) language use implies indissoluble solidarity, a "nexus," of language and cultural circumstance; and (c) cultural circumstance is itself inevitably a local phenomenon, of such a kind as to resist generalization and reduction to rule.

A reason why it has been possible for so long to conceive language pedagogy as the acquisition of skills in the absence of concern for pragmatic adaptability is, perhaps, that we teachers have ourselves tended to misrecognize the degree of local cultural difference that exists among people (such as the English and the French, or Americans and the French) whose social practices are those of Western modernity, and this both despite and because of a certain fascination with the will-o'-the-wisps of supposedly national "character" and national "culture." At the same time we have failed until quite recently to take account of the way world languages fulfill the communicational needs of people of widely divergent cultures, whose insertion in the culture of modernity may differ significantly from that of Westerners. The first requirement of a pedagogy oriented toward pragmatic adaptability would therefore be that it correct these two forms of misrecognition: Raymonde Carroll's excellent book, *Evidences invisibles*, is a fine starting point (precisely because it condones the concept of "national" cultures) for dealing with the first of these. But once the degree to which local cultural differences affect linguistic communication *has* become evident, the next problem becomes this: how does one (learn to) negotiate interactions that are governed by an assumption of cultural difference rather than of similarity?

The operative word here is "negotiate," for as I've already hinted, there is no requirement that in such interactions one participant should commit a kind of suicide of cultural subjectivity in order to conform to the expectations of the other, say the "native speaker" or the "culturally French" subject. For one thing, those assumptions aren't necessarily retrievable (indeed, they are likely to be opaque to all the participants, especially in the heat of action). For another, and more importantly— the assumptions of many French speakers themselves with respect to the primacy of a "national" culture notwithstanding—cultural authority is likely to vary according to the social identities of the participants and the hierarchical relations that are perceived to pertain between them (adults and children, men and women, and so forth) as well as the perceived genre of the interaction (say, a friendly gossip session as opposed to a formal examination or an after-dinner speech). It becomes necessary to understand that *part of the point* of many interactions will lie in the working out, between the participants, of the conditions of the interaction's possibility, that is their joint figuring out, as they make their discursive moves, of what it takes to make the particular interaction they are engaged in "work."

And to this understanding, finally, is attached an intellectual bonus, which lies in the possibility it offers of discovering that such circumstances are not necessarily the "exceptional" or "unusual" case, applicable only when cultural difference—as opposed to an assumed "norm" of similarity—is presupposed or becomes evident. It is more likely the case, for good theoretical reasons, that communication is regularly governed by differential relations, including relations of cultural difference—relations that of course imply *some* degree of cultural similarity as well as of difference—than that it depends on transparency. After all, the only reason what we call "communication" is actually necessary at all (we might otherwise rely on mental telepathy) is that differences, all of which in the final analysis can be classified as cultural, exist. As a result, communication is always, in a certain sense, a negotiation of difference and so concerned, inevitably, with a (usually unself-conscious) exploration of its own conditions of possibility. And that insight, in turn, sounds as if it could provide a nice starting point for any form of cultural studies that seeks to understand itself as linguistically (but I would rather say discursively or semiotically) grounded, since it means that we can examine *any* supposedly "linguistic" exchange as, simultaneously, a culturally mediated negotiation and a negotiation about culture—one that has culture (and its synonym, cultural difference) as at least one of its stakes.

I'll try to do just that in a moment, by way of exemplifying what I mean, taking an interaction in which I once participated as a kind of acted-out "comment" on its own cultural conditions of possibility. Not unexpectedly, perhaps, in view of what I've already foreshadowed, these will turn out to have been forms of sensitivity to difference and of flexibility in handling it in which, in the event, both of the participants on this particular occasion proved to be deficient. For, of course, our "successful" acts of communication (scare quotes because we don't know, in fact, how successful or unsuccessful they are) have nothing to teach us; it's our communicational failures that are instructive.

CULTURE AS PRESUPPOSITION

But let me first explain my understanding of the language-culture nexus, which can be approached through the concept of presupposition. More precisely, I propose that the ability to recognize that a cultural difference is active has to do with *sensitivity to presupposition*, while the ability appropriately to negotiate a situation of cultural difference has to do with the particular form of presuppositional understanding that is genre, specifically with the possession of a rich *genre repertoire* and the ability to be *generically flexible*.

It is impossible to use language in social circumstances without making presuppositions and without assuming that one's presuppositions are shared by one's interlocutors. Although some would argue that not all presupposition is cultural (there being, as it were, "situational" presupposition and "cultural" presupposition), it is enough for my present argument to point out that it can be, and frequently is, cultural in kind. If I say: "The weather is clearing up" (implying something like: "Let's go on our planned picnic after all!" but presupposing that picnics are better held in fine weather than in wet), the presupposition is perhaps of such a degree of commonsensicality as to be transcultural. If my stockbroker says to me (or I to her): "Buy low, sell high!"—the presupposition being that it is desirable to get rich quick— we are referred, obviously enough, to the culture of capitalism, whose common sense, fortunately enough, is (so far) not universally shared. If I complain to my shrink that "my mother never loved me" (presupposition: mothers should love their children), one might hesitate over the status of the presupposition: are there people who do not have a cultural understanding, and so presuppose, that mothers should love their children? (I'll bet there are.)

Where presuppositional common sense becomes significant, however, from the point of view of the language-culture nexus, is in those cases where it is *clearly* cultural in kind because presuppositional differences turn out to be active, and to be causing trouble, in communicational events. I worked for many years in a multicultural department before realizing that some of our stresses and strains were being caused by the fact that, although all of my colleagues presupposed, as did I, that a well-functioning department requires "teamwork," the concept of teamwork itself, for some of us, presupposed something like collective responsibility while for others it was more a matter of simple division of labor. So some of us were, constantly and with the best of intentions—but oblivious to our colleagues' anger—impinging on areas that others liked to think of as their own personal terrain of action and responsibility. Such frictions might have been avoided if there had been greater sensitivity, on either side of the divide, to the possibility of cultural difference.

Now all the examples of presupposition I have given so far are *propositional* in kind. They are a precondition for understanding what the proffered statements actually signify in the context of their utterance ("The weather is clearing up" means "Let's revive our plan for a picnic"). *Generic* presupposition, on the other hand, concerns the kind of interaction itself in which the uttering subjects are engaged. Thus, where propositional presupposition mediates the understanding of "statements" (in Benveniste's vocabulary, language as *énoncé*), generic presupposition mediates the "use" of language as a relational phenomenon (language as *énonciation*). And since no *énoncé* can occur without simultaneously constituting an *énonciation* (and vice versa), it follows that neither kind of presupposition occurs in isolation: each entails the other.

The importance of the distinction to my argument, however, lies in the fact that where propositional presuppositions are cultural givens, generic presupposition offers room for pragmatic maneuver. The kind of sensitivity to presupposition that makes for skill in recognizing when cultural differences are at work entails the ability to recognize the effects of *both* propositional presupposition (which is where differences in "subjective intention" will show up) and generic presupposition (which is where differences concerning the understanding of "what is going on" intersubjectively will appear). But I can do little about the other person's propositional presuppositions, beyond learning to recognize when differences arise because of them. Nor, indeed, can I prevent the other from making generic presuppositions that differ from my own. Genre, though—I am following here the work of Anne Freadman—is a terrain that has the particularity of being singularly fluid and of lending itself easily to negotiation, so that it offers a greater chance of corrective behavior when a discrepancy in generic presupposition has become evident. If I realize that my interlocutors are saying teamwork but thinking division of labor whereas I myself am thinking collective responsibility, the best we can do, probably, is to agree to differ (and that's a worthwhile step). If I see that my companions are (mis-) taking my "philosophical musings" for specifically targeted "personal attacks" on their character, lifestyle, career profile, or life project, there's still time—this is a "best case" scenario!—to repair the damage through some sort of mutual adjustment in our collective sense of the interaction. That's because the interaction is in fact still going on, and remains open, therefore, to the possibility of generic redefinitions.

It was Derrida who made it clear that generic situations are always and necessarily mixed, so that genre shifting is always potentially an option. Obviously, we don't always take advantage of that fluidity, or need to. Every time I get my hair cut, I fall into the same kind of conversation with my hairdresser. But it's always possible to change genres, or—what amounts to the same thing—for one's understanding of what is entailed, for example, by the genre called "conversation with one's hairdresser," to change. (By mutual agreement, or even by a *coup de force*—after all, I'm the customer, who is "always right"—I can segue from "chat" into "serious discussion" with my barber, and back to chat again, without its being necessarily a big deal, or indeed without its being necessary for either of us to realize what has happened.) Genre is thus the terrain on which, in situations where cultural difference is an active factor, it is theoretically possible for concessions to be made, agreements worked out, or alternatively (as in the story I'm about to tell), for rigidities to be displayed and communicational disasters to arise.

The latter will occur either because of a simple failure, on one or both (or all) "sides" of an interaction, to recognize that presuppositional difference is at work, or else from generic rigidity, which itself can arise either through simple unwillingness to change genres (even though one might) or from an insufficient genre repertoire on one or both (or all) sides, with a consequent difficulty for the participants to find common generic ground. Generic give-and-take, conversely, depends on at least one of the participants' having both a good genre-repertoire and a disposition inclined to flexibility. Thus, a simple form of genre shifting, and one that frequently arises in cross-cultural circumstances, consists of drawing attention to presuppositional differences of a propositional kind—"That's funny, when you said teamwork, I thought you meant something like division of labor but now I'm beginning to see you meant collective responsibility—what a weird misunderstanding!"—so that the participants can move generically, say, from "holding a conversation" to something more like "doing philology" about the conversation they are having, and establish an *entente* (which of course includes the possibility of disagreeing) on that basis.

I am suggesting, then, that for the purpose of understanding the relation of language (-use) to culture, one can understand culture as a vast field of propositional and generic presuppositions, that is, of understandings that are so self-evident to cultural subjects that in many circumstances they don't need to be recognized, let alone made explicit or addressed. With any given person, I as a cultural subject may share n degree of overlap in the area of propositional presuppositions (resulting, perhaps, from similarities of class and education, even though we may speak different languages) and n degree of overlap (but not necessarily for the same value of n) with respect to the kinds of social interaction we recognize as valid. With respect to a certain number, perhaps quite large or perhaps quite small, of other propositional and generic presuppositions, we may be quite out of synch, however. (We may, for example, readily agree that mothers should love their children without having to discuss the issue, but get into strife because what to one is a "friendly dinner party" is, to the other, an occasion for "political activism," or because, although we may agree that this is a "friendly dinner party," that generic concept entails for each of us quite different understandings about, say, the degree of formality and informality that should prevail among the guests.) The success or otherwise of my interactions with that person will depend on my ability, and hers, to recognize *both* the propositional and the generic presuppositions we have in common, *and* those we don't share. But it will depend also, beyond that kind of recognition, on our common—if perhaps unequally shared—ability to negotiate such differences, which itself rests on genre-flexibility, including both the number of genres we may have more or less in common, and our willingness and ability to be generically adaptable.

I'm not forgetting my earlier point that misrecognition of difference as similarity is presumably rife, or that misrecognition thrives most easily when different cultural subjects share a common language. But in the end cultural difference matters only when (either because misrecognition doesn't occur, or because it isn't mutual) active misunderstandings and actual conflict arise (a misrecognized misunderstanding isn't functionally a misunderstanding at all). It is in those circumstances that sensitivity to presupposition becomes important, because it makes it more possible to identify a problem, actual or potential; and it is then that the rhetorical skills of genre flexibility can come into play, as a way of eluding the problem, or of negotiating it, by redefining the nature of the interaction. I can look for a genre that I share with my interlocutor(s) either genuinely or by misrecognition (but who can tell the difference?); or, if that fails, find a genre of my own that corresponds well enough to what my interlocutors' seems to be for a misrecognition to occur that enables the interaction to continue. ("Hmm, this seems to be a more formal occasion than I thought, not the friendly dinner party I assumed: I'd better mind my p's and q's.")

The anthropologist Eric Michaels describes a group of Warlpiri Aboriginals, culturally still close to their traditional "law," watching a Rocky movie and speculating about who is looking after the hero's mother-in-law and who, of the cast of characters, might have a classificatory identity suitable for marriage with Rocky's sister. Through misrecognition, they have adapted the genre of the Hollywood movie to that of the Warlpiri story, and Michaels points out both that the movie lends itself to the adaptation (it was, in potentia, a Warlpiri story as well as a Hollywood movie from the start), and that such borrowing of cultural items (traditionally songs, stories, designs, and rituals) along so-called "song-lines" and as fragments of a Dreaming to which no one has total access, has been one of the secrets of Aboriginal cultural continuity and stability for at least forty thousand years. If the Warlpiri are right, and Michaels correct in his analysis, the adaptability inherent in the phenomenon of genre may well be a major clue, then, both to understanding how "cross-cultural" communication can occur, and to making it happen.

A SORRY STORY

The occasion on which I (and my interlocutor) displayed mutual inability to adapt occurred at a *réception* I attended a few years ago in a provincial city in the Rhône valley. I found myself talking with a woman I didn't know, whom I'll call Simone (I never really caught her actual name). I had been teaching at a summer school, which was culturally speaking its own little autonomous heterotopia, and mixing with a group of friends who were very largely of the species "expatriate intellectual," and inclined therefore to tolerance with respect to one another's cultural assumptions. Nothing had happened to remind me that in France one can still encounter quite rigid cultural expectations. Simone, though, was very *bourgeoisie de province*: perhaps sixty, carefully dressed, coiffed, and made up, with (I thought) more grooming than style and slightly overdressed for the occasion (she must have thought me over-casual and unkempt). Clearly at ease in the genre of *mondanités*, it was she who launched the conversation; she did so by mentioning that she had seen me on other occasions and noticed that I was given to wearing a wide-brimmed hat, of which she made gentle fun: was I addicted to it? was it a fetish? had I made some kind of vow? I recognized the genre and it was up to me to respond in kind—that is, in the mode of "banter"—with perhaps a well-turned comment on her own outfit, and then to segue, as party chat requires, into some other harmless topic. But she had accidentally pushed some of my buttons, tapping into both a personal anxiety and a political concern of mine. I heard myself expounding to her the high incidence of skin cancer, especially among Australians of Anglo-Celtic extraction, and waxing indignant about the failure of governments, worldwide, to take responsible measures to correct the damage to the earth's ozone layer, or even to warn their citizens of its effects. Neither disease nor the criticism of authority are necessarily appropriate topics in Simone's milieu for an insignificant conversation on a festive occasion with someone you are unlikely ever to meet again. She made an attempt—symptomatically, I've forgotten what she said—to bring the talk back to a lighter register. But I was launched, and proceeded to share with her some alarming news I had recently learned, concerning an epidemic of melanoma among Torres Strait Islanders and Australian Aboriginals in the far north of the country, people who erroneously believe themselves immune to the effects of ultraviolet rays.

This time Simone, still trying to correct what to her (but not to me) was my persistent genre-infraction, was led to take more heroic measures. Maintaining perfect poise and with a very large smile, still in the semi-bantering tone with which she had begun the conversation, she refused the tone of "concern" (in which I was stuck) and reasserted the register of pleasantry with a joke: "*Mais, Monsieur, vous voilà bien débarrassés, vous autres*" ["*But sir, then you will be well rid of them*"].

For my part—recognizing that it was a joke but thinking it in the worst possible "taste"—I was unable for a moment to respond at all; and when finally I did so I launched blindly into an angry lecture on the history of colonial settlement and race relations in Australia (understanding myself to be addressing the question of who might appropriately wish to get rid of whom). But it was now clear to both of us that, as party conversation, our interaction had failed disastrously and within a few moments we parted company by unspoken mutual consent, I simmering with rage and she, I presume, likewise simmering over my unconscionable uncouthness.

Obviously, racism is an issue here. But so too, as I realized much later, is my failure to pick up on her clear signals that (a) I had failed to appreciate the implications of the generic situation as she viewed it; and (b) that she had no intention of compensating for my deficiency by backing away from her own generic presuppositions as they had been signalled from the start. It would be tempting to say that the conversation failed because of a political incompatibility: whereas I am "concerned" about racial issues, Simone turned out to be a racist. But that is too easy, since I too am a racist as, in the culture of modernity, all cultural subjects (alas!) inevitably are. It does no good to "know" that race is an ideological construct; one still can't live in the world without making racial identifications every day, and my own segue from the "plight" of white Australians to the epidemic among black Australians, and my "concern" on their behalf, are clearly a case in point. The question to ask about racism, therefore, is not who is and who isn't racist, but to what social uses the ideology is put.

Simone's projection onto Australia of a certain Le Penist analysis of conditions in France (a country of sixty million people allegedly "invaded" by a few million immigrants from Africa and their descendants) is grotesque. But then, in her own understanding, she presumably wasn't proffering it as social analysis; rather, she was, doubtless slightly desperately, making a move in a conversational relation that, again from her angle of vision, had gone seriously awry. Her joke was a compromise formation between a certain conversational coherence rule (it was I who had brought up racial questions), the desire to signal to me the appropriate tone for a party conversation, and doubtless, at this point, a desire to punish me for my recidivism in genre-infraction. It doesn't follow that I should have *agreed* with her crazy analysis, just to be pleasant, just as it doesn't follow that I should simply have given in to her generic insistence on levity. But in responding at the level of ideology critique to her signal I was both demonstrating a generic rigidity of my own and, as it turned out, depriving myself, as a result, of any further opportunity to have input into Simone's thoughts and world view. The political conflict between a guilty-white-liberal racist and a Le Penist racist arose only because I had behaved, at a social gathering, like a pedantic intellectual (playing the Proustian role of Brichot, as opposed to the suave Swann, among the Verdurin "clan"). It was this cultural infraction, a form of genre-rigidity (rather than my political views, which she must have readily guessed) that was upsetting to Simone and in the end what she was no longer willing to tolerate.

I'm suggesting, then, that had I played my rhetorical cards better, we *could* have had a quite productive "political" conversation. Simone and I weren't in generic disagreement about the nature of the occasion and neither of us had an expectation of engaging in anything other than cocktail talk. Our difference related to what that generic understanding entailed: for me it did not exclude the possibility of "serious" topics arising and being seriously discussed, whereas for Simone the most important thing of all was that nothing "important" be said. Flexibility would have entailed either a redefinition of the genre itself ("Oops!" Simone might have thought, "this isn't a party conversation at all, this man thinks he's a talking head on TV"), or a revised understanding of what our generic agreement presupposed ("Whoa!" I could have said to myself, "this woman wants small talk and nothing but small talk"). By steering a middle course between Simone's generic presuppositions and my own, with a degree of give-and-take on each side, there was a chance, perhaps, for us to have had something like what she wanted (an amicable chat) without my eyes glazing over from sheer boredom (my major motivation on such occasions).

How might this have happened? Genre, to use Michael Halliday's vocabulary now, entails the regulation of "field," "tenor," and "mode." That is, there is a *semantic* domain that is thought appropriate on a given occasion (is it okay to discuss disease and death, for example, or to raise political issues?). A certain type of *interpersonal* relation is assumed, involving matters of power and/or solidarity (issues of status, prestige, hierarchy, and so forth, deriving from class, gender, race, level of education, and other markers of social identity). And finally, the generic agreement regulates *vehicular* options, matters of discursive medium and tonal register (or "level of style"): should I deal with this by phone or send a letter? is it appropriate to use coarse language? may I, or my interlocutor, "hold forth" at length, or is rapid turn-taking, with frequent shifts of matter, the rule? That there is a degree of mutual implication among field, tenor, and mode, is what genre conventions exist to make us think: Simone wanted the field to be inconsequential, the tenor noncommittal, and the mode correspondingly light, and I committed infractions, from her point of view, in each of these respects. But that such generic coherence is always loose, is what enables negotiations to take place and generic innovations to arise. If I've always called my boss "Ma'am," avoided bad language and refrained from mentioning my personal problems to her, I may one day get away with saying "shit" or mentioning that I have a headache, as long as I continue to say "Ma'am." In exchange for my adopting a bantering tone and a less concerned demeanor, consistent with the inconsequentiality of the relation between us, Simone might have been willing to countenance some expansion of the field of topics our conversation embraced. Had she in fact made a concession of that kind, I in turn might have been willing to be more playful in tone and less buttonholing in manner—less the "dreary pedant" she got and more the *mondain* she expected.

However, neither of us displayed that kind of flexibility. In holding forth as I did, in assuming that the relation between me and Simone was like that I had with my expatriate intellectual friends, and in insisting on raising the most "delicate" of topics (delicate in terms of her genre expectations), I was infringing all of her understandings of what the occasion of our meeting was all about. She similarly was infringing mine by insisting that everything—the topics of conversation, the degree of our engagement each with the other, the general tone— be kept "light." The result, since neither of us made the slightest concession, was the nasty standoff I've related, one that has stuck in my memory and left me with a nasty taste in my mouth for a number of years.

FROM PRAGMATIC PROFICIENCY TO CULTURAL STUDIES?

Reader, are you feeling that my essay, generically speaking, is itself a bit slippery? I am slithering around between the conventions of the allegorical anecdote (it means something, but I'm asking *you* to figure out its implications), the position paper (whose author knows all the answers) and the think piece (in which more or less pointed questions get asked, without its being clear what the answers might be). That makes concluding dicey, since there are a few questions I want to leave artfully hanging in the air, and a great many I don't know how to answer (or even, perhaps, how to pose correctly)—and yet I *am* trying to develop an argument and make it stick. Let's go back to the pedagogical issues I raised at the outset: how to teach a language such as French for cultural interaction, and the possible relation between such teaching and a "French cultural studies" that itself remains to be invented.

From the foregoing, it's fairly clear how I think such teaching should *not* be conceived. There being no possibility of identifying a single "target" culture (i.e., a single set of presuppositions, propositional and generic) that would be automatically associated, wherever and whenever, with speaking the French language, it can make no sense, pedagogically or otherwise, to attempt to isolate and describe—that is, in fact, to construct—such a culture, either with a view to teaching students to conform to its expectations when speaking French, or with a view to teaching them to make allowances for its differences from "their own" culture (what would *that* be?). There is no mileage, for example, in teaching the cultural component of the language-culture nexus as a set of supposedly major genres (major for whom?) that would be available for interaction whenever English-speaking North Americans and French-speaking people of whatever provenance got together, no likelihood of cataloguing those genres in terms of field, tenor, and mode, and then *drilling* them.

Instead, we might want to think about an education in the pragmatics of language use and, for our specific purposes, in the pragmatics of using a foreign language. This would entail developing pedagogical strategies aimed at emphasizing situational, and therefore strictly local, appropriateness of use as much as correctness of speech (the latter being in fact a function of the former). These strategies, I suggest, would seek to develop an awareness of presupposition and to encourage sensitivity to its role as the mode whereby culture—that is, cultural difference—is operative in every use of language (every social interaction), presupposition being understood, in turn, as both propositional and generic. In the case of the latter, we should emphasize, not a prescriptive catalogue of genres, but the infinite resources for flexible interaction that genre offers, that is, the fluidity and diversity of genres, their always potential otherness from "themselves," and thus seek to encourage the supple resourcefulness a pragmatics of interaction in intercultural conditions would entail. These qualities, in turn, would become the criteria for a new understanding of linguistic proficiency, as the ability not so much to produce a supposedly universally correct form of speech independently of circumstance, as to recognize situations in which there is a significant difference between the assumptions and expectations the different participants bring to them, and to make rhetorical moves accordingly.

So far, so good. But now the questions arise to which I don't have answers: how, in detail and as a practical matter, to go about this? The most important how-to problem has been defined by Anne Freadman in her extremely lucid lecture on "Models of Genre in Language Teaching," the direct inspiration for the present piece. It resides in the culture of the classroom itself, a culture that has its own genres ("drill," "conversation practice") and which mediates all uses of a foreign language that occur under its aegis, turning them relentlessly into fictional examples of language use, "classroom exercises" (with real-life stakes approaching zero). (Roland Barthes pointed out a long time ago that the phrase *quia ego nominor leo* in a textbook states "for my name is Lion" but signifies, in situation: *"je suis un exemple de grammaire"* [*"I am a grammar example"*].) If the challenge of a pragmatic understanding of linguistic proficiency lies in the ability to operate appropriately under generic circumstances one has not (been) prepared for, because they are inevitably local and so new, unforeseen, and unexpected, then that challenge *begins* with the transfer of language use from the pedagogical circumstances of the classroom to nonfictional, extra-classroom uses, and it is such a "pedagogy of transfer" we will need to develop. It's a paradoxical concept, I know—pedagogy is asked to supervise its own death—but then, education itself (which, in its widest sense, is oriented toward the moment when the services of the educator no longer make sense, education as such having been superseded) is subject to the same paradox. I think we might begin by thinking *hard* about what it means that "living" in another language tends to produce pragmatically proficient users of second and foreign languages, while classroom language teaching tends to produce people whose knowledge of "the language" (as a grammar, a morphology, a phonology, a lexicon, and so forth) is extensive but who, when it comes time to make use of it, turn out to be tongue-tied and uninventive. Then we may be able to invent ways of making classroom genres (which, by axiom, cannot be "pure") more permeable than they currently are to extrapedagogical modes of language use: through field work projects, for example, but also through forms of play and the exercise of the imagination.

And what has all this to do, finally, with "French cultural studies"? I've argued elsewhere that French studies brings with it a set of disciplinary axioms that are intellectually, and if it comes to that politically, at odds with the understandings about culture that are characteristic of much "cultural studies" work (on this issue see also Petrey); consequently, I've suggested, the only place for a "French cultural studies" within French studies would be as an "invaginated" site of "post-disciplinary" critique of the discipline itself. That's a possible, but perhaps not very probable, development. On the other hand, "cultural studies," as it has evolved under historical circumstances of its own, isn't necessarily the only possible model. One of the surprising gaps in contemporary cultural studies as it is practiced in many English-speaking countries (and some others) in the wake of the Birmingham school, lies precisely in its indifference to the language-culture nexus. One can speculate about the reasons for such indifference, which are perhaps not unrelated to the quite similar cultural studies habit of leaving the study of elite genres to the established disciplines, in favor of popular and everyday manifestations. But it's conceivable, nevertheless, that, were French studies (or some similar discipline) to reinvent its own conceptualization of the language-culture nexus so as to orient it toward a pragmatics of language use, as the culturally mediated vehicle of social interactions, such a turn could provide a model and a starting point for new and important developments within cultural studies itself.

There is a chance, in other words, of something genuinely helpful emerging, not only for French studies but also for cultural studies, and of its emerging, not from the existing literary and civilizational wings of French studies—which, I fear, are anxious only to appropriate the "cultural studies" aura without reexamining their own assumptions and practices—but from what has always been our bread-and-butter field, that of language pedagogy.

Works Cited

Althusser, Louis. "Ideology and State Ideological Apparatuses: Notes Towards an Investigation." *Lenin and Philosophy and Other Essays.* New York: Monthly Review Press, 1971, 127–186.

Anderson, Benedict. *Imagined Communities: Reflections on the Origin and Spread of Nationalism.* New York and London: Verso, 1983.

Benveniste, Emile. *Problèmes de linguistigue générale.* 2 vols. Paris: Gallimard, 1955, 1974. (Esp. "L'homme dans la langue," II, 195–238).

Carroll, Raymonde. *Evidences invisibles.* Paris: Seuil, 1987. Translated as *Cultural Misunderstandings: The French-American Experience.* Chicago: U of Chicago P, 1988.

Chambers, Ross. "Cultural Studies as a Challenge to French Studies." *Australian Journal of French Studies* 33, 2 (1996): 137–156.

Derrida, Jacques. "La loi du genre." *Parages.* Paris: Galilée, 1986, 249–287. Translated as "The Law of Genre." *Acts of Literature.* Ed. Derek Attridge. New York & London: Routledge, 1992: 221–252.

Freadman, Anne. "Untitled (On Genre)." *Cultural Studies*, 2, 1 (1988): 67–99.

_____. "Models of Genre in Language Teaching." Sonia Marks Lecture, University of Sydney, 1988. (Obtainable from Department of French Studies, University of Sydney, Sydney NSW 2006, Australia.)

Freadman, Anne, and Macdonald, Amanda. *What Is This Thing Called "Genre"?* Mount Nebo (Qld): Boombana Publications, 1994.

Halliday, M. A. K. *Language as Social Semiotic.* London: Edward Arnold, 1978.

Michaels, Eric. "Hollywood Iconography: A Walpiri Reading." *Bad Aboriginal Art. Tradition, Media, and Technological Horizons.* Minneapolis: U of Minnesota P, 1994.

Petrey, Sandy. "French Studies/Cultural Studies; Reciprocal Invigoration or Mutual Destruction." *French Review* 68, 3 (1995): 381–392.

4

Creolized North Africa

What Do They Really Speak in the Maghreb?

Alawa Toumi

On May 26, 1993, Algerian poet and journalist Tahar Djaout was murdered by Islamic fundamentalists in front of his two little daughters. He was thirty-nine. His crime, according to the murderers, was that he wrote in French. On the first anniversary of his death writer Rachid Boudjedra explained that French and Algerian intellectuals were partly responsible for this murder since they had accused Djaout of "collaboration" with France on a French television program; since they had found him guilty of "writing in French" (Boudjedra, 63). According to the Islamists and their supporters, Djaout, as an Algerian, a Muslim, and therefore an Arab, should have written in his native language, Arabic, not in French, the language of the colonizer.

The purpose of this chapter is to demonstrate that this seemingly impeccable logic is flawed and to argue that, being a matter of life and death in Algeria today, the language issue deserves to be examined closely. To that effect I will explore two related questions: what do people really speak in Algeria and why do most North African intellectuals still write in French?

HISTORICAL BACKGROUND

The first inhabitants of North Africa[1] called themselves *Imazighen*—plural of *Amazigh*—which means "free man." The Roman colonizers of

69

the second century B.C., who considered that everything foreign was barbarian, called the native North Africans "Berbers."[2] The actual Maghreb, which the Romans called Africa, was divided in two parts: Numidia, to the north of the city of Constantine, and Mauritania to the west. Massinissa, Jugurtha, and Saint Augustine, the author of *The Confessions*, were neither Roman nor Arab but *Imazighen*. These people spoke *Tamazight*, or Berber, as their mother tongue, yet wrote in Latin.[3]

Coming from Spain, the Vandals invaded North Africa in 429 A.D.. One century later, in 533, the Byzantines arrived in North Africa and remained there until the end of the sixth century. In the middle of the seventh century, in 647, Arabs—people who came from the Arabian peninsula—settled down in North Africa. According to historians,[4] the Arabs who left Mecca numbered fewer than 35,000 soldiers. After crossing the Gulf, the Middle East, and conquering Egypt a fraction of this army arrived in North Africa. Their first contacts with the *Imazighen*, who outnumbered them, were peaceful and soon after the Arabs' arrival, several Berber tribes converted to Islam. Nonetheless, one of those new converts, the Berber Koceila, led a rebellion against the Arabs and after his death, a woman called Dihya, better known as La Kahina, organized the resistance against the Arabo-Islamic colonizers, killing their leader Okba.[5] The Berber population of the seventh century has been estimated at about 400,000 people. Since the Arabs who had come from the Arabian peninsula represented less than 5 percent of the total population at the time, it is reasonable to assume that the dominant *Amazigh* character of the population remained unchanged. After the death of Kahina, other Berber tribes converted to Islam.[6] Nevertheless, the Muslim religion did not firmly establish itself as the dominant religion until the conquest of the Ottoman Turks in the sixteenth century,[7] and when it did, it adapted to the local customs and ancestral traditions.[8] Its strictures, for instance, were superseded by diverse honor codes.[9]

After 1830, French colonialism cut new boundaries in North Africa. Roman Numidia and Mauritania became French *départements* called Algeria bordered by two colonies, Morocco and Tunisia. Each parcel of land was divided according to regions. Colonialism was very careful to draw up boundaries so as to exacerbate ancient tribal quarrels and entertain old hate. The fall of Greater Kabylia in 1878, which had never been colonized prior to that date, followed by the *décret Crémieux* of 1880[10] succeeded in conquering the last Berber resistance, a situation that lasted until the beginning of the Algerian war in 1954.

Ethnically speaking, the Berbers, who exhibit a wide variety of physical features, are native North Africans. Although they have blended with many different colonizers from the Romans to the French, North Africans have struggled for centuries to preserve their language and culture. They cannot, therefore, simply be categorized as "Arabs."[11]

DIGLOSSIA

If the question, "which language do they speak in North Africa?" appears rather trivial at first, it is because it seems to beg one answer and one answer only: well, Arabic, of course. Just asking the question, in fact, can be viewed as a ridiculous challenge because of the commonly held notion that there exists one homogeneous, united, Arab people whose language is Arabic. It is also common knowledge, of course, that there still are people in North Africa who speak, write, and publish in French, and whether it is so because of their inability to let go of the colonial past or not, does not change much. From my vantage point, however, both views fail to account for the complex linguistic situation of the Maghreb. As I would like to argue, it is just as problematic to replace the erroneous notion of a linguistically homogeneous North Africa with that of a region linguistically polarized between Arabic on the one hand, and French on the other.

Like Kateb Yacine before him, the Moroccan sociologist Abdelkebir Khatibi suggests a more accurate and satisfying answer to the question raised above (What do they really speak in North Africa?) in the following lines from *Maghreb Pluriel*:

> Mauvaise plaisanterie, nous les Maghrébins, nous avons mis quatorze siècles pour apprendre la langue arabe (à peu près), plus d'un siècle pour apprendre le français (à peu près), et depuis des temps immémoriaux, nous n'avons pas su écrire le berbère. C'est dire que le bilinguisme et le plurilinguisme ne sont pas dans ces régions des faits récents. (Khatibi, 179)

The linguistic situation Khatibi describes here is one of diglossia. Frequent in communities that differentiate between at least two types of languages—one usually associated with the social elite, one with the common people[12]—diglossia is characterized by the coexistence within the same geographic region of a wide variety of linguistic practices. In North Africa, this includes Arabic and its dialect, Berber, as well as various forms of French and even Spanish. Of particular importance here is the distinction between classical Arabic and its various "dialects," a distinction that has serious political implications and therefore tends to be deemphasized these days. Some linguists, however, have long been aware of it. Moroccan linguist Mohammed Chafik points to it, for instance, when he wonders—in an article entitled "Structure socio-linguistique de l'arabe-marocain"—why Arabic speaking Middle Easterners do not understand the Arabic spoken in Morocco and elsewhere in North Africa.[13] North Africa is indeed very diverse and his question is a complex one.

From a historical point of view, *Tamazight,* or Berber, was spoken from the beginning of time until the seventh century, when Arab-Bedouins arrived and introduced Arabic. Several generations later some of the Moors spoke a mixture of Arabic-Berber, a hybrid form. At that time already, then, there were not two, but three languages: Berber, Arabic, and a first sabir, a spoken Arabo-Berber. After the Turkish, and especially the French colonization, this sabir was to undergo a second major hybridization with the language of Descartes. It would become a *pataouete*, a North African creole, a type of Franco-Arabo-Berber referred to as *Farabé,* with a multitude of words borrowed from Turkish, Spanish, and Italian.[14]

In his article "Quand tout un pays vit à l'heure du trabendo," the deceased novelist Rachid Mimouni described very accurately the Arabic spoken by the *"trabendistes,"* the little street vendors: "En Algérie, on ne parle ni l'arabe ni le français, mais un nouveau et succulent pataouete fait d'un curieux amalgame d'expressions arabes, françaises, berbères, et de suaves néologismes" (Mimouni, 94). It is this *"pataouete,"* this creolized form of Franco-Arabo-Berber spoken by North Africans, that Egyptians, Saudis, and other Middle Easterners do not understand. This very vivid example of diglossia has been largely ignored by scholars. Today, political forces are also inclined to deny the existence of this hybrid language, even as they obsessively attempt to purify *Farabé* from its Berber and French components. This creole Arabic is to classical Arabic what Yiddish is to Hebrew, what French is to Latin. Perhaps the best analogy is Afrikaan in South Africa, a creole form of Dutch intermingled with African, Portuguese, English, and Malay.[15]

Berber and *Farabé* (creole Arabic) are the two spoken languages of Algerians, Moroccans, and Tunisians. No one in North Africa has classical (Middle Eastern) Arabic as a native language. Just as being Spanish, French, or Italian does not mean that you can converse freely in Latin, so being North African does not mean that you are fluent in classical Arabic—unless, of course, you have studied it as a second or a third language in school. Studying classical Arabic is becoming a necessity in Algeria today because it is the official language, the language the president uses in his speeches, the language used for broadcasting news on national radio or television. But it is a foreign language for North Africans and not, by contrast, for the overwhelming majority of Arabic-speaking Middle Easterners. For them the difference between the classical Arabic they learn in schools and the Arabic dialect they speak at home is minimal—in part because the language of their ancestors did not go through various phases of hybridization.

A good way to emphasize this point is to consider that Egyptian, Syrian, and Palestinian elites consistently use classical Arabic while the North African intelligentsia still tends to use French instead. Granted, Nobel Prize laureate in literature Naguib Mahfouz does publish and makes public declarations in Arabic. But Moroccan Tahar Ben Jelloun provides a good counterexample: he won the 1987 Prix Goncourt, the French equivalent of the Pulitzer Prize, for his North African novel *La nuit sacrée*. Still, even if we accept the controversial notion that most North African intellectuals are still more at ease in French than in any other language, a perplexing question remains: why they don't write in their own native dialects?

OF LANGUAGES, SPOKEN AND WRITTEN

In *L'aliénation linguistique* Henri Gobart classifies languages according to four dimensions, or functions: *vernacular* (the language spoken at home before entering the school); *vehicular* (the language used for economical exchanges); *referential* (the language used for cultural information); and *mythical* (the language used by religion, in a synagogue, a church, or a mosque). In France, except for Corsican and Breton pockets, French is at the same time the vernacular language (both at home and outside) and the vehicular language of the streets, the schools, and the lycée. It is also the language used in the universities, by the media, the intellectuals, and in official discourse. Except for a few priests who still use Latin, French is also the religious language. But more importantly, it is a language that is both spoken and written at the same time. It has a recognized alphabet, which is taught beginning in primary school.

Applying Gobart's classification to the North African context (see chart below), makes it possible to clarify an important point, namely that there are (at least) four languages used in that region, not two: classical Arabic, French, French-creole-Arabic (*Farabê*), and Berber. In terms of language speakers, this gives "classicophones"—for classical

Arabic—francophones, farabophones, and berberophones. The most important problem stems from the wide extension of the term "arabophone" which is usually used to designate both farabophone and classicophone. But to make the situation even more complex, Berber and *Farabé* are vernacular languages, spoken in the streets and at home, among families and friends, but they are not written. *Farabé* has no alphabet and while Berber has one, it has been outlawed for a variety of political reasons. But if *Farabé* and Berber are not languages one writes, they still carry oral traditions which are much very alive, notably in modern songs and in popular theater.

FOREIGN	
1. ARABIC (classical) written; *not* spoken	2. FRENCH spoken and written (language of science and technology)
VERNACULARS	
3. FARABE (creole) spoken; *not* written	4. BERBER spoken; *not* written

Classical Arabic remains a written language and it is not spoken by North African families either at home or outside. Even in families that consider themselves to be "purely" Arab, no one speaks classical Arabic with one's mother, father, sister, or brother. As unbelievable as it may seem, classical Arabic is no one's native language in the Maghreb. To claim that classical Arabic is the native language of North Africans is about the same thing as saying that Latin is the native language of Italians, French, and Spaniards, or to make a better analogy, that Spaniards or Latin Americans speak Latin at home (and then to substantiate this claim by arguing that they are Latins and Christians and that the Bible was written in Latin).

In general, these "Arabic-speaking" families speak *Farabé* or Berber but not classical Arabic at home. In the streets, at the market place, they speak *Farabé* with the accent of Algiers, Tunis, or Rabat. Amazingly enough, though, classical Arabic is the language foreigners typically learn when they travel to North Africa and want to communicate with people. Some French and Americans make an honest effort and study the language seriously only to find out that they learned the wrong language. They are sometimes bewildered and even embarrassed to hear some North Africans amused, answering them with a half teasing tone of voice: "But, we don't talk like this. It is the Egyptians, the Syrians, and the Saudis who talk like that."[16]

In his book *Le Gone du Chaâba,* Azouz Begag describe this language in these terms:

> A la maison, l'arabe qu'on parle ferait certainement rougir de colère un habitant de la Mecque. Savez-vous comment on dit les allumettes chez nous par exemple? Li zalamite. C'est simple et tout le monde comprend. Et une automobile? La taumobile. Et un chiffon?- Le chiffoun. Vous voyez, c'est un dialecte particulier qu'on peut assimiler aisément lorsque l'oreille est suffisamment entraînée. (Begag, 213)

Similarly, the rural population of Kabylie, the Rif, or Atlas does not speak classical Arabic or even *Farabé,* but rather Berber languages— respectively, Kabyle, Rifain, or Chleuh, and this regardless of the fact that many of these Berber peasants are devout Muslims. To tell Kabyles that they are "Arabs" amounts to telling Irish people that they are English, or Basque people that they are Spanish. It is, in other words, to negate their cultural identity.

While international stars such as Idir and the all-women group Djurdjura sing in the Berber language from Kabylie, Cheb Khaled and Cheb Mami are among the most famous Arab-Algerian singers in France and Europe. They both sing raï music, a reggae-rock type of music that blends with North African and oriental rhythms with a touch of southern Spain.[17] Love is often the main theme of their songs, but as opposed to Egyptian or Lebanese stars,[18] raï singers do not compose their lyrics in classical or Middle Eastern Arabic. When Michel Field asked Cheb Mami about his lyrics on a French program, Mami gave the following response: "C'est en arabe, mais pas en arabe de la poésie. C'est dans le language de la rue."[19] Asked a similar question by another journalist, Cheb Khaled's reply was: "In charabia"! Raï, in other words, is sung in *Farabé.* Since this creole Arabic does not have its own alphabet, raï singers transcribe "Arabic" lyrics using the French alphabet. The product of various types of hybridization, linguistic as well as musical, raï music is perhaps the ultimate creolized art form and as such, it brings a vivid refutation to an official discourse bent on cultural and linguistic homogenization. It is therefore no accident that Islamic fundamentalists have banned this type of music, put Raï singers on a death list, and even murdered one of them, Cheb Hasni.

If the streets of North Africa are either Farabophone or Berberophone, school is a universe that is even more interesting to examine. In the classroom, the primary school teacher uses classical Arabic or French, not Farabé or Berber, thus in effect instructing students in two completely foreign languages (imagine students in the United States using Shakespeare's English or Latin). Once they're out of the classroom, school children and high school students switch back to the vehicular Farabé, Berber, or even French. Classical Arabic is not an option in this case.[20] Now, to the extent that creole Arabic is universally called "Arabic," these students are, in a sense, speaking Arabic. But the failure to acknowledge diglossia has the negative effect of misleading many of them into thinking that they are speaking classical Arabic when they are, in fact, speaking creole Arabic. As a result, a whole generation of Algerian students is now being referred to as *"illéttrés bilingues"*— bilingual illiterates: they do not know French as well as their elders did and they have not yet mastered classical Arabic, as Middle Easterners generally do.

During the 1960s and 1970s the overwhelming majority of North African intellectuals were trained in French schools, particularly in Algeria. Most of them did not know any classical Arabic since French was the only language taught in schools. As their ancestors had done before them, they simply used the language they knew best, which also happened to be the last linguistic legacy in a long history of colonization. Just as Saint Augustine had gone from Berber to Latin, Ibn Khaldoun[21] went from Berber to classical Arabic; Kateb Yacine went from Farabé to French and Mouloud Mammeri from Kabyle (Berber) to French. In my mind, therefore, to single out Francophone Algerian intellectuals and to accuse them of continuing to write in the language of their master, is to distort history. For as Boudjedra puts it, determining which language to use is not a matter of personal choice in the context of colonization: "Pour moi, Algérien, je n'ai pas choisi le français. Il m'a choisi, ou plutôt il s'est imposé à moi, à travers des siècles de sang et de larmes et à travers l'histoire douloureuse de la colonisation" (Boudjedra, 30).

During the French colonization another deterrent to learning and using classical Arabic was that almost all colleges of Arts, Sciences, and Technology provided instruction in French—in fact, most of them still do today. There was no way to become a physician, an architect, or an engineer without French since these "modern" topics were all taught in French. Apparently, scientific subjects are not easily taught in classical Arabic, so that even in the Middle East today most colleges use English for these disciplines instead. In that regard, therefore, forcing students to study classical Arabic only is to exclude them from colleges of medicine, engineering, architecture, etc . . . Even pan-Arabists and

Islamists recognize this. But when they argue that what they want to do is to replace French with English, the logistics of the operation appear fuzzy at best. How can the switch from French to English be accomplished overnight without financial and pedagogical means—since, right now, the Maghreb is deeply sinking under foreign debts?

If the policy of eliminating French at all costs appears unreasonable for economic reasons, it is also immoral. First, because it has given extremists the leeway to murder Francophone intellectuals—who, again, write in French because they can't write in their native language, Farabé or Berber; and second, because it is hypocritical. While openly criticizing French, France, and the Western world, children of "*le pouvoir*," of the party apparatchiks and even of Islamist leaders, attend French and Francophone lycées, then go abroad to graduate schools in the West. As Khalida Messaoudi writes: "Je défie quiconque de me trouver un seul de leurs enfants avec une bourse d'études ailleurs que dans les pays occidentaux"(Messaoudi, 57). The claim that eliminating French will bring along a return to the "authentic" Arabic heritage and thereby provide better educational opportunities for children of the lower social strata does not hold. In reality this policy excludes most of these children from the best colleges and thereby also substantially reduces the competition privileged children would undoubtedly experience if they were included.

CONCLUSION: NORTH AFRICA OF THE THIRD ZONE

The Maghreb finds itself at the crossroads of two vast linguistic worlds, Francophonie and Arabophonie. While in the Middle East the linguistic signifier "l'Arabe" designates Middle Eastern or classical Arabic, in North Africa it means, creole Arabic or Farabé. The three North African language pariahs, Berber, Farabé, and French must be recognized, along with classical Arabic. Everyone, citizen or native North African must be allowed to speak freely the language(s) he or she knows best.

If North African intellectuals still write and express themselves in French, it is because their native Farabé is not a written language and because written Berber is banned. While the language policy of the government claims to be "Arabic (classical) only," in reality it denies and tries to eradicate the real "native Arabic," Farabé and Berber. Because of diglossia between creole Arabic and classical Arabic, Francophone intellectuals are often wrongly perceived as being far away from their people since they are not classicophones. In Algeria they are systematically viewed as "*le parti de la France*" and therefore treated as collaborators—even by those who used to collaborate with various colonizing and postcolonizing powers. They are unjustly accused of not expressing themselves in their native language, they are censured and brutally murdered by the new colonizing power, the Islamists.

As the Algerian civil war rages on, spilling over into neighboring countries, a solution to North Africa's cultural problems can only be found if all aspects of its long history are acknowledged, if all facets of its identity are recognized. North Africa will not find peace and serenity if it leaves out its African-Berber and Mediterranean-Farabé heritages.

Notes

1. North Africa is called Amazighie or the land of Amazigh in Berber.

2. The origin of the term is still a subject of passionate debates.

3. It is important to point out that the linguistic impact of colonization is not a new phenomenon in Algeria.

4. See, for instance, Belvaude, *L'Algérie*, 211.

5. A mythical woman and a symbol of resistance against all colonizers, Kahina came from the Jerawa tribe of the Aures mountains in the east of Algeria. According to the historian Ibn Khaldoun, she preached judaism. This red-haired woman ruled over North Africa for more than fifty years and is said to have had an army of women. Kateb Yacine paid a tribute to her in his banned play *La Guerre de 2000 ans*. Many women activists still look up to her as their idole. Today, many Berber families still name their daughters Kahina.

6. They would provide the bulk of the Moor army that colonized Spain during eighth century.

7. The fall of Tunis was in 1534.

8. Contrary to Saudis, who are Muslims of the Handbalite rite, and to many Middle Easterners, who are of the Chafeism rite, North Africans are of the Malekite rite. This branch of the religion allows for a certain degree of freedom in interpretation and therefore flexibility in practice.

9. In Kabylia, women do not veil themselves. They have never worn a veil and will probably never wear one, despite the actions of some Islamist leaders. Villages do not have a chief or head of the village but elect assemblies that have ruled democratically for thousands of years.

10. For example, French colonialism gave citizenship to Sephardic Jews but not to the rest of the population, which led to the alienation of this "second class" of citizens and to the revival of antisemitic sentiment. According to André Chouraqui, Sephardic Jews are of Berber descent. In Algeria, the Kabyles, who still refuse adamantly to be Arabized and who publicly claim that they are not Arabs, are treated as Jews by many Arabists and Islamists

11. In France and in Europe North Africans are "perceived" as belonging to a minority—the racism deployed against them speaks to this—but they are

not treated as such. Paradoxically, the situation is reversed in the United States: minorities are granted some privileges through affirmative action but North Africans are officially classified as white—and therefore denied minority status.

12. For instance, in the Antilles, they speak French and Creole. The creole languages are a mixture of two or more languages, that resulted from the contact between French, Spanish, and Portuguese and the indigenous languages.

13. Middle Easterners find the North African Arabic accent so difficult to understand that Algerian movies have to be subtitled (in Arabic) before being shown in Egypt.

14. See Alawa Toumi, *Langue française et identité nord-africaine dans l'oeuvre d'Albert Memmi et de Kateb Yacine.*

15. I would like to thank Dr. Andrew Sessions, from the political science department of the University of Wisconsin-Madison, for his expertise and helpful comments.

16. I am quoting professor Leslie Bold-Irons of Brock University and professor Patricia Geesey of the University of Florida.

17. See Reporters Sans Frontières, "Cheb Khaled ou le raï du ras-le-bol" in *Le drame Algérien*, 52.

18. For instance, in classical Arabic, the texts of Egypt's Oum Kalssoum and Lebanon's Fairouz could be considered poetry. It is not the case of Khaled and Mami.

19. *Le cercle de minuit*, du 27 Mars 1994, avec la participation de Rachid Boudjedra, Benjamin Stora, Omar Belhouchet, et Khalida Messaoudi.

20. This would be a very interesting topic to study. When asked why they do not use classical Arabic among themselves, many answer: "It's too long and too complicated." Simplicity and shortness of expressions seem to be the two main reasons.

21. Ibn Khaldoun is the author of *Histoire des Berbères* and *L'Introduction*—for which he is considered one of the fathers of modern sociology.

Works Cited

Aktouf, Omar. *Algérie entre l'exil et la curée*. Paris: L'Harmattan, 1989.

Arnaud, Jacqueline. *La Littérature maghrébine de langue française*. Paris: Publisud, 1986.

———. *Le Cas de Kateb Yacine*. Paris: Publisud, 1986.

———. *Kateb Yacine: L'oeuvre en fragments*. Paris: Sindbad, 1986.

Begag, Azouz. *Le gone du Chaâba*. Paris: Seuil, 1986.

Ben Jelloun, Tahar. *La nuit sacrée*. Paris: Seuil, 1987

Belvaude, Catherine. *L'Algérie*. Paris: Khartala, 1991.

Boudjedra, Rachid. *Lettres Algériennes*. Paris: Grasset, 1995.

Chafik, Mohammed. "Structure linguistique de l'arabe marocain." *Tifinagh*. (Rabat: SARL), no 2 (fev-mar 1994): 5–10.

Chaker, Salem. *Berbères aujourd'hui.* Paris: L'Harmattan, 1989.

Gobard, Henri. *L'Aliénation linguistique.* Paris: Flammarion, 1976.

Mimouni, Rachid. "Quand tout un pays vit à l'heure du trabendo." *Jeune Afrique.* Paris: Jeune Afrique, 1990.

Khatibi, Abdelkebir. *Maghreb pluriel.* Paris: Denoël, 1983.

Messaoudi, Khalida. *Une Algérienne debout.* Paris: Flammarion, 1995.

Ouerdane, Amar. *La Question berbère.* Québec: Septentrion, 1990.

Reporters Sans Frontières. *Le drame Algérien.* Paris: La Découverte, 1994.

Toumi, Alawa. "Langue française et identités nords-africaines dans l'oeuvre d'Albert Memmi et de Kateb Yacine." Diss. U of Wisconsin-Madison, 1993.

Turin, Yvonne. *Affrontements culturels dans l'Algérie coloniale.* Paris: Maspero, 1971.

5

Rap Music and French Cultural Studies

For an Ethics of the Ephemeral

Mireille Rosello

*Quand on crie la sentence d'un livre, les ouvriers de l'imprimerie disent:
"Bon, encore une édition."*

—Diderot, Sur la Liberté de la presse.[1]

FRENCH CULTURAL STUDIES AS CHRISTMAS

I wonder. Perhaps French cultural studies is like Christmas in predominantly Christcommercialized areas: damned if you do go along, but certainly damned if you don't. I confess to having some envy and respect for all the Scrooges of the world because I certainly do not have the courage to spend three months muttering to myself that Christmas music is naff or asserting less sneakily what I (of course) take to be my very legitimate suspicion of regular Christmasy or disciplinary agitations. And if our shared narratives of what happens to Scrooge are any indication, his is a lost cause anyway so that I had better not waste my time trying to boycott institutionally sanctified moments when genuine enthusiasm and creative thinking are authorized even if the context is artificial. After all, it is not that I don't want the intellectual excitement of rethinking corpuses, methodologies, values, and French studies, it's just that I would like to have that all the time, not once a year or every five or ten years. So, even if the feast is tainted, incomplete, exclusionary, commercial, even if, in other words, there is perhaps no good reason to rejoice, I have no option but to cling to the belief that yet again, this time, this decade, something is happening that is meaningful and generous and intellectually stimulating. So, French cultural studies it is—for now. Too bad if I am painfully aware that it would be just as intelligent to be able to reflect on the future of disciplines, on the acquisition of foreign languages and cultures without adhering to this necessarily restrictive label (why "French" rather than "Francophone," and aren't the French "Europeans" now? Why not "in French"? Isn't "cultural" included in "French studies" or "studies in French"?). After all, I am even more puzzled by those who seem to believe that (any version of) French cultural studies is a heretic enterprise, an attempt at upsetting a perfectly adequate organigram of experts in French (and sometimes Francophone) "literature(s)," "culture(s)," or "civilization," and "politics." And I do welcome those voices who suggest that the move toward a reassessment of the role played by words such as "French," "cultural," and "studies" is important even if I do agree that the new combination of words cannot be seen as a solution, merely as the identification of serious theoretical and pedagogical difficulties (LaCapra 1995).

Literature? Yes of course literature, why on earth not? Literature is part of so many cultures and if we are talking about French-speaking areas, how can its importance be overrated? But should I opt for *either* literature or culture? Are they "complementary" as some would suggest and consequently mutually exclusive in our daily teaching practices (Rifaterre 1995)? I am not so sure. I cannot conceive of French studies (or studies in French) without literature, and, because there is no culture without literature, it would probably be nonsensical to try and teach culture without literature. On the other hand, and just as importantly, there is no literature outside (at least one) culture and, more crucially our definitions of literature are the products of the learning environments that allowed us (if we were lucky enough to get an education) to form an opinion about what literature is and why literature is (or is not) valuable. Some of us (readers of this piece) did have the fortune or misfortune to be made to read Sartre's *What Is Literature?* in high school. Some of us memorized La Fontaine's "La cigale et la fourmi," Corneille's "*O rage! ô, désespoir...*" (*Le Cid*, I, 6), or "*Que vouliez-vous qu'il fît contre trois...?*" (*Horace* III, 6).[2] What we do with the reminiscences, as I shall try to show in this chapter, is not necessarily a matter of literature.[3]

Besides, I am not sure that those who seek to preserve borders between "culture" and "literature" are policing the most sensitive territories. Most of the time, I think that it is not so clear whether we can afford to separate literature *and* culture from an even more problematic field called, loosely, politics. In fact, I suppose that it would be nice if I *could* be indifferent to politics when I do literature/culture. Then, I would have the opportunity to really ask myself whether I *wish* to separate literature and culture from politics. But I am tempted to suggest that politicians should begin: why don't *they* keep politics out of literature (another way of saying this would be, perhaps paradoxically: why don't they do more literature)? Often, governments intervene before universities. Long before Western canons stopped to consider whether the Martinican journal *Tropiques* was worth teaching and whether this rich eclectic collection of poems, translations, essays about tropical fauna and flora fell into the category of culture or literature, the representatives of the Vichy government in Martinique had banned the review.[4] Today, other texts are coming under fire.

FRENCH CULTURAL STUDIES AND CANONICAL POETRY: MC SOLAAR AND RIMBAUD

Le dormeur du val ne dort pas, il est mort et son corps est rigide et froid.

—MC Solaar, "La Concubine de l'hémoglobine"

Consider the following example: a few months ago, I was wondering about the advantages and disadvantages of developing a course that would focus primarily on French rap music and on nineteenth-century poetry. One of MC Solaar's songs had triggered the dream. Because he quotes "Le Dormeur du val" in one of his texts, it occurred to me that it might be interesting to actually devote an equal amount of time and attention to Rimbaud and MC Solaar in the first two-thirds of the semester, while the last third would focus on an analysis of *what type* of connection is established by MC Solaar and on whether or not the course duplicates or modifies the relationship thus created. I was wondering how to frame a meaningful comparison between rap music and contemporary or earlier poetry, between French rap music and American rap music, between MC Solaar and other French rap groups, between rap music and other manifestations of urban cultures. I had mixed feelings and anxieties about being too trendy and possibly superficial,[5] I worried about indulging in demagogic gestures. Surely, if my role consisted exclusively in elucidating MC Solaar's literary allusions for students born and raised in a country other than France, the enterprise was not worthwhile.

Even if we dug further, would I have to confess that I don't know what to make of MC Solaar's insistence that Rimbaud's soldier is "dead" and not asleep? Isn't it painfully obvious, at first, that the song constitutes a rather crude flattening of the poem? Is rap music turning poetry into banality?[6] After all, as everybody knows, one of the most striking decisions made by Rimbaud in the poem is precisely to ignore the soldier's death until the very last line. No reader of "Le Dormeur du val" can possibly forget the sharp contrast between the beginning of the poem where the soldier is described as though he was merely relaxing in a calm and refreshing landscape (*"C'est un trou de verdure . . . Les pieds dans les glaïeuls, il dort"*), the gradually more disturbing hints (*"Souriant comme sourirait un enfant malade"*) and the breathtakingly matter-of-fact denouement: *"Il a deux trous rouges au côté droit,"* a line that still manages to avoid any mention of death. Anyone teaching the poem may well have to reinvent that wheel, at least for a few minutes. But, in a sense, MC Solaar's song is both accepting to reinvent the wheel and going farther (or at least somewhere else), using a shock tactic that could prove quite as memorable as Rimbaud's structure. After all, why not take seriously Solaar's obviously provocative metaphorical reterritorialization? Rimbaud's invitation to get closer and closer to a young, unthreatening, child-like body and the subsequent shattering of the illusion may elicit mixed feelings of compassion and disgust, tenderness and horror. Like Baudelaire's "Une Charogne" (which we might decide to look at), "Le Dormeur du val" will not let us draw a clean line between (our) life and (his) death and the poem lures us toward the object from which our imagination may have wanted to recoil.

Solaar's rewriting is brutal but, in his song, there is no deceptive beginning: *"Le dormeur du val ne dort pas/Il est mort et son corps est rigide et froid."* Is the rapper refusing to set a narrative trap? In which case, what would be the point? Are postmodern readers expected to be more mature and more willing to confront violent images? Or are we, on the contrary, expected to be so blasé as to need shock treatment? Is poetry aligning itself with violence-saturated news bulletins?

Perhaps the critique of Rimbaud's poem is directed at its status as high culture? Isn't the desire to call a spade a spade normally expected from "ordinary" people? And, depending on the context, someone can either praise their courageous no-nonsense wisdom, or regret their anti-intellectual knee-jerk reflexes. But wouldn't it be too facile to assume that French *banlieues* are allergic to poetry?[7] Would some students point out that Solaar both knows the poem well enough to quote it, understand it in a conventionally literary way, and then depart from Rimbaud's imaging strategies? Should Solaar's refusal to beat around the bush be interpreted as a rejection of Rimbaud's aesthetics or should we insist on the reappropriative and inclusive gesture? After all, he includes and rewrites, rather than ignores, Rimbaud's poem, a courtesy, I realize, that I was not quite willing to extend to Solaar's song when I was first put off by his demystifying interpretation.

Even if I could satisfy myself that the comparison between Solaar and Rimbaud was promising, however, other difficulties remained. It was rather depressing to think about how much time it would take to educate myself should I decide that it was imperative to find out much more about corpuses that, as a student of twentieth-century French and Francophone cultures, I am usually allowed to ignore. I suspected that nineteenth-century poetry was not the only possible "forefather" of rap.[8] And if diachronic explorations seemed mandatory, the same was true of synchronic and interdisciplinary incursions into other types of music: the history of raï music suddenly appeared like an absolute must. A quick look at a recent book on raï music had convinced me that it was crucial to compare the different types of subversiveness expressed by rap and rai music.[9] As for medieval poetry, I would not even have known where to begin to substantiate a vague intuition that rap music may be listened to in parallel with medieval texts if a colleague had not generously shared my curiosity and helped me build bridges. In the end, the link proved even more fruitful than I thought. Catherine Léglu pointed out, for example, that rap music's borrowings (samplings or self-quotations, allusions to proverbs and other rappers) and its tendency toward ritualization could be compared to "medieval satirical texts, which are overwhelmingly formulaic and 'rewrite' each other often." She suggested that revealing parallels might be formulated through a simultaneous reading of MC Solaar and Occitan satirists such as Marcabru while "more 'visceral' invective (NWA or French NTM or I/AM)[10] can be found in corpuses [she] tends to call 'insult songs,' i.e., expressing rage, invective attacking language as much as specific targets."[11]

While the corpus widened, however, another difficulty arose: I was also wondering if the theoretical and methodological tools and reflexes acquired when studying literature, or linguistics, or theory (the previously worshiped dominant disciplines) would do justice to an analysis of such arguably completely different discursive formations as rap music and nineteenth-century poetry. So that, in the end, both my corpus and my methodology had become sources of questioning and anxiety.

I was not sure the corpus I had in mind could be described as cultural studies (after all, what is more canonical than nineteenth-century literature or Occitan troubadours?), or as "French"cultural studies: what was so exclusively French about it? I knew, for example, that my search for ancestors would certainly lead me back to English and the United States. I could hardly look at French rap without studying American rap.[12] As for raï music, it is written neither in French nor in English so that I could not rely on the often implicit assumption that there is always a way of doing cultural studies in "translation" (i.e., in English) rather than in the original (i.e., supposedly European) language. This whole project was beginning to look like Lichtenberg's proverbial knife: it does not have a blade and is missing its handle. Not only was my corpus missing but I was not even sure how to handle that threatening absence. I knew the course could be developed, I just did not think that it was represented by the structure of our departments or disciplines.

In a sense, I was saved by the gong: here I was trying to articulate several possible bridges between different and perhaps competing definitions of literature and music, popular culture and the canon, performance and bookish knowledge, literary culture and its more or less legitimate usages. I needn't have worried. In retrospect, my questions appear as a luxury I can no longer afford. It is now obvious that the course on rap music will have to work more urgently on a re-articulation of the links not between culture, literature, and poetry but between literature/culture/poetry and politics/power/governments.

FRENCH CULTURAL STUDIES AND POLITICS:
RAP MUSIC AND THE LAW

On November 14, 1996, a judge in Toulon found the two singers of the rap group Suprême NTM guilty of "*outrages à personnes dépositaires de l'autorité publique dans l'exercice de leurs fonctions*"[13] because of comments they made on stage after singing their song "Nick [sic] la Police." It is not the first time that a rap group finds itself threatened with legal procedures. In the United States, we all remember the 2 Live Crew trial and the FBI's tense relationship with Public Enemy.[14] In France, in 1993, Suprême NTM had already been asked to present themselves following the release of the song "Police," the same song they sang at La Seyne-sur-Mer during the performance that led to their arrest. When

Ministère Amer contributed to the soundtrack of Mathieu Kassovitz's *La Haine* the *Ministère de l'Intérieur* decided to press charges against them in 1994. That case against two songs, "Sacrifices de poulets" and "Brigitte femme de flic," is still pending.

Rap music has always had virulent detractors but when NTM is condemned in Toulon, it is of course difficult to treat as a coincidence the fact that Toulon is one of those southern towns whose mayor belongs to the Front National, or that the concert during which the singers committed their crime was organized by SOS Racisme as a protest against the election of that very same mayor in 1995.

In an article published in the *South Quarterly Review*, critic Alan Light once said that "[w]riting about rap always has a certain dispatches-from-the-front-lines quality" (Light, 870). This, he says, is due to the rapidly evolving sounds and styles of the genre. I would also suggest that the reception of rap music by its multiple audiences is another front line that moves continuously. The metaphor also implies that some sort of cultural war is going on and I suggest that it is important to both retain and significantly qualify that image of rap music as a cultural war zone and the rapper as antisocial rebellious poet.

Suprême NTM, short for "Nick ta mère" (not very tasteful perhaps, but I would not jump to the conclusion that this has anything to do either mothers or sex), had already run into trouble when they released a song called "Police" in 1993. What *Libération* described as *"[u]n jugement stupéfiant de sévérité"* (Simmonot, 2) involves a three-month prison sentence, an additional three-month probation, heavy fines, and an unheard of *"interdiction d'exercer la profession de chanteurs de variétés pendant six mois,"* in other words, censorship.

Now, in the interest of time, let me make my position clear. I do have an opinion about the judge who returned that verdict. But that is not what I want to talk about. I suggest that what was most interesting in the days that followed the announcement of the verdict by the press, was not the difference between what was said by those who approved of the judgment and by those who disapproved of it. It was not even who took which side. All that was rather predictably determined by the old Left-Right watershed. I think that what was most remarkable was the unanimous feeling among those who responded that whether or not the group should have been condemned, it was urgent to defend the principle of their freedom of expression and not that song in particular.

No one wanted to hear that song. Even those who opposed the sentence considered it unacceptably aggressive and their argument was

generally that it should be protected as fiction, as literature (therefore
as politically harmless, the old "*affaire Aragon*" syndrome). The socialist party declared that the lyrics were probably excessive or clumsy.[15]
Sode Sylla, president of SOS Racisme, explained that "he prefers MC
Solaar's cool rap."[16] Guy Bedos said: "Je ne me souviens pas d'un seul
titre de chansons de NTM. . . ."[17] And those who wanted to celebrate
NTM's creativity seemed bent on erasing their specific position as poets
of the *banlieue* in the 1990s: NTM became the latest version of some
Lagarde et Michard's figure of the *poète maudit.* Jack Lang, ex-*Ministre
de la Culture*, who loves a good quote, brought in the soon-to-be-
pantheonized André Malraux to the rescue. Lang reminded us ("pomp-
ously," Johannes says in *Libération*) that Malraux once defended Jean
Genet's play *Les Paravents* by "reading some terrible texts by Baudelaire,
quoting Madame Bovary, . . . before concluding: "Il faut toujours choisir
la liberté."[18]

In the past, Jack Lang had subsidized NTM tours because according
to him, rap music is like "commedia dell'arte as it was practiced in the
sixteenth and seventeenth centuries."[19] And I wonder if this is a case of
politics being influenced and defined by literature or a case of literature
being influenced and defined by politics. I wish I were as certain as Jack
Lang that "commedia dell'arte" is comparable to rap music. I confess that
that is an avenue of research I have not pursued and I am obviously
green with envy that the Minister of Culture should be so well informed
about all art forms in all centuries. And even if I give up on envy and
sarcasm, I cannot help but fear that such comparisons are dangerous in
the context of a trial where contemporary artists have been found guilty
as charged.

It is indeed quite tempting to compare NTM to all the poets who
were once accused of antisocial behavior. But what I find slightly
disturbing in the gesture of comparing rap groups with people such as
Georges Brassens, Boris Vian, or Charles Baudelaire and Arthur Rimbaud
is that crucial elements have to be left out at each end of the comparison for the analogy to work. When we remember that Baudelaire or
Verlaine were not exactly typical *petit bourgeois*, I wonder if we are
saying that it is therefore acceptable for rap singers to be ostracized.
Does the fact that Baudelaire's work is now canonized somehow add
glamor to a type of transhistorical marginalization? Are we to understand that Rimbaud's *bohème* justifies NTM's *galère*? The comparison
does suggest that it is quite possible that NTM's songs will eventually
be taught in schools but I wonder if such arguments are the best
possible use of an interdisciplinary study of politics and literature.

Reading Oscar Wilde's work today hardly redeems the years he spent in prison.

On the other side of the comparison, I wonder if what is more or less systematically erased by those endless comparisons with famous French *poètes maudits* is not the group's ethnicity. Reactions to the group's condemnation have included references to the fact that the two singers are French of Portuguese and Caribbean origins. Somehow, that element does not seem to come into play when literary forefathers are invoked. Not to mention that it may well be a mistake to interpret NTM's rage as a known form of insubordination. It is not because Rimbaud was a rebel that it is all right not to adapt policies to today's situations. Literary recognition in the future is not a substitute for political intervention today.

And I suggest that Lang's own narrative of what he is subsidizing or defending is not so much guilty of cooptation or reappropriation. I think he misses the point. He wants to celebrate a form of idealized rebelliousness that is not there, and he refuses to hear a different type of rebellious message that the group desperately tries to get across: that the song is fiction not because of its excess of violence but because it minimizes and poeticizes the level of antipolice violence present in the *banlieue*. This song is a euphemism. To be fair, Lang is imposing familiar models of *poète maudit* upon an admittedly confusing cultural phenomenon. I would argue that it is difficult to underestimate the as yet little theorized radicalness or at least the historical originality of this combination of virulent rage against the State and conventional or even conservative thinking.

First of all, NTM's public persona has nothing to do with the romanticized ideal of the *poète maudit*. They even refuse to be compared with more recent *engagés* singers. When a journalist from *Le Nouvel Observateur* asks them: "Certains disent que vous prenez la relève des chanteurs anars, Bruant, Brassens, Vian, Ferré," the answer is: "Ils sont forts ceux-là. Nous, on n'est pas de cette trempe. On n'a pas cette subtilité" (Etchegoin, 44). And I am not sure that this should be interpreted only as modesty. They are obviously aware of at least some of Boris Vian's work: *J'irai cracher sur vos tombes* is overquoted in the song called "Sur 24 pistes" where, in a typical example of cross-Atlantic "dissing," NTM ritually insults other artists whose rap is supposedly contaminated by commercialism or obsolescence: "On va les enterrer pour pouvoir aller chier sur leurs tombes" ("Sur 24 pistes").

While some would like to rehabilitate rap in the name of some hidden subtlety, NTM treats subtlety as an undesirable element: "on n'a

pas les moyens de finasser" (Etchegoin, 44). Unlike singers associated
with raï music, rappers are no revellers. Unlike Khaleb, one of the best-
known representatives of raï whose public image is that of an exuber-
ant and happy troublemaker, Bruno Lopez and Didier Morville, also
known as Kool Shen and Joey Starr, construct their lives as boring
conventional bourgeois narratives. When asked if they feel that fame
and money have somehow alienated them from their *banlieue*, the
singers calmly explain that money will help them buy a house, support
their wife and kid, and leave the *banlieue* to raise them in a quiet
neighborhood (Etchegoin, 45). The journalist, obviously outraged and
horribly disappointed, exclaims: "Mais c'est le plus commun des rêves"
(Etchegoin, 45). Kool Shen's answer, I think, is a rather striking shift of
paradigm. He takes full responsibility: "Je ne me pose pas ce genre de
questions. Je fais ce que je dois faire." In other words, I doubt that they
would be flattered to be compared to Verlaine if they did go to prison
even for three months and not for two years. And, for all their talk of
guns and bombs, they never did shoot anyone, let alone their gay
lover. The song "J'appuie sur la gachette" is about a desperate man
who commits suicide—not about delinquents or *banlieusards*.

   Not only is their perception of their social role completely
unglamourous, their own criticism of their art is very conventional. It
is certainly far from confirming the image of rap music as the perfect
emanation of postmodern poetics. Maxwell says, for example, that
"[r]ap, after all, appears to be a music built upon the pastiche counted
by Linda Hutcheon, Fredric Jameson, Fred Pfeil and many others as a
defining feature of postmodern cultural forms" (Maxwell, 6).[20] NTM
uses all the musical techniques that have been seen as examples of
bricolage, recycling. Like their American counterparts, French rappers
have adopted the method of sampling and punch phrasing: they rap
on preexisting, prerecorded musical fragments. They do not compose,
they reappropriate. Their samples implicitly question the value of au-
thorship and cultural property. As for the most eclectic web of references, the often casual allusions to other songs, other groups, other
texts, films, TV programs, commercials, and proverbs that pepper NTM's
texts, some will no doubt deplore that they represent the epitome of
postmodern cultural hodgepodge. Finkielkraut's dreaded *défaite de la
pensée* comes to mind when we encounter ghastly comparisons between Proust's *madeleine* and Prost, the Formula One racing driver:
"L'allégorie des Madeleines file, à la vitesse de Prost" ("Obsolete").

   But when NTM talk about their texts, there is nothing postmodern
about their vision. They obviously disapprove of approximations, they

are quite determined to be quoted accurately and they have very specific ideas about what their texts mean. They will not allow what they perceive as sloppy interpretations. When a journalist suggests: "Vous dites, quand même, dans une de vos chansons: 'des balles pour la police municipale,'" Joey Starr immediately corrects her: "On retient toujours une seule phrase. Si vous dites ce qu'il y a avant et après ce n'est plus pareil: 'Traquer les keufs dans les couloirs du métro/Tels sont les rêves que fait la nuit Joey Joe/Donne-moi des balles pour la police municipale . . . ' " (Etchegoin, 45).

Now, even if their position strikes us as hopelessly naive, we can perhaps agree that the determination not to be quoted out of context does not go very well with a postmodern reverence for endless slippage and reappropriation. And NTM does not seem to care much for polysemy and ambiguity either. The day after *Le Monde* published the text of "Police" the newspaper had to print a *rectificatif*: some "transmission errors" had resulted in alterations in the lyrics of the song. "Vos papiers" had become "Faux papiers" and "matrice décervelée" had become "matrice d'écervelés." And, perhaps the juiciest mistake, "Eduquons les forces de l'ordre" had become "Eh du con! Les forces de l'ordre." NTM had obviously no desire to rejoice in the fact that their texts could be heard in two different ways, they were not interested in the humor of a possibly Freudian slip theory of why *Le Monde* would want to see their texts as more aggressive than they are. They were apparently not impressed by the inevitability of "transmission errors" in a noisy cultural system. They value clarity and they want to increase the volume not blur the message.

If there is a literature of the *banlieue* imagining itself here, it bears little resemblance to Césaire's wish to be "la bouche des malheurs qui n'ont point de bouche" (*Cahiers d'un retour au pays natal*, 88). Kool Shen and Joey Starr do not want to be spokespeople or representatives. Nor do they want to be leaders of the people or inspired prophets, and they are not romantic rebels, either. As they put it bluntly, they want to be "*hauts-parleurs*," loudspeakers (Etchegoin, 44). The image is most prosaic and perhaps self-deprecating. It dehumanizes the singer and turns him into a ventriloquist's puppet. On the other hand, it does make an important point about those who listen to NTM's songs: silencing the group will not silence the song. For if turning off a loudspeaker may reduce the noise level for a while, it is probably both silly and dangerous for a tribunal to assume that once NTM is turned off we no longer need to pay attention to the voices that come from the *banlieue*. Given the amount of controversy generated by rap groups such as NTM, it is becoming obvious that different *publics* are hearing different things. But when the difference bears on words such as "violent" or "violence," no one is willing to agree to disagree. The phenomenal number of NTM's records sold both before and after the free publicity campaign graciously offered by the right-wing judge makes it clear that rap music is not exclusively consumed by the *banlieues.* Accordingly, rap music may be a good place to start looking for different protocols of listening.

FRENCH CULTURAL STUDIES, HISTORY, CONSUMERISM, ETHICS:
RAP MUSIC AS PERISHABLE PRODUCT

Such protocols of listening will have to take into account the fact that rap music is listened to by people who belong to vastly different socioeconomic backgrounds but also that such dissemination is not the result of shared literary canons. What allows the circulation of NTM's lyrics is its commercialization, the fact that they have signed a contract with Sony, one of the most powerful production and distribution companies. NTM's popularity places the group in the delicate position of artists whose voice is both amplified but also controlled by the media and the profit-making private companies who support them. In other words, a right-wing judge is not the only force capable of turning the loudspeaker of rap music on or off.

In "Challenging Conventions in the Fine Art of Rap," Richard Shusterman proposes a metaphor that could be an important contribution to the search for a protocol of reception, not only of rap music, but of all the postmodern genres that find themselves inextricably intertwined with the issues of commercialization and commodification. Shusterman suggests that rap music can be seen as an ephemeral product whose quality may well depend on a certain degree of "freshness." As he hastens to add:

> [R]ap's postmodern aesthetics, the ephemeral freshness of artistic creations does not render them aesthetically unworthy, no more than the ephemeral freshness of cream renders its sweet taste unreal. For the view that aesthetic value can only be real if it passes the test of time is simply an entrenched but unjustified presumption, ultimately deriving from the pervasive philosophical bias that equates reality with the permanent and the unchanging. (Shusterman, 192)

At first, I was tempted to resist Shusterman's conclusion that the "test of time" is always, or only the result of an untheorized philosophical prejudice. And to be fair, there is here no indication that the critic proposes to simply replace one bias with another: he is obviously not suggesting that we systematically embrace the ephemeral at the expense of whatever cultural production has enjoyed lasting esteem and/or canonization. On the other hand, likening rap music to perishable goods has quite interesting implications if we choose to take the metaphor seriously. It first occurred to me that here, rap music is treated like a product, that is, something sellable and disposable. In a sense, the allusion is hardly a new or revolutionary critical comment: rare is the article on rap music that does not at least mention and most typically worries and frets about the dangers of commercialism, cooptation, taming, or crossover. On November 16, 1996, the day Suprême NTM was sentenced, Plantu's daily cartoon on the front page of *Le Monde* represented a courtroom where two symmetrical characters were allowed to speak in unison. A lawyer asks the judge: "Doublez la peine," while a representative from Sony, speaking on a portable phone, says: "Doublez les ventes de disques." Both those who approved and those who disapproved of the sentence for ideological reasons were quick to point out that the strategic side of the verdict was self-defeating: the amount of publicity generated by the much-publicized verdict not only added to the group's fame but it also resulted in an increased circulation of the supposedly offensive lyrics.

What is, however, not only more original but much more interesting about the organic image used by Shusterman is the fact that it implicitly contains a narrative of how the audience can respond to the commodification of rap music. Perishable products are subject to very strict and very explicit protocols of industrial stocking and they belong to the type of goods that require a certain level of cultural competence. Individual customers know that purchasing a carton of cream involves paying attention to the date after which it should not be consumed anymore. Even if this element of vigilance is minimum, some activity and some thinking and planning are necessary. Otherwise the customer will eventually have to throw the cream away (losing the right to consume that his or her purchasing power had originally secured) or will make him or herself sick (and deprive them of whatever pleasure principle was supposed to be gratified by the consumption of a fresh and sweet tasting cream).

Shusterman's metaphor suggests, I think, a politics of the ephemeral that, if applied to cultural productions, constitutes an ethics of consumption. In the case of Suprême NTM for example, the image warns us against the temptation to treat the compact disk as a dead object: perhaps the music will go sour if we store it too long. And perhaps we need to wonder if there is an equivalent to the dates printed on the packages of fresh products. What kind of awareness and attention to some of the specificities of rap songs would constitute responsible handling?

An attention to micro history? For example, in 1995, Suprême NTM released an album called *Paris sous les bombes*. Deceptively, the title does not refer to bombs but to cans of spray paint ("bombes" in French). The title song is an almost nostalgic account of the singers' previous career as graffiti artists: "C'était l'épopée graffiti qui imposait son règne/Paris était recouvert avant qu'on ne comprenne. . . . Où sont mes bombes, où sont mes bombes/Avec lesquelles j'exerçais dans l'ombre/ Quand nos nuits étaient longues/Et de plus en plus fécondes." I would suggest that we may lose much of the song's cultural flavor if we do not appreciate that it was released in 1995, in a particularly delicate context: other bombs were exploding in Paris, in the subway or in crowded market places, and the fear of terrorism was paramount. The song still makes sense now that the terrorist campaign has stopped but layers of meaning have disappeared from the untheorized connection between the title and the atmosphere that reigned in Paris at the time.

Another way of respecting the value of perishability would be to welcome the apparent thinness of certain of the puns and sound games used in the lyrics of the songs. It could be argued that some of the word plays are meant to be heard and appreciated in one second, like some jokes that lose all their interest if the storyteller must explain or belabor the point. Ethical consumption, in this case, would consist of refraining from the reflex of conserving, storing, keeping for later, reusing (in a quotation for example). Solaar's Prostian *madeleine* comes to mind again.

Perhaps this is precisely one of those literary/popular references that should be apprehended in exactly the same way as a spectator of a Grand Prix sees and hears cars racing in front of him or her. By the time the noise recedes, the car has already come and gone not to be seen again for another lap. Maybe a Prostian *madeleine* can only be appreciated at the speed of light. Rap music would thus propose a model of listening as well as a model of writing urban poetry. Internal rhymes or verbal puns that look appallingly simplistic on paper ("Arizona où Henry zona" in MC Solaar's "Nouveau Western,"or "la guerre niqua Guernica" in "La concubine de l'hémoglobine" or "la dèche au Bangladesh . . . la déroute à Beyrouth," in "Matière grasse contre matière grise") take on strangely hypnotic qualities when inserted in the rapid and vibrant chanting that alternatively shortens or lengthen syllables, inventing a syllabic beat that the French language does not have. I am not only talking about the difference between a script and a live performance, I am talking about the rapid pace of rap delivery, which forces the listener to adapt to its pace and sometimes give up on rational meaning. Sometimes, words themselves function like musical samplings, or even scratching when the sounds of words are privileged. With a sentence such as "j'suis un MC d'attaque, sans tic, authentique, pas en toc," (MC Solaar's "Qui sème le vent récolte le tempo"), an ephemeral listening would pick up on a series of very similar sounds ([tak], [tik], [tik], [tok]) which the audience's minds may recombine to hear other words besides those chosen by Solaar (at first, I kept hearing "tactique" and "tic-tac" as if a clock or a bomb was ticking through the song).

CONCLUSION: FRENCH CULTURAL STUDIES
AS A STRANGE ATTRACTOR

Inventing a course, or a unit of research, or a reading group, that would focus on the NTM trial while insisting on exploring in depth every various avenue of research that an interdisciplinary frame of mind offers, would possibly be a successful example of French cultural studies. It would not solve every problem, but it would certainly redefine the parameters of what is defined as knowledge, literature, culture, as well as politics, responsibility, and aesthetics in this end of the twentieth century. If such a course is eventually developed, I don't think that the surrealist knife will have been reunited with a blade but at least, we may perhaps claim to have, provisionally, for a few years, chosen a handle.

As for the question of whether this type of French cultural studies would boost enrollment in "French" departments, I am not willing to take for granted that I had, at some point, unknowingly, accepted that mission. It may well be that the project I have described here would encourage some students to learn French (as a language) and to study other areas of French or Francophone cultures. But it does not necessarily follow that such research would be an instant solution and an excuse not to redefine our corpuses. It is doubtful, for instance, that a study of NTM's trial would fit quite "naturally," so to speak, within a traditional departmental structure, and although I have as much of a vested interest in the survival of "French departments" as the next guy, I am sure that other exciting teams of scholars are possible. Besides, I can't help thinking that it is slightly cynical to assume that the aim of theoretical disciplinary reflections is to "recruit" more students to "our" departments. I think I have made it clear that monolingualism is a shame, but more than a shame, it is often a lack of privilege. In other words, I simply cannot see the point of certain articles that describe

French cultural studies as imminent apocalypse—not to mention that certain implications are rather scandalous.[21]

Another constructive way of looking at French cultural studies would be to visualize our research and teaching universe as the temporary computer-generated image produced by the calculation of one given chaotic equation, knowing that graphs are short-lived imaginary constructions if we accept to modify the variables of the equation for each project we embark on. Jill Forbes and Mike Kelly, authors of *French Cultural Studies, an Introduction*, suggest, for example, that the question of "identity" can function as the generating equation that will create patterns within the diversity of French-speaking corpuses (Forbes and Kelly, 1).

Depending on what original variables we choose to consider (in this text, the key words were "rap music," "*banlieues*," "satirical poetry," "censorship," "France and the United States," "medieval ballads," "a theory of allusions," etc. . . .), the imaginary computer-generated graph would spew out different clusters of what chaos theory calls strange attractors, a vortex of unpredictably related interests, related specialists. Unlike the territories defined by our current specializations, the general forms and location of the strange attractor could only be revealed at the end and not at the beginning of the research: it would not be determined by the shape of a preexisting corpus (sixteenth-century poetry) and, contaminated as it would be by the commodification of every area of knowledge, it might well be some sort of perishable goods that have to be consumed by a certain date. Only in retrospect could we then survey, name the area of our ephemeral passion, interest, work. That non-territory would have its own explicit and hidden agendas, it would be a temporarily magic zone of increased agitation, encounters, friction, from which, at certain junctures (after ten years or perhaps even five) we could always stray at will to reach another cluster of both connected and disconnected points. In practice, it may well be that all disciplines have always functioned like attractors, but time was supposed to be the touchstone of intellectual validity. As a result, difficulties systematically arose when certain groupings were perceived as new or emergent or radical disciplines: their legitimacy was sometimes virulently questioned to the tune of tales of loss and decadence. And while it could be argued that the nature and logic of the borders of older structures of knowledge (departments organized around centuries, national cultures, literary genres) were always just as unstable and chaotic as those of the new ones (how do we cross Francophone cultures with queer interventions and a study of new technological means of disseminating knowledge?), it seems that at any given historical moment, conventions have endowed certain attractors with enough institutional power to authorize the illusion that only they are naturally self-contained territories.

Thinking of French cultural studies as a provisional and temporary attractor would allow us to dispense with arguments about whether we are engaged in a typically limited "add-on" enterprise (which, some will hasten to point out, leaves the canon unchanged) or in a probably doomed (and I would argue potentially reactionary) attempt to replace one eternal canon with another immortal set of intellectual and social values. If we accept the invention of an ethics of the ephemeral, the question of borders and canons does not cease to be a theoretical quicksand but the whole issue may lose its urgency: for example, if it is legitimate to start from the NTN trial, then it seems almost pointless to wonder if raï music, which falls outside the most broadly defined domain of French or Francophone cultures, should be part of the project. I am not proposing to canonize raï music or to become a specialist of raï (it may or may not be the case that this project forces me to learn Arabic for example) but I am suggesting that the strange attractor produced by questions about the trial of a rap group in the South of France in 1996 are the opposite both of provincialism (and its rampant xenophobic reflexes) and of globalization (which tends to obey the laws of the market): such topics force us to start from a regional context (Toulon as one of the few towns whose mayor belongs to the National Front) and will just as logically lead us to Oran, New York, and Los Angeles rap groups. After all, there is no reason why global and transnational flows of information and knowledge should continue to be hijacked exclusively by multinational worshipers of the Gods of Trade and Profit. Paradoxically, this theory of ephemerality would suppose that we accept spending more time on a supposedly unique and self-contained project than we normally do. If so-called "current" affairs require that we go back to the Middle Ages for suitable background, a few weeks or even a semester will not be enough.

And it is not exclusively a question of transnational cultures either. For I certainly do not see why I would want to assume that French cultural studies starts after 1950. French cultural studies would certainly benefit from the presupposition that history is one of the disciplines that simply cannot be forgotten, especially if we combine our respect for history with an attention to the narratological constraints that apply to every historical discourse. My interest in the ethical dimension of the ephemerality of a rap music is, after all, a reflection on how time should be theorized as part of our conception of knowledge and culture. A different approach to time units might be useful. After all, we all know that it was always already a (historically accepted) illusion to declare ourselves specialists of a given century. Until recently, it was quite convenient (except for medievalists). Perhaps it does not have to be anymore. For example, ephemerality also means accepting the challenge and the pleasure of starting from scratch every time. If I decide to write on rap music, it might be the first time that I have to study medieval ballads, commedia dell'arte, and Rimbaud seriously. My serious endeavor will of course remain woefully inadequate, especially in the eyes of specialists, but as more generations of trained interdisciplinary scholars learn how to cope with the challenge of uncharted territories, this may become a moot point (not to mention that it may be quite a useful exercise to worry once in a while about whether or not we *are* frauds). Like comparative literature, French cultural studies is and should be "anxiogenic," as Bernheimer puts it (Bernheimer, 1).

I thus suspect that French cultural studies would be just adequately served by ad hoc teams formed around a given project (a paper, an article, a course, a book, a CD Rom, a reading group) as by departments or sections. The team could accept disbanding either after a given time period or after reaching a commonly formulated objective. Such ephemeral teams would not need to become a hegemonic model: as Bruno Latour has demonstrated, hybridity will thrive when purity dominates (Latour 1993). Interdisciplinarity may be more relevant when disciplines erect fortresses around them. It is obvious to me that the type of studies I propose would be facilitated rather than hindered if scholars who are used to devoting their time and energy to strongly delineated territories continued to do so. In fact, French cultural studies would only encounter an insuperable obstacle if its own model became so hegemonic that chaos theory for example, or surrealism became the only possible metaphor for the discipline. Needless to say, I doubt that might happen in the foreseeable future.

Notes

1. Quoted in Chartier, 70.
2. Even if nothing proves that the two singers of the rap group NTM have been exposed to the same type of corpus, the lingering memory of fables and scenes from seventeenth-century tragedies may influence the way in which we hear the lyrics of popular songs. In "Plus rien ne va," a critique of French politicians' empty rhetoric, the singers exclaim: "Alors que voulez-vous que je fisse, Face à ses fils. . . ." Whether or not the facetious echo is deliberate or not, to a whole generation of ex-French students, the unexpected imperfect of the subjunctive may function as a reminiscence from a familiar scene in

Corneille's *Horace*, where the father of the three apparently defeated Horaces, thinking that his last surviving son has fled, curses his lack of courage and wishes him dead:

> Julie: Que vouliez-vous qu'il fît contre trois?
>
> Le Vieil Horace: Qu'il mourût
>
>   Ou qu'un beau désespoir alors le secourût
>   (*Horace*, III, 6).

3. Rap music in French is obviously haunted by the distorted ghost of La Fontaine's fables, popular proverbs, and famous canonized quotations.

4. After only a few years of regular publication, the journal was banned in 1945 for racism, sectarianism.

5. For specific and interesting answers to such questions in a different context, see Susan Mendelsohn's account of her experiment: "an adaptation of Euripides' *Electra* incorporating rap music, developed with students at a New Haven high school" (Mendelsohn 1992, especially 11, where she mentions as a possible model the "Joint Stock collaborative approach that Cary Churchill used in creating new pieces").

6. Naturally, notions of banality and crudeness may be seen as judgments passed by a hopelessly philistine audience that cannot appreciate the deliberate rejection of subtlety. According to William Maxwell, "like early punk, early rap was performed by and for a traditionally voiceless group of lower and working-class urban youth who self-consciously insisted upon their music's marginality and crudeness" (Maxwell, 5).

7. And why would it be legitimate to suggest that rap needs to be poetry in order to be acceptable? For a careful unpacking of such assumptions see Henry Louis Gates's article on the New York movement "rap meets poetry" (Gates 1995). In an attempt to answer the question "Is rap necessarily poetry? Isn't it enough that rap is well, rap?" (37), Gates notes: "Most rap lyrics can be scanned as tetrameters, allowing for a lot of syllabic compression between those four stressed beats. But how is it that rhyming, an activity that was discarded as too effete by a generation of wan modernists, has now been taken up by b-boys with Kangol caps?" (Gates, 37). For a study of rhyme patterns in American rap see also Pieter Remes.

8. The search for "forefather" in this case being an attempt both at inserting rap music within a historical frame and also at questioning the rules that traditionally govern the frame in question: would it make rap more authentic and more legitimate if I could formulate links of resemblances with medieval poetry? Or would I simply be pandering to my own desire for sameness, for a chronological tidy cultural history?

9. In *L'Aventure du raï* Bouziane Daoudi and Hadj Miliani point out that the reason Western journalists were in a position to generalize about the supposedly subversive potential of raï music was precisely that some songs had been cleaned up before being allowed to cross Algerian borders. See especially chapter 7: "De l'institutionalisation à l'internationalisation," 211–222.

10. NWA (Niggers with Attitude) is the American rap group whose 1989 song "Fuck da Police" can hardly be ignored as one of the possible influences on Suprême NTM's 1993 "Nick la Police." I/AM is a multicultural and multiracial group based in Marseilles, whose lyrics are respectfully quoted by MC Solaar in "La Concubine de l'hémoglobine": "En campagne électorale dans mes magazines/Jovial mais bancal le politicien s'installe/Comme le dit I/AM 'c'est un hold-up mental/ Je les dose avec le prose combat." The friendly quote is worth noting in a cultural universe where the protagonists are much more likely to insult and threaten each other.

11. I want to thank Catherine Léglu who helped me build potential bridges between troubadours and rap music. I am practically quoting verbatim from a series of e-mail messages we exchanged after I mentioned the project. She suggested *Les poésies du troubadour Marcabru* as further reading (including the forthcoming edition prepared by Linda Paterson, Simon Gaunt, and Ruth Harvey).

12. See especially Tricia Rose's *Black Noise* and Houston Baker's *Black Studies, Rap and the Academy*. See also "Planet Rap: Notes on the Globalization of Culture" (Gates 1996).

13. *Le Monde*, 16 November 1996, 9.

14. For analyses of the 2 Live Crew's trial, see William Brigman's article where the author refuses to be reassured by the acquittal of the group. He disagrees with Richard Goldstein who suggested, in the *Village Voice,* that "right-wing depression is a paper tiger in America today" (Goldstein, 49, quoted in Brigman, 55). See also Lisa Jones's "The Signifying Monkees: 2 Live Crew's Nasty Boy Rap on Trial in South Florida" and Houston Baker's *Black Studies, Rap and the Academy.*

15. *Le Monde*, 17–18 November 1996, 7.

16. *Le Monde*, 17–18 November 1996, 6.

17. *Le Monde*, 16 November 1996, 9.

18. Johannes (1996, 2).

19. Jacques Lang, quoted in Labi, 40–41, and Gross et al., 24.

20. Maxwell writes, for example, that rap music is a "popular genre that is able to negotiate with the postmodern without succumbing to it" (Maxwell, 4). He points out that "[t]hose who worry about the connection between rap music and crime do have a point: there is thievery at rap's musical core. Rappers are notoriously unanxious about their refusal to accept the logic of private artistic property" (Maxwell, 4).

21. Consider the following remark: "While French programs benefit from student involvement in the high culture of European civilization, I cannot see how anything except an accelerated decline in French enrollments can come from increased interest in the popular arts and post-colonial struggles addressed by most research in Cultural Studies. For whether we like it or not, American students have traditionally studied French because of the association with the elitist tradition of European hegemony, and much of the appeal for Cultural Studies comes from its forceful demand for alternatives to that tradition" (Petrey, 386). Perhaps "whether we like it or not" is not the right way of formulating

the problem; perhaps those of us who teach French studies have (sometimes) been instrumental in linking "elitist traditions" and "our" discipline. Surely, some of us, at least, are interested in the "alternatives to that tradition." Why would students be less receptive to that teaching if they were so influenced by previous cultural stereotypes?

Works Cited

Baker, Houston A. Jr. *Black Studies, Rap, and the Academy.* Chicago: The U of Chicago P, 1993.

Baudelaire, Charles. "Une charogne." *Les Fleurs du mal.* Paris: Garnier, 1961, 34–36.

Begag, Azouz. *Le Gone du Chaâba.* Paris: Seuil, 1986.

Berheimer, Charles. "The Anxiety of Comparison." *Comparative Literature in the Age of Multiculturalism.* Baltimore: The Johns Hopkins UP, 1995, 1–20.

Brigman, William. "Pornography, Obscenity, and the Humanities: Mapplethorpe, 2 Live Crew, and the Elitist Definition of Art." *Rejuvenating the Humanities.* Ed. Ray B. Browne and Marshall W. Fishwick. Bowling Green, Ohio: Popular, 1992, 55–56.

Césaire, Aimé. *Cahier d'un retour au pays natal. Notebook of a Return to My Native Land.* Trans. M. R. and Annie Pritchard. Edinburgh: Bloodaxe Books, 1995.

Chartier, Roger. *Les origines culturelles de la Révolution Francaise.* Paris: Seuil, 1990.

Corneille. *Le Cid. Oeuvres Complètes*, Vol. 1. Paris: Gallimard, 1980.

———. *Horace. Oeuvres Complètes*, Vol. 1. Paris: Gallimard, 1980.

Daoudi, Bouziane, and Hadj Miliani. *L'Aventure du raï.* Paris: Seuil, 1996.

Dejeanne, J. M. L., ed. *Les Poésies du troubadour Marcabru.* Toulouse: Privat, 1909.

Etchegoin, Marie-France. "On est ce qui se passe." Interview with NTM. *Le Nouvel Observateur*, 21–27 November 1996, 44–45.

Finkielkraut, Alain. *La Défaite de la pensée.* Paris: Gallimard, 1987.

Forbes, Jill, and Michael Kelly. *Introduction to French Cultural Studies.* Oxford: Oxford UP, 1995.

Gates, Henry Louis. "Sudden Def." *New Yorker*, June 19, 1995: 34–38, 40–42.

———. "Planet Rap: Notes on the Globalization of Culture." *Fieldwork.* Ed. Marjorie Garber, Rebecca L. Walkowitz, and Paul B. Franklin. New York and London: Routledge, 1996, 55–66.

Gross, Joan, David McMurray, and Ted Swedenburg. "Arab Noise and Ramadan Nights: Raï, Rap, and Franco-Maghrebi Identity." *Diaspora* 3, 1 (1994): 3–39.

Johannes, Franck. "Condamnation des deux chanteurs de rap par un juge toulonais." *Libération*, 16-17 November 1996, 2.

Jones, Lisa. "The Signifying Monkees: 2 Live Crew's Nasty Boy Rap on Trial in South Florida." *The Village Voice* 6 (November 1990): 44.

Labi, Philippe, Marc Daum, and J.-M. Crazy. "Jack Lang: Je crois à la culture rap." *VSD* 31 (October 1990): 40–41.

LaCapra, Dominick. "Approaching 2000: An Odyssey of the Discipine." Paper presented at the MLA Convention, 1995.

Latour, Bruno. *We Have Never Been Modern.* Translated by Catherine Porter. London: Harvester Wheatsheaf, 1993.

Light, Alan. "About Salary or Reality? Rap's Recurrent Conflict." *South Atlantic Quarterly* 90, 4 (1991): 855–870.

Lipscomb, Michael. "Can the Teacher be Taught? A Conversation with KRS-One and Michael Lipscomb," *Transition* 57 (1992): 168–189.

Maxwell, William. "Sampling Authenticity: Rap Music, Postmodernism, and the Ideology of Black Crime. "*Studies in Popular Culture* 14, 1 (1991): 1–15.

MC Solaar. "Matière grasse contre matière grise." *Qui sème le vent récolte le tempo.* Polydor France, 1991.

———. "Obsolete." *Prose Combat.* Polydor, France, 1994.

———. "La Concubine de l'hémoglobine. "*Prose Combat.* Polydor France, 1994.

Mendelsohn, Susan. "The Rap on Euripides." *Theater* (New Haven, Conn.) 23, 2 (1992): 6–11.

Petrey, Sandy. "French Studies/Cultural Studies: Reciprocal Invigoration of Mutual Destruction." *French Review* 68, 3 (February 1995): 381–392.

Remes, Pieter. "Rapping: A Sociolinguistic Study of Oral Tradition in Black Urban Communities in the United States." *Journal of the Anthropological Society of Oxford* 22, 2 (1991): 129–149.

Rifaterre, Michael. "On the Complementarity of Comparative Literature and Cultural Studies." *Comparative Literature in the Age of Multiculturalism.* Baltimore: The Johns Hopkins UP, 1995, 66–73.

Rimbaud, Arthur. "Le Dormeur du val" (1888). *Oeuvres complètes.* Paris: Gallimard, 1972, 32.

Rose, Tricia. *Black Noise: Rap Music and Black Culture in Contemporary America.* New Hampshire: University Press of New England, 1994.

Simonnot, Dominique. "Un jugement stupéfiant de sévérité." *Libération,* 16 November, 1996, 2.

Suprême NTM. "Paris sous les bombes." *Paris sous les bombes.* Sony Music Entertainment (France) SA, 1995.

Tropiques. Paris: Editions Jean-Michel Place, 1978 (facsimile of no. 1-13/14, avril 1941–1945).

6

In Search of a Postmodern Ethics of Knowledge

The Cultural Critic's Dilemma

Michèle Druon

CULTURAL CRITICISM AND THE POSTMODERN LEGACY

A major part of the "politics of difference" advocated by cultural criticism could be defined as a fight for the "right to representation" of the cultural groups considered discriminated against, marginalized, silenced, or oppressed by the socially dominant groups or by "hegemonic" cultural structures. It has been described, in this function, as representing the "voice of the Other."[1] Since cultural criticism is now produced in great part by the very groups it seeks to defend—as attested by the feminist, Afro-American, Chicano, gay, postcolonial critics, etc. . . . that compose its discourse—it does appear to represent the point of view of the alienated. At this level, cultural criticism can be said to speak *as* the Other: the Other's voice, in its discourse, appears unmediated.

But a problem arises whenever cultural criticism speaks *for* the Other, for those whose voice is silenced, for the "disempowered" of society. For the voice of these "others" is necessarily mediated—represented or reconstructed—by critical discourse. The ethical and epistemological problem created by this mediation originates in the junction

103

between a specific model of culture, now prevalent in cultural criticism, and the "postmodern" model of knowledge. Contemporary cultural criticism theorizes culture as a series of (relatively) discrete "fields" of signifying practices, thus inscribing between them not only the liberating space of "difference," but also the separating space (to use Bourdieu's terms) of "cultural distinction." The valorization of cultural difference associated with this model of culture is linked to the postmodern devaluation of all "metanarratives" as a form of rhetorical or cultural imperialism: unified, "homogenized," or "organic" conceptions of culture[2] are politically suspect metanarratives, since they imply the denial or levelling of cultural differences. The devaluation of metanarratives is in turn related to the post-structuralist/postmodern deconstruction of the logocentric and ethnocentric "arrogance" of Western reason, both in its epistemological pretension as a universal model of rationality, and as a universal foundation of moral transcendence. In this perspective, knowledge is not legitimated by a universal reason, but by the consensus of "local" (historically and culturally relative) institutions. Which implies, among other consequences, that our knowledge of other cultures can no longer be legitimated by *our* conception of reason. The problem raised by this epistemological "isolationism," which has become a central debate in contemporary philosophy and human sciences—particularly in sociology, ethnology, and anthropology[3]—could be (schematically) summarized in the following question: if knowledge is relative to "local" conceptual frameworks, how is it possible to step "outside" these frameworks to make any kind of legitimate epistemological assertion?[4]

By sharing its epistemological premises, contemporary cultural criticism also shares the predicament of postmodern relativism, especially when it speaks about cultures considered foreign or external to the critic's society—in which case it assumes the same epistemological position as anthropology or ethnology. But cultural criticism simultaneously "internalizes" this predicament by re-inscribing it, in accordance with its own cultural model, *within* the critic's society: the insistence on "difference" in the internal organization of culture not only implies the recognition of different values, different tastes, or different "habitus," but also the "local" legitimation of these different fields of signifying practices, which leads in turn to the recognition that each cultural group, or practice, obeys a different "reason" than the other groups. This implication necessarily applies to the "culture" of cultural criticism: for in spite of the pluralization of its own discourse (through the integration of different cultural voices), cultural criticism is both produced and legitimated by an academic culture that is institutionally and stylistically "incommensurate" to the cultures it constitutes as its object of study. These encompass not only "popular" or "everyday" cultures but all the cultural actors of signifying practices (including ethnic, sexual, or other colonized minorities) who are not enacting the culture of our present academic world. Even more basically, each of our cultural models "reframes" and captures our cultural Other, thus paradoxically negating its cultural difference. Cultural criticism thus structurally and "internally" reproduces the epistemological dilemma, or aporia, central to postmodern thought. The question it raises at this level bears on the epistemological right of any cultural group to represent, describe, or speak about any other cultural group.

Many answers, many strategies have been proposed to solve this dilemma in different fields of contemporary thought ranging from epistemology, ethical philosophy, philosophy of science to anthropology, ethnography, sociology, and cultural criticism itself: some propose to correct the "absolute" relativism of postmodern thought by a "weak" relativism that maintains a minimal model of universal rationality;[5] specific strategies of communication or interpretation have been advocated, Gadamer's historical hermeneutics or Bahktin's dialogics, for instance. Richard Rorty, on his part, seems to hesitate between a pragmatic or functionalist model of understanding other cultures, and a more "romantic" emphasis on "imagining" (rather than "knowing") the Other.[6] Clifford Geertz sees ethnography as a process of interpretation, or discursive mediation across cultural codes.[7] Jürgen Habermas imagines an "ideal speech" situation,[8] while Francois Lyotard, in *The Differend*, attempts to bridge the "abyss" created by the heterogeneity of "phrase regimens" through a paradoxical (and Kantian) notion of the "sublime." To this (nonexhaustive) list could be finally added the rejection of cultural relativism in favor of an emphasis on the interrelations of cultures, as exemplified by the attempt of the French anthropologist Jean-Loup Amselle to define a "*logique métisse,*" a hybrid cultural space that would bridge the communicational and representational gap created by cultural differences.[9]

I do not have the intention—or the arrogance—of adding one more solution to this dilemma. But I would like to bring attention to the fact that cultural criticism adds its own specific resonance to it by relocating its aporetical site in the hybrid conceptual space of "cognitive justice." For the question raised by cultural criticism is simultaneously epistemological and ethical, as made obvious by its political and moral valorization of the Other's difference. More specifically, it does not only raise the problem of how we can legitimately speak *about* other cultures, but also of how we can legitimately speak *for* other cultures, when they represent for us a disempowered Other, when we feel it is our moral and political responsibility to speak *for* those who do not have the power to speak for and about themselves. By reinscribing the question of the representation of other cultures in this particular ethico-political dimension, cultural criticism "dramatizes" the dilemma of postmodern thought and articulates it to the conditions of possibility of justice in the construction of knowledge. It also reinscribes the question of "cognitive justice" in the context of specific cognitive "postures": for the act of speaking "for" the Other involves a different "posture"—a different relation to the representation of the Other—than the act of speaking "about" the Other. When we speak *for* the Other, we symbolically occupy the position of the witness, and our cognitive relation to representation is invested with the dimension of a moral or legal *obligation* which charges it with a specific affective resonance. Speaking *about* the Other, by contrast, involves a more detached position, which defines a colder, or more analytical relation to representation.

My intent in this chapter is to show that cultural criticism oscillates between these two "cognitive postures," which can alternately be defined as partial or impartial, interested or disinterested. In this oscillation can be read a conflict between models of cognitive justice, of which I will emphasize here only the ethical, and not, for reasons of space and clarity, the legal aspect. I will show how this conflict is articulated, first at the level of different models of representational justice, and secondly at the level of the antithetic cognitive postures constituted by the analytical and political stances of cultural criticism. My attempt to delineate how certain aspects of cultural criticism "reframe" the postmodern epistemological dilemma in a specific dimension of cognitive justice cannot be other than "sketchy" in the space allotted for this essay. The few specific examples I use to illustrate my argument are emblematic and thus obliterate the nuances as well as the variety of points of view—the difference—represented by the multiplicity of cultural critics. By referring to the "discourse of cultural criticism," I am guilty of the very generalization, or "metanarrative," that is denounced by cultural critics as a negation of plurality, or as a disembodiment of the cultural groups they represent. I could say in my defense that the very concept of "culture," however articulated, is a generalization; or that the genericity of the term "Other," often used by cultural critics, also disembodies and undifferentiates the groups it represents. But the felt insufficiency of these arguments is itself a symptom of the ethico-epistemological dilemma that haunts cultural criticism and our ethics of knowledge.

My only justification, ultimately, is the belief that this dilemma is *felt* by many of us in the academic world; or more specifically, that the dilemma told by the cultural critic also resonates in the personal and impersonal dimension of our "inner scene." By this, I do not necessarily refer to the (Lacanian) scene of our unconscious, but to the space where any text, any story—even theoretical ones—acquires an affective or ethical resonance, where it reincarnates itself in the world of desires, drives, emotions, and passions, as well as feelings of moral obligation that animate our inner life.[10] I also believe, with Emmanuel Levinas, that "the subject is a host," that I am inhabited by multiple Others, or by an Other with multiple (and potentially reversible) figures. I will thus use the generic concept of the Other in this paper as a figure playing multiple parts in our personal/collective scene, as a moral allegory delineating a conflict in the hybrid space of our cognitive ethics.

REPRESENTATIONAL JUSTICE

In its search for recognition of the Other, cultural criticism pursues a certain model of social justice whose content is sometimes elusive, but can still be minimally defined as democratic and "differentialist" (in the sense that "difference," as well as equality, constitute its basic values). Implicated in this search is the founding metaphor of cultural criticism: culture is a Text; social organization (the political) is shaped (or "mediated") through a series of "signifying practices" (the symbolic) that include verbal and visual representations, artistic, mediatic, scientific, and pedagogical discourses or narratives, as well as other forms of cultural organizations or "habitus," such as the structuration of urban or domestic space,[11] consumers' usages, sports, or other rituals, in short all the "banalities" of our everyday life.[12] As it encompasses all the signifying practices that construct the meaning of our life, "culture," in this perspective, becomes synonymous with the "text" of our reality: it defines the way in which our entire reality is mediated or "encoded" through different forms of signification.

   In this framework, the search for recognition of the Other, along with its implied model of social justice, becomes necessarily transcribed or "textualized" on the symbolic level, and thus gives shape to a search for what could be defined as "representational justice." This is evidenced by the explicit conversion of the "politics of difference" into a "politics of representation" that involves both an intervention on, and a transformation of the cultural text. This politics of representation is not only motivated (and justified) by its ethical and political goal, it is also epistemologically and ideologically grounded in a second aspect of the theorization of culture which can be defined, in Stuart Hall's terms, as "the constitutive and political nature of representation" (Hall,

285). Since the search for representational justice is intrinsically linked to this particular conception of representation, I will briefly outline what this conception entails, along with some of its implications.

In accordance with Antonio Gramsci's model, the signifying practices that give meaning to social organization are conceived as the site of "hegemonic" and "counterhegemonic" strategies, which constantly alter their content as social or historical conditions change. Alternately articulated through Bakhtin's "dialogics," Gadamer's "hermeneutics," Austin's "speech acts," Bourdieu's notion of "cultural distinction," or yet again Lyotard's "agonistic" language games, the production of meaning is seen in cultural criticism as engaged in power relations either between centralized hegemonic structures and culturally dominated groups, or between and within the different cultures that constitute our "global village," or even more simply, and more radically, between any two individuals engaged in a communicative exchange. Reflecting the dominance of the "pragmatic" model of communication borrowed from Austin or from the Palo Alto school of communication, cultural criticism—and most contemporary critical theory—emphasizes the "strategic" and the "performative": to communicate is to convince, seduce, manipulate or "entrap" the Other. As strikingly formulated by discourse analyst Simone Bonnafous, language in the political/public space is "a differed weapon" (68).

The conception of power relations in the production of meaning may take the mild form of a "negotiation" (for instance in Gadamer's model); their violence may be neutralized by the playfulness of a "game" (as in Lyotard's model); or, on the opposite, exacerbated (as in Bonnafous's perspective) in the notion of a linguistic or representational "capture" of the Other. In all cases, however, the construction of representation involves at least minimally a relation of power over the Other. It also frequently involves, as mentioned above, the notion of an ideological "project" concealed in the (mediatic, artistic, pedagogical, scientific) discourses surrounding us, and destined to pursue either political, economical, or symbolic interests.

Significantly, this conception of representation also involves the production of knowledge. As previously mentioned, the model of culture now prevalent (or dominant) in cultural criticism merges with the "postmodern" model of knowledge which forms the epistemological "consensus" of most critical theory today. Some of the characteristics of this model—the emphasis on the historical, the local, the contingent as determining conditions of the production of knowledge—are directly imported in the cultural critic's politics of representation.[13] The status of this "postmodern" model is ambiguous since it presents itself as both epistemological and ideological. This peculiarity originates in the premises that the production of knowledge cannot be neutral or disinterested. Knowledge is fundamentally ideological since, at the most general level, it is overdetermined by the set of beliefs and values consciously or unconsciously inscribed in the "episteme" dominant in a given culture at a given historical moment. At a "local" level, knowledge is validated by the consensus of experts who consciously or unconsciously reproduce the interests of the (educational, scientific, mediatic) institutions to which they belong. One of the most important effects of this model is that it "de-neutralizes" the production of knowledge: it implies that all our cognitive constructions (including, logically, the postmodern model itself) are ideologically "situated," and that our conception of reason itself is an ideological construction.

The "de-neutralization" of knowledge in the postmodern model coincides with its symmetrical reinvestment by power. In Michel Foucault's (or Lyotard's, or Feyerabend's) analysis of knowledge production in our late-capitalist societies most, if not all, cognitive productions (including the scientific) are "interested" in acquiring power over our physical and social environment—over our planet, over other societies, and in its most radical form, over people in any society. For Michel Foucault, knowledge, along with other signifying practices, is a "form of governmentality." A corollary assumption of this perspective (also developed in Antonio Gramsci's conception of "hegemony") is that, like Big Brother, power sees all, but is not seen. In order to govern people's life, power must hide its constructions under the mask of a universal Reason, or that of a permanent, or natural, "order of things." Knowledge, when used to legitimate any representation of reality as an "order of things," must conceal its own interests under a deceptively neutral or objective appearance. In this light, the apparent "naturalness" of our cultural representations, as well as the "false neutrality" (or disinterestedness) of knowledge, become "structures of dominance."[14]

Thus the "text" of culture—the text of our reality—appears entirely permeated or "seized" by relations of power. Power is in ideology, in the apparent neutrality or naturalness it gives to our representation of reality; power is in seduction: in the pleasure or "consent" produced in us by the seductive use of certain discourses or images; power is in language, in the rhetorical devices used to manipulate, persuade, conquer, or captivate its addressees; power, above all, and in all the preceding manifestations, is in the hidden interest lurking everywhere in the text of culture to shape and construct the spectator-auditor, the reader-consumer of culture, making of him/her, in the process, a (disempowered) cultural actor.

De-neutralized, the text of our (knowledge about) reality thus becomes "intentionalized": it is haunted by the hidden intention of an Other that is the shadow of power, and which not only surrounds us but also necessarily inhabits us, since we are not only the actors of culture but its authors, its producers—as shown (among other evidence) by our, and the cultural critic's, ability to construct "counter-hegemonic" strategies. This role reversal is also implied by the theorized "positionality" of cultural identity: our identity is a construction that changes as we change positions in the social text, leading to the potential reversal of the dominant into the dominated, and reciprocally. Thus, to construct discourses is *also* to further the cause of our own interests; to represent is to "capture" a portion of reality, in a relation of competition with the rival constructions produced by others; to give form and meaning to our life is to produce "cultural distinction;" to reappropriate our cultural identity or "habitus" against others. Which also suggests that there are two "Others" in the cultural text, which we alternately represent as actors and authors of culture, and which we simultaneously externalize and internalize in the ethical figures of master or victim of power. Against this epistemological and ethical background, the search for representational justice implied in the politics of representation of cultural criticism already appears quasi-impossible, or at least fraught with ambiguities and difficulties. An outline of the general dynamics of this search will confirm that it does indeed constitute a major site of tension in cultural criticism, which points to a crucial dilemma, or conflict, in our conception of cognitive justice.

THE CULTURAL CRITIC'S ETHICO-EPISTEMOLOGICAL PARADOX

The search for justice in and through representation first manifests itself "negatively," through the denunciation of certain representational injustices, which takes shape in a dual operation of deconstruction/reconstruction of the representation of the Other. This dual operation essentially involves two types of injustice, which often merge or overlap, but which I will characterize, for analytical purposes, as the underrepresentation and the misrepresentation of the Other. The explicit desire, in cultural criticism, to become "the voice of the Other" is directly linked to a dynamics of reinscription, in the cultural text, of the groups who are silenced or "disempowered," and thus considered underrepresented. As clearly formulated by Jennifer Daryl Slack and Laurie Ann Whit in "Ethics and Cultural Studies": "Cultural studies advocates for the disenfranchised and has served as a voice for those individuals and groups who are variously seen as subjugated, silenced, repressed, oppressed and discriminated against. It speaks not just for those 'here' but for those 'there,' that is, for those anywhere without a voice in the dominant discourse and without a place in the dominant and economic hierarchy" (*Cultural Studies*, 573).

The mission of bringing to recognition the underrepresented often takes the shape of a "recovery" of working-class culture, which must be rescued "from the enormous condescension of posterity."[15] At the same time, commercial or "banal" forms of cultural production traditionally deemed unworthy of interest by the "official" academic culture—such as crime fiction, action movies, mail order culture, or the use of the Walkman[16]—are reintegrated in the critical text—or in the literary canons—as valuable objects of study. The democratic model manifest in this attempt to equally redistribute "cultural capital" translates on the symbolic level into a specific form of representational justice that could be defined as equality in representation: all cultural groups and their cultural productions should be equally recognized— hence given equal value—on the cultural scene.

While this form of representational justice seems to involve less the content of each representation than the equal "space" given each of them in the cultural scene, it nevertheless supposes that equal value is attributed to them, which necessarily implies a distancing from particular preferences in the (theoretical) cultural agent constructing these multiple representations. In other words, the egalitarian ethics implied in this model of representation prevents the possibility of giving any advantage to one group over the others, or of declaring one inferior to another. The first problem created by this implication is that it seems to involve a constitutive "disinterestedness" in the point of view of the agent constructing these representations, which would thus seems detached from, or uncontaminated by any cultural determination: a theoretical impossibility given the "situatedness" of all cognitive positions postulated by the postmodern perspective. The suspension of preference associated with this position in fact coincides with a "classical" cognitive posture, commonly known as "impartiality."

In his discussion of the Kantian foundation of practical reason, philosopher Bernard Williams shows that the rational agent's ability to make *just* ethical choices depends on the "standpoint" of impartiality: "[The rational agent] stands back from his own desires and interests, and sees them from a standpoint that is not that *of* his desires and interests. Nor is it the standpoint of anyone else's desires and interests. That is the standpoint of impartiality" (*Ethics*, 65–66). Williams goes on to specify that this impartial standpoint, in the Kantian model, is constituted "not only in decisions to act but also in theoretical deliberations, thought about what is true" (66). The utilitarian model of impartiality, also explored by Williams in "Styles of Ethical Theory," similarly supposes a detachment from personal interests, through identification with the point of view of an "Ideal Observer," an "omniscient" and "ideally reflective agent . . . who acquires everybody's preferences" (83). In both cases, however, impartiality depends on a transcendental and monological conception of reason which is invalidated by postmodern epistemology: if, as mentioned earlier, our conception of reason is historically and culturally constructed, we cannot be impartial because the reason with which we identify is only one among several other possible conceptions of reason. But if we cannot be impartial, from which standpoint can we be just and give equal weight and value to the representations of other cultural groups?

Another prevalent operation of the politics of representation advocated by cultural criticism consists in "redressing" or "correcting" the misrepresentations (the "stereotypes," "biases," "prejudices") associated with the social groups marginalized or ostracized within or outside the critic's society. The terminology quoted here to describe this operation is pervasive in the discourse of cultural criticism. Since I obviously cannot demonstrate the frequency of its occurrences here, I will use two articles chosen for their emblematic value: they "typify" the dual operation of deconstruction/reconstruction of the representation of the Other prevalent in cultural criticism, as well as crystallize its inner tensions and ambivalences.

In an article entitled "Cultural Theory, Colonial Texts: Reading Eyewitness Accounts of Widow Burning," the feminist/postcolonial critic Lata Mani develops a critique of the colonial/European accounts of "sati"—the practice of burning widows on their spouses' funeral pyres. Mani's purpose is to "draw attention to the partiality of the [colonial and eyewitness] descriptions" of sati, which have constructed the Indian woman "not as someone who acts, but as someone to be acted upon" (397). While there is "insurmountable evidence that women were coerced, drugged and tied to the pyre," they were presented either as "heroines able to withstand the raging blaze of the funeral pyre, or else as pathetic victims coerced against their will into the flames" (396–397). The unfairness of this representation is not situated in its lack of truth, but in its "discursive and ideological consequences" (396), which robs Indian women of their full "agency." At this level, Mani's position aligns itself with the "nonessentialist" conception of cultural (and personal) identity prevalent in cultural criticism: since identities are "positional" or relational, the strategy adopted to "redress" the representational injustice committed against the Other is thus to construct not "truer," but "better" (strategically more efficient, or self-empowering) representations. In Mani's case, this strategy consists in reading the accounts of sati "against the grain," "to produce a richer conception of the widow's agency" (396). This form of representational justice could be defined as "preferential," since the criterion apparently guiding its construction is not truth, but a preference for the effects produced by the chosen representation.

Yet, the injustice also consists in the "disembodying" glare of the colonizer's scrutiny, which negates the reality of the widows' suffering and the reality of the violence committed against them. At this level, Mani's analysis unravels "the evidence to the contrary that [the colonial texts] themselves contain" (395). Reading "against the grain," then, also implies uncovering the facts in these accounts, which allow the reconstruction of a "truer" representation of the sati, a representation that would be more faithful to the reality of the widows' suffering. (Mani also significantly designates the colonial accounts as "fictions" compromised by her "readings" [403].) The denunciation of the "partiality" of colonial accounts of widow burnings thus oscillates on two levels, creating a theoretical ambiguity that we find recurrent in cultural criticism.

A similar ambiguity can be discerned in an article by Douglas Crimp entitled "Portraits of People with AIDS." In this article, Crimp identifies the "fears, prejudices and misunderstandings," the "racist presumptions and class biases," created and maintained by television programs such as CBS's *60 Minutes* and *Frontline* about PWA (people with AIDS), and apparently motivated by the benevolent intention of "giving AIDS a face" (120–123). In Nicholas Nixon's and Rosalind Solomon's photographs, he similarly denounces the "unfairness" of the "prejudices" and "false stereotypes" (125–126) betrayed by their apparently objective portraits of homosexuals. Following this denunciation, Crimp states his theoretical position in terms similar to Mani's: "We must continue to demand and create our own counter-images, images of PWA and self-empowerment. . . . But we must also recognize that every image of a PWA is a representation, and formulate our activist demands not in relation to the 'truth' of the image, but in relation to the conditions of its construction and to its social effects" (126).

As a "counter-image," Crimp proposes the more personalized representation on a home video of a PWA called "Danny." Besides reintroducing the dimension of the personal in its images, the video also emphasizes PWA's sexuality—an element that had been obliterated in the previously described photographs and television programs, and which is at the center of the "fears" and "prejudices" they betray. The value given this "counterrepresentation" is ambiguous, as was Mani's counterreading of colonial texts. On the one hand, it justifies itself not as a "truer" reading but as a "more complex" representation of PWAs. Yet on the other hand, the reinscription of sexuality in the counterimage of the PWA is "preferred"—as was the reality of the Indian widows' suffering—because its omission in photographs exhibits, and television programs constitutes a "prejudice," in short, because the "preferred" representation corrects this misinformation by being "truer" to the life of the PWAs. The alternately "truer" or "preferred" status here attributed to the proposed "counter-images" of the oppressed groups indicates an ethico-epistemological hesitation, or oscillation which is pervasive throughout the general dynamics of deconstruction/reconstruction of the Other's image in cultural criticism. A symmetrical ambivalence can also be discerned—with essential implications—in the very definition of the cultural critic's program.

In an article entitled "The New Cultural Politics of Difference," Cornel West defines "demystificatory" criticism in the following terms: "I call demystificatory criticism 'prophetic criticism'—the approach ap-propriate for the new cultural politics of difference—because while it begins with social structural analyses it also makes explicit its moral and political aims. It is partial, partisan, engaged, and crisis centered, yet always keeps open a skeptical eye to avoid dogmatic traps, prema-ture closures, or rigid conclusions" (213). The self-asserted "partiality" of the cultural critic's political program is here ambiguous because, as implied by its "demystificatory" or deconstructive vocation, it simulta-neously defines its project as a critical or "skeptical" reading of the social text, which seems to imply a detached, uncommitted analytical stance. The dual dimension contained in this program is reiterated through-out the discourse of cultural criticism, which usually characterizes itself as "engaged analysis." In "Putting Policy into Cultural Studies," Tony Bennett notes that "however divergent they might be in other respects, [cultural studies] share a commitment to examining cultural practices from the point of view of their intrication with, and within, relations of power" (33). Culture is thus "examined," it is an object of study and analysis, but it is also a site of political critique and intervention.

The relation between the critical/analytical and political dimension of cultural criticism is usually perceived as instrumental, rather than problematic. Thus, for instance, Tony Bennett asserts that "the key instrument of politics here is criticism" (24). Yet, the critical/analytical and the political vocations of cultural criticism imply two different modes of reading the cultural text, as made apparent by the terminol-ogy used to describe the two operations. To analyze the text of culture is to "study," "examine," "scrutinize," "interrogate," or "articulate insights" about the processes that constitute it. This mode of reading is itself supported by a series of practices explicitly defined as analytical—such as "discourse analysis," semiotics, content analysis, psychoanalysis—as well as various ethnographic techniques (interviews, surveys, "participant observation," etc.). By contrast, the political reading of the cultural text proposes to "intervene" on it, so as to "reproduce, resist and transform the existing structures of power";[17] to "designate sites of resistance" against these power structures within the cultural text; to "critique" the normative, or essentialist constructions of gender, identity, nation, race as well as culture itself. And finally, as previously described, to "construct" counterrepresentations to "undermine" or "redress" these very constructions.

As suggested by the above description, the analytical and political modes of reading the cultural text, while generally collapsed in the same operation, coincide in fact with two distinct cognitive relations to this text, which define two antithetic cognitive postures. One is clearly partial, since it explicitly presents itself as oriented or "intentionalized" by specific political interests. As it seeks to "transform" or "intervene on" the cultural text, it also necessarily claims power over it. On the other hand, the critical/analytical reading of the cultural text maintains the observer's distance in relation to it, and remains symptomatically "unaffected" by the political interest (or passion) of which it is nevertheless the "instrument." The cognitive posture implied, while also transforming its "object of study" (as does any form of reading), is not presented as an aggressive intervention on the cultural text, but rather as a "description" or "examination." As such, it implies an affective distancing from the object of study,[18] a conscious or voluntary disjunction of the cognitive gaze from the observer's emotions, passions, and interests. While declaring itself "interested" (since instrumental to the pursuit of political goals), critical analysis thus remains an impersonal, detached, neutral cognitive posture which bears the appearance of disinterestedness and impartiality.

The oscillation between partiality and impartiality that we attempted to delineate throughout cultural criticism here converges into two antithetical cognitive postures, between which the cultural critic's discourse seems poised or suspended. The dilemma it suggests can be traced, at the more apparent level, to a conflictual relation with power and its interests. The assertion of representational power in cultural criticism is justified—made just—by the nature of its enterprise, which is to seek the "reempowerment" of the disempowered. The construction of counterrepresentations is "interested" in political power, but this power is justified as a tool of emancipation of the dominated. Dominance, in other words, is only justified as a "site of resistance" against dominance, acts of rhetorical power only legitimated as "depotentiation" of power. The authority of one's own discourse over a (dominated) Other is never fully assumed, or it is assumed only when the Other on which it exerts its authority is a figure of power.

The ethical tension apparent in the political posture of cultural criticism is symmetrically inverted in its analytical dimension. In its relentless unmasking or demystification of the biases and interests concealed in representations, cultural analysis *is* politically interested—but it is symptomatically (and circularly) interested in the deconstruction of the interests of representation. While cultural criticism "de-neutralizes" all our signifying productions by theorizing them as forms of power (and one must admit, taking it at its own word, that this theory of "interest" is itself interested), it simultaneously denounces and deconstructs these very forms of power as a central form of injustice. Most importantly, it associates this specific form of injustice with deceit. As shown in my earlier examples, a major part of the political and analytical enterprise of cultural criticism consists in unmasking the deceptive representational strategies (the ruses of the media, the misinformation produced by colonial texts, the seductive ploys of the market, or the false "naturalness" of institutional discourses ...) that entrap and manipulate us. The interest or intention concealed in our representations is associated with the scandal of deception, and relentlessly denounced as an insidious form of violence that robs us of our freedom.[19] If power is in deceit, if injustice is in the capture of one's own representation by other interests, it seems to follow that representational justice lies in the opposite conception: in the construction of true, objective, disinterested representations of the world, ourselves, and others.

The denunciation of deceit as political and ethical injustice seems to imply a symmetrical demand for the justice of truth, as something that is equally owed to ourselves and others. But this demand is here paradoxical since truth, neutrality, objectivity are simultaneously denounced as masks of power. At this point, the ethico-epistemological paradox delineated by cultural criticism could be condensed in the following terms: in order to be just, I must tell what I believe is true to the Other; but what I believe is true is that my truth is necessarily "local," partial, interested; I thus cannot tell what I believe is true without being unjust to the Other. The paradox not only involves the cognitive posture implied in speaking *to* the Other, it also implies the "witness" posture, which can be defined as speaking *for* the Other: when I speak for the Other, I am morally obligated (to him/her) to tell the truth about him/her. But telling my truth about them denies the right I simultaneously grant them to a different truth. I thus cannot speak the truth about the others without "colonizing their reality"— without asserting my power upon them.

At the most fundamental level, the dilemma seems to be created by a conflict between two mutually exclusive ethico-cognitive imperatives. The first imperative is a central tenet of our democratic conception of justice; its principle is egalitarian: to be fair, justice must be equally (without prejudices or preferences)—hence universally—distributed. By implication, to be just, truth must be equally—hence impartially—said to/about all others. Hence also the association of truth with objectivity and disinterestedness. The second imperative is specifically "postmodern": its central tenet is the Other's right to Difference—which includes the right to a different reason, and a different truth. At this level, the universality "built in" the egalitarian principle becomes totalitarian. The structural generality of the impartial standpoint merges with the figure of a universal Reason, thus assuming the violence of a general prescription which becomes a symbol of epistemological imperialism.

The untenable position created by this dilemma reframes the epistemological aporia central to postmodern thought as a conflict in the hybrid dimension of cognitive justice, where the moral, legal, epistemological, and affective dimensions of our ethics of representation intersect. To the epistemological dimension of the aporia, it adds the ethical dimension of a search for justice in our construction of knowledge about the Other, which is itself inspired in us by the Other's intractable ethical demand. Some, such as Homi Bhabha, recognize the symptom of our "postmodern guilt" in our moral passion for the Other. But the guilt we may feel when asserting our knowledge *about* the Other is not dissociable from the responsibility we feel in speaking *for* the Other. This suggests—as evidenced by the culture of cultural criticism itself— that among the complex web of pulsions, desires, interests that intentionalize the texts of our reality are also moral passions, such as the passion for justice, which capture us with a force at least equal to that of our interests.

But the dilemma is created by the impossibility of giving a content, a representation to this passion for justice. This is why in cultural criticism, cognitive justice is never asserted positively, in the construction of just representations. Its "political" or "preferential" stance leads to "counterhegemonic" representations, which merely inverse and reproduce the partiality simultaneously denounced in other discourses. Yet justice is relentlessly sought, albeit in a negative mode, through the ever-renewed deconstruction (or "engaged analysis") of representational injustice. If cognitive justice is present, it is in the inaugural moment of deconstruction itself, in the "skeptical" moment of analysis, when the critical gaze opens the fracture of doubt in our representations, thereby necessarily disengaging us from the interests we and others have invested in them. In this fleeting moment when disbelief becomes "disinterestedness," the figure of impartiality seems resurrected. But it is only fugitively resurrected, in the evanescent form of a cognitive *posture* disjoined from the power it would assume if asserted as a positive cognitive content. At this level, cultural criticism seems haunted by a figure of impartiality that can no longer embody itself, but can only exist as a shadow of itself, nostalgically, or as the ghost of an impossible neutrality. Perhaps, ultimately, the only form that cognitive justice can take at this particular moment of our postmodern conjuncture lies in the very *experience* of the dilemma it creates in us. For in the simultaneously felt necessity and impossibility of being just in our knowledge also lies the felt obligation to continue searching for a yet unnamed way of knowing the Other justly.

Notes

1. The expression is used, among others, by Simon During: "As cultural studies became the voice of the Other, the 'marginal' in the academy, it absorbed a radical wing of anthropology . . . " (17).

2. By emphasizing the prevalence of this contemporary model of culture, I naturally omit the many nuances and variations it actually encompasses in the wide variety of approaches taken by cultural critics. I also omit the successive cultural models that have prevailed since the birth of cultural studies in Great Britain, in the fifties. I "justify" myself on the genericity on my approach a little further in this essay.

3. On the junction of the discourse of cultural studies and that of the "new" anthropology and ethnology, see: Clifford and Marcus; Geertz; Rosaldo; and Marcus and Fisher.

4. J. H. M. Beattie puts it this way: "We cannot jump out of our own cognitive skin (so to speak) into someone else's" (19).

5. As argued by J.H.M Beattie, 1–20.

6. See Balslev, 19–20.

7. See *The Interpretation of Culture* and *Writing Culture.*

8. In Habermas, *Theory of Communicative Action* and *De l'Ethique de la Discussion.*

9. The "hybridization" of cultural productions is a recurrent strategy in contemporary cultural criticism: it is used to bridge the gap between popular and academic cultures, or heterogeneous discourses; the "hybrid" created by Donna Haraway's "cyborg" is also destined to "trouble" gender differences, as

do the figures of the transvestite and the transsexual, now frequent in the cultural critic's discourse (see Garber, for instance). As it often coexists with a valorization of cultural differences, this attempt at "hybridization" of our cultural productions reflects a tension that is related to the ethico-epistemological conflict I intend to delineate in this essay. However, I do not have the space to develop its implications.

10. At this level, I align myself with the "affective" thought of Roland Barthes, along with other cultural critics, such as Homi Bhabha.

11. See de Certeau, for instance.

12. I am specifically referring here to Meaghan Morris's article: "Banality in Cultural Studies."

13. See, for example, Cornel West: "Distinctive features of the new cultural politics of difference are to trash the monolithic and homogenous in the name of diversity, multiplicity and heterogeneity; to reject the abstract, general and universal in light of the concrete, specific, and particular; and to historicize, contextualize and pluralize by highlighting the contingent, provisional, variable, tentative, shifting, and changing" (204).

14. Already denounced in Barthes's *Mythologies* (1957) the "false neutrality" of ideology is an omnipresent theme in cultural criticism. Stuart Hall's conception of its "naturalizing" effect as a "structure of dominance" sums up many of its aspects: "The operation of naturalized codes . . . produces apparently 'natural' recognitions. This has the (ideological) effect of concealing the practices of coding which are present" ("Encoding, Decoding," 95).

15. An often-quoted phrase from E. P. Thompson in *The Making of the English Working Class*.

16. I am referring to a particularly representative essay by Rey Chow, "Listening Otherwise . . . ."

17. Grossberg, quoted by J. D Slack and L. A Whitt, 572.

18. Commenting on the "new" ethnographer's reading of culture Meaghan Morris notes that "[t]he 'understanding' and 'encouraging' subject may share some aspects of that culture, but *in the process of interrogation and analysis* is momentarily located outside it" (22).

19. To wit, Adorno's seminal essay "The Culture Industry: Enlightenment as Mass Deception."

Works Cited

Adorno, Theodor, and Max Horkheimer. "The Culture Industry: Enlightenment as Mass Deception." *Dialectic of Enlightenment*. Trans. John Cumming. New York: The Seabury Press, 1972.

Amselle, Jean-Loup. *Logiques Métisses: Anthropologie de l'Identité en Afrique et Ailleurs*. Paris: Payot, 1990.

Balslev, Anindita Niyogi. *Cultural Otherness, Correspondence with Richard Rorty*. Shimla: Indian Institute of Advanced Study in collaboration with Munshiram Manohar Lal, New Delhi: 1991.

Beattie, J. H. M. "Objectivity and Social Anthropology." *Objectivity and Cultural Divergence.* Ed. S. C. Brown. Cambridge: Cambridge UP, 1984.

Bennett, Tony. "Putting Policy into Cultural Studies." *Cultural Studies.* Ed. Lawrence Grossberg, Cary Nelson, and Paula Treichler. New York: Routledge, 1992, 23–37.

Bhabha, Homi K. "Post-Colonial Authority and Postmodern Guilt." *Cultural Studies.* Ed. Lawrence Grossberg, Cary Nelson, and Paula Treichler. New York: Routledge, 1992, 56–68.

Bonnafous, Simone. "Analyse du discours, lexicométrie, communication et politique." *Langages, Les Analyses du Discours en France* 117 (Mars 95): 65–74.

Bourdieu, Pierre. *La Distinction. Critique sociale du jugement.* Paris: Minuit, 1979.

Certeau, Michel de. *The Practice of Everyday Life.* Translated by Steven Rendall. Berkeley: U of California P, 1984.

Certeau, Michel de. *L'invention du quotidien. I. Arts de faire.* Nouv. éd. établie et présentée par Luce Giard. Paris: Gallimard, 1990.

Chow, Rey. "Listening Otherwise, Music Miniaturized: A Different Type of Question about Revolution." *Writing Diaspora.* Bloomington: Indiana UP, 1993, 144–164.

Clifford, James, and George E. Marcus. *Writing Culture: The Poetics and the Politics of Ethnography.* Berkeley: U of California P, 1986.

Crimp, Douglas. "Portraits of People with Aids." *Cultural Studies.* Ed. Lawrence Grossberg, Cary Nelson, and Paula Treichler. New York: Routledge, 1992, 117–133.

Derrida, Jacques. *La Force de Lois.* Paris: Galilée, 1994.

During, Simon. "Introduction." *The Cultural Studies Reader.* Ed. Simon During. London & New York: Routledge, 1993.

Garber, Marjorie. *Vested Interests.* New York & London: Routledge, 1992.

Geertz, Clifford. *The Interpretation of Culture.* New York: Basic Books, 1973.

Habermas, Jürgen. *Theory of Communicative Action.* Vol. 1. Boston, Mass.: Beacon Press, 1984.

———. *De l'Ethique de la Discussion.* Paris: Cerf, 1992.

Hall, Stuart. "Theoretical Legacies." *The Cultural Studies Reader.* Ed. Simon During. London & New York: Routledge, 1993, 277–294.

———. "Encoding, Decoding." *The Cultural Studies Reader.* Ed. Simon During. London & New York: Routledge, 1993, 90–103.

Haraway, Donna. *Simians, Cyborgs, and Women.* New York: Routledge, 1991.

Lyotard, Jean-Francois. *The Differend, Phrases in Dispute.* Minneapolis: U of Minnesota P, 1986.

Mani, Lata. "Cultural Theory, Colonial Texts: Reading Eyewitness Accounts of Widow Burning." *Cultural Studies.* Ed. Lawrence Grossberg, Cary Nelson, and Paula Treichler. New York: Routledge, 1992, 392–408.

Marcus, George E., and Michael M. J. Fisher. *Anthropology as Cultural Critique*. Chicago & London: U of Chicago P, 1986.

MacIntyre, Alasdair. *Whose Justice, Which Rationality?* Notre Dame: U of Notre-Dame P, 1988.

Morris, Meaghan. "Banality in Cultural Studies." *Logics of Television*. Bloomington: Indiana UP, 1990, 14–43.

Rosaldo, Renato. *Culture and Truth*. Berkeley: U of California P, 1989.

Slack, J. D. and L. A. Whitt. "Ethics and Cultural Studies." *Cultural Studies*. Ed. Lawrence Grossberg, Cary Nelson, and Paula Treichler. New York: Routledge, 1992, 571-592.

Thompson, E. P. *The Making of the English Working Class*. New York: Vintage, 1963.

West, Cornel. "The New Cultural Politics of Difference." *The Cultural Studies Reader*. Ed. Simon During. London & New York: Routledge, 1993, 203-217.

Williams, Bernard. "Styles of Ethical Theory." *Ethics and the Limits of Philosophy*. Cambridge, Mass.: Harvard UP, 1985.

7

The "Popular" in Cultural Studies

Marie-Pierre Le Hir

[D]iscourses on the "popular" cannot be elucidated without recognizing that this notion is first and foremost a stake of struggle in the intellectual field.

—Pierre Bourdieu

It is in the struggles around popular culture that social identities and groups are constructed.

—Lawrence Grossberg

In contemporary critical discourse, cultural studies is often "associated with contemporary popular culture" (Nelson, *PMLA*, 276), but so far the perception that cultural studies is "about popular culture," reinforced by the fact that many Cultural Studies[1] projects focus on "popular culture," has led to a problematic result: the reversal of the hierarchy of values attributed to "high" and "low" culture in literature departments, the "implicit bias in favor of the productions of international mass media" making literary studies appear "as hopelessly elitist and retrograde" (Trumpener, Maxwell, *PMLA* Forum, 262). As readers' responses gathered in a "Forum" in *PMLA* illustrate, just raising the question of the "potential relations between cultural studies and the literary" can have the paradoxical effect of giving new legitimacy to the issue of high and low culture that has always haunted literary studies.[2] Obviously, cultural studies cannot be "about popular culture" and at the same time claim to be "committed to the study of the entire range of a society's arts, beliefs, institutions and communicative practices" (*Cultural Studies*, 4), that is, among other things, to overcoming the high/low culture dichotomy. How, then, can this goal be achieved and, first, is it an important objective for cultural studies and why?

Cultural Studies, which I take to include "French cultural studies" in the form of Bourdieu's reflexive sociology,[3] revolves around the task of "understanding practice" (Bourdieu, "Scholastic," 380), a seemingly impossible project that seeks to retrieve "lived experience" but can only do so from within a world that is by definition a retreat from the urgencies of lived experience and from its temporal constraints, the world of research. How is it possible to reconcile the project of understanding subjective, lived experience when the academic mode of thinking necessarily entails constructing the world as object, as "things to be deciphered," as spectacle to be decoded? Or, as Lawrence Grossberg puts it in a chapter devoted to the "Mapping [of] popular culture," how can we face the "challenge . . . that confronts contemporary cultural analysis—to understand what it means to 'live in popular culture'—" (*We gotta*, 69) given academics' tendency to "treat everything—whether works of art, profane cultural objects, social events, or even natural objects—as things to be considered in isolation, as embodiments of formal principles of construction" (73)?

These questions and the fact that the "will to knowledge" that animates Cultural Studies is driven by the attempt "to respond to history, to what matters in the world of political struggles" (Grossberg, 18) form the core assumptions of Cultural Studies. Beyond that, however, marked differences exist between Anglo-American Cultural Studies and Bourdieu's brand of cultural studies, particularly on the issue of the conditions and modalities of political intervention, Bourdieu's cautious stand being often viewed as an embrace of the status quo, which makes him appear, to more "radical" cultural studies practitioners such as Bruce Robbins, "as a new and fashionable guide for an anti-progressive strain of cultural studies" (197).[4] Examining Bourdieu's rejection of "the concept of the popular"[5] and contrasting his position with the one that, within Anglo-American Cultural Studies, grants it primary importance, seems to me a worthwhile project insofar as it might contribute to dissipating some misunderstandings between the two "schools." In the process, it should also become clear that reducing Cultural Studies to the study of "popular culture" can only detract from the project of a general economy of sociocultural practices—which is, after all what Cultural Studies is supposed to be about.

CULTURAL STUDIES AND "THE PEOPLE"

The importance Cultural Studies grants to the study of the "popular" has a lot to do with the ethical, Marxist imperative to side with the "people." When Jennifer D. Slack and Laurie A. Whitt argue, in "Ethics and Cultural Studies," that the "people" question cannot be dissociated from the overall project of "moral and political critique of late capitalism, and more generally of oppressive cultural and social formations" (572), it is this ethical commitment to "the people" they are recalling: "Cultural Studies advocates for the disenfranchised and has served as a voice for those individuals and groups who are variously seen as subjugated, silenced, repressed, and discriminated against" (573). But as they also point out, the term "the people" has evolved over time, from its original definition of "the people" as "working class"—in E. P. Thompson's and Raymond Williams's works—[6] to a more inclusive understanding of "the people" as being also made up by "*other* human subspecies [*sic*], differentiated according to different criteria (notably, subculture, gender and race)" (577). In the process, they note, a "subtle shift" has occurred, "away from the concern of the working class as being disenfranchised politically toward the celebration of various 'styles' of semiotic resistance to the 'styles' of the parent and dominant cultures" (578).

In this newer version, Cultural Studies emphatically rejects the intellectualist critique of "mass culture," and in particular "the picture the Frankfurt School provided of a populace of dopes, dupes, and robots mechanically delivered into passivity and conformity by the monolithic channels of the mass-media and the culture industries" (Ross, *No Respect*, 52). These newer projects are founded on the ethical and political imperative of demonstrating that the opposite is true—that "popular" culture can be positively valued, that "the people" are not cultural dopes—or, in Bourdieu's terms, in the attempt "to convert the stigma into an emblem" (*In Other Words*, 151). In the United States, for instance, John Fiske's name has become associated with the trend that defines "popular culture" in relation to cultural products' ability to "bear the interests of the people" (*Understanding*, 23). But in a more subtle way, Michel de Certeau's "science of the ordinary" (*L'Invention*, 29) also belongs to this affirmative conception of "popular culture." Premised on a similar understanding of "the people" as "the weak," his attempt to show that "users" are no docile, disciplined subjects,[7] is an invitation to celebrate the ingenuity, the ruses of the "people." Of late, however, this affirmative conception of "the people" has come increasingly under attack, the celebratory mode prevalent in some sectors of the field being perceived by some critics as a deterrent to Cultural Studies' overall political and ethical project.

Relating the tendency, within contemporary cultural studies, to revel in "the celebration of the popular" (584) to a "loss of criteria for moral judgment" brought along by the "postmodernist challenge" (581), Slack and Whitt deplore the trend that has led critics "to abandon the commitment to struggle against oppressive social and political formations and to find and celebrate essentially 'semiotic resistance' in virtually any manifestation of popular culture" (584). To describe cultural practices as "sites of resistance," even if it is with the intent of redeeming them, so the argument goes, should not detract from the larger project of "articulating those practices to larger political positions" (584). Another critique of the unconditional embrace of "popular culture" as site of resistance has been formulated by Stuart Hall, who warns that "popular culture, commodified and stereotyped as it often is, is not at all, as we sometimes think of it, the arena where we find who we really are, the truth of our experience," but rather "an arena that is *profoundly* mythic" ("What is this 'black' in black popular culture?" 474).[8]

But a potentially more radical critique comes from increased attention to the role of the cultural critic. In *Cultural Studies and Cultural Value* John Frow declares himself "deeply suspicious of this claim that 'the people' can speak through the position of the cultural analyst" (65). In *We gotta get out of this place* Lawrence Grossberg points out that "[d]eclaring oneself of the side of the oppressed too often serves as a way of avoiding the more difficult task of locating the points at which one already identifies and is identified with those who hold power in society" (65). In *No Respect* Andrew Ross casts his refusal to dissociate the history of popular culture from the history of intellectuals against the backdrop of "the enthusiastic, and often, uncritical appraisal of popular culture as an authentic *expression* of the interests of the people" (4). In "Banality in cultural studies,"[9] Meaghan Morris argues that "once the 'people' are both a source of authority for a text and a figure of its own critical activity, the populist enterprise is not only circular but (like most empirical sociology) narcissistic in structure" (23). Taking issue with John Fiske, she points out that if Cultural Studies' goal is "to understand and encourage cultural democracy," it cannot be well served by "'voxpop' techniques common to journalism and empirical sociology" (22). For her, rather than disproving the thesis of "cultural dopes," this type of analysis reinforces it.[10] But her more powerful argument comes from her critique of De Certeau. As opposed to Frow and

Grossberg, who also criticize him, but mainly for failing to understand "the complexities and confusions of hegemonic struggle,"[11] Morris singles out as target of her criticism his lack of self-reflexivity, his failure to interrogate the place from which his knowledge is secured.[12] Yet, for all their insistence on the importance of taking into account the critic's place of enunciation, no one elaborates on how this can be done. Yet, for all their protest against the facile association of "the people" with cultural value and political resistance, no one is willing to let go of the concept of "popular culture." What is "popular culture," then, once it is no longer understood as a valorization of "the culture of the people," and why is it important to retain the concept?

"Popular culture," as studied by Lawrence Grossberg, Andrew Ross, or John Frow, has little to do with what is commonly understood as "popular culture," that is as a culture "usually defined in explicit opposition to the 'legitimate' culture of the intelligentsia" (Grossberg, *We gotta*, 75). John Frow's starting point in *Cultural Studies and Cultural Value*, for instance, is that, in "the advanced capitalist world . . . there is no longer a stable hierarchy of value (even an inverted one) running from 'high' to 'low' culture, and that 'high' and 'low' culture can no longer, if they ever could, be neatly correlated with a hierarchy of social classes" (1). Frow justifies his claim by arguing that the distinction between "high" and "low" culture cannot be made: 1) by invoking different modes of production—since all cultural products are now commodities; 2) by relying on the authority of those who have traditionally assigned value to cultural products—since their authority has been successfully challenged by the authority of the mass media; 3) by distinguishing between different types of audiences—since the constitution of mass audiences has eroded the social landscape and made it hard, if not impossible, to distinguish between social classes; or 4) by continuing to believe in "the modernist fantasy of self-definition through opposition to a degraded mass culture" (25), not so much because this pessimistic approach to popular culture has been replaced by a more optimistic approach, but rather, as already mentioned, because both approaches construct "the people" as an idealized category.

If, for me, none of these reasons are good ones,[13] the rejection of the "high/low" culture dichotomy provides nonetheless a rationale for questioning the value of disciplinary classifications, and it also explains why Cultural Studies research projects tend to cover a much wider range of disciplinary "objects" than traditional disciplines do. Once "popular culture" can no longer be defined "formally (as formularized), aesthetically (as opposed to high culture), quantitatively (as mass culture), sociologically (as the culture of 'the people') and politically (as resistant folk culture)" (Grossberg, *We gotta*, 75–76); once it is accepted that "culture is never a fixed set of objects, and [that] the meaning of 'the popular' as a qualifer is always shifting" (77), cultural studies is no longer constrained by any kind of disciplinary boundaries. My point here, however, is not to draw attention to Cultural Studies' "hegemonic politics" in the academic field, but rather to relate the central place "the popular" occupies in cultural studies to the theory of hegemony cultural studies borrows from Gramsci.

The crucial role the "popular"—a concept apparently defined negatively that refers to nothing in particular—plays in this theory of culture becomes clearer in that context. A modified version of the theory of class struggles and its understanding of domination as imposed from above by "the ruling class," the theory of hegemony explains the power of a dominant bloc to dominate by its ability to win consent from the "people," from the dominated masses. What must be emphasized here, is that, according to Cultural Studies, the only terrain on which such consent can be won is the "popular," or more precisely, the "complex and contradictory terrain, the multidimensional context, within which people live out their daily lives" (Grossberg, *We gotta*, 247). For Stuart Hall and Lawrence Grossberg, therefore, any hegemonic struggle has "to ground itself, or to pass through 'the popular;'" "[h]egemony always involves a struggle to rearticulate the popular" (247).[14] This general theoretical framework seems to be informed by an understanding of the social world as a bipolar structure,[15] but some cultural critics insist that it is no longer the case, that the "popular" is not to be conceived in opposition to something else. Having moved away from the issue of "class struggle" (or rather "power bloc" versus "the people," as in Hall's "Notes on Deconstructing the popular") the focus of examination of the "popular," they claim, is on relations, processes, ways in which "different cultural domains are continually being redefined and challenged" (Grossberg, *We gotta*, 77). It is therefore understood as a site of construction and struggle over meanings and values in which no authentic, or pure practices are produced, but also as a realm that matters deeply to people who feel and live it passionately.[16]

On the basis of Grossberg's work on the popular, it seems perfectly legitimate to argue that "the popular" is the term used by Cultural Studies "people" to refer to "lived experience," to what Bourdieu calls "practice": at the core of both cultural studies projects is the notion that no theory of society or culture can afford to disregard the immediate, lived experience of "agents" for Bourdieu, of the "people" for Cultural

Studies. Both have in common the goal of understanding "the popular," "practice." There is, however, no agreement on how to reach that goal. In what follows, I would like to revisit some of the points just discussed from Bourdieu's perspective.

BOURDIEU, PRACTICE, AND THE "POPULAR"

Bourdieu's work can only disappoint those who approach it with the expectation of figuring out his stand on trendy theoretical issues or those who read it as a purely theoretical work. Its greatest merit is nonetheless to offer a sophisticated mode of thinking that can be appropriated for research in virtually any area of the humanities or the social sciences. For this kind of appropriation to occur, however, all aspects of his work, not just parts of it, must be considered. The opposite is usually the case: discussions of it tend to be fragmented, cut off from the general theoretical framework and from the specific mode of thinking that inspired it.[17]

John Frow offers a good example of this kind of partial reading (although he still is, with Andrew Ross, one of the few Cultural Studies people who do not reduce Bourdieu's work to *Distinction*) and unfortunately also, of the type of inaccurate statements that have given others the means to attack Bourdieu as a politically "antiprogressive" thinker. For instance, when Frow writes that "without a more complex analysis of the political and ideological functions of intellectuals, Bourdieu is unable to theorize relations of domination as relations of contested hegemony" (45), he does not seem to realize that the term *hegemony* does not belong to Bourdieu's vocabulary for a good reason:[18] namely, that he has developed a more sophisticated way of theorizing "practice" and its logic than the general, bipolar model the theory of hegemony rests on—and that, in the absence of anything better, Cultural Studies accepts reluctantly, especially in the United States. Through the tools he has come up with—field, habitus, and symbolic capital—Bourdieu has also given himself and others the means to *analyze concretely* not "the political and ideological function of intellectuals," that is, the universal function of a universal category, but the specific functions of historically constituted groups of agents variously positioned within specific, historically constituted social fields. Short of referring to the three copious works Bourdieu has devoted to the French intellectual field (*Homo Academicus, The Nobility of State,* and *Rules of Art*), Frow could have used the following passage from "For a Corporatism of the Universal"—since he discusses that very essay toward the end of his book—to show, that contrary to what he asserts, Bourdieu has a very good understanding of the complexities of fields of cultural production and that he grants a central place to their analysis throughout his work:

> When we speak as intellectuals, that is, with the ambition to be universal, it is always, at any moment, the historical unconscious inscribed in the experience of a singular field which speaks through our mouths. I think that we only have a chance of achieving real communication when we objectify and master the various kinds of historical unconscious separating us, meaning *the specific histories of intellectual universes which have produced our categories of perception and thought.* (*Rules,* 344, my emphasis)

Whereas Frow's attempt to come to grips with "the political and ideological function of intellectuals" rests on an absolute faith in the ability to solve the question in a thoroughly theoretical manner, Bourdieu's approach is to consider the whole issue as a concrete problem (how can intellectuals better communicate across these various intellectual universes of which they are the products?) to be solved concretely (by taking this central fact into account in one's analysis and thereby neutralizing it).

Another major problem with Frow's reading of "For a Corporatism of the Universal" is that it creates an artificial opposition between Bourdieu's scientific practice, on the one hand, and his politics on the other. When he argues, for instance, that Bourdieu "uncharacteristically abandons the skeptical detachment of the sociologist in order to argue directly for the necessity of a corporatist politics of intellectuals" (166), he overlooks one of the central points Bourdieu tries to make in that article, namely, that:

> Far from there existing, as is customarily believed, an antinomy between the search for autonomy (which characterizes the art, science or literature we call "pure") and the search for political efficacy, it is by increasing their autonomy (and thereby, among other things, their power to criticize the prevailing powers) that intellectuals can increase the effectiveness of a political action whose ends and means have their origin in the specific logic of fields of cultural production. (*Rules,* 340)[19]

Bourdieu's entire project rests on the recognition that there is a fundamental difference between "the practical mode of knowledge which is the basis of ordinary experience" (*Logic,* 25) and modes of knowledge that owe their condition of possibility to "this sort of bracketing of temporal emergency and of economic necessity" (Scholastic, 381) that is typically the rule in the academic world.[20] This retreat from the ordinary world has a serious impact on all the thinking that it makes possible, Bourdieu says, particularly when the object of this thinking is practice itself: "the scholastic vision destroys its object every time it is applied to practices that are the product of the practical view . . . " (Scholastic, 382). Rock n' roll, for instance, matters in different ways to Lawrence Grossberg, the cultural critic who "wants to locate culture in its articulation to and within the contexts of postwar culture" (Grossberg, *We gotta*, 132) and to his students who "oppose classes on rock because . . . it will become increasingly a meaningful form to be interpreted rather than a popular form to be felt on one's body . . . "(79). As opposed to the students, the cultural critic "brackets all practical interests and stakes," he injects "meta- into practice" (Scholastic, 382–383). When "the popular" falls under the sway of the scholastic point of view, as soon as rock enters Grossberg's classroom or the Cleveland Rock and Roll Hall of Fame—it ceases to be "lived experience."

Cultural Studies critics are aware of the problem Bourdieu addresses— as Morris's critique of de Certeau illustrates. But self-reflexivity itself remains an undertheorized area of Cultural Studies whereas it constitutes Bourdieu's single most important contribution, not only in theoretical, but also in practical terms. As Loïc Wacquant points out, "reflexivity does not involve reflection *of* the subject *on* the subject" (40), it requires rather "a veritable critique of scholarly or scholastic reason to uncover the *intellectualist bias* that is inscribed in the most ordinary instruments of intellectual work . . . and in the posture that is the tacit condition of their production and of their utilization" (Scholastic, 385). The question Bourdieu raises to illustrate this point provides both a clarification and a condensed version of what he has to say about "popular culture":

> What do we do, for instance, when we talk of "popular aesthetics"or when we want at all costs to credit "the people" (*le peuple*), who do not care to have one, with a "popular culture?" Forgetting to effect the *épocbé* of the social conditions of the *épocbé* of practical interests that we effect when we pass a pure aesthetic appreciation, we purely and simply universalize the particular case in which we are placed or, to speak a bit more roughly, we, in an unconscious and *thoroughly theoretical* manner, grant the economic and social privilege that is the precondition of the pure and universal point of view to all men and women. . . . (385–386)

For Bourdieu, as for Meghan Morris, Andrew Ross, and many others, the "anti-elitist" move by which "popular culture" is discovered by scholars as "the culture of the people" is more elitist than it first appears. The intellectualist desire to grant "the people" a culture ends up reinforcing the idea of "the people" as "cultural dopes" and, actually, essentializing that difference.

Bourdieu's focus, however, is on the fact that such a project, and all such projects, can only be conceived by "cultured" minds working from a scholastic point of view. What matters, for him, is not only to recognize "that the commendable concern to *rehabilitate . . .* can end up yielding the opposite result, *pushing them [the people] further down,* by converting deprivation and hardship into elective choice" (387), but also to realize that "most of the works we are accustomed to treating as universal—law, science, the fine arts, ethics, religion, etc.—cannot be dissociated from the scholastic point of view . . . " (386). Cultural Studies' version of this insight is its critique of disciplinarity, a critique limited to the recognition that "the disciplinary practices of the academy . . . carry with them a heritage of disciplinary investments and exclusions and a history of social effects" (*Cultural Studies,* 2). The response, which is also a weak one in my mind, is to declare cultural studies an "interdisciplinary, transdisciplinary, and sometimes counter-disciplinary field" (4), to act, in other words, "as if" disciplines did not matter. For Bourdieu, by constrast, the only way to neutralize the scholastic point of view is to tackle that problem head on, to "unearth the epistemological unconscious" (Wacquant, *Invitation* 41) of "fields of cultural production."[21] The fact that scholars, artists, and all other professionals of thought are positioned (*and engaged in struggles*) in such fields is of tantamount importance because these agents "have in common the *privilege* of fighting for the monopoly of the universal, and thereby effectively to cause truths and values that are held, at each moment, to be universal, nay eternal, to advance" (386).

The methodological consequence of this analysis is to subject any research project to an examination of the external constraints that bear on representations and interactions related to it. This means rejecting at first the terms of a theoretical discussion as they are given ("Cultural Studies" versus "literature"; "high" versus "low" culture) and finding out instead in which space of positions "the popular" and "Cultural Studies" are deemed important. Mapping out the field, this exercise in self-reflexivity, leads to the realization that Cultural Studies' primary function is not to replace literature in English departments, or even to change "society" or to save the "people," but, as I would like to suggest, to try and modify the power balance between the humanities and the social sciences in American universities.

In that respect, it is interesting to note, as Herman Gray does,[22] that the social sciences are not particularly interested in Cultural Studies, but also to contrast that insight with Ben Agger's observation that although "[t]he American social sciences . . . have not been well fertilized by

European theory" (87), a few Continental thinkers such as Pierre Bourdieu have nonetheless had a "significant impact on American cultural studies" (87). For Agger, this curious state of affairs—Bourdieu's success as a Cultural Studies person in the social sciences and Cultural Studies' failure to make an impact in these disciplines—can be explained by the fact that "a great deal of his [Bourdieu's] work utilizes techniques of empirical data that are much more familiar to the Americans than are the obscurities of Derrida" (87). If we add to this brief analysis, Benjamin Lee's critique of the social sciences' methodologies ("derived from natural science and statistics," 571) and Meaghan Morris's expressed disdain for "empirical sociology," empirical research clearly emerges as Cultural Studies' unconscious Other. Just as from a social science perspective, the humanities can be reduced to "pure theory"—to "the obscurities of Derrida"—so too, from a humanities perspective, the social sciences can be reduced to mere "empirical research," to facts and numbers.

The merit of thinking about Cultural Studies from Bourdieu's perspective, that is, of relating it to its "sites of enunciation" in today's American academic field rather than viewing it as a "theory of cultural practices" only, is in part to provide an explanation for its current success in the humanities. By contesting the monopoly of discursive practices on the social world held (or perceived to be held) by the social sciences, Cultural Studies reaffirms the importance of the knowledge produced by the humanities and therefore also the central role "intellectuals"—the term *humanists* has a dusty connotation—should continue to play "in all matters of social consequence" (Ross, *PMLA* Forum, 286). Cultural Studies, however, does not give itself the means to reach that kind of insight, that is, to acknowledge its role in this particular, historical, academic struggle. Even as it recognizes sites of enunciation as a significant theoretical issue, it fails to apply that insight to itself. This is a crucial point: for if Cultural Studies truly represents an attempt to try and modify the power balance between the humanities and the social sciences in American universities, as I am claiming here, what are the consequences of this blind spot for the Cultural Studies research agendas?

Cultural Studies' ambivalent response to Bourdieu's work—which translates into a lot of silence and misunderstandings, even in the obligatory references to *Distinction*—can be attributed to the impossibility of classifying him as a "pure theorist." But the point of Bourdieu's scientific project is precisely to overcome ordinary oppositions between "pure theory" and "empirical research," "between quantitative and qualitative methods, between statistical recording and ethnographic observation, between the grasping of structures and the construction of individuals" (quoted in Wacquant, 27), because "beyond their antagonism, methodological inhibition and the fetishism of concepts can conspire in the organized abdication of the effort to explain existing society and history" (Wacquant, 33).[23] Seen that way, the question then becomes: can Cultural Studies produce something other than a *theory* of culture? Can it practice a self-reflexivity it advocates and thereby contribute to a *science* of culture?

As we saw, there are many problems with John Frow's appropriation of Bourdieu's work in *Cultural Studies and Cultural Value*,[24] but his comment that Cultural Studies "in defining itself by means of a renunciation of the aesthetic concerns of literary or cinematic or art-historical studies, and in adopting some of the rhetoric and some of the founding assumptions, if not the instruments of the social sciences, . . . tends to repeat, and so be caught within, that opposition of fact to value which has always haunted the latter" seems to imply the necessity of overcoming that very opposition. Unfortunately, Frow's book stops short of fulfilling that promise: it remains thoroughly theoretical. The questions he raises are nonetheless important ones—they center on what he calls the issue of "cultural value" and the role of intellectuals in relation to that question. I will use them here to illustrate the difference between Cultural Studies' theoretical, and Bourdieu's "scientific" approach.

To go back to "popular culture," self-reflexivity would enable Frow to avoid false antinomies like the double aporia he creates to summarize the dilemma of the cultural critic: "the impossibility either of espousing, in any simple way, the norms of high culture, in so far as this represents the exercise of distinction which works to exclude those not possessed of cultural capital; or, on the other hand, of espousing, in any simple way, the norms of 'popular' culture to the extent that this involves, for the possessors of cultural capital, a fantasy of otherness and a politically dubious will to speak on behalf of this imaginary Other" (158–159). What reveals Frow's dilemma to be a "purely theoretical" one is that it disappears if it is examined as the set of concrete questions he himself raised at the beginning of his book—"What do we teach? High Culture and low culture, or some mix of the two? And what basis can there be for our decision?" (Frow, 15). But it disappears *only* if these questions are raised from the multiple and diverse positions the persons asking them occupy in a given field. For one thing, counterbalancing the impulse to theorize with an empirical approach brings out the correlation that exists between the degree of freedom professors enjoy in their teaching and the position they occupy in the field. Frow's aporia, by contrast, assumes absolute freedom for all in curricular matters, it generously grants equally to all college professors the will and the liberty to make curricular decisions that are in practice the exclusive privilege of the most autonomous agents, who are usually those who occupy key positions in a given field. In a similar way, Frow also overlooks how much being able to collapse one's responsibility as a teacher, which is a responsibility to students, with one's responsibility as researcher, which is a responsibility to peers, is a privilege, a privilege that only exists for those whose students are, for all practical purposes, already peers, that is, doctoral students. No less significant in this case is the dubious association of college students—who are obviously not the ones excluded from the "culture of the universal"—with the "dispossessed."

By contrast, how to understand and make those who lack cultural, social, and economic capital heard and understood, how to help the subaltern speak, is the practical agenda set by Bourdieu and the team of researchers who collaborated on the project that led to the publication of *La Misère du Monde* (1993). Conceived as a "political act" (923), the project aimed at bringing to the attention of the public what never has access to the public sphere, at least not in the form of a publication: the personal stories of ordinary people, of their daily experiences, stories that owe their existence and their "dramatic intensity and their emotional force" (Bourdieu, *Misère*, 922) not only to the fact that they are told by individual people, but also to a sophisticated theorization of the interview situation and to the concrete means devised, as a result of this theoretical labor, to neutralize the effects of this artificial (nonordinary) situation.[25]

If it is true, as Andrew Ross claims, that "many cultural forms, devoted to horror and porn, and steeped in chauvinism and other bad attitudes, draw their popular appeal from expressions of disrespect for the lessons of educated taste," and if these "bad attitudes" are "articulated through and alongside social resentments born of subordination and exclusion," then projects like *La Misère du Monde* certainly represent a way to "rearticulate the popular, resistant appeal of the disrespect" (Ross, 231–232) if only because they are unthinkable without fieldwork, without a concrete encounter between "real people" that has, potentially at least, the ability to destroy stereotypes such as the ones Ross studies and deplores. Here again, bringing practice into the equation leads to the awareness that the issue of the relations between "intellectuals" and the "people" cannot be solved in a purely theoretical fashion. The vexing question of finding a "way out of that politics of the alibi whereby intellectuals claim the right to speak from a position of relative power on behalf of the powerless and the dispossessed" (Frow, 168), for instance, finds a satisfying, concrete solution in *La Misère du Monde* because it is no longer approached solely as an theoretical issue but also as a concrete set of problems to be solved concretely. Focusing attention on individual agents—and not on a presumably homogeneous "class"—reveals the theoretical nature of the concept of "the people" by bringing to light the very different ways in which similar social conditions can be experienced and recalled by "real" people. This "reality check" practice entails is crucial to the extent that it makes theoretical questions that would otherwise be deemed all-important disappear into thin air. In *La Misère du Monde* the issue of the relation between intellectuals and "the people" is therefore not so much ignored as it is rephrased, redirected: the ethical imperative for scholars, researchers, intellectuals is no longer to address the "people" question, or to stand and speak for the "people," but to contribute to the task of universalizing access to the universal in a concrete fashion. Once ethics is no longer a theoretical question alone but a practical one also, time otherwise expended on gruelling soul searching can be usefully spent on identifying the obstacles that usually prevent ordinary people from being heard and on finding the means, the tools to neutralize them.

But the task of universalizing access to the universal need not take just one form. In fact, Bourdieu's reminder that intellectuals owe their specific authority in part to the type of cultural capital they engage in their field seems to me a useful warning against the temptation to reduce cultural studies to the type of sociological project I have just described. Rather than changing fields, which would be the logical consequence of embracing projects such as *La Misère du Monde* as the cultural studies panacea, individual responses should be devised within specific fields. As a literary critic, I see at least two ways of practicing cultural studies in Bourdieu's spirit: first, by continuing to question some of the most sacred assumptions in my field, as I did in my work on the "popular" genre of melodrama, in other words, by contributing to a new history of literature; and second, by making use of my knowledge of literature and literary criticism to examine this new literature (born) of sociology—the stories told in *La Misère du Monde* or Abdelmalek Sayad's *L'Immigration*—that might very well be the only type of truly "popular" literature ever published.

CONCLUSION

As this examination of the issue of "the popular" in cultural studies illustrates, the type of cultural studies developed by Bourdieu and his followers provides a better, more practical way of addressing the thorny issue of the relation between intellectuals and "the people" than (Anglo-American) Cultural Studies. What is gained by neutralizing the distorting effects of the scholar's lens that is usually used to retrieve and account for the daily practices of "others," that is, by going beyond a purely theoretical recognition of the significance of the critic's site of enunciation, is the ability to identify the implicit assumptions that guide scholarly investigation, to find out to what extent a given project is inspired by the logic of the academic field rather than the logic of scientific inquiry.

From what precedes it should be clear, for instance, that for those of us who work on France today, "the object of inquiry," "cultural studies," cannot be dissociated from us, the subjects of the inquiry, as Pierre Bourdieu would put it: reflecting on cultural studies at this point in time and in this institutional setting cannot be reduced to a neutral, scholarly way of contributing to French studies; it is also to participate in a struggle over the future of the discipline. Self-reflexivity is a tool that makes it possible to recognize how much the project of writing about "the popular in cultural studies" owes to the current struggles in the American academic field, or more specifically to the rise of Cultural Studies as the dominant critical theory in the humanities and at the same time to the perceived demise of the discipline of French; and thereby also to realize that the acceptance of Cultural Studies as the dominant theory in the humanities is premised on a doxic assumption that needs to be spelled out, namely the notion that French theory is *passé*.

As professors of French, the job of convincing ourselves that it is still okay to be in "French," and to convince others that they still have something to gain from studying what we teach, entails a rejection of the absurd claim of the "end of the intellectuals" in general, and of French intellectuals in particular—a notion dear to some French "intellectuals" whose claim to fame is linked, paradoxically, to the vulgarization of that assumption. Like all stereotypes, this one equates the particular (a certain kind of French theory) with the universal (all theoretical work from France) and it has had the chilling effect of instilling the erroneous belief that nothing good, in terms of theory, can come out of France anymore. In more than one sense, Bourdieu's work offers effective ways to counter this notion.

Notes

1. Cultural Studies is capitalized throughout this essay when the term refers to Anglo-American cultural studies.

2. An early example could be Nisard's 1833 manifesto against "la littérature industrielle."

3. See Le Hir, "Defining French Cultural Studies." For a critique, see Stivale, 84. In claiming that Bourdieu's theory of practice represents the French cultural studies tradition, I do not mean that Bourdieu's work was developed "under the aegis of British cultural studies," but rather that it represents a related endeavor, and a valuable alternative to the array of critical practices associated with cultural studies. My position may seem more paradoxical given Bourdieu's recent critique of cultural studies as a media hype, and of French cultural studies as a publisher's invention ("Sur les ruses de la raison impérialiste," 114). While Bourdieu's fears about the publishing industry's control of research agendas may be well-founded, I view the emergence of French cultural studies in the United States differently, namely as a healthy reaction on the part of a discipline threatened by forecasts of doom—the alleged death of French theory; the end of the discipline of French in the US; the end of France as a super power, etc. . . . In that context, making Bourdieu the representative of the French cultural studies tradition seems to me not only logical, for the reasons presented in this article, but also necessary, if only to counter the claim of the "death of French intellectuals."

4. "[D]espite his loud anti-populism, his theory so flatteringly resembles the cynicism or fatalism of everyday non-elite opinion: the theory that nothing ever changes" (Robbins, 197).

5. See in particular, "The Scholastic Point of View"; "The Uses of the People"; and other texts in Language and Symbolic Power.

6. "Thus, in the early period of this development of cultural studies, the ethical commitment to the disenfranchised is directed largely to the working class as a group of atomistic individuals recognized as possessing intrinsic, non-instrumental value. The members of the working class are treated almost as a privileged subspecies within the human species, by virtue of their intrinsic value, subordinated status, and comparative moral worth" (Slack and Whitt, 577).

7. In the general introduction to L'Invention du quotidien, de Certeau writes: "La recherche . . . est née d'une interrogation sur les opérations des usagers, supposés voués à la passivité et à la discipline" (xxxv).

8. See also Stuart Hall's "Notes on Deconstructing the popular."

9. "I get the feeling that somewhere in some English publisher's vault there is a master disk from which thousands of versions of the same article about pleasure, resistance and the politics of consumption are being run off under different names with minor variations" (Morris, 21).

10. "The problem is that in antiacademic pop-theory writing . . . a stylistic enactment of the 'popular' as essentially distracted, scanning the surface, and

short attention span, performs a retrieval, at the level of *enunciative* practice, of the thesis of 'cultural dopes'" (Morris, 24).

11. See Frow, 55–59; Grossberg, *We Gotta*, 119.

12. "The analytical scene for de Certeau occurs in a highly specialized, professional place. Yet in contrast to most real academic institutions today, it is not already *occupied* (rather than nomadically crossed) by the sexual, racial, ethnic, and popular differences that it consitutes as 'other.' Nor is it squarely *founded*, rather than 'disrupted,' by the ordinary experience at its frontiers. It is a place of knowledge secured, in fact, by precisely those historic exclusions. . . . [t]he immediate practical disadvantage of his construction of analysis is to reinscribe *alienation* from everyday life as a constitutive rather than contingent feature of the scholar's enunciative place" (36–37).

13. The first assumption is simply inaccurate because it entirely disregards the perhaps paradoxical, but nonetheless real importance of art, the economic and symbolic weight of the art world in today's "advanced capitalist society." Second, the implied distinction between "capitalist" and "*advanced* capitalist world" has to be critically examined, not just taken for granted, especially when it comes loaded with the thesis of radical rupture. But more importantly, one must ask from where the distinctions Frow makes are made: none of the criteria are the product of a reality "out there," they are produced by the professionals of thought.

14. As Frow points out, "Hall's conception of the popular is deeply indebted to Ernesto Laclau's work on populism" (75). See Frow, 75–80.

15. See for instance, Ben Agger's claim that "the Birmingham group has managed not to lose touch with class struggle (although Hall would agree that the agenda for late twentieth-century leftists is precisely to broaden class struggle into a host of different theaters of struggle heretofore off-limits to the left)" (88). Although Agger's radical leftist appropriation of cultural studies does not represent the mainstream, his book provides good insights into the baby boomers' narcissistic attraction to cultural studies. His "Culture Is Us" (6–7) stand, which he presents as exemplifying cultural studies' "attitude of reflexivity" (7), provides a stark contrast with Bourdieu's understanding of reflexivity.

16. See Grossberg, 69–87.

17. Although summarizing this work is a daunting task, beginning with Loïc Wacquant's concise overview of it, in the following statement, might be useful: "Bourdieu has steadfastly argued the possibility of a *unified political economy of practice* and of symbolic power in particular, that effectively welds phenomenological and structural approaches into an integrated, epistemologically coherent, mode of social inquiry of universal applicability—an Anthropology in the Kantian sense of the term, but one highly distinctive in that it explicitly encompasses the activities of the analyst who profers theoretical accounts of the practices of others" (Wacquant, 4).

18. Bourdieu's "symbolic violence" resembles Gramsci's theory of hegemony to the extent that for him also "[a]ll symbolic domination presupposes, on the part of those who are subjected to it a form of complicity . . . " (*Language*,

50–51). But it differs from it because "it is neither passive submission to external constraint nor a free adherence to values" (*Language*, 52). Consequently, the "legitimation of the social order is not the product . . . of a deliberate and purposive action of propaganda or symbolic imposition; it results, rather, from the fact that agents apply to the objective structures of the social world structures of perception and appreciation which are issued out of these very structures and which tend to picture the world as evident" (*Social Space and Symbolic Power*, 210).

19. There is also a discrepancy between Frow's wide extension of concept of "intellectual"—which can almost be replaced by the term "college professor"—and Bourdieu's very specific and restricted use of it: "Intellectuals are two-dimensional figures who do not exist and subsist as such unless (and only unless) they are invested with a specific authority, conferred by the autonomous intellectual world (meaning independent from religious, political or economic power) whose specific laws they respect, and unless (and only unless) they engage this specific authority in political struggles" (*Rules*, 340). Frow does acknowledge that there is a difference between his concept of intellectual and Bourdieu's when he objects to Bourdieu's distinction between "real" intellectuals and "pseudo-intellectuals"—which is not the central distinction Bourdieu makes. The reason Frow gives for his objection is nonetheless worth commenting on: it can only destroy, he says, "any notion of the possible unity of the class fraction of intellectuals" (168). Here, the static understanding of class Frow imputes to Bourdieu elsewhere turns out to be Frow's own, clearly not Bourdieu's dynamic concept of field, and the way Frow interprets Bourdieu's concept of intellectual ends up totally essentializing it.

20. This claim might sound outrageous to the many American professors who experience academic life as anything but "serious play," "gratuitous leisure," or "freedom from economic constraints." Bourdieu's "scholar" obviously does not fit that profile, and is, in fact, in that regard at least, the "master critic" Sosnoski opposes to the "token professional." Nonetheless, Sosnoski's opposition only confirms Bourdieu's notion of the life of research as privilege of the few.

21. Disciplinary boundaries do not necessarily delimit a field. In the United States, for instance, two distinct fields, language and literature, intersect in departments of French, English, German, Spanish, and other national literatures.

22. Herman Gray points out that "humanities departments like Literature, English, American Studies and Film have been quite a bit more receptive to the presence of cultural studies" (210) than the social sciences, where it "has been received with interest and engagement in some limited quarters of American sociology" but with "considerable suspicion and wariness" almost everywhere else (209).

23. In my case, giving serious consideration to Bourdieu's claim that such dichotomies are not only reductive, but detrimental to the production of knowledge means that it is insufficient to assert that Cultural Studies is an attempt to unsettle the power balance between humanities and social sciences. Empirical research to that effect has to be considered. For reasons of space, however, this part of my analysis has to be omitted. Based on data provided by the

National Research Council I argue that it might be wise to question the commonly accepted notion of the "crisis of the humanities" if only because the number of Ph.D. recipients in the humanities has increased, not decreased between 1986 and 1990, as opposed to a decade earlier.

24. See for instance his partial reading of *Distinction*, his unacceptable critique of Bourdieu's concept of class and the ensuing accusation of essentialism (27–47). Compare with Bourdieu, "A Reply to Some Objections," in *In Other Words* (106–139).

25. These theoretical and practical problems are presented and discussed by Bourdieu in a chapter called "Comprendre," in *La Misère du Monde* (903–925).

Works Cited

"Forum: Relations between Cultural Studies and the Literary." *PMLA* 112, 2 (March 1997): 257–286.

Bourdieu, Pierre. "Le point de vue scholastique." *Raisons Pratiques. Sur la théorie de l'action*. Paris: Seuil, 1994: 221–236. Translated as: "The Scholastic Point of View." *Cultural Anthropology* 5, 4 (November 1990): 380–391.

———. "The Uses of the 'People.'" *In Other Words*. Stanford: Stanford UP, 1990.

———. "For a Corporatism of the Universal." *The Rules of Art: Genesis and Structure of the Literary Field*. Stanford: Stanford UP, 1995, 335–348.

———. *Language and Symbolic Power*. Ed. John B. Thompson. Trans. Gino Raymond and Mattew Adamson. Cambridge: Harvard UP, 1991.

———. *The Logic of Practice*. Stanford: Stanford UP, 1990.

———. *La Misère du Monde*. Paris: Seuil, 1993.

Bourdieu, Pierre and Loïc Wacquant. "Sur les ruses de la raison impérialiste." *Actes de la Recherche en Sciences Sociales* 121–122 (March 1998): 109–118.

———. *An Invitation to Reflexive Sociology*. Chicago: The U of Chicago P., 1992.

Certeau, Michel de. *L'Invention du quotidien. 1. Arts de faire*. 1980. Paris: Gallimard, 1990. Trans. Steven Randall. *The Practice of Everyday Life*. Berkeley: U of California P, 1984.

Fiske, John. *Understanding Popular Culture*. Boston: Unwin Hyman, 1989.

Frow, John. *Cultural Studies and Cultural Value*. Oxford: Clarendon Press, 1995.

Gray, Herman. "Is Cultural Studies Inflated? The Cultural Economy of Cultural Studies in the United States." *Disciplinarity and Dissent in Cultural Studies*. Ed. Cary Nelson and Dilip Parameshwar Gaonkar. New York and London: Routledge, 1996, 203–216.

Grossberg, Lawrence. *We Gotta Get Out of This Place: Popular Conservatism and Postmodern Culture*. New York: Routledge, 1992.

———. "History, Politics, and Postmodernism: Stuart Hall and Cultural Studies." *Stuart Hall*. Ed. Morley and Chen, 151–173.

Hall, Stuart. "Notes on Deconstructing the 'Popular.'" *People's History and Socialist History*. London: Routledge & Kegan Paul, 1981, 227–240.

————. "The Emergence of Cultural Studies and the Crisis of the Humanities" *October* 53 (1990): 11–23.

————. "What Is This 'Black' in Black Popular Culture?" *Stuart Hall: Critical Dialogues in Cultural Studies.* Ed. David Morley and Kuan-Hsing Chen. London and New York: Routledge, 1996, 465–482.

Lee, Benjamin. "Critical Internationalism." *Public Culture* 7, 3 (Spring 1995): 559–592.

Le Hir, Marie-Pierre. "Defining Cultural Studies." *M/MLA* 29 (1996): 76–86.

————. *Le Romantisme aux Enchères: Ducange, Pixerécourt, Hugo.* Amsterdam: Benjamins, 1992.

Morris, Meaghan. "Banality in Cultural Studies." *Logics of Television.* Ed. Patricia Mellencamp. Bloomington: Indiana UP, 1990, 14–43.

Nelson, Cary, Paula A. Treichler, and Lawrence Grossberg. "Cultural Studies: An Introduction." *Cultural Studies.* Ed. Nelson, Treichler, and Grossberg. New York and London: Routledge, 1992.

Nisard, Désiré. *Essais sur l'école romantique.* 1833. Paris: Calmann-Lévy, 1891.

Robbins, Bruce. "Double Time: Durkheim, Disciplines, and Progress." *Disciplinarity and Dissent in Cultural Studies.* Ed. Cary Nelson and Dilip Parameshwar Gaonkar. New York and London: Routledge, 1996, 185–200.

Ross, Andrew. *No Respect: Intellectuals and Popular Culture.* New York and London: Routledge, 1989.

Slack, Jennifer Daryl, and Laurie Anne Whitt. "Ethics and Cultural Studies." *Cultural Studies.* Ed. Grossberg, Nelson, and Treichler, 571–592.

Sosnoski, James. *Token Professionals and Master Critics: A Critique of Orthodoxy in Literary Studies.* Albany: SUNY P, 1994.

Stivale, Charles J. "On Cultural Lessons." *Contemporary French Civilization* 21, 2 [Special issue "Cultural Studies, Culture Wars."] (Summer/Fall 1997): 65–86.

PART II

Negotiating Postcolonial Identities

Beyond Disciplinary and Geographic Boundaries

INTRODUCTION

In the United States today the debate over the relations between cultural studies and the more historically entrenched academic disciplines rages on, fuelled most recently by an exchange of (thirty-two) letters addressing the place of cultural studies in the field of literary criticism and appearing in the March 1997 issue of the *PMLA*. Concerned more specifically with the controversies arising from the introduction of cultural studies as a discipline into the programs of American college and university French departments, the essays in the first part of this volume focus on both the disciplinary angst arising from the blurring of boundaries cultural studies entails and the productive tensions within the field created by interdisciplinary or in some cases antidisciplinary approaches. Asking such provocative questions as: "What is the relationship between language and culture in French studies?" and, "Is an endorsement of postmodern techniques of analysis in cultural studies at odds with the search for cognitive justice?," these essays explore issues involving critical theory, textual and cultural practices, as well as the historical, institutional, and political conditions that inevitably give shape to the questions considered.

Borrowing their analytical tools from the highly diversified stockpile currently available to researchers in the interdisciplinary fields of gender studies, ethnic studies, and postcolonial studies, the contributors whose essays are included in Part II investigate a broad spectrum of topics drawn from the field of French and Francophone studies. Ranging from a reevaluation of Baudelaire's poetic interlude in the Mascarene Islands to a discussion of Patrick Chamoiseau's fictional blueprints for Caribbean resistance, from an analysis of Pius Ngandu Nkashama's disillusioning postindependence encounters with the French to a critique of Marguerite Duras's textual reterritorialization of colonial Indochina, these essays propose a remapping of all manner of boundaries. Calling into question fixed epistemological categories (defining gender, racial, ethnic, and national differences, for example), their authors also challenge time-worn disciplinary optics, often reifying constructions of knowledge that, despite their fundamentally arbitrary origins, are quite real in their material consequences.

In the spirit of both the subtitle of this collection, "Criticism at the Crossroads," and the guiding principle it presumes: the exploration of new approaches to the increasingly complex questions that confront us as literary and cultural critics, let us begin our introduction to the essays that constitute Part II—at the end—with Khatibi's (and Réda Bensmaïa's) image of the Third World writer as "professional traveler." It seems to us that Khatibi's composite portrait of the "bi-langual" writer, inhabiting transnational spaces of identity located between languages and "different temporalities," could serve as a model for the position adopted by the contributors to this section, whose fundamental goal as critics might mirror Khatibi's own: "to cross borders with an openness of mind" (Khatibi, *Un été à Stockholm,* 9–10). Although we must acknowledge, in a concession to Michèle Druon's convincing arguments, the epistemological and ethical dangers faced by scholars who seek to place themselves in the critical stance of the "exote" ("exiled person"), we nevertheless believe that the essays assembled in the following pages offer worthy examples of critical practices that more often than not avoid the impasse Druon cautions against by measuring their findings with the yardstick of "practice," the everyday lived experience upon which Bourdieu insists.

Take for example Françoise Lionnet's essay, "Reframing Baudelaire: Literary History, Biography, Postcolonial Theory, and Vernacular Languages," offering noncanonical readings of several poems Baudelaire wrote following a youthful voyage to the Indian Ocean. Contending that previous readings of the poems have been obscured by "the emergent theoretical practices of postcolonial criticism and its vaguely nationalistic agendas," Lionnet clears away the fog of postcolonial rhetoric, grounding her own readings in historical and biographical sources. Her research leads to the discovery of undeniable, if veiled, references in Baudelaire's poems to Mauritius and Reunion, providing evidence of the islands as important "crucibles of globalization." In arguing that Baudelaire's poetry bears traces of the complex cultural terrain that characterizes these island-nations, Lionnet seeks to correct misreadings that overlook the signs of geographic specificity in a rush to focus on the more obvious exoticizing aspects of his writing.

Her successful search for signs of the transcultural in *Les fleurs du mal* reflects what might be seen as a common theme in her scholarly work, an insistence upon viewing cultural contact (even within a co-lonial setting with its dramatic imbalance of power) as a dynamic process "whereby all elements involved in the interaction would be changed by that encounter" (Lionnet, 102).[1] Thus, for Lionnet, Baudelaire's texts, canonical though they may be, are so richly infused with traces of his Indian Ocean travels that the indelible mark of the poet's cultural and linguistic encounter has been left on the French literary imagina-tion through his poems, *being that they are canonical.* She concludes her essay by advocating a historicized, multicultural approach to criti-cism, one based on the acceptance of the importance of local realities, as an antidote to the "problematic search for unity" that too often guides current critical practice.

With Cilas Kemedjio's essay, "Performance, Departmentalization, and Detour in the Writing of Patrick Chamoiseau," we shift our focus from the irrepressible heteroglossia of the Mascarene Islands to strate-gies of resistance structured around oral performance in the Caribbean novels of Patrick Chamoiseau. Kemedjio prefaces his discussion of Edouard Glissant's concept of "detour" as a popular response to domi-nation with a pointed warning about the risks involved in embracing too quickly the current critically sanctioned rhetoric of subversion. His admonitions bring us back to the primordial role practice must play in assessing theoretical choices. He cautions, for example, that social crit-ics and observers who engage in a celebration of the tactics of resis-tance may unwittingly divert attention from the ultimate goal of resis-tance, which is to say, the redistribution of power.[2] Basing his discus-sion on two novels by Chamoiseau, *Solibo Magnifique* and the widely acclaimed *Texaco,* Kemedjio identifies successful instances of "detour" as defined by Glissant, examples that illustrate the power of the spoken (creole) word. In *Texaco* then, the city planner's failure to complete his project of urbanization marks, perhaps ironically, the success of another project: the "re-apprenticeship" of this Western-trained urban architect, who eventually comes to the realization that he must learn "to think creole before he even thinks." In this instance, "thinking creole" quite obviously extends beyond the narrowly defined linguistic to encompass the Caribbean realities bodied forth in the oral performance Kemedjio highlights.

In "Addicted to the Race: Performativity, Agency, and Césaire's *A Tempest*," Timothy Scheie is interested in yet another aspect of performance, or perhaps it would be more accurate to say he is concerned with the intersection between two possible sites of performativity: theatrical performance and identity. Taking as his starting point the underlying premise of Judith Butler's arguments in her groundbreaking critique, *Gender Trouble: Feminism and the Subversion of Identity*, that identity is not fixed but the ever-evolving product of (repeated) performative gestures, Scheie wonders what the implications of this postdiscursive notion of identity might be for the dramatic *oeuvre* of a committed writer such as Aimé Césaire. More specifically, he asks, do Césaire's staging strategies in his play, *A Tempest*, successfully reveal the constitutive instability of racial identity, or do they allow for an external agency proscribed by Butler's theories, thoroughly grounded as they are in a Foucaldian concept of an impersonal, yet all encompassing, power structure? Convinced of the historicity of fixed racial categories, Césaire relies upon the use of arbitrarily assigned masks in his play in order to destabilize racial identification. Yet, as Scheie notes, the ploy of cross-race casting serves only to reinforce the "real" of unperformed race in comparison with its illusory theatrical version. He therefore concludes that "to qualify as performative, a stage performance would have to take Brecht a step further, displacing not only the performed character, but the performer as well to reveal both as a result of a performative gesture."

If Caliban's disappearance at the end of the play throws the colonial dialectic into crisis by eliminating one of the necessary categories for its continued existence, his invisible unmasking may signal that Césaire's "postracial utopia" remains unrepresentable. Scheie is, of course, not alone in recognizing the difficulties of representing difference otherwise. Since he cites Sue-Ellen Case as one of the critics expressing reservations about the strategic potential of the concept of performativity, we would simply note that Case identifies strategies of absence as one defense avant-garde feminist playwrights call upon in their efforts to subvert the patriarchal bias of stage tradition.[3] According to Case, feminist playwrights have sought to undermine the essentializing function of visibility by destabilizing the subject position, in order to avoid having woman reduced to a sign of difference in representation (e.g.,

Tolstoy's "shadow of a beauty mark").[4] Motivated by desires not unlike Césaire's, these playwrights may perhaps be hoping to locate a similarly elusive "post-*gender*" utopia.

Dana Strand's essay, "'Dark Continents' Collide: Race and Gender in Claire Denis's *Chocolat*," extends the discussion of representations of racial identity to include issues of gender, while shifting the venue from the stage to the screen. As Catherine Portuges observes, Denis's film is one of several autobiographical film narratives by French women filmmakers that, in the past fifteen years or so, have probed France's ambivalent relationship to its colonial past through an emphasis on gender-specific topics (Portuges, 82). Although working within the limits of classical narrative cinema, Denis nevertheless destabilizes certain ideological operations of mainstream films, a tactic that has implications for a postcolonial understanding of her work. Strand's reading of *Chocolat* actually engages with two intersecting stories told by the film: the first, the highly personal one filtered through a white Frenchwoman's memories of her childhood in colonial Cameroon; the second, the *representation* of that experience staged within a colonial geography that resists the camera's efforts at mythologizing (and exoticizing).

While critics have tended to focus on the details of the personal story the film tells (the failure to recover the lost paradise of the colonial childhood, the confrontation with white guilt), thus stressing the important issue of the material oppression that haunts the colonial period and its aftermath, Strand is the first to underscore the challenge to oppression in representation the film launches. Relinquishing the controlling (hegemonic) gaze of conventional filmic narrative, Denis's film seems to sound the alarm for Godard's prescient warning: "A photograph is not the reflection of reality, but the reality of that reflection."[5] If her narrative of colonial power in decline seems at times oddly "off,"[6] it is perhaps because she has chosen to abandon what Teresa de Lauretis calls "the oedipal logic of narrative." For de Lauretis, this "inner necessity or drive of the drama" implies a "'sense of an ending' inseparable from the memory of loss and the recapturing of time" (de Lauretis, 125). Since, despite its acknowledgment of the memory of loss, Denis's film denies the possibility of recapturing a time (and place) to which her protagonist never had a legitimate claim, the colonist's story is also deprived of the reassuring sense of an ending. And as for the story of the colonized, her discretion in this regard no doubt signals her tacit acceptance that it too is not hers to tell.

In Jeanne Garane's essay on Marguerite Duras's *The Lover*, "'Cette enfant blanche de L'Asie': Orientalism, Colonialism, and *Métissage* in

Marguerite Duras's *L'amant*," questions of female identity constructed in relation to colonized space are linked to issues of racial and cultural difference through a discussion of Duras's approach to textual and cultural hybridization. After citing the critical tradition that views the Durassian text as inscribing a practice of writing as "différance," Garane goes on to discuss the means by which Duras exploits hybridization in the dual (and contradictory) sense evoked above, both to undermine racial and cultural identity and to reinforce orientalized images of Otherness. In *L'amant*, the protagonist's refusal to identify with the dominant order, which sets in motion what Garane calls "the process of hybridization," culminates in her affair with the Chinese man. Brazenly embracing a "liberating alterity," the girl is both object and subject of desire, disdaining colonial society at times, while at others, enjoying its access to privilege. Garane concludes that Duras's text ultimately reveals the ambiguity of her protagonist's rebellious gesture, since her oscillating position allows her to undermine hegemonic structures without foregoing her right to participate in the politics of oppression.

Garane's postcolonial reading of Duras contributes an important chapter to the critical corpus devoted to her work. If we are to judge by the evolving image of the writer the critics have produced, Duras is herself something of a hybrid. Labelled at first a New Novelist, she was soon discovered by feminist critics, who found her writing to provide fertile ground for exploring questions of sexual difference and "écriture féminine," although a few skeptics have questioned her feminist credentials.[7] Recently, scholars have examined Duras's work from a postcolonial perspective, more often than not finding that her novels, films, and plays expose the bankruptcy of colonial society.[8] The reservations Garane expresses here, through her analysis of the uses *and* abuses of hybridity in which the Durassian heroines engage, represent a significant corrective to the dominant course of Duras criticism today.

If, as Garane suggests, Duras's use of intertextuality can be viewed as a deconstructive strategy, through which she indefinitely postpones closure in her narratives by ceaselessly rewriting them, Pius Ngandu Nkashama's allusions to Senghor's poetry serve quite another purpose. As Janice Spleth illustrates, in her essay entitled "African Intellectuals in France: Echoes of Senghor in Ngandu's Memoirs," Ngandu sets up Senghor's work as a subtext so as to critique the poet, an enthusiastic proponent of the Negritude movement, from the perspective of a postcolonial African intellectual. Where, for example, Senghor uses the quest structure in his poetry to reaffirm his identity as an African,

Ngandu calls upon the same motif to demystify the West. Furthermore, as Spleth's careful intertextual reading reveals, where Senghor fabricates a myth for his generation of African students, Ngandu unravels that myth and, through the clever use of parody and irony, challenges the underlying premises supporting Senghor's unfulfilled dreams for a revitalized Africa. The two writers' approach to African art is indicative of their fundamentally different outlooks. As Spleth notes, "While Senghor evokes the glories of a generalized Africa as a reminder of his heritage and a promise of the future, Ngandu's [view on the place of African art in the West] is imbued with the pain of the neocolonial present and continued economic exploitation." Senghor's unshakable optimism is here, as elsewhere, countered by Ngandu's fatalism, a function of his disillusionment with the deplorable state of affairs in the postindependence era. Spleth concludes that Ngandu, as an African intellectual grappling with his historically specific "anxiety of influence," is compelled to confront a legacy that, for all the decidedly impressive impact it had in its time, seems today to be lamentably outmoded.

What prompted Leslie Rabine to ask the questions she addresses in her essay, "Interdisciplinarity, Knowledge, and Desire: A Reading of Marcel Griaule's *Dieu d'eau*," was the very doubt Bourdieu recommends as a defense against unreflective acceptance of disciplinary models of knowledge production.[9] Rabine first compares the Biblical story of Adam and Eve with the myth of the origin of clothing and knowledge in the cosmology of the Dogon of Mali. Although she finds both epistemologies join knowledge to desire, she underscores considerable differences between the two systems in the articulation of that fundamental link. Having based her analysis of Dogon cosmology on the field work of the French ethnographer, Marcel Griaule, Rabine decides that, before she can pursue her own cross-cultural research on clothing, she must first turn a critical eye towards the methodological problems raised by Griaule's study, *Dieu d'eau*, his report of a series of interviews he conducted with Ogotemmêli, an expert in Dogon initiatory knowledge. As she enters into the ongoing debate among anthropologists and scholars of Dogon culture surrounding unresolved issues of ethnographic writing raised by Griaule's report, Rabine cites five examples to illustrate her claim that this jointly produced document might be considered a model for "intercultural knowledge." She observes that while it may be impossible to have unmediated access to another culture, the process of exchange, contaminated though it may be by the effects of human intervention, may result in a model of knowledge as informal commerce that yields "a fabric more than the sum of its threads."

And now, our peregrinations through the critical pathways of this volume lead us back to Abdelkébir Khatibi, via Réda Bensmaïa's essay, "Political Geography of Literature: On Khatibi's 'Professional Traveller.' " Bensmaïa examines several of the Maghrebian writers' texts in order to show how they redefine ethnic, national, linguistic, and cultural "borders of belonging." Returning to a chord struck earlier by Françoise Lionnet, he stresses the modern prevalence of a transnational notion of identity, suited to populations that are best defined as culturally hybrid. He acknowledges however that the unsettling effects of the economic processes of deterritorialization and globalization in these emerging "ethnoscapes" can result in a backlash of nationalist or even fundamentalist sentiments. In this dangerous political climate where fortifying geographic and cultural boundaries more often than not leads to horrifying consequences, Khatibi proposes that francophone writers should adopt the position of the "professional traveller." Embodying a new relation to language as well as ethnic and cultural identity, Khatibi's "professional traveller" is both nomad and foreigner. Able to negotiate between terms from a liberating third space, the willingly dispossessed writer thus continually runs the risks (and reaps the benefits) of productive encounters with the Other.

Given the dual focus of this collection of essays, we would like to encourage readers to consider the issues raised in Part II in the light of the theoretical debates outlined in Part I, as we have occasionally done, albeit very briefly, in these introductory remarks. Those who pursue this line, will benefit from the opportunity to participate in an ongoing dialogue testing theory against practice, practice against theory, a process that ultimately should underscore the importance, if not the necessity, of constantly reassessing the efficacy (both intellectual *and* ethical) of our critical methodology. For example, Alawa Toumi's insistence upon recognizing diglossia as a defense against linguistic and ethnic hegemony is echoed by Françoise Lionnet when, in the name of "créolité," she reclaims the island vernacular, less from the poet Baudelaire than from contemporary critics who, she argues, may have sacrificed geographic and historical realities to political expediency. Or, to cite another example, Mireille Rosello's belief that studying aspects of everyday life may lead to significant insights on important cultural issues is resoundingly affirmed by the epistemological implications of Leslie Rabine's fascinating investigation into the symbolic function of clothing in a cross-cultural perspective. While we could cite numerous other possible sites of exchange, we prefer to leave the discovery of those intersections to our readers, whom we invite to plot their own itinerary across the critical frontiers we have opened up before them.

Notes

1. In a highly suggestive footnote to her discussion of the new paradigms for understanding intercultural exchanges that postcolonial writers have created, Lionnet mentions a historical study suggesting that African notions of time and space were eventually incorporated into the Southerner's world view (116).

2. Feminist critics have certainly been prone to celebrate the subversive tactics of heroines who, for all their strategies of resistance, have fallen victim to unspeakable mental and physical torment, even onto death. Michel de Certeau's notion of "microresistances" has also appealed to some critics as a model for a kind of subversion that, Kemedjio has argued in another context, does little to disturb the social and economic (im)balance of power (de Certeau, *L'invention du quotidien*).

3. In "From Split Subject to Split Britches," an essay included in *Feminine Focus: The New Women Playwrights*, ed. Enoch Brater (Oxford: Oxford University Press, 1989), Case analyzes the way in which the Marguerite Duras play *India Song* makes use of this theatrical strategy.

4. Here, we repeat the example Case borrows from Lacan's psychoanalytic explanation of women's "natural" place in the object position. Case writes, "[Lacan] cites 'certain passages of Tolstoy's work; where each time it is a matter of the approach of a woman, you see emerging in her place, in a grand-style metonymic process, the shadow of a beauty mark, a spot on the upper lip, etc.'" As cited in Case, 137.

5. As cited in Sylvia Harvey, *May '68 and Film Culture* (London: British Film Institute, 1977), 71.

6. Christine Anne Holmslund uses this term to describe the refracted images of colonial power in Marguerite Duras's films. See her "Displacing Limits of Difference: Gender, Race, and Colonialism in Edward Said and Homi Bhabha's Theoretical Models and Marguerite Duras's Films," *Quarterly Review of Film and Video* 13 (1991): 12.

7. See, for example, Trista Selous's monograph, *The Other Woman: Feminism and Femininity in the Work of Marguerite Duras* (New Haven: Yale University Press, 1988).

8. One recent publication that examines the postcolonial implications of Duras's writing is Lucy Stone McNeece's *Art and Politics in Duras' India Cycle* (Gainesville: University Press of Florida, 1996).

9. For a thorough discussion of Bourdieu's views on this issue, we refer the reader to Marie-Pierre Le Hir's essay in Part I of this volume.

Works Cited

Butler, Judith. *Gender Trouble: Feminism and the Subversion of Identity.* New York and London: Routledge, 1990.

Case, Sue-Ellen. "From Split Subject to Split Britches." *Feminine Focus: The New Women Playwrights.* Ed. Enoch Brater. Oxford: Oxford UP, 1989.

De Lauretis, Teresa. *Alice Doesn't: Feminism, Semiotics, Cinema.* Bloomington: Indiana UP, 1984.

Holmslund, Christine Anne. "Displacing Limits of Difference: Gender, Race, and Colonialism in Edward Said and Homi Bhabha's Theoretical Models and Marguerite Duras's Films." *Quarterly Review of Film and Video* 13 (1991).

Khatibi, Abdelkébir. *Un été à Stockholm.* Paris: Flammarion, 1990.

Lionnet, Françoise. "'Logiques métisses': Cultural Appropriation and Postcolonial Representations." *College Literature* 19.3/20.1 (1992/1993).

McNeece, Lucy Stone. *Art and Politics in Duras' India Cycle.* Gainsville: UP of Florida, 1996.

Portuges, Catherine. "'Le colonial féminin': Women Directors Interrogate French Cinema." *Cinema, Colonialism, Postcolonialism: Perspectives from the French and Francophone Worlds.* Ed. Dina Sherzer. Austin: U of Texas P, 1996.

Selous, Trista. *The Other Woman: Feminism and Femininity in the Work of Marguerite Duras.* New Haven: Yale UP, 1988.

8

Reframing Baudelaire

Literary History, Biography, Postcolonial Theory, and Vernacular Languages

Françoise Lionnet

In *A Room of One's Own*, Virginia Woolf quips: "History is too much about wars; biography too much about great men"; literary history, she might have added, is too much about sons murdering their fathers.[1] Canonical readings of the canon have often insisted on the vaguely Freudian (if not Biblical) model of literary creation susceptible both to "anxieties of influence" and to creative revisions imposed by strong misreadings. Criticism has followed the same reactive pattern in order to clear new ground for further research: the debate between "traditionalists" and proponents of "cultural studies" all but repeats this familiar and combative dialectic. Between formalist and sociopolitical readings, French texts have been mined by many different critical trends; but the perspectives that do not fit neatly into one or the other of these agonistic moves tend to be left out. Dominick LaCapra has suggested that "one issue for readers today is whether a different, 'noncanonical' reading of the canon, which resists symbolic resolutions as well as narrowly formalistic interpretations, may be one force in reopening texts to the[ir] broader sociopolitical effects (LaCapra, 731).

In the case of Baudelaire, the way to do this "noncanonical" reading might well be to go back to a discursive field that includes biography and oral histories, and to resist the temptation either to eulogize the innovations of the poet of modernity or to denounce the patent racism of his images. The challenge today is to return to the scene of writing and the conditions of production of the early poetry—in other words, to look at the text from *outside* of conventional literary, critical, or cultural history, to reclaim it for *our side*, that of a more global *francophonie*. To do so might mean to map out once again the contested terrain of culturally and politically sensitive readings such as the ones Christopher Miller and Gayatri Spivak claim to do. Their readings, however, do not take into account the residual cultural element of the poetry, that is, the vernacular language it appropriates. This language is all but buried beneath the emergent theoretical practices of postcolonial criticism and its vaguely nationalist agendas.[2] Critics have tended to look for symbolic resolutions and to settle cultural scores at the expense of historical and geographical specificity, despite claims to the contrary.

The facts of Baudelaire's youthful travels in the Indian Ocean have remained relatively obscure. While doing research in the islands of Mauritius and Reunion on two separate occasions during the past few years, I came across written documents and watercolors that helped me reconstruct the historical and visual contexts that appear to have been Baudelaire's in 1841. By reexamining the criticisms that have been lodged against the exoticizing rhetoric of his poetry, I want to foreground the links between the Creole culture with which Baudelaire became familiar and the now canonical texts he produced. These links can allow us to bypass the sterile opposition between "literary studies" and "cultural studies" or between aesthetics and politics; they demonstrate the urgency of re-visioning the canon not just from the perspectives of its margins, but as an important source of muted cultural knowledge. The questions with which I begin, then, are the following: where did Baudelaire actually go on his travels in 1841? and why does this matter to the field of French studies?

∾

> Il faut en finir avec la légende de l'Inde parcourue par Baudelaire. Elle était séduisante, Gautier l'a adoptée, Banville ne l'a pas négligée. . . . Mais la vérité vraie est que Baudelaire, embarqué malgré lui, brûla la politesse à l'Inde. . . . Peut-être Baudelaire abandonnait-il complaisamment au commun public ces bruits de longues pérégrinations en pays fabuleux, parce qu'il en tirait, avec des couleurs de mystère, l'air de revenir de loin. Dans tous les cas, il ne nous parlait jamais de ces voyages. A peine, à son retour, nous dit-il quelques mots d'une station dans l'île Maurice ou l'île Bourbon.

(It is time to put a stop to the legend of Baudelaire's trip through India. It was seductive, Gautier adopted it, Banville did not neglect it. . . . But the real truth is that Baudelaire, embarqued in spite of himself, avoided India. . . . It is possible that Baudelaire obligingly fed the public rumors of his long peregrinations in fabulous countries because it gave him the mysterious appearance of having returned from far away places. In any case, he never talked about these voyages. Upon his return, he scarcely mentioned to us his brief stay in Mauritius and Reunion.)[3]

This comment made by Ernest Prarond, a friend from Baudelaire's youth, sums up the facts: Baudelaire never went "en pays fabuleux," that is, he did not set foot in those legendary continents that have nourished the imagination of Europeans since Marco Polo. He was, however, careful to construct his own myths around these travels.

Who can blame him? India, Africa: these were the stuff of his youthful dreams. Having settled for Mauritius and Reunion, exotic but little-known islands instead of fabulous continents, he must have felt that his experiences did not live up to his contemporaries' expectations. For the inhabitants of island-colonies, the feeling is a familiar one: islands are "dust on the ocean" and "confettis of Empire"[4] and their peoples suffer from "traumata of insignificance."[5] Islands do not have the same status imaginatively or politically as the larger continents of Africa and Asia. Islands do not bestow on the traveller the same aura of acquired knowledge or esoteric wisdom; they are mythical, seem unreal, and tend to be seen as places of escape and rest, hideaways onto which an infinite number of desires can be projected. They do not appear to have any cultural integrity of their own, unlike older civilizations. They are seen as the residues of Europe's dream of empire, *tabulae rasae,* which need not be taken very seriously.

Baudelaire's strategies of avoidance ("il ne nous parlait jamais de ces voyages") can perhaps be explained by the fear of ridicule. His journey dead-ended in exotic tropical islands that profoundly influenced his sensibility, but the traces of Africa and India that he found there would have been hard to explain without a general theory and a history of métissage as would be developed by twentieth-century thinkers.[6] His lack of precision regarding his destinations has led both his contemporaries and his critics to contruct their own imaginary geographies of the "far away lands" he visited. Christopher Miller has even collapsed dissimilar locations and their inhabitants into vaguely substitutable entities. Miller engages twice with Baudelaire's writings, and twice errs in his understandings of the poet's strategies of representation, first in his 1985 book, *Blank Darkness: Africanist Discourse in*

French, then in a 1995 essay, "Hallucinations of France and Africa in the Colonial Exhibition of 1931 and Ousmane Socé's *Mirages de Paris*." Miller discusses two poems, which I will call Baudelaire's Indian Ocean poems: "A une dame créole," "La Belle Dorothée"; he also focuses on "A une Malabaraise" and "Le Cygne," as does Gayatri Spivak, and they both misread crucial elements of the text. Miller fails to discriminate among distinct places while proceeding to expose what he perceives to be Baudelaire's contributions to nineteenth-century exoticism and other myths of alterity and femininity. Gayatri Spivak, in "Imperialism and Sexual Difference," chooses "Le Cygne" as a pretext for uncovering "a curious tale" (230), that of the disappearance of the "Malabaraise" or Indian woman behind a vaguely "African" one. Like Miller, she denounces Baudelaire's misnamings and his use of European poetic conventions that subsume historically specific female subjects; but she too fails to address the exact historical details of Baudelaire's Indian Ocean voyage and the people he encountered there. Her strategy, which is to "reveal the degree to which imperialist discourse homogenizes and misnames its others . . . risks the very carelessness for which it indicts Baudelaire," as Laura Chrisman puts it (Chrisman, 499–500). This approach is symptomatic of a larger problem, that of the status of local histories in the production of knowledge, of the erasure, neglect, or sheer invisibility of local knowledges in mainstream academic discussions of topics that relate to "marginal" areas of investigation—such as the southwestern Indian Ocean and its "poussière d'îles," the Mascarene Islands of which Mauritius and Reunion are part.

In this paper, I want to suggest that the poet contributed more to making other cultures and languages visible and present within mainstream French literature than his critics are willing to grant, and that he is more important to francophone studies than either Christopher Miller or Gayatri Spivak understand. I will argue that the Mascarene Islands are the repressed of Baudelaire's travels, and that they return in the form of a feminine voice to which these critics are not attuned. Miller mistakenly takes this voice to be linguistic "noise" whereas Spivak's rush to render the Indian woman visible behind the African denomination (the word "négresse" in "Le Cygne") impairs her ability to focus on the specificities of these insular regions. This results in both critics' failure to do justice to the oral contexts of the Mascarenes and to the regional realities that Baudelaire echoes. I want to stress, like Miller or Spivak, that nineteenth-century European literature cannot be fully understood without in-depth knowledge of the geographies and historico-cultural arenas that marked and inspired the writers and travellers of that epoch. But my goal is to add a greater density of details and specificity to that context. Though Spivak is sensitive to this particular issue, her approach eliminates the possibility that a poem can be the site of a multiplicity of voices, including the reported or indirect speech of the local women. Spivak thus loses an opportunity to recognize and honor those voices, however mediated they may be. Finally, I will make a plea for a more sustained and historicized "multiculturalism": one without which literary criticism of classic texts runs the risk of creating embarassing misunderstandings and wiping out islands as crucibles of globalization from the history of intercultural exchanges.

Let me then rehearse some of the neglected facts of Baudelaire's biography before demonstrating the ways in which the Creole cultures of the Indian Ocean made their mark on his poetry.

On April 18, 1839, at the age of eighteen, Baudelaire is suspended from the *collège* Louis-Le-Grand in Paris where, as an *interne*, he is preparing the *bachot*. He must enroll in another school, and he spends the summer studying. He becomes *bachelier* in August. Free at last, he starts living a dissolute life in the Quartier Latin in the company of a young Jewish prostitute named Sara, also known as "La Louchette" while making his first contacts with writers and artists, including Nerval and Balzac (Pichois and Ziegler, 126). His *bourgeoise* mother is worried, his step-father, the strict Général Aupick, is not pleased with this bohemian lifestyle. Aupick has many contacts in the merchant marine, and arranges to have the young Charles embark on a ship that is sailing to India. The family hopes that the change of scene and *l'air du large* (the sea air) will cure him of his "melancholia," and his excessive interest in literature: the purpose of the voyage is to interest him in "reality," to blunt his excessive love of words. The *Paquebot des mers du Sud* sets sail from Bordeaux to Calcutta on June 9, 1841. Under the watchful eye of Captain Saliz, Baudelaire remains a recalcitrant passenger: he does not respond to the cure as planned. As Saliz writes to Aupick:

> Dès notre depart de France, nous avons pu voir à bord qu'il était trop tard pour espérer faire revenir M. Beaudelaire [*sic*] soit de son goût exclusif pour la littérature telle qu'on l'entend aujourd'hui, soit de sa détermination de ne se livrer à aucune autre occupation.

> (We could see on board the ship that it was too late to hope to change either M. Beaudelaire's exclusive taste for literature as it is defined today or his determination to engage in no other occupation.) (Pichois and Ziegler, 150)

After almost three months at sea, the *Paquebot* arrives in Mauritius on September 1, 1841. There, in Pamplemousses, the young Charles is

FIGURE 1. *Débarcadère de Saint-Denis* (c. 1830). Prosper Eve, *D'une colonie agricole à une colonie industrielle.* La Nouvelle Réunion [St.-Denis: Conseil général, 1996, ed. Wilfrid Bertil, 31. Propriétaire-Conseil général. Archives départementales de La Réunion.

the guest of a magistrate and planter named Gustave-Adolphe Autard de Bragard and of his wife Emmeline who was famous for her beauty. On September 18, the *Paquebot* sets sail for Bourbon. On September 19, Baudelaire disembarks in Saint-Denis with all of his belongings. The *Feuille hebdomadaire* of St.-Denis dated September 21, 1841, recounts the following anecdote:

> Au moment de débarquer du vaisseau ancré en rade, le jeune Charles Baudelaire n'agrippe pas assez rapidement l'échelle de corde du débarcadère. Gêné par les livres qu'il porte sous les bras, et dont il n'a pas voulu se séparer, il est happé par une lame au moment où il surplombe la mer, et tombe à l'eau. On le repêche non sans mal et surtout non sans dommages pour ses précieux livres (see fig. 1).

> (As he was attempting to disembark from the ship anchored in the harbor, the young Charles Baudelaire fails to grasp quickly enough the rope ladder connecting to the wharf. Impaired by the books he was carrying under his arms, and which he would not entrust to anyone else, he is caught by a wave at the moment when he is suspended over the sea, and falls in the water. He is rescued with some difficulty and with much damage to his precious books.)
> (Maurin and Lentge, 2:446)

Another version of these incidents is also related in *La Chronique de Paris* dated September 13, 1867:

> A l'arrivée à Bourbon, il se passa un fait qui peint bien les allures de Baudelaire. On sait qu'à Saint-Denis de Bourbon, à cause de la rudesse habituelle de la mer et des difficultés qu'offre le seul point possible d'atterissage, le débarquement s'opérait jadis au moyen d'une échelle de corde suspendue, à l'extrémité d'une jetée en pilotis, à une sorte de gigantesque potence. Pour débarquer, il faur saisir les échelons au moment où la vague qui se soulève et s'abaisse alternativement est à sa plus grande élévation.
>
> Bien que renseigné sur cette précaution nécessaire, Baudelaire s'obstina à monter à l'échelle avec des livres sous le bras . . . et gravit l'échelle lentement, gravement, poursuivi par la vague remontante. Bientôt la vague l'atteint, le submerge, le couvre de douze à quinze pieds d'eau et l'arrache à l'échelle. On le repêche à grand'peine; mais, chose inouïe, il avait toujours ses livres sous le bras. Alors seulement il consentit à les laisser dans le canot qui se tenait au pied de l'échelle, mais en remontant il se laissa encore une fois atteindre par la vague, ne lâcha pas prise, arriva sur la rive et prit le chemin de la ville, calme, froid, sans avoir l'air de s'apercevoir de l'émoi des spectateurs. Son chapeau seul avait été la proie des requins.

(The circumstances surrounding the arrival in Bourbon clearly revealed Baudelaire's demeanor. It is well known that in Saint-Denis de Bourbon, because of rough seas and the difficulties presented by the only possible landing spot, disembarkment used to proceed by means of a rope ladder tied to a kind of gigantic gallows built at the extremity of a pier built on piles. To disembark, one needs to catch a rung of the ladder just when the wave which goes up and down is at its highest elevation.

Though informed of this necessary precaution, Baudelaire obstinately resolved to climb the ladder with his books under his arm . . . and he climbs slowly, solemnly, while the next wave approaches. It soon reaches him, submerges him, covering him under twelve to fifteen feet of water and making him fall off the ladder. He is rescued with great difficulty; and incredibly, he is still holding on to his books. Only then did he consent to leave those in the canoe still roped to the foot of the ladder, but while climbing, he was hit by another wave, did not fall off, arrived ashore, and made his way to town, calm, cold, without appearing to notice the emotions of the spectators. Only his hat had become food for the sharks.) (Cited in Pichois and Ziegler, 150)

The scene described in these papers evokes very well the recalcitrant young traveller, the loner, ill at ease, but stubborn, refusing assistance and unable to adapt to the exigencies of the moment. Baudelaire is getting off the *Paquebot des Mers du Sud* and abandoning Captain Seliz and his crew because he has the firm intention of catching the next ship back to France—rather than continue on to India as originally planned. But he will have to wait for some forty-five days, until November 4, 1841, for the next ship—*L'Alcide*—which is returning from India—to set sail from Saint-Denis on its way back to Bordeaux. Baudelaire's first contact with Bourbon is a very wet and unpleasant one—and he will later deny ever having set foot there. In a letter to the Parnassian poet Leconte de Lisle, a native of the island, with whom he will correspond later on in Paris, he declares:

> Je n'ai jamais mis les pieds dans votre cage à moustiques, sur votre perchoir à perroquets. J'ai vu de loin des palmes, du bleu, du bleu, du bleu, du bleu . . .

> (I have never set foot in your mosquito-ridden cage, in your nest of parrots. I have only seen palm trees from afar, and vast expanses of blue, blue, blue.) (*Mémorial*, 446)

Whereas in Mauritius Baudelaire is welcomed with open arms by the local elite, in Bourbon, he seems to have spent his weeks frequenting black prostitutes and writing. On October 20, 1841, Baudelaire sends the poem, "A une dame créole," dedicated to Emmeline de Bragard, in a letter to her husband. This original version differs slightly from the later one published in Paris first in *L'Artiste* in 1845, and then in the 1857 edition of *Les Fleurs du mal*:

Le 20 octobre 1841

Mon bon monsieur A., vous m'avez demandé quelques vers à Maurice pour votre femme, et je n'ai pas oublié. Comme il est bon, décent et convenable que des vers adressés à une dame par un jeune homme passent par les mains de son mari avant d'arriver à elle, c'est à vous que je les envoie, afin que vous ne les lui montriez que si cela vous plaît.

Depuis que je vous ai quitté, j'ai souvent pensé à vous et à vos excellents amis.—Je n'oublierai pas certes les bonnes matinées que vous m'avez données, vous, Madame A., et M. B.

Si je n'aimais et si je ne regrettais pas tant Paris, je resterais le plus longtemps possible auprès de vous, et je vous forcerai à m'aimer et à me trouver un peu moins *baroque* que je n'en ai l'air.

Il est peu probable que je retourne à Maurice, à moins que le navire sur lequel je pars pour Bordeaux (l'Alcide) n'y aille chercher des passagers.

Voici mon sonnet:

Au pays parfumé que le soleil caresse
J'ai vu dans un retrait de tamarins ambrés
Et de palmiers d'où pleut sur les yeux la paresse,
Une dame Créole aux charmes ignorés.

Son teint est pâle et chaud; la brune enchanteresse
A dans le cou des airs noblement maniérés;
Grande et svelte, en marchant comme une chasseresse,
Son sourire est tranquille et ses yeux assurés.

Si vous alliez, Madame, au vrai pays de Gloire,
Sur les bords de la Seine ou de la verte Loire,
Belle, digne d'orner les antiques manoirs,

Vous feriez, à l'abri des mousseuses retraites,
Germer mille sonnets dans le coeur des poètes,
Que vos regards rendraient plus soumis que des noirs.

Donc je vais vous attendre en France.
Mes compliments bien respectueux à Madame A.

C. Baudelaire.

(21 October 1841

My dear Monsieur A., you asked me, in Mauritius, for a few verses for your wife, and I did not forget you. Since it is good, decent, and appropriate that verses addressed to a lady by a young man should be handed to her husband before reaching her, I am sending them to you, so that you may only show them to her if you so desire.

Ever since leaving you, I have often thought about you and your excellent friends.—I shall certainly never forget the wonderful mornings that you granted me, you, Madame A., and M. B.

If I did not love and miss Paris so much, I would stay as long as possible in your company, and I would force you to love me and to find me a bit less *baroque* than I seem.

It is unlikely that I will ever return to Mauritius, unless the ship that is taking me back to Bordeaux (the *Alcide*) should need to fetch passengers there.

Here is my sonnet . . .

So I will be waiting for you in France.
My respectful compliments to Madame A.

C. Baudelaire)[7]

The *published* version (1845) reads as follows:[8]

A Une Dame Créole

Au pays parfumé que le soleil caresse,
J'ai connu sous un dais d'arbres tout empourprés
Et de palmiers d'où pleut sur les yeux la paresse,
Une dame créole aux charmes ignorés.

Son teint est pâle et chaud; la brune enchanteresse
A dans le cou des airs noblement maniérés;
Grande et svelte en marchant comme une chasseresse,
Son sourire est tranquille et ses yeux assurés.

Si vous alliez, Madame, au vrai pays de gloire,
Sur les bords de la Seine ou de la verte Loire,
Belle digne d'orner les antiques manoirs,

Vous feriez, à l'abri des ombreuses retraites,
Germer mille sonnets dans le coeur des poètes,
Que vos grands yeux rendraient plus soumis que vos noirs.

(For A Creole Lady

Off in a perfumed land bathed gently by the sun,
Under wide trees tinged with a crimson trace,
A place where indolence drops on the eyes like rain,
I met a Creole lady of unstudied grace.

This brown enchantress' skin is warm and light in tone;
Her neck is noble, proud, her manner dignified;
Slender and tall, she goes with huntress' easy stride;
Her smile is tranquil, and her eyes are confident.

Madame, if you should come to the true place of pride and
    glory—
Beside the green Loire, or by the pleasant Seine,
Adorning ancient mansions with your stately ways—
There in the shelter of the shady groves, you'd start
A thousand sonnets blooming in the poet's hearts,
Whom your great eyes would render more servile than your
    slaves.)

The poems "Bien loin d'ici" and "La Belle Dorothée" both published later in Paris, are specifically about his experiences in Bourbon.[9] In this slave-owning plantation culture of the French colony, the
still adolescent and rebellious poet is not an attractive or sought-after
guest. Very different historical circumstances from those of Mauritius

can help explain why the *Bourbonnais* have a dim view of French intruders. At the time, the Franco-Mauritians—such as the Autard de Bragards—are living under British rule, and make every effort to hold on to any vestige of French culture. Visitors from France are always welcome, even sought after. In 1841, the francophone elite is already fast becoming a cultural as well as a numerical minority: the surrender to the British crown in 1814 has resulted in emancipation in 1835 followed by the arrival of large numbers of indentured laborers from India.[10] In Bourbon, by contrast, slavery still exists and the local planters are suspicious of intellectuals, rebels, and *libres-penseurs* (free-thinkers) from France. The Revolutionary Convention, under the leadership of Danton, had decreed the abolition of slavery on the 16 Pluviôse An II (4 February 1790). But the local Colonial Assembly did not comply with this decree, and in 1801, it threatened to secede from France if the ruling was imposed. Revolutionary ideas, and the intellectuals who are always under suspicion of transporting them, were not welcome on the island, nor were they in Martinique and Guadeloupe. Unlike Haiti, which became the first independant black nation in 1804, the Mascarenes do not seem to have embraced or fought for any kind of revolutionary agenda. The Colonial Assembly's aim was primarily to protect the interests of the landowners—mostly white planters but comprising also a certain number of free-born *métis*. In 1841, outsiders from France—who are still nicknamed the "z'oreilles" today—continue to be perceived as potential troublemakers, especially if they are, like Charles, too visibly bohemian, rebellious, and at loose ends. The planters are worried about their future, haunted by the spectre of emancipation. The slave revolt of 1811 had been severely repressed, but the phenomenon of *marronnage* was becoming more and more widespread. The mountainous interior of the island provided ideal hiding places for maroons (or runaways). When Baudelaire arrives in 1841, abolition is a mere seven years away and figures such as Sarda Garriga—the counterpart of abolitionist Victor Schoelcher in Martinique—are causing planters plenty of worry. Despite the fact that Baudelaire spends twice as long in Reunion as he did in Mauritius, he seems to have been completely ignored by the locals. The 1840s correspond to a period of intense endocentric and endogenous attitudes on their part and their chilly reception may well have caused the poet's denials.

These denials may explain why critics such as Miller are confused by the colonial cartographies that emerge from the poetry, or why they are given to blurred chronologies and hazy geographies. Baudelaire sets up his readers for critical confusion, "fogs" or "mirages," to use Miller's critical vocabulary (See "Hallucinations"). But such denials, and the resulting blindness of critics, is more pointedly a symptom of the difficulty in thinking about French literary history in terms of local knowledges and the impact they may have had on the conditions of production of the literature. This problem is made manifest by the persistent inablity to theorize what Mireille Rosello has called "the insularization of identities," and to invent new identifications on the basis of those fragments of local stories that help to undermine the problematic search for unity that Edouard Glissant has called the "obsession of the One."[11] The unfinished and fragmentary quality of the colonial past and the epistemologies that derive from it can begin to be contextualized once we shed light on the historical frameworks and the motivations of writers such as Baudelaire. When one looks at the cultural history of the 1840s, it becomes fascinating to realize that Baudelaire himself is an "exote"—a young man from post-Revolutionary France—in the eyes of endogamous planters and their entourage, and this "exote" will be viewed differently in the context of each of the two islands. The direction of the exoticizing gaze is not initially what we have assumed, what we have been trained to see: it is in fact Baudelaire who has been put in the place of an "other" from across the seas. His own reversal of this exoticizing gaze, his focus on the black cultures of the islands reflects an initial identification that cannot be understood in terms of simple binarisms as critics have done.

Thus, when Miller discusses "A une dame créole" in a chapter of *Blank Darkness*, he shows how the rhetoric of nineteenth-century "Africanist discourse" functions to negate Creole realities and to construct absence and void as the paradigmatic themes and motifs emerging from encounters with non-Europeans. His general argument is valid and convincing. However, he negates Baudelaire's actual encounter with the Creole realities and prejudices that the poetry actually conveys very well. Miller misreads the poem's context, stating:

> The poem is *about* ambiguity and the possibility of moving along a scale of colors and places, from the purple islands where ignorance rains from the trees, to the banks of the Seine and the green Loire: from the Ile de la Réunion, where the sonnet was written to the Ile de France, the center of the center. (101)

Oddly, Miller never once mentions Mauritius which had been known as the Ile de France before 1814, when it was ceded by Napoleon to the British who changed its name back to Mauritius, the name given by the earlier Dutch colonists.[12] But in Miller's reading Mauritius has disappeared from history. He actually confuses and conflates Mauritius, Reunion, and the kind of imaginary Africa that he takes the poetry to be representing. He assumes that M. and Mme. Autard de Bragard were Baudelaire's hosts in Réunion (rather than Mauritius—*Blank* 98) and does not distinguish between the different kinds of places that are either evoked or actually mentioned by the poet.

Nowhere in this poem does Baudelaire mention the "Ile de France" by name. Yet Miller extrapolates and infers a comparison between "purple islands" and "the Ile de France, the center of the center," that is, the area around Paris, "sur les bords de la Seine" where Baudelaire returned soon after leaving the Mascarene area. But, as I have pointed out, "Ile de France" was also the earlier name of Mauritius given by the French settlers between 1715 and 1814. So when Baudelaire writes about the "vrai pays de Gloire/Sur les bords de la Seine," the irony for his *dédicataire*, Mme de Bragard, must have been obvious, because behind the "vrai pays de Gloire," the metropolitan Ile de France, we have an implicit reference, in filigree, to the other Ile de France, its namesake in the antipodes where the "dame créole" resides, and where the Franco-Mauritians, now defeated and subjugated to the British, are holding on to their connection to France, the "vrai pays de Gloire." Here we see that local history resists marginalization, and meaning emerges along a chain of significations that include differential understandings of "France" or "Ile de France" as nodes in a complex network of linguistic correspondances that could not have been lost on the author of "Correspondances," nor on his *destinataires*.

The prose poem "La Belle Dorothée" also offers a precise instance of cultural and linguistic hybridization which critics have failed to recognize, and which reinforces the specificities of the geographical area that inspired it. The next to last paragraph reads as follows:

> Peut-être a-t-elle un rendez-vous avec quelque jeune officier qui, sur des plages lointaines, a entendu parler par ses camarades de la célèbre Dorothée. Infailliblement elle le priera, la simple créature, de lui décrire le bal de l'Opéra, et lui demandera si on peut y aller pieds nus, comme aux danses du dimanche, où les vieilles Cafrines elles-mêmes deviennent ivres et furieuses de joie; et puis encore si les belles dames de Paris sont toutes plus belles qu'elle.

> (Perhaps she is going to meet some young officer, who on far-off shores heard of the famous Dorothy from his mates. Without fail the simple creature will beg him to describe the Opera, and will

ask him if one can go there with bare feet, like at the Sunday
dances, where the old Cafrines themselves get drunk and furious
with joy; and again, if the most beautiful ladies of Paris are more
beautiful than she.)

Miller picks up on Baudelaire's use of the term "Cafrine." He speculates
that it "may have been Baudelaire's invention." He searches for clues
about the word *cafrine* in the *Grand Larousse*, the *Littré*, or the *Grand
Robert*, where, he notes, the word "is not to be found" (*Blank*, 120 n.
35), adding, "[The word] represents an unnecessary insistence on the
feminine gender" (120). According to the French dictionaries Miller consults, the adjective *cafre* serves both as the masculine and feminine forms
of the noun *cafre* from the Arabic *kafir* or "infidel" (see figure 2).[13] Miller
speculates that the suffix *-ine* would therefore appear to add an excessively feminine quality to the description. He deduces that the rhetoric
of the poem thus devalorizes and overracializes the black woman. "The
double feminine," he explains, "coincides with [Baudelaire's] most frankly
Africanist scene" (122), thus buttressing the general argument of his book
that the Africanist topos in Baudelaire is coded as absence and void—
as also happens to be the case in Gobineau and in a long Western
tradition within which Africa is represented as a feminized void. But this
argument bypasses any understanding of the local cultures which
Baudelaire is in fact able to communicate to his readers, despite his
refusal to acknowledge having ever "set foot" in those countries.

I want to suggest that the word "Cafrine" in the prose poem
actually gives us the sound of the voice of the black woman herself,
a voice Baudelaire knew, had heard, and that he lets us hear in the
reported speech or indirect discourse of the sentence: "elle lui demandera
si on peut y aller pieds nus, comme aux danses du dimanche, où les
vieilles Cafrines elles-mêmes deviennent ivres et furieuses de joie . . . "
(she will ask him if one can go there with bare feet, like at the Sunday
dances, where the old Cafrines themselves get drunk and furious with
joy). Indeed, if Miller had looked for clues in a different archive from
the ones produced in France—the French dictionaries he consults—he
might have found out that "Cafrine" is a word from the local Creole
language that is still spoken today and he thus would not have dis-
missed it as "noise" produced by Baudelaire's exotic imagination. Robert Chaudenson's *Le Lexique du parler créole de la Réunion* gives the
following explanation:

> les néologismes créoles formés par suffixation (-e) et (-in)
> (comprennent le mot) cafrine/(kafrin): femme de race noire, de type
> africain; le mot sert de féminin à "cafre," prononciation créole: [kaf].

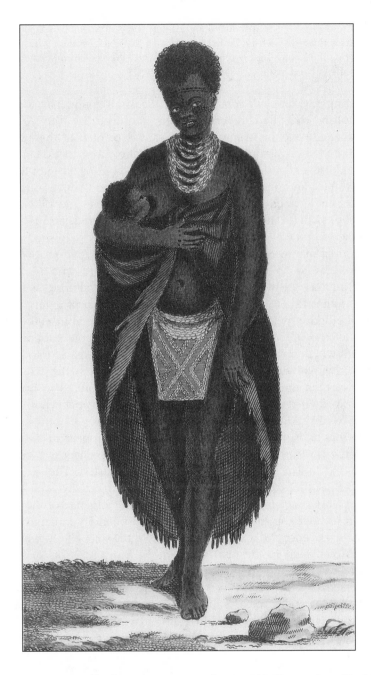

FIGURE 2. *Femme Caffre*, from François Levaillant's 1791 *Voyage dans l'intérieur de l'Afrique* and reprinted in Miller's *Black Darkness* (121). Baudelaire was familiar with this work.

(Creole neoligisms produced by adding the suffix [-e] or [-in] include the word cafrine/[kafrin]: woman of the black race, of African type; the word is the feminine of "cafre," creole pronunciation: [kaf]) (Chaudenson, 2:1041).

During my research in the Indian Ocean, I found two series of watercolors that had recently been acquired by the Archives Départmentales de La Réunion. The first was painted in the 1860s by Hyppolite Mortier, Marquis de Trévise, Secrétaire d'Ambasssade in China, who made several journeys to Reunion. The second is by Jean-Baptiste Louis Dumas, an engineer who was director of the Ponts et Chaussées in Reunion between 1829 and 1831. They illustrate the different female "types" that Baudelaire would have encountered during his stay there (see figures 3, and 4). I also found postcards published for the mass tourist market which use the words "ti kafrine péi" (native black girl) to refer to an exoticized young female figure who is offering sweet fruits as she welcomes the tourists with her alluring smile (fig. 5). It is interesting to note here that the image is that of a very young, child-like figure, who is wearing a cook's apron: her youthfulness and domestic appearance is belied by the alluring Creole caption. One wonders whether the intent is to lure Western adult males into blissful domesticity with underage females? Would this be what Baudelaire himself saw in the young black women he encountered in Bourbon, women in their teens and barely younger than the poet who had just turned twenty that year?

Be that as it may, Creole languages, as they appear in the poetry and in the postcards, are the product of a creative encounter between African and Indian languages and those of the masters. The site of this encounter is the site of production of both subjectivity and agency. "Cafrine" in Baudelaire's poem is the point of emergence of the *other's* voice in his text, the site of heteroglossia and hybridity in language, "le lieu par excellence de la capture de l'autre" (the very site at which the other is contained in the text) (Felman, *La Folie*, 128), or "le lieu où le poète se laisse traverser par de l'autre" (the site at which the poet is traversed by otherness) (Cixous, 158), the place where Baudelaire is both seduced by the voice of the woman, and enshrines her, imprisons her self-designation within his own discourse. If, as Shoshana Felman argues, "la *place* du sujet . . . ne se définit pas par *ce* qu'il dit, ni par ce *dont* il parle, mais par le lieu *à partir d'où* il parle" (the location of the subject is not defined by *what* he/she says, nor by what he/she talks *about*, but by *the site of enunciation*—the place from which he/she speaks) (50), then the word *Cafrine* registers a locus of enunciation

FIGURE 3. *Une Cafrine et son petit*, watercolor by Hyppolite-Charles-Napoléon Mortier, Marquis de Trévise, who traveled to Ile Bourbon in 1861 and 1865–66 while he was Secretary of the Embassy and attaché to the Mission in China. Propriétaire-Conseil général. Archives départementales de La Réunion.

170

FIGURE 4. *Malabare créole, Malgache,* watercolors by Jean-Baptiste Louis Dumas, Directeur des Ponts et Chaussées, Ile Bourbon, 1829–31. They both are dated 1830. Propriétaire-Conseil général. Archives départementales de La Réunion.

FIGURE 5. I picked up the postcard in a bookstore in Saint-Denis, La Réunion, in September 1996. It reads: "My lichees are sweet like our native girls . . . don't be shy, come and taste! . . ." The sexual innuendoes show the degree to which the native woman continues to be exoticized for the purposes of global tourism. This does not, however, take away the fact that "ti kafrine" (in Creole) continues to be a term of endearment.

that is geographically quite specific and at the same time hybrid. "Cafrine" is the trace of the encounter between two subjectivities, a masculine one and a feminine one, the latter echoing across the centuries thanks to the poetry of a rebellious young traveller who immortalizes her while screening out the dominant voices of the French colony—the ones that had sketched him in their chronicles as this awkward, "nerdy," bookworm from beyond their shores. In so doing, he contains the "Cafrine" within his representation of her, but he also delivers her to posterity in *her own* Creole language—something no historiography has yet done.[14]

To recognize the Creole origin of "Cafrine" in this classic text is to engage in what Peter Hulme has called a form of "local remembering." In his reading of Jean Rhys's *Wide Sargasso Sea*, Hulme insists on the need to find "geocultural frameworks which will allow us to make connections that transcend the usually national or colonial categories.... Local history [he adds]... still remains largely untold, and its connections with literary production largely unexplored" (Hulme, 15–17). Hulme calls for a "politics of locality" that remains sensitive to two needs: "to treat the history of 'local' places like Dominica [the setting of *Wide Sargasso Sea*] as worthy of serious historical investigation" and "to recover the colonial and imperial dimensions of . . . canonical literature" (17). Only by attending to both of these needs will we reach an understanding of the local as part of "a network which is anything but local," he concludes.

The word *Cafrine* is a node in just such a network of signifying practices that can help us arrive at a more global understanding of "French" literary history. Baudelaire's use of the local dialect in this prose poem is an undeniable clue about the conditions of production of the poem, and the contexts within which it acquires meaning. By allowing local history, geography, and gendered language to persist (and to resist limited definition from within the pages of the *Larousse* or the *Littré*) Baudelaire is better able to validate the existence of local political realities than are his contemporary critics. Even if, in a fit of anger at the white Creoles who snubbed him, Baudelaire denies ever having set foot in Bourbon, his text speaks a different truth, transgressing his wish to disavow his experiences, and serving instead as a rare locus of memory for the colonized female subjects of the island. As Felman states, "Le scandale en littérature c'est que l'altérité surgit, se donne à voir, là où on s'y attend le moins" (The scandal in literature is that alterity emerges, becomes visible, where you expect it the least).[15] The otherness of the local vernacular produces hybridity within the poetic text. The irony in Miller's interpretation is that he misses the deconstruction of standard French that Baudelaire performs in "La Belle

Dorothée" more than a century before such deconstruction will become the trademark of francophone writers (such as Ahmadou Kourouma, Simone Schwarz-Bart, Axel Gauvin, and Patrick Chamoiseau) in their literary practice. If Hedi Abdel-Jaouad can argue that Isabelle Eberhardt is the precursor of several generations of Maghrebian writers because of her "linguistic 'corps-à-corps' with French to make it express a [different] ontology," then we can perhaps claim Baudelaire as the elusive precursor of many francophone writers who search for a thematics and a stylistic practice that will correspond to their hybrid identities and thus generate a new ontology (Abdel-Jaouad, 116–117).

Ten years after the publication of *Blank Darkness*, in his 1995 essay, Miller once again rehearses the colonial topos in Baudelaire's poetry. This time, he makes reference both to what he terms the "Africanist" poems ("Le Cygne," "La Belle Dorothée," " A Une dame créole"), and to the one titled "A une Malabaraise."

from Le Cygne

Un cygne qui s'était évadé de sa cage,
Et, de ses pieds palmés frottant le pavé sec,
Sur le sol raboteux traînait son blanc plumage [lines 17–19]
. . .
Je pense à mon grand cygne, avec ses gestes fous,
Comme les exilés, ridicule et sublime,
Et rongé d'un désir sans trêve! [lines 34–36]
. . .
Je pense à la négresse, amaigrie et phthisique,
Piétinant dans la boue, et cherchant, l'oeil hagard,
Les cocotiers absents de la superbe Afrique
Derrière la muraille immense du brouillard; [lines 41–44]

(The Swan

A swan who had escaped from his captivity,
And scuffing his splayed feet along the paving stones,
He trailed his white array of feathers in the dirt
. . .
I think of my great swan, his gestures pained and mad,
Like other exiles, both ridiculous and sublime,
Gnawed by his endless longing!
. . .
I think of a negress, thin and tubercular,
Treading in the mire, searching with haggard eye
For palm trees she recalls from splendid Africa,
Somewhere behind a giant barrier of fog;)

from A une Malabaraise

Pourquoi, l'heureuse enfant, veux-tu voir notre France,
Ce pays trop peuplé que fauche la souffrance, [lines 17–18]
. . .
Comme tu pleurerais tes loisirs doux et francs,
Si, le corset brutal emprisonnant tes flancs,
Il te fallait glaner ton souper dans nos fanges
Et vendre le parfum de tes charmes étranges,
L'oeil pensif, et suivant, dans nos sales brouillards,
Des cocotiers absents les fantômes épars! [lines 23–28]

(To A Malabar Woman

O happy child, why do you want to see
Our France, a country reaped by misery,
. . .
How you will cry, regretful of the trip,
If, in the brutal corset's crushing grip,
You have to sell your beauty in the street,
Out of this muck to glean some food to eat,
While through our filthy mists your vision sees
The phantom spars of absent coco-trees.)

Referring to these passages, Miller claims that:

> In "Le Cygne," cultural and temporal barriers are everywhere, exile
> is pandemic, and the African woman is enfolded within an appar-
> ently *universal* problem. Difference is everyone's proccupation and
> labour. In "A une Malabaraise," a single cultural barrier is built up
> between France and a colony (in this case the French enclave on
> the coast of India); the world is bisected and difference is a matter
> of categories and exclusion. ("Hallucinations," 41)

Quoting the following lines from "A Une Malabaraise": "Pourquoi, l'heureuse enfant, veux-tu voir notre France/Ce pays trop peuplé que fauche
la souffrance," Miller adds: "The single Malabarese woman is an alien,
while the speaker is a natural/national (from the same root) belonging
to *notre* France. The woman is advised to stay where she belongs" (41).
I do not want to quarrel here with Miller's interpretation of the exclusions to which immigrants are subjected in France and that, in his
reading, the poem prophetically outlines. I do want to propose a
somewhat different articulation of the oppositions that the poem constructs. For Miller, these exclusions are revealed through the binary
opposition between a "citizen" and an "alien." Because his goal is to

make Beaudelaire's poetry function as an *instrument* for his critique of hybridity, "métissage culturel," and the "fog of intercultural space" that the encounter between France and Africa generates, Miller adds that "nationalism claims to blow [the fog] . . . away in order to establish clear boundaries and claim 'Africa for Africans'" (41).

Two clarifications are in order: first of all, as I have already indicated, Baudelaire's referent in his Indian Ocean poems is neither Africa per se, nor "the French enclave on the coast of India" as Miller puts it. This French enclave was, to be precise, Pondicherry, on the southeastern coast. It became a legal part of India in 1963. The poet never went there and he indicates no connection to that colony. The islands with which he is familiar were—and are today—inhabited by women of African and Indian descent such as the one described in the poem. Secondly, the *Malabaraise* may ethnically be from the Malabar coast (on the west and not the east coast of India), the point of origin of many of the Indian immigrants of Dravidian background. According to Claude Pichois's annoted edition of the "Malabaraise" poem, it refers to a woman who worked as a kitchen maid in the Autard de Bragards' house in Mauritius. The reference to the "Malabaraise" who wants to see "notre France," I would propose, does not imply an opposition between "them" and "us," the alien woman and the national subject from France, the colonized figure and the French-born poetic voice. Instead, I think we should read "notre France" as an implicit opposition to something like "ton Ile de France," in the same way that "A Une dame créole" opposes the two "Iles de France" in a subversive counterpoint that undermines the distinction between the center and the margin, the metropole and its periphery, between the local meaning of "France" and the imperial or global one. Just as "La Belle Dorothée" does, this poem performs a deconstruction of stable meaning by putting into question all continental forms of identity, be they French, African, or Indian, and reconstructing them as hybrid, insular, and local.

Gayatri Spivak makes specific reference to the Mascarene Islands in her discussion of "A une Malabaraise" and "Le Cygne," but goes on to say that "the original of the negress in 'Le Cygne' is a textual palimpsest of the original of the agonist of 'A une Malabaraise,' one of two women Baudelaire encountered in Mauritius and the island of Reunion respectively" (230). She rightly points out that lines 41–44 of "Le Cygne" echo lines 27–28 of "A une Malabaraise," and this, she argues, is sufficient indication that behind the "negress" of the first poem is in fact the "Malabaraise" or Indian woman of the second, a "vague woman, encountered on either one of the two colonial possessions, mis-named by white convention" since Indian immigrants to the Mascarenes "are not necessarily, not even largely, from India's Malabar coast" (230). She critiques Baudelaire for shifting the origin of the "negress" "on an imagined native place as generalized as 'Africa,' " and she seems unaware that Baudelaire would have indeed encountered women of both African and Indian origin in the Mascarene Islands. For Spivak, the "negress" is only a figure for "generalized otherness" (Chrisman, 500), or more specifically "generalized darkness," or as Miller puts it more suggestively, "blank darkness." That these dark females figure rhetorically as dark others of an exotic femininity has been amply demonstrated. But my point is that these "figures" correspond to actual historical subjects whose visual presence had been recorded by chroniclers of the time (see fig. 3 & 4). There is indeed an intertextual echo between "Le Cygne" and "A une Malabaraise," but the geographical referents are plain and simple: Africa is mentioned only in "Le Cygne," and Baudelaire puts in relation the plight of two women, one possibly from Africa (or from Madagascar?—see fig. 4, right), the other from India (fig. 4, left). In both cases, however, it is most likely that they would have been "Creoles," that is, born and raised in the colony.[16] They might also be of mixed parentage: African and Indian. The only thing we know for sure is that these "dark" women who fascinated Baudelaire were Creole-speaking, and that the *Malabaraise* lived in Mauritius. When one looks at the visual representation of figures 4 and 5, what is striking is that, in all the cases, the actual origin—African or Indian—is not easy to determine. Thus, in the postcard printed for the 1990s tourist market, the "ti kafrine péi" has straight hair and could be part Indian. In the 1830 watercolor representation by Jean-Baptiste Dumas of the "Malabare Créole" (fig. 4), the woman's features and her headdress suggest "créolité" rather than "indianité."[17]

Furthermore, from within the Mauritian historical and colonial context, the poem "Le Cygne" has a specific connotation that may justify a reading of its bird and female allegories as another site of hybrid imagery. In the course of its colonial history, Mauritius was briefly settled by the Portuguese who called the island *Ilha do Cirne* or Island of the Swan. They occupied the area for a time during the sixteenth century and discovered the indigenous dodo birds, a now extinct creature that looked like a short-winged swan (fig. 6). They named the island after this unusual and flightless bird. In the late eighteenth century, and throughout the nineteenth and twentieth century, the main newspaper of the island echoed this Portuguese naming: it was called *Le Cernéen* (from *cirne*, swan) and it had a picture of a swan on its front page, above the title which was followed by the subtitle "Petite revue africaine" (fig. 7), since Mauritius has always been included in the general geographic area of the African continent. *Le Cernéen* began as a weekly in 1773, stopped publication in 1790, resumed in 1832, and became a daily in 1852. We can speculate that Baudelaire would have seen it. It was widely read by all those who considered themselves educated, and Baudelaire's hosts, the Autard de Bragards are very likely to have shared its contents with their guest whose choice of poetic imagery would later echo these experiences.

In "Le Cygne," the poetic association between a swan, "un cygne qui s'était évadé de sa cage" (a swan who had escaped from his captivity), and a black woman, "la négresse, amaigrie et phthisique" (a negress, thin and tubercular), both exiled in Europe, finds its counterpart in the "matelots oubliés dans une île" (sailors forgotten on an isle), men such as Baudelaire who lived his sojourn in the Indian Ocean as an extended prison sentence, feeling caged and flightless in the antipodes.[18] Canonical readings of this poem have stressed its allegorical elements, and shown how the plight of the bird and that of the negress are linked, both becoming figures for the lost sailors and for the poet's own anxieties. Rejecting those interpretations, Spivak notes that

> whereas Baudelaire, inscribing himself as poet within the tradition of European poetry, is *meticulous* about the specificity of that tradition, the inscription of himself as an admirer of negresses can only be deciphered by guesswork outside of the boundaries of the poem. It is seemingly irrelevant to the poem's proper functioning. And it is mired in a conventionally sanctioned *carelessness about identities*. (230, my emphasis)

She adds that what "troubles" her the most is Edward Ahearn's suggestion that "the negress is somehow Baudelaire's dark double." This reading, she says "perform[s] a lie" (231), and she goes on to discuss Andrew Bush's Bloomian reading which, in her view, is "perfunctory."[19] Her point is that the actual Indian women who were encountered by Baudelaire in 1841 are being falsely represented as "African" or as figures for Jeanne Duval, his black mistress in Paris, and thus their very existence is negated by this naming process which conflates all of them as "products of hegemonic false cartography" (230).

As my research shows, however, the swan/dodo bird points to a very precise but hybrid geographical locus: one in which the dodo might be legible only as a swan—and the swan only as a dodo, depending on which perspective one adopts: the poetic or the historical one. Yet, even this distinction between the "poetic" and the "his-

Figure 6. Dodo, as exhibited in the Museum of Natural History in Port-Louis.

torical" becomes unstable, as the swan is but a historical palimpsest for the dodo bird, and an embellished version of the indigenous fauna. The instability of this referent further points to the hybrid local identities of the colonial subjects, and to the colonial wish to transform and "purify" Creole realities as a means of dealing with the fear of degeneration connoted by the concepts of métissage and hybridity. Baudelaire's poetry reveals an acute (if implicit) understanding of the complicated genealogies that have been the legacy of slavery and indentured labor in New World colonies. The intertextual link between "Le Cygne" and "A une Malabaraise" thus simply underscores the fluidity of identities shaped by the imposition of colonial rule within these insular regions of the Mascarenes.

Did Baudelaire's imagination transform the somewhat grotesque dodo into a poetic swan, as the Portuguese had? He does refer to this swan as a creature both "ridicule et sublime" (ridiculous and sublime), thus "signifying" (as Henry Louis Gates Jr. would say) on the Portuguese colonizers' naming of the island (see Gates). If indeed Baudelaire *signifies* on the Portuguese word *cirne*, the canonical interpretations of

FIGURE 7. Front page of *Le Cernéen* dated 29 Feb. 1833.

the poem can now be seen in a different historical light which allows us to re-inscribe the geographical contexts of the "negress" *within* the rhetorical texture of the poem. The poet's identification with the bird and the woman thus does not reveal his "carelessness about identities" but his astute understanding of the visual and discursive fields within which his experiences as a poet and a traveller took shape, and about which he is historically and culturally quite "meticulous."

∞

My point in this essay has not been to recover "some concealed radical message from ostensibly reactionary writing" as Spivak says, quoting Lisa Jardine (231). Baudelaire's rhetoric of exoticism *is* distorting and serves a particular "Africanist" purpose within the field of European literary representation. Thanks to feminist cultural critiques, postcolonial studies of imperialism such as Spivak's and Edward Said's, and Miller's analysis of Africanist discourses, we have learned to suspect both the causes and the effects of representational structures that overlap with imperial and colonial agendas. But I can read Baudelaire today and know that he speaks to us, Mauritians, of realities that *historians* have failed to record, and that his poetry is a valuable intervention which ought to give critics pause when they carelessly assume that its residual cultural images have no historical or geographical validity. It is the critics' epistemological standpoint that turns out to be more limited than Baudelaire's.

Just as Shakespeare's Caliban has been part of the *imaginaire* of anglophone, hispanophone, and francophone Caribbean writers, fragments of Baudelaire's texts continue to become parts of the narratives we tell in the literary and cultural discourses of *francophonie*. Think, for instance, of Aimé Césaire's use of the phrase "comique et laid" in the *Cahier [Notebook of a return . . .]*, a phrase from Baudelaire's *L'Albatros* that he slips into his text and upon which he then signifies (Rosello, 182–184). Think also of Césaire's *Une tempête*, Roberto Fernandez Retamar's *Caliban*, and Georges Lamming's *The Pleasures of Exile*. Figures invented by Baudelaire and Shakespeare map a location that we keep on visiting and analyzing, although "critical" distance and cognitive grounding are sometimes hard to achieve when you are yourself closely implicated in the imaginative discourses (and the exotic fantasies they spin) that have become substitutes for historical knowledge.

We might do well to learn from Baudelaire to discriminate between continents and islands, between Africa, India, the East Indies, and the Mascarene Islands, in other words, between *continental* nationalist agendas, and the status of island-nations which have always had "hybrid" identities. The intercultural space that is the familiar territory of island-nations (in the Caribbean as well as the Mascarenes) is not coded as "fog" or "mirage" by their inhabitants and writers. It is a space of *painful lucidity*: one in which one is forced both to recognize the differences among different local communities and to articulate anew the hybrid, heteroglossic, site of their encounters and their practices of everyday life.

The nationalist agendas of these islands have been articulated around a set of vernacular discourses developed by Frantz Fanon and Césaire, Glissant and Lamming, Fernando Ortiz and C. L. R James, Benítez-Rojo, Dev Virahsawmy, and Khal Torabully. The vocabulary of these theorists includes terms such as *transculturacíon, contrapunteo, métissage, antillanité, créolité, indianité*, and most recently *coolitude*.[20] These words have become instruments for describing the processes that obtain in those islands. This vocabulary presages recent developments in postcolonial theory in general which have foregrounded these models as possible approaches to an emancipatory politics. Miller argues that hybridity and *métissage* are coded as "mirage" by some African writers and critics of the assimilationist ideologies of French colonial and post- or neo-colonial discourses. I do not quarrel with that. But Baudelaire was and continues to be the wrong place to begin if one wants to analyze the rhetoric of "Africanist" discourses and the "manifestations of the 'fog' between cultures that French colonialism engendered" ("Hallucinations," 41). On the other hand, Spivak's accusation that Baudelaire's "carelessness about identities" must be countered by "a strategy rather than a theory of reading that might be a critique of imperialism" (230) does little to illuminate the complex and multifaceted identities that were taking shape in this outpost of the empire and that Baudelaire's poetry echoes.

When properly contextualized, *Les Fleurs du mal* can actually help to dispel the "fog" created by critical discourses that fail to discriminate between distinct geographical entities where a variety of continental identities have come together to create the island peoples and the island-nations that were a part of Baudelaire's own *imaginaire*. As Illena Rodriguez has recently shown, hybrid *insular* spaces have generally been coded as feminine, and hence negative, in relation to more "virile"—masculine and continental— forms of nationalism that insist on the separate and distinct identities of their subjects. In her analysis of Simone Schwarz-Bart's *Pluie et vent sur Télumée Miracle*, Rodriguez writes

> The denationalization of the representation of woman in these narratives is the consequence of their exclusion as subjects of law

in liberal republics, and of plotting the construction of nation as a series of male acts. . . .

In these senses, the only one who can claim to belong is . . . paradoxically, the destitute Télumée [we might read "Dorothée" here] for she has absolutely *nothing to claim.* (196, my emphasis)

The *island* as hybrid locus of the feminine is a very old topos of exotic poetry that contemporary francophone writers like Césaire and Edouard Maunick both reactivate. But the surprise is that comtemporary critics also fall into this trap—and emphasize the virtues of national identity as negations of hybridity, as "denationalizations" of insular or feminine identities that they subsume under more muscular "continental" rubrics. The answer to these agonistic critical debates is to be found in the elements of the poet's biography such as they appear in his own poetic rhetoric. Perhaps the time has come to reconsider Baudelaire's poetry as one of the first places of emergence of the native Creole woman's voice, a ventriloquized voice to be sure, but the only one we have from the first half of the nineteenth century.

Notes

1. I wish to thank the American Philosophical Society, the Social Science Research Council, and the Fulbright Foundation for their generous grants which made it possible for me to travel and do research in the Indian Ocean and Mascarenes in 1988 and in 1997–98. I also thank Ross Chambers, Gerald Mead, Sylvie Romanovski, Mireille Rosello, and Sidonie Smith for their comments on earlier versions of this essay. My feminist reading group at Northwestern University has provided much support over the years: thanks especially to Susan Manning for bringing us all together on a quarterly basis, and to Hollis Clayson, Tracy Davis, Margaret Drewal, Madhu Dubey, Sandra Richards, and Jane Winston. This paper was first read to audiences at the University of Iowa, the University of Pennsylvania, Duke University, UCLA, and Cornell University. I thank colleagues there for inviting me to share my work and for their useful criticisms and comments.

2. My use of the terms *residual* and *emergent* follows that of Raymond Williams, *Marxism and Literature* (New York: Oxford University Press, 1977), 121–127.

3. Letter dated 1886 by Ernest Prarond to Eugène Crépet, the poet's first biographer, as cited in Emile Dayre and Claude Pichois, *La Jeunesse de Baudelaire vue par ses amis,* W. T. Bandy Center for Baudelaire Studies, Vanderbilt University, Nashville 1991, 76–77. Although "La Réunion" became the official name of "Bourbon" in 1793, the locals continued to refer to it under the previous name well into the twentieth century.

4. See Jean Morisset and Eric Waddell, "La Francophonie océane: Le souffle des îles lointaines," *Géographies et cultures* 15 (1995): 85–103 (89).

5. The phrase is Patrick Bellegarde-Smith's. See my discussion in *Auto-biographical Voices: Race, Gender, Self-Portraiture* (Ithaca, Cornell UP, 1989), 6.

6. Carmen Bernand and Serge Gruzinsky, *Histoire du nouveau-monde II: Les Métissages* (Paris: Fayard, 1993); Edouard Glissant, *Poétique de la Relation* (Paris: Gallimard, 1990); Jean-Loup Amselle, *Logiques métisses: Anthropologie de l'identité en Afrique et ailleurs* (Paris: Payot, 1990); Homi Bhabha, *The Location of Culture* (London: Routledge, 1994); Françoise Lionnet, *Autobiographical Voices: Race, Gender, Self-Portraiture* (Ithaca: Cornell UP, 1989).

7. Letter published in *Le Cernéen*, 22 juin 1866. Reprinted in Pichois and Ziegler (153–154). The poem differs from the later version in the following respects:

line 2: "I have seen under the branches of amber colored tamarinds"

line 9: Glory with a capital G

line 14: "Whom your gaze would render more servile than slaves."

8. The poems are from Baudelaire, *Les Fleurs du mal*, trans. James McGowan, *The Flowers of Evil* (New York: Oxford UP, 1993). I have modified the translation when it wanders too far from the literal meaning I am interested in stressing.

9. See Claude Pichois's commentary in Baudelaire, *Oeuvres complètes* (Paris: Gallimard/Pléiade, 1975), 1119.

10. By 1850, one-third of the total population of 180,000 is Indian. Today, about 68 percent of the population of 1.2 million is Indo-Mauritian.

11. The contrast between "insularity" as static essentialized identity and "insularization" as dynamic, provisional, and tactical identity formation is discussed in Rosello, "Caribbean Insularization of Identities in Maryse Condé's Work from *En attendant le bonheur* to *Les derniers rois mages,*" *Callaloo* 18 (Summer 95): 565-578 (see in particular 571-577). The critique of homogeneity and the "One" is in Glissant, *Le Discours antillais*, trans J. Michael Dash, *Caribbean Discourse* (Charlottesville: UP of Virginia, 1989). See 29–32 especially.

12. See Baudelaire, *Oeuvres complètes* (Paris: Robert Laffont, 1980), preface by Claude Roy, p. v. See also Pichois and Ziegler, 147–155.

13. See also Pichois and Ziegler, 155.

14. I am well aware that the etymological origins of the word *infidel* do not point to a "positive" view of the African "infidel" as defined by the Islamic conqueror and then taken up by the European colonizer. Nonetheless, this is the case of a term that has been reappropriated and transformed by the logic of Creole grammar into a feminine term still used by Creole women today in La Réunion. See also Alain Lorraine, *Tienbo le rein* and *Beaux visages cafrines sous la lampe* (Paris : IDOC-France, 1975), with drawings by Geneviève Koenig-Durieux.

15. Statement made during the discussion after her lecture "Rereading Femininity" at the University of Michigan, March 1980. See also Felman, "Rereading Femininity," *Yale French Studies* 62 (1981): 19–44.

16. Spivak states that "the islands of Mauritius and Reunion, terrains of military colonial exchange between France and Britain, have a sizeable population of Indian origin as a result of the British import of indentured labour" (230). But the fact is that already under French rule, Indian slaves were being brought to Mauritius.

In 1806, there were 6,162 Christianized Indians on the island. See Lehembre, 41 n. 14, and Beejadhur. My point is that the "Malabar" woman encountered by Baudelaire in 1841 could well have been born and raised on the island.

17. Or "coolitude" as Khal Torabully has recently put it, making reference to the coolies who emigrated as indentured laborers in the nineteenth century: see his "Coolitude." For an understanding of *créolité* in the islands of the Caribbean (and to a lesser degree, those of the Mascarenes), see the manifesto by Bernabé, Chamoiseau, and Confiant, *Eloge de la créolité*.

18. See the entry on the "Dodo" in the 1911 edition of the *Encyclopedia Britannica*, 370–372. When captured dodo birds made their way to Europe, they were exhibited in cages. Sir Hamon Lestrange recounts how he saw such a bird while walking around London in 1638. Is this the inspiration for the "cygne évadé de sa cage"?

19. See Spivak, 239 n. 15, Ahearn, and Bush.

20. See in particular the recent work of Edouard Glissant, *Tout Monde* (Paris: Gallimard, 1993), Antonio Benítez-Rojo, *The Repeating Island* (Durham: Duke UP, 1992), Dev Virahsawmy, "Doktèr Hamlet" in *Maurice: Demain et Après/Beyond Tomorrow/Apredimé*, ed. Barlen Pyamootoo and Rama Poonoosamy (Port-Louis: Immedia 1996).

Works Cited

Abdel-Jaoud, Hedi. "Isabelle Eberhardt: Portrait of the Artist as a Young Nomad." *Yale French Studies* 83 (1993): 93–117.

Ahearn, Edward. "Black Woman, White Poet: Exile and Exploitation in Baudelaire's Jeanne Duval's Poems," *The French Review* 51 (1977): 212–220.

Amselle, Jean-Loup. *Logiques métisses: Anthropologie de l'identité en Afrique et ailleurs*. Paris: Payot, 1990.

Baudelaire, Charles. *Les Fleurs du mal*. Trans. by James McGowan. *The Flowers of Evil*. New York: Oxford UP, 1993.

———. *Oeuvres complètes*. Paris: Gallimard/Pléiade, 1975.

———. *Oeuvres complètes*. Paris: Robert Laffont, 1980.

Beejadhur, Aunauth, *Les indiens à l'Ile Mourice*. Port-Louis, 1935.

Bernabé, Jean, Chamoiseau Patrick and Raphaël Confiant. *Eloge de la Créolité*. Paris: Gallimard, 1989.

Bernand, Carmen and Serge Gruzinsky. *Histoire du nouveau monde II: Les Métissages*. Paris: Fayard, 1993.

Bhabha, Homi. *The Location of Culture*. London: Routledge, 1994.

Bush, Andrew. "Le cygne ou El cisne: The History of a Misreading." *Comparative Literature Studies* 17, 4 (December 1980): 418–428.

Chaudenson, Robert. *Le lexique du parler créole de La Réunion*. 2 vols. Paris: Honoré Champion, 1974.

Chrisman, Laura. "The Imperial Unconscious? Representations of Imperial Discourse." *Colonial Discourse and Post-Colonial Theory: A Reader*. Ed. Patrick Williams and Laura Chrisman. New York: Columbia UP, 1994, 498-516.

Cixous, Hélène. *La jeune née*. Paris: UGE 10/18, 1975.

Dayre, Emile and Claude Pichois. *La jeunesse de Baudelaire vue par ses amis*. Nashville, Tennessee: W.T. Bandy Center for Baudelaire Studies, Vanderbilt U, 1991.

Felman, Shoshana. *La Folie, la chose littéraire*. Paris: Seuil, 1978.

———. "Rereading Femininity." *Yale French Studies* 62 (1981): 19-44.

Gates, Henry Louis. *The Signifying Monkey*. New York: Oxford UP, 1988.

Glissant, Edouard. *Le discours antillais*. Paris: Seuil, 1981.

———. *Poétique de la Relation*. Paris: Gallimard, 1990.

Hulme, Peter. "Postcolonial Theory and the Politics of Locality: An Approach to *Wide Sargossa Sea*." *A View of Our Own: Ethnocentric Perspectives in Literature*. Proceedings of Conference at Universiti Kebangsaan, Malaysia November, 1994. 1–17.

LaCapra, Dominick. "1857: Two Trials." *A New History of French Literature*. Ed. Denis Hollier. Cambridge: Harvard UP, 1989.

Lehembre, Bernard. *L'Île Maurice*. Paris: Karthala, 1984.

Lionnet, Françoise. *Autobiographical Voices: Race, Gender, Self-Portraiture*. Ithaca: Cornell UP, 1989.

Lorraine, Alain. Tienbo le rein suivi de Beaux visages cafrines sous la lampe. With drawings by Geneviève Koenig-Durieux. Paris: IDOC-France, 1975.

Maurin, Henri and Jacques Lentge, eds. *Le Mémorial de la Réunion*. St.-Denis, Réunion: Australe Editions, 1979.

Miller, Christopher. *Blank Darkness: Africanist Discourse in French*. Chicago: U of Chicago P, 1985.

———. "Hallucinations of France and Africa in the Colonial Exhibition of 1931 and Ousmane Socé's *Mirages de Paris*." *Paragraph* 18 (March 1995): 39-63.

Morisset, Jean and Eric Waddell. "La Francophonie océane: Le souffle des îles lointaines." *Géographies et cultures* 15 (1995): 85-103.

Pichois, Claude and Jean Ziegler. *Charles Baudelaire*. Paris: Fayard, 1996.

Rodriguez, Ileana. *House, Garden, Nation: Space, Gender, and Ethnicity in Post-Colonial Latin American Literatures by Women*. Durham: Duke UP, 1994.

Rosello, Mireille. "Caribbean Insularization of Identities in Maryse Condé's Work from En attendant le bonheur to Les derniers rois mages." Callaloo 18 (Summer 95): 565–78.

———. "One More Sea to Cross: Exile and Intertextuality in Aimé Césaire's *Cahier d'un retour au pays natal*." *Yale French Studies* 83 (1993): 176-195.

Spivak, Gayatri. "Imperialism and Sexual Difference." *Oxford Literary Review* 8 (1986): 226-240.

Torabully, Khal. "Coolitude." *Notre librairie* 128 (Oct.–Dec. 1996): 59–71.

Williams, Raymond. *Marxism and Literature*. New York: Oxford UP, 1977.

9

Performance, Departmentalization, and Detour in the Writing of Patrick Chamoiseau

Cilas Kemedjio

This paper proposes to analyze strategies of resistance structured around oral performance in the texts of Patrick Chamoiseau, specifically *Solibo Magnifique* and *Texaco*. The concept of detour, as theorized by Edouard Glissant, constitutes the departure point for this analysis:

> Diversion is the ultimate resort of a population whose domination by an Other is concealed: it then must search elsewhere for the principle of domination, which is not evident in the country itself: because the system of domination (which is not only exploitation, which is not only misery, which is not only underdevelopment, but actually the complete eradication of an economic entity) is not directly tangible. Diversion is the parallactic displacement of this strategy. (19–20)

Detour is neither a systematic refusal to see, nor a flight from reality. On the part of the community that resorts to it, detour implies the recognition of its relative position of weakness in a state of unequal distribution of power. It is the articulation of a resistance conscious of being in the minority: "the weak, with ruses or diversions, make do the best they can" (*Lettres,* 57). Seen in this way, detour suggests more a project of survival than a forthright questioning of the distribution of power. The use of detour implies a scrambled message, a confusion,

185

and, on the part of the oppressed, an impossibility of clearly grasping the entire picture of domination. The practice of detour necessitates in its practitioners an ignorance of its mechanisms: invisibility, the condition of possibility for detour, hinders the unveiling of resistances in the consciousness of the resistors. Any discourse about detour carries with it two main risks in relation to the fundamental exigency, which, to my mind, is the reduction of inequalities and their impact on the life of oppressed communities. The theoretical tendency to ignore these two imperatives derives from the tendency to move from a misunderstanding of domination to a unilateral celebration of detour as a tactic without calling into question its relevance in terms of the ultimate objective of ameliorating the conditions of the resisting person. The sublimation of the indirectness of detour as a tactic of resistance, of its Brer Rabbit–like reliance on guile (Confiant), risks becoming a celebration of a quasi-mythological dissidence of dissimulation, an estheticization of invisible resistance. Tactic is celebrated in and of itself, as a value in and of itself, leading to a marginalization of the ultimate goal of all resistance: a redistribution of power.

The first risk can be summed up by what I will call a romanticism of tactic. Glissant's novel, *Malemort*, is an inventory of the practices of survival, such as the black market and the informal modes of production practiced by the Martinican people under Vichy occupation during World War II. Glissant celebrates the actions of heroes of survival, for whom a multitude of menial odd jobs provides subsistence. The popular resourcefulness exemplified by these characters (contrasted with the collective passive irresponsibility that predominates in Martinique today) is a result of the total denial of their existence by the Vichy regime, which is not without echoes of the system of slavery. Glissant, though, acknowledges that the listing of these multiple practices of survival can appear to be a celebration of what he calls "leur misérabilisme" ("their sordid state"): "I do not sing a hymn to their abject poverty, because it remains true that these same children are dying of malnutrition, that wounds are dressed with boiling water, and that old people are dying silently. But the Martinican people resisted and knew a unanimity in those days that has surely been forgotten" (40). Glissant's treatment of survival does not fall into the trap of sublimation because, as with slaves, for Martinicans under Vichy occupation, indirect resistance was the only possible option. The historical exigency of the situation precludes any romanticization.

The aggrandizement of detour constitutes the second risk. In this case, the practice of deflected resistance is linked to the revalorization of popular practices. Detour becomes an argument for delegitimating elitist discourse. This approach is taken mainly by the proponents of Créolité who use detour as a response to what they refer to as the Cesairian model of resistance. "Marronnage" (2), resistance that is violent, heroic, and very visible, all form a part of what these apologists for Créolité call the Cesairian model. The fort of Christophe, the death of the heroic rebel in *Et les Chiens se taisaient* (*And The Dogs Went Silent*) or *Une Saison au Congo* (*A Season in the Congo*), and the development through rapid building of the city of Fort-de-France are manifestations of this spectacular model of self-assertion. At the heart of the work of Chamoiseau and Confiant, two of the most outspoken writers of the Créolité movement, lies detour as the antithesis of the Cesairian model: their project is that of demystifying other forms of resistance and the political and intellectual exploitation they engender. In their model, detour can be read as a revalorization, one may say as a mythification, of Creole resistance: "While there were maroons in the hills, there were also people living a life of maroons even within the midst of plantations." (*Texaco*, 63). Unlike the maroon who opts for the hills in the quest for freedom, the slave engaged in the practice of detour chooses the earth (lying low, banality, invisibility), the cultures of subsistence. From this position, his/her action can be none other than "a gleam of authority from under lowered eyelids" (97). One of the narrative voices of *Texaco* emphasizes this aspect of dissimulated resistance that took place within the plantation:

> The maroons would break from the confrontation, but the land slaves would remain in formation, standing over mud as best as they could, a bit like those waterlilies of the blind marshland, you had to hold on, hold on, and moor the bottom of your heart in the sand of deep freedom, without noble gestures, just like a dry seed arrives on the beautiful alluvial lands riding the train. (81)

In the works of the proponents of Créolité, the practice of detour becomes as much a tactical as a political position, especially when read as a statement of opposition to Césaire and négritude. Following Antoine Bory (1982), Raphaël Confiant argues in *Aimé Césaire, une traversée paradoxale du siècle* that it is the inability of Antillean intellectuals to connect with popular sites of resistance that leads them to celebrate excessively overt modes of resistance. For Confiant, such an orientation in Césaire is explained by a "lack of confidence in Créolité" (149), or in other words, an inability of the francophone leaders to recognize the silent resistances already put in place by the Antillean people to deflect, and not necessarily to confront, diverse forms of domination. Césaire has no confidence in the Martinican people because he cannot locate those sites of resistance "which are not always directly in conflict, or verbally vehement and emphatic, but which are situated instead in deflection, in a stubborn daily marronnage, silent, masked, but unquenchable" (171).

For Confiant, Césaire's municipal politics largely ignored the thirty years of popular organization of space until an architect-urbanist of the PPM (Progressive Party of Martinique, founded by Césaire following his "Lettre à Maurice Thorez" and subsequent break with the French Communist party) put forward concepts of the "urban mangrove" and "urban diglossia," ideas that are "wholly Creole, breaking with the European urban planning methods which have been applied in a brutal fashion throughout many quarters of the capital (Fort-de-France)" (150). Staking out a position in opposition to the Cesairian project, however, leads Chamoiseau and Confiant to adopt a stance that, in an excessive revalorization of deflected resistance, risks erasing even the existence of domination: "And so, many of the slaves were never enslaved. Rich with secret dignity, they were, often more so than the maroons, the source of what we are" (*Lettres*, 61). It is important however to recognize that in the case of Chamoiseau and Confiant, the valorization of detour as a mode of resistance occurs within the very practical project of trying to reconceptualize Caribbean discourse, and to bring about fundamental cultural and political reforms.

This analysis examines two examples of performance as detour. In the first case, I will consider to what extent the speech of Solibo Magnifique (or Solibo the Magnificent), as related by his last audience, deflects and distracts the police officers charged with leading the investigation into the death of the storyteller. Solibo's performance, which he shares with his listeners, who become suspects as well as the inheritors of his ridiculed legacy, is presented as a modern practice of detour which diverts the police (an incarnation of the departmental strategy) (3) away from their official mission toward a function unforeseen by the letter of the law and toward the path of Creole orality. The second performance, that of Marie-Sophie Laborieux, the narrator/story-teller of *Texaco*, similarly succeeds in deflecting a city architect charged with renovating, that is, destroying, the Quarter of Texaco. Performance in *Texaco* also deflects geometric architecture which culturally, historically, and politically, is a function of the French hegemony in its efforts to transform the Creole landscape: "the urban planner who comes to raze the insalubrious Texaco Quarter finds himself in a creole circus and faces a matadora's word" (*Texaco*, 7). The patience of the residents of the Creole quarter distracts the representative of the departmental order from his primary mission. Initially called "the Plague" by the inhabitants of Texaco, the urban planner becomes a Christ-like figure who saves Texaco from "renovation." Speech preserves the Creole profusion that is characteristic of Texaco from being built over with concrete blocks, a symbol of departmentalization. In both these texts, performance as a practice of detour is situated as a reinvention of "marronnage" that patiently infiltrates the cracks it has succeeded in opening in the departmental walls. How does such an infiltration work? What causes the cracks in the departmental edifice? Why do the agents of departmental power succumb to these tactics of a new "marronnage"? These are some of the questions that shape my analysis, but before they can be addressed, it is necessary to explore the political context, because it is only within this context that the oppositional profiles of Solibo Magnifique and the police take on their full significance. In the absence of these oppositional stances determined by relations of political power, detour becomes regression, a waste of time, or at least a phenomenon that does not address the unequal distribution of power, that is, diversion from the imperative of resistance.

The economic context is that of the eradication of production brought about by what Glissant calls the economic assimilation of the mid-1970's. Glissant describes this process as the eradication of the Martinican entity from the world scene by suppression of its economic density. From this follows a remaking of all Martinicans into the role of passive consumer. In *Solibo*, the character of Congo illustrates the consequences of this economic erasure. Congo has a long history of combating what he calls "Bateau France." He was condemned in 1900 for setting fire to the field of a white planter as part of a strike and in 1935 was again held for several days for his role in instigating another historic strike. This system that Congo protests increasingly marginalizes him through processes that later came to be called economic assimilation.

In the present of narration, Congo makes manioc graters which he sells in the markets, but manioc increasingly is replaced by imports "made in France." Congo becomes an "anachronistic shadow" (*Solibo*, 204), a museum piece despite himself, an addition to the tourist repertoire as his trip to Fort-de-France during the carnival shows: "Congo was well amused; the tourists thought he was in costume. They applauded, laughed even when he was playing the clown, and took his picture" (*Solibo*, 205). "The flour of France powdered our dreams," writes Glissant in *La Case du commandeur*. The rhythm of time is no longer that of traditional work. The concept of time is determined instead by the assimilation program:

> Richard Coeurillon and Zaboca used to talk of the times of harvests
> and factory smoke stacks. In that time, one handled a machine and
> the other grasped a cutlass, those were the days. But nowadays if
> the fields are empty, if the whistles of the factory no longer give
> rhythm to the day, if hands no longer know how to moor down,
> to braid together, to screw tight, or to cut off, where does time go,
> Inspector? They say it's in France. (*Solibo*, 146)

The time of production gives way to a time of exacerbated dependence, of consumption of that which is "made elsewhere" (*Solibo*, 146).
This is literally the import and export of a concept of time. The wiping
out of production is one of the most controversial aspects of departmental status. In *Texaco*, the urban planner draws a connection between the obliteration of production and the violence of the urban
space:

> Urbanity is violence. Town spreads with one violence after another.
> Its equilibrium is violence. In the Creole city, the violence is harder
> than elsewhere. First, because around her, murder (slavery, colo-
> nialism, racism) prevails, but especially because this city, without
> the factories, without the industries with which to absorb the new
> influx, is empty. (148)

Texaco, a city with "a negative balance sheet," is structured by the
needs of the military and the import/export trade. The inability of the
unproductive city to channel those descending from the hills into productive activity or to regulate patterns of habitation within it leads to
a progressive marginalization of bodies freed from slavery in the housing projects located at the urban and social peripheries. The former
slaves undertake an infiltration of the city despite the watchful eye of
the bureau of city services (*Texaco*, 314). Texaco is, then, a gathering
place for the victims of the shock wave of the agricultural disaster, that
is to say the victims of the obliteration of production:

> The communists had understood that their old troops from the
> fields and from the central factories had taken the colonial roads,
> forgetting the Trails, to pile up here, right in City's mouth. A
> proletariat without factories, workshops, and work, and without
> bosses, in the muddle of the odd jobs, drowning in survival and
> leading an existence like a path through embers. (314)

The political context of the story is that of departmentalization, or more
accurately, the absence of sovereignty. Sosthène Versailles, one of the
suspects in Solibo's death and an anticolonialist militant with the Progressive Party of Martinique, considers his detainment and interrogation as a
deliberate effort to sabotage the next municipal elections, an elaborate

masquerade meant to while away the time he had meant to consecrate to the discussion of "the fundamental distinction between what Césaire labels In-dependence and a-dependence" (*Solibo*, 189). According to Sosthène, Solibo Magnifique's speech and anticolonialism participate in the same resistance to dispersal: "We are on a path to dispersal and I resist this. Solibo also resisted in his own way, maybe even more effectively than I can with my tracts and posters" (189). An increasingly anticolonial atmosphere provides the perfect pretext for not responding to the questions of Inspector Evariste Pilon: "Ti-Cal took refuge in abstruse politics. But what kind of era was that? What kind of time? Without Autonomy or Independence, there is nothing but tempest or dead time . . . "(145). Solibo does not necessarily represent a call for independence; in fact Solibo's speech, in the face of the mobilization of the forces of the assimilation program, inscribes itself in detour, in a dissimulated resistance that much prefers to circle around the sites of power, to outwit obstacles rather than to enter into a direct and spectacular confrontation:

> The authorities in charge of Cultural Action had often solicited his participation in staged story-telling events, but Solibo, fearing this sort of conservation effort in which one gives up living for the gift of artifice, always claimed unspecified obligations. Only an ignorant fool, he says, provides the rope that hangs him. (23)

The act of the collective voice holding its breath through the silence of the storyteller draws out the camouflage used by the enemies of the Martinican people. Cultural Action is an official structure whose ostensible goal is to promote culture, or to accomplish the work necessary to preserve local cultures under attack. The official function is one of survival, but the real project, most notably the propagation of folk culture for purposes of attracting tourists, is in effect one that exacerbates the devolution of culture. The tourism industry depends on standardization in the extreme, an eradication of local industry and other factors that contribute to the diminution of Martinique as a nation on the global scale. Solibo, in refusing the Cultural Action's proposals of salvage, indicates an understanding, if somewhat muddled, of this ambiguity. His refusal is nevertheless an indirect one: he does not confront the Cultural Action program; he invents excuses in order to escape it, since the practice of detour is dependent upon an enemy formulated in such a way as to render direct and unambiguous resistance impossible.

The Creole storyteller, according to Chamoiseau and Confiant's *Lettres créoles*, is "the artist of the cry, the receptacle of its poetics, the 'papa' of the literary path" (35) who, in the heart of the fields and sugar refineries, took up as his burden the contestation of the colonial system, using his art as both a mask and a didactic tool. In the midst of the plantation system that circumscribed the lived experiences of slaves, the storyteller, like the slaves, had to disguise his speech born of the cry of refusal through confusing the paths of its guile: "The slave adjusted to the forced labor and relocations, to the systems of slavery and colonialism, all the while contesting them through the minutia of indirect resistance" (39). The storyteller, who spends his days in a cocooned revolt, presides over the night, forging a language constrained by the "ambivalences of creolization, the opacity of detour necessary to survive and the unwritten knowledge of the Creole culture" (41). He is the spokesperson of a "dynamic questioning that accepts and refuses" (57). The speech of the plantation storyteller shifts around the obstacles of consciousness in order to diffuse, in both senses of the word, opposition to slavery, to the colonial ideology, to dehumanization. The storyteller then, has as his mission, the creation of the maroon's hills in the midst of the plantation. A tactician of survival, the storyteller does not attack but instead lays out traps and mines. The necessity to disguise the message dictates dissimulation, an element of all poetics of detour that can lead to disappearance. The storyteller is also an expert of digression, a strategy that redirects the attention of the party supposed to be in a superior position in order to gain the time to slip through the chinks in his armor. Digressions create opportunities, though parasitic. Digression embodies the tactic of detour in its fullness of discourse, multiplying the chances to fool the vigilance of the guardians of the status quo. Solibo's audience, now suspects in the police inquiry, resorts to a systematic use of diversion, of ulterior motives: the interrogation becomes a chance to insinuate themselves into the police system with the ultimate goal and effect of rendering marginal the inquiry itself. Digressions around the subject of the inquiry lead the police away from their principle objective and for Evariste Pilon, open up horizons of Martinican life that had been iced over by his Parisian background. Marie-Sophie Laborieux, in *Texaco*, also resorts to speech riddled with digressions in order to deflect the urban planner, sent by the modernist municipality of Fort-de-France, from his official mission of either "architecturally normalizing" or destroying Texaco, toward a compromise that takes into account the exigencies of the modern city and the Creolité of the location.

An oppositional structure cuts through *Solibo Magnifique*: the character of Solibo both subtly and openly opposes the structures whose goal is to promote the official culture, whether they are represented by the Cultural Action or the police. As a child, Solibo is pushed into the hills by the death of his father Amédée and the consequent decline of his mother Florise. Deprived of the help of his biological parents, Solibo becomes a child of slave speech or those still held to it:

> Some of the old women of the market where he camped out in his distress named him Solibo, meaning: one who has fallen in the deepest crack without a ladder to climb out. As was the case in these kinds of situations, the old women, during their periods of rest, offered him words, words of survival, words of resistance, all types of words that the slaves had forged in the heat of the old days in order to lift their decline to the sky. (78)

This initiation into speech made Solibo an uncontested master of the word, from whence his second name, Magnifique. The displacement of Solibo into the back country establishes an analogy between Solibo and the maroon that places him firmly in the trace of the historical and political tradition of maroon resistance:

> During his life, Solibo Magnifique was like someone at war: always alert. Get the békés to tell you the old stories of the maroons that no dog could track. The Negroes who did hide themselves in forests as big as birdhouses and still none could figure out where they were. The old hunters and the békés of yesteryear called them warriors! Solibo Magnifique was one of them. You can't assassinate one of those warriors, Inspector. (196)

In order to turn aside the customary assaults of the police, the residents of Texaco set up guard posts. A reflex inherited from the long-ago days of the maroons, to be on watch is a practice revived among the fringes of a population that, in a postslavery society, has taken the place of the slaves and the maroons. Being on alert protects against potential attacks while allowing one to take advantage of any opportunity to infiltrate the sites of power. By neutralizing the serpents, which, in the Antillean imagination, symbolize the ghost of the slave master, Solibo's speech contests slavery's project of domination: "Companions, you know this, the long-beast terrifies us. It killed us so often in the fields, it carries in its slithering so many ancient meanings, that its presence empties us" (74–75).

Solibo Magnifique represents the Antillean speech that yet escapes the regimentation of decrees, of the official edict: "On the ground in Fort-de-France, he had become an uncontested Master of the Word, not by decree of some folklore authority or Cultural Action (the only places in which one still celebrates the oral) but by this taste for words, his uninterrupted discourse" (26). Solibo is also the site of institutional interference, a symbol of resistance to the legitimation that comes from official decrees and departmental dependence. Solibo in and of himself symbolizes a cultural space where speech develops without the aid of official, departmental edict. The speech of Solibo is unofficial/unedited: it is unforeseen (or rather it was not programmed) by the texts of the colonial or departmental edicts. Circling around the authorities of Cultural Action works to preserve this speech from the impulse toward normalization that shapes all edicts, all legal and bureaucratic writing. The death of Solibo leaves him without defense against departmental edicts: the revenge of the edict against Solibo, the anti-edict par excellence, is thus posthumous. Even at this moment in his life, however, detour prevents the edict, embodied this time by the police, from appropriating Solibo.

The departmental system, of which the police are a part, constructs itself in opposition to the anticolonial and independence movements. The police, representing the law "made in France" (*Solibo,* 50), come to resemble parts of the slave system when they find themselves in conflict with marronnage. The story multiplies the connections between the Martinican police force and colonialism. The narrator, for example, talks of the "nature of these fanatics who shred the police in order to destroy colonialism" (*Solibo,* 55). The stratification of the police corps reproduces that of the plantation society by following a hierarchy imported from France: "Around here, the officers of the judicial police are France-whites, and the plain uniform officers—more native than the natives" (*Solibo,* 104). The association of the police and the slave becomes evident in this description of the Brigadier chief Bouaffesse:

> That man, it must be said, is stuff of chiefs. On the slave ships it was he who bathed us in salt water, disinfected cankers with boiled vinegar, rubbed us with oil just before the sale. On the plantation, he was the one who set the pace of work in the field, and then later became overseer. He was made to be a chief, but on the side of the law. To be in charge of, for example, a band of disreputable maroons would not have interested him. (83)

Evariste Pilon, the officer of the judicial police charged with the inquiry into the death of Solibo, is presented in the text as an important detective, but the narrator quickly says that this honor is accorded to him by the newspaper *France Antilles,* in contrast with the consecration of Solibo Magnifique, which comes from the local cultural norms. Implicitly in the text, the criminal affairs of Martinique come to be associated with the irrational, unlike the Cartesian police procedures that Pilon was taught during his training in France. The slippage between his training (French) and the exigencies of the local criminal scene are symptomatic of a methodological incompatibility or malaise between the theories of policing and the lived Martinique reality. The police then also come to represent a system of knowledge (and power) poorly adapted to the Martinican experience: "Never police when there's a scooter accident, stray cattle, Dominicans without papers, chicken thieves, or merchants with rigged scales, no. No, only those types with dark glasses who cast shadows over people in favor of independence" (118). The profile of Inspector Evariste Pilon reveals a personality riddled with cultural, intellectual, and political ambiguities:

> During the Solibo affair, he was living with a chabine, petitioning for Creole in the schools but taken aback when the children used it to address him, revering Césaire the poet without having read him, wearing a sun hat with winter boots, venerating the Caribbeanness of the Théâtre de Juillet and dreaming of the avenues of Jean Gosselin troop, commemorating the liberation of the slaves by themselves and shivering at the rites of the Godlike liberator Schoelcher, refusing to set up a Christmas tree but dusting his Filao bush with artificial snow, memorializing Fanon, but judging him effective only in the countries that lay over the horizon, voting Progressive in the municipal elections and crying "Long live de Gaulle" at the presidential ballot-box, mustering up a sob at independence, a beating of the heart at the idea of Autonomy and all the rest for Departmentalization. (119)

The police inquiry into Solibo's death can be read as the revenge of the written disciplinary code (edict) of departmental order over his autonomous and rebellious speech of resistance. Deploying a strategy of camouflage that tries to throw a wrench into the works of daily life of Martinicans, the inquiry participates in the criminalization of Solibo's audience, the only people who, in a context of political, economic, and cultural standardization, give Solibo a chance to be heard. At the same time, the police, in a technical manner, justify the inculpation or suspicion of the Cultural Activity under the unlikely pretext of finding the motives and authors of Solibo's death. The criminalization of his performance, of the relation between him and his audience, borders on a transformation of the community of storytelling (storyteller, performance, audience, audience participation, and an entire esthetic of participation) into a criminal society: the necessary communion and interaction between the storyteller and his listeners is recast in the language of criminal conspiracy. The community participation in the performance of

Solibo Magnifique becomes a collective assassination (148). The official criminalization of the performance also leads to a judicial and funerary identification of Solibo, and a criminal identification of his listeners. In the attempt to render the death of Solibo a banality, one can see the workings of a bureaucratic code that follows from departmentalization to treat with suspicion everything that does not emerge as a function of its own system. Ambiguity is introduced by the police presenting themselves as Solibo's ally, even though their respective goals are divergent, if not directly opposed. The mechanical procedures of the police humiliate his corpse as if he were part of the "trash of life" (25), thus contributing to what one could call the second death of Solibo: "around his corpse, the police set up an obscure death: injustice, humiliation, disdain. It carried with it all the absurdities of power and force: terror and madness" (27). If the cultural and symbolic death is a result of the conditions created by the departmental system, the second death is also provoked, or at least anticipated, by the disciplinary order of departmentalization.

Michel de Certeau tells us that tactic depends on time. The inquiry into the death of Solibo provides the time needed for the performers of the word to initiate Evariste Pilon into the Martinican experience and landscape, to transform the methods of inquest, to detour them onto the path of a quest for identity, toward a search for self inherent in the search for the meaning of his own name, Pilon. In general, the inquest is a span of time controlled by the inquisitor who reserves the right to pose the questions, implicitly determining the responses. In principle, the interrogated are at the mercy of the logic of the inquest. However, in the course of the inquiry into the death of Solibo, although Inspector Evariste Pilon and his team are technically in charge, the responses to their questions and the events that shape the inquest literally escape them. There are no answers to their questions, especially to the central question, who killed Solibo?

In place of the police inquiry's central question, the Inspector finds another question literally imposed by the suspects, which becomes his central preoccupation: who was Solibo? Such a change in focus represents an appropriation of the process of inquiry by those who are supposed to figure simply as suspects. For one of the suspects, Pierre Philomène, the central question is simply irrelevant: "Then, leaning towards Pilon, he said, 'without telling you how to do your job (you are a boss in the police, I know), looking for who killed Solibo will never lead to any truth. The real question is: who is Solibo? . . . and I'd add, Why Magnifique? . . . ' " (185). The question "who was Solibo?"

introduced by the suspects, calls into question the methods of investigation used by the police, and is thus a methodological critique:

> Excuse me Inspector, I don't want to teach you your job, but it's been forty years that I've crawled through the mud of Fort-de-France, I know all the bad habits of the gangster vagabonds, the godless, these people who respect nothing, I know what they are capable of, . . . So you want to know what I think? It's a small thing for me: Inspector, we don't kill story-tellers. (188)

Philomène Soleil, in the above passage, gives directions to the police while at the same time denying that his suggestions have any didactic purposes. Having done this, he takes up again the linguistic strategy of the storyteller articulated around an "ambiguous language wherein the truth of a statement is affirmed and transmitted in the development of its opposite" (*Lettres*, 60). Inspector Evariste Pilon seems to have recognized the message produced by the slippage between the methods of inquest and the criminal motivations in Martinique. After many interviews in the city that lead nowhere, the inquiry shifts to the back country, a move that echoes those of the maroons. Pilon, however, is not looking to explore paths that are not described by the methodological and theoretical characteristics of police inquiries. That he makes these changes is directly due to the influence of the words of the suspects:

> In the head of Evariste Pilon, the whole business took hold, sinuous, empty, laughable, bearing as its only fruit a name, a silhouette: Solibo Magnifique. What the suspects said about this man, and what little he heard, arranged itself in his memory, until a flood from a new source irresistibly insinuated itself into the river. After having demanded. an answer to the simple question "who killed Solibo?", he found himself bound to the other question: "who was Solibo and why Magnifique?" (219)

Rather than respond to the questions of the police, the companions and admirers of Solibo turn the inquiry into a wake, a time and place to celebrate the Magnificent One. The celebration of Solibo takes on the guise of the story of his life, a declaration of the impact of the Magnifique's stories on their lives. The supposed suspects thus infiltrate the time of the inquest, appropriating it as the time of a wake, going so far as to impose their own logic on Evariste Pilon. The questions become for them a pretext to celebrate the life of the Magnifique. The police are dispossessed of their own time, their power.

The protocol of a criminal inquest as it is formalized in the investigative report that takes place at the beginning of the novel, becomes here the call of duty: "We have begun a criminal inquiry, so no negro mumbo-jumbo, just French logic . . . " (105). Yet, the practice of detour consists precisely of working around the rigid French paths of inquiry toward the paths of negro mumbo-jumbo. The reversal occurs when the spoken precedes the written. The mystery of the Master of the Word fascinates Evariste Pilon, turning him away from the call of duty: the suspects lead the inquisitor, the inquisitor is led by the suggestions and words of the suspects, the written, the standardized, disciplinary code of interrogations is led by the flux of proliferating words. The police inquisition and its resulting terror for the last companions of the Magnifique yield the stage to a recreation of the character of the Master of the Word. The police, abandoning the arrogance born of their official function, which is entirely dependent on a crystallization of Parisian forms, submit to the voices of this place, relearn the essence of the word of Solibo, and thus themselves participate in the celebration of Solibo. Evariste Pilon becomes the inspiration for a written record of the words of the Magnifique, his personal witness and testament, after having criminalized participation in his last performance. In the absence of a wake, the novel and the entire process that leads to a written record of the last moments in the life of the Magnifique figure the literary wake of the storyteller: "the strategy of detour can therefore lead somewhere when the obstacle for which detour was made tends to develop into concrete 'possibilities' " (*Glissant,* 23). Detour, continues Glissant, is "not a useful ploy unless it is nourished by reversion: not for a return to a longing of origins, to some immutable state of Being, but a return to the point of entanglement, from which we were forcefully turned away; that is where we must ultimately put to work the forces of creolization, or perish" (Glissant 26). Detour, in *Solibo Magnifique,* leads to a questioning of a dependence on French conceptual frameworks, a questioning of the ways in which questions are formulated in an Antillean space, a reflection on the status of the storyteller and orality, and an expression of the agony in the voice of the Master of the Word. Detour forces the police, representatives of the departmental order, to relocate their practice in the exigencies of the Martinican landscape, constrained by the community of the story to take the actions that are ineluctably mutated, to move from the written to the oral. The site where the written and the oral meet, mediated toward the end of the text by the "sign of the word," represents the fullest realization of detour undertaken by the friends of Solibo; but also the moment where detour reaches its limits.

The novel *Texaco* puts into motion another modality of detour, anchored in speech, as is the case with *Solibo Magnifique*, and which, as we will see, borders on the recognition, by the modernist Cartesian, and by the conquering city of Fort-de-France, of the fact that Texaco "spells out the other urban poem" (*Texaco*, 143) that is new, disruptive, and remains to be decoded. The colonial edict, the law of slavery (*Le Code Noir*), the writing of the housing registry enter into conflict with the speech of the storyteller who is figured as anti-edict, anti-law, anti-writing. The speech of the storyteller is unedi(c)ted. Texaco also belongs to the order of the unedited, that is to say, part of that which is not programmed by the edicts of slavery, colonialism, or departmentalization, part of that which escapes the regimentation of the written, writing being here the mark of a civilization that sees itself as unique and normative, and thus also assimilationist: "We from Texaco, last to join the wreath of the old Quarters, we reinvented everything: laws, urban codes, neighborhood relations, settlement and construction rules" (317). The unedited is seen as a menace to the order of the edict. It is nothing but a heap of unhealthy shacks, inimical to public order. Texaco figures, on the outskirts of the city, a sort of determination to survive, a metaphorical reproduction of the ancient war between the slaves and the masters of the plantations. In the plantations, dogs were used to intimidate the slaves and sniff out the maroons, now, it's the highway (Pénétrante West) that presages an ultimate "police crackdown to make us clear off" (*Texaco*, 10). As Marie-Sophie Laborieux, the elderly founder of Texaco confides, the battle comes down from afar: "Texaco, my work, our Quarter, our field of battle and resistance summed up my interest in the world. There we kept up the fight to be part of City, a century-old battle. And this battle was the beginning of a final confrontation in which the stakes were either life as we knew it or our definitive defeat" (125). The metaphor of conquest echoes the assaults of the slave masters against the sallies of the maroons. Just as the body of Solibo Magnifique is wrapped up in the links of the police inquiry, in the French techniques of investigation, Texaco is trapped in the same logic of conquest. Just as with Texaco, the body of Solibo figures a site of conquest, as symbol of resistance (of disorder, of the indecipherable) that is to be mastered by the modern and rational project, represented in the novel by the urban planner and the city of Fort-de-France.

The urban planner is presented by Marie-Sophie Laborieux as "one of those agents of the modernizing city council which destroyed poor quarters to civilize them into sacks of projects" (10). A whole series of qualifiers describing the bullies of the center city such as "vanguard of a police crackdown" (19), "the riders of our apocalypse," "the modern municipality's angel of destruction" (25), invite a comparison between the actions of the police in the Solibo affair and those of the city planner. Evariste Pilon and the city planner were calcified into the same Parisian forms by their training: "This angel of doom whom I [Marie-Sophie] would make our Christ was preparing an urban planning thesis at the Institut de Géographie at the Paris Fourth District campus, under the direction of professor Paul Chaval, that for now he worked in the urban services bureau created by the modernizing city council that wanted him to rationalize space, and conquer the pockets of insalubrity which were a crown of thorns around it" (*Texaco*, 26). Urbanization is here seen as a project of violence, a violent conversion of the landscape according to Western norms: "In the center, memory subsides in the face of renovation, before the cities which the Occident inspires" (170). The coming of the urban planner announces a project of conquest, an architectural normalization. The Westernized city incarnates a project of order and discipline charged with the normalizing reduction of the Creole space: "Around it: a boiling, indecipherable, impossible crown, buried under misery and History's obscured burdens" (184). The geometric grid of a dominating urban grammar (184) recalls the mathematical French of Brigadier Bouaffesse: "In the center, an occidental logic, all lined up, ordered, strong like the French language. On the other side, Creole's open profusion according to Texaco's logic" (220). The conquering municipality of Fort-de-France becomes the figure for French calculations that seek to neutralize the proliferation of the Creole "mumbo-jumbo" that represents Texaco, "that site of savagery that no civilized map completely details." The attempt to control the periphery that remains ungraspable, anarchic, and obscure is also assimilable to a project of transparency.

Texaco opens with the annunciation "in which the urban planner who comes to raze the insalubrious Texaco Quarter instead finds himself in a Creole circus and faces a matadora's word" (7). To the open war against the unhealthy conditions of popular neighborhoods as defined by the city, Marie-Sophie Laborieux opposes the ancestral practice of survival: "I had suddenly understood that it was I, around this table with poor old rum, with my word for my only weapon, who had to wage— at my age—the decisive battle for Texaco's survival" (27). The city is compared to a Master's house of the slavery epoch, with the same mystery and the same power, thus making relevant the strategies used in those days of slavery to be reactivated or reinvented and put into operation by Texaco, which figures the slave's shack in modern times.

The construction of Texaco inscribes a practice of detour. The ceremonial obedience displayed by Mano Castrador, the guardian of Texaco, (the gas company from which the neighborhood derives its name), contrasts with an invisible indocility, characterized by the appropriation of building material from the gas station. Detour is also visible in the seizing of opportunities: the construction of makeshift houses, as with the storyteller's performance, takes place during the night: "We worked together in Upper Texaco, in Lower Texaco, until broad daylight. And by the time the oil béké arrived, he'd lost his guardian angel. Our hutches had bloomed from the rubble with more stubbornness than the tough wild grasses" (340–341). Mano, the guardian, plays a double game: he allows the residents of Texaco to take the béké's water between five and six in the morning. The day belongs to the slave master, the night is the realm of the storyteller. The day belongs to the béké of the gas company, the night to residents of Texaco.

The defense of Texaco seems to rely on the adversary's loss of time. For the residents, it is a case of delaying the inevitable visit that also means destruction of their huts, the issue is "to gain some time, to swindle some time from them" (337). The lawyer commissioned by the communist party to defend the residents of Texaco against the assaults of the police, the prefecture, and the béké of the gas company adopts the same tactic: it was he who led the béké of the gas company, the police, the entire prefect in a blinding mass of reversals, suspensions, deliberations, appeals, and procedures to delay until a day that would never come, and then started up the same legal circus all over again. It is significant that Marie-Sophie Laborieux compares the pleading of their defender to a legal circus, an expression that is used in the beginning of Chamoiseau's text by the narrative voice to describe Marie-Sophie's performance. The lawyer also resorts to digression, as is shown in his association of the residents of Texaco with the other wretched of the earth under the paradigm of a devastating imperialism such as colonialism, slavery, the exploitation of man by man, genocide of the American Indians, the massacre in Madagascar, the thousands of death along the Congo-Ocean railroad, the dirty tactics of the Indochina wars, and the torture of Algerian nationalists. A similar tactic of digression and diversion allows the lawyer to waste the time of the judge and to win time in order to delay the destruction of Texaco. The performances of Marie-Sophie Laborieux and the lawyer are exemplary manifestations of detour.

The survival tactics deployed by the inhabitants of Texaco also resemble a quest for self-knowledge. The first sight of the urban planner shows well that, in the eyes of the municipality of Fort-de-France, Texaco is the negation of what a city is supposed to be: "Texaco. I see here cathedrals of shafts, arcades of scrap iron, pipes carrying poor dreams. A non-city of soil and gas" (115). The urban planner, in the beginning identified as a plague by the residents of Texaco, is by the end considered a Christ, or Savior, by the very same residents. Through the detour of the words of Marie-Sophie Laborieux, the "angel of destruction" is transformed into Christ. The metamorphosis in the characterization of the urban planner is not without resemblance to the transformation of Inspector Evariste Pilon whose conflictual relations with the audience of Solibo Magnifique progressively give way to a fruitful collaboration in memorializing the life of the storyteller. The pacification of relations between representatives of order and the community is the product of a practice of detour, inscribed in oral performance.

The resistance of the residents of Texaco, provoked by the necessity to survive, raises an important question on a cultural and conceptual level: how can one conceive of an urbanization that is in accord with the laws of the area (les lois du lieu) while at the same time responding to the exigencies of Antillean modernity? Listening to the history of *Texaco* leads the urban planner to a realization of the inherent lack in his unconnected practice, from whence this confession: "We have to understand this future, knotted like a poem before our illiterate eyes. We have to understand that this Creole has been dreamt—I mean engendered—by its plantations, our plantations, by every Big Hutch of our Hills" (115–116). The time of performance becomes for him an apprenticeship, a coming to historical and cultural literacy: "She taught me to reread our Creole city's two spaces: the historical center living on the new demands of consumption; the suburban crowns of grassroots occupation, rich with the depth of our stories" (170). The derailing of the official project of normalization and destruction is in fact a pedagogical undertaking. To listen leads to a consciousness that the proliferation of Texaco is not an aberration. Beyond the unhealthiness, it is important to see the poetics put into play by the Creole city. The time of performance, the time of coming to literacy, is also a time stolen from the municipality via the distraction of the urban planner from his official mission. The questioning of his theoretical knowledge, of Western theories of urbanization, border on a re-apprenticeship into his occupation: "I understood suddenly that Texaco was not what the Westerners would call a shantytown, but a mangrove swamp, *an urban mangrove swamp*"

(263). The reinvention of terminology, a reconceptualization under-taken in the new light of the landscape indicates the rebirth of the former architect-plague who can now become the Christ whose new mission is the redemption of Texaco:

> The western urban planner sees Texaco as a tumor on the urban order. Incoherent. Insalubrious. A dynamic contestation. A threat. It is denied any architectural or social value. Political discourse negates it. In other words, it is a *problem*. But to raze it is to send the problem elsewhere or worse, not to consider it. No, we must dismiss the West and re-learn how to read: learn how to reinvent the city. Here the urban city planner must think Creole before he even thinks. (269–270)

The rethinking of his approach is a realization on the part of the urban planner of the need to take into account the question of Caribbean modalities of interpretation and action. The death of Solibo Magnifique precipitates the movement of one official into the lived Martinican experience. The attempt to discipline that life by the mechanical impo-sition of legal knowledge and police techniques coming from Paris progressively converts the representatives of glacial knowledge to the Creole tropicalities of the Martinican space. The project of assimilation in the practical work of officialdom runs up against the resistance of the lived, the mystery of Solibo, which in turn assimilates officialdom to itself. The energy spent in trying to solve the mystery in metropolitan fashion, the misunderstandings that characterize the interrogations, multiply the time that the police dedicate to it. The project of Evariste Pilon ceases to be the search for Solibo's cause of death according to the dependent/departmental order of knowledge and power but in-stead an unveiling of his own identity, constituting a theft of time from the departmental order. Detour can be defined as a supplement of energy and time required by those resisting power in order to arrive at the zone of compromise where hegemony abandons its pretensions of domination, where resistance can open up possibilities of a less precarious survival. The death of Solibo Magnifique maroons the de-partmental order on the frontiers of such a zone by imposing on the police the time necessary to engage in truly human interactions. The detour of proliferating Creole discourse leads the representatives of law and order to realize the urgency of exploring in depth the Caribbean realities, be it the speech of a storyteller or the space of a Creole quarter, all of which come in part from the plantation system. Detective Evariste Pilon and the urban planner come to discover the necessity of working toward cultural and historical literacy. The power of detour through oral performance is to have constrained the agents of the official edict to acknowledge the existence of the speech of *Solibo Magnifique* and of *Texaco* as phenomena that are unedited, carriers of their own significations.

Works Cited

Bory, Antoine, "Crise de la société—Crise de la pensée aux Antilles." *Présence africaine* 121–122 (1er et 2e trimestre 1982):27–52.

Chamoiseau, Patrick. *Solibo Magnifique.* Paris: Gallimard, 1988.

———. *Texaco.* Paris: Gallimard, 1992. Trans. Rose-Myriam Réjouis and Val Vinokurov. *Texaco, a Novel.* New York: Pantheon Books, 1996.

———, et Raphaël Confiant. *Lettres créoles.* Paris: Hatier, 1991.

Confiant, Raphaël. *Aimé Césaire, une traversée paradoxale du siècle.* Paris: Editions Stock, 1993.

Glissant, Edouard. *Malemort.* Paris: Seuil, 1975.

———. *Le Discours antillais.* Paris: Seuil, 1981 Trans. Michael Dash. *The Caribbean Discourse, Selected Essays.* Charlottesville, 1992.

———. *La Case du commandeur.* Paris: Seuil, 1981.

10

Addicted to Race

Performativity, Agency, and Césaire's A Tempest

Timothy Scheie

A profound sense of spectacle pervades the dramatic writings of Aimé Césaire. Unabashedly political in their critique of simplistic, accepted readings of racial and national identity, these plays do not preach to the spectator, nor do they purport to mirror a reality through the conventions of mimetic theater. A ludic and frequently ironic deployment of theatricality lends them a complexity that resists a realist *mise-en-scène*, and that leads theater practitioners and spectators alike to ponder the implications of the foregrounded performance of identity. In both the characters represented and the gesture of their representation, Césaire questions complex and unstable racial categories inflected by the colonial and national backdrop against which the action of his plays unfolds—King Christophe's Haiti, the newly independent Congo, and most remarkably, the thinly disguised Caribbean island of *Une tempête* (1969). Translated as *A Tempest*, this last play, a rewriting of Shakespeare's *The Tempest*, prescribes in its stage indications a self-conscious performance where characters exist only within a play of masks, and the parody of a canonical text generates both humor and a pointed commentary on the factitiousness of familiar racial categories.

For the 1990s spectator, *A Tempest*'s portrayal of racial identity as performance might evoke the now-familiar notion of a performative identity. The idea that identity is not stable or fixed but performative, and that it might therefore be performed differently and presumably in a less harmful or unjust manner, has sparked a great deal of discussion both by zealous subscribers and cautious critics. The theorization of performativity, most extensively articulated in the work of Judith Butler, would seem to inform an assessment of how Césaire's prescribed staging tactics disturb accepted readings of racial identity.

If the performative has provoked a great deal of excitement, however, the notion has also come under intense critical scrutiny. Caveats concerning the strategic potential of performative acts have been echoing with increasing urgency, effectively tempering the zeal of those who might glibly invoke performativity as a panacea to the ills of patriarchy.[1] Indeed, one need look no farther than Butler's own writings to find numerous qualifications that sharply restrict the sweeping agency some would attribute to the performative.[2] Furthermore, the status of theater in relation to the performative is far from clear. Butler often defines the performative *against* the conventions of the theatrical performance of a dramatic text, even one replete with apparently subversive staging strategies such as Césaire's; *A Tempest* consequently serves as an excellent site for assessing the import of the performative for theatrical practice. Furthermore, if the performative informs our understanding of Césaire's racial politics, *A Tempest*'s formulation of race through the metaphor of an incurable addiction in turn sheds light on the performative's limits as the theoretical justification for an activist theater's strategy. After articulating the troubled relationship between the performative, agency, and live theater practice, the discussion that follows will explore the potential for a subversive performativity in *A Tempest*, specifically in the final scene's enactment of racial identity as addiction.

In the fields of literary, cultural, and performance studies, few notions have sparked as much interest as the performative. Launched in the 1950s by philosopher and linguist J. L. Austin, the term served as a target of Derridean deconstruction before achieving wide circulation with the publication of Butler's *Gender Trouble: Feminism and the Subversion of Identity* (1990), and discussions of performativity have been proliferating ever since. The performative's current appeal might not seem evident in its initial formulation. Austin used the word to describe an utterance whose act of enunciation accomplishes something or somehow transforms the world: the priest's act of saying, "I now pronounce you man and wife," is often cited as the quintessential example. Butler, however, brings this notion to bear on questions of identity, arguing that gender likewise results from a similar performative gesture, or more precisely from sustained repetition of this performative gesture which generates the illusion of a fixed gendered identity.[3] Derrida's earlier deconstruction of the term only furthers her demonstration of gender's instability. The notion that identity results from a performative gesture, rather than being grounded in fixed and stable categories of the subject, offers a much desired theoretical direction for the efforts of writers, critics, and others who seek to change a repressive and patriarchal status quo and who, in our post-poststructuralist world, can neither triumphantly announce the dissolution of subjectivity nor fall back on essentialist or determinist accounts grounded in a purportedly truthful "real."

Despite its apparent liberatory potential, however, the performative does not easily serve the interests of an activist, counterhegemonic agenda. If it radically disturbs oppressive identity categories, the performative also destabilizes the agent who seeks to subvert them and necessitates a rethinking of agency as it is defined in familiar theoretical models for *engagé* theater practice. Two related qualifications of agency inhere in the performative, and restrict or even preclude its invocation to subversive ends. First, the performative does not recognize an individual's autonomy, perhaps best emblematized in the existentialist heroes of Sartre's dramas, to choose new identities or even to misperform identity transgressively in original or deviant ways. An impersonal power structure strictly regulates the constitutive gesture of identity's performance. "Power" must here be understood in the Foucaldian sense: not a privilege wielded by someone who has power, but a diffuse network of institutionalized constraints that coerce the performance of identity into naturalized configurations and that include mechanisms for censuring performances that do not comply. All actions, even those apparently in opposition to the identity categories of the power structure, are always already a function of it.[4] Secondly and moreover, a performer who invokes the performative further relinquishes the ability to recast identity at will, for it is precisely such "wills" that performativity calls into question. A willful intent to transgress the sanctioned categories of identity, however imaginary, posits a subject whose identity precedes and motivates the performance. An individual who claims to "perform" transitively an identity therefore betrays a misunderstanding of the performative mode, for that "who," a "subject" in both a philosophical and grammatical sense, is always already the product of a constitutive gesture. The performative consequently forecloses the possibility of agency wherever this term implies an autonomous agent with claims to prediscursivity. There is no autonomy, no exterior to which one can escape; to "be" a subject at all implies compliance with an epistemological regime of power relations.[5]

Paradoxically, this same injunction to repeat the performance of identity along sanctioned lines constitutes the performative's subversive potential. Identity "is" nowhere other than in its repeated performance, and Power not only exacts sustained compliance, but also depends on it in order to pull off the sleight of hand which causes the ephemeral performances to be misrecognized as a fixed identity. Power is needy; one could say it is *addicted* to such iteration. This dependence is, for Butler, a purportedly stable identity's Achilles heel:

> Agency is the hiatus in iterability, the compulsion to install an identity through repetition, which requires the very contingency, the undetermined interval, that identity insistently seeks to foreclose. . . . And yet, the future of the signifier of identity can only be secured through a repetition that fails to repeat loyally, . . . a disloyalty that works the iterability of the signifier for what remains non self-identical in any invocation of identity, namely the iterable or temporal conditions of its own possibility. (*Bodies That Matter,* 220)

A performance that could draw attention to the repeated gesture of identity's constitution would reveal that this repetition is neither self-identical with its imaginary source nor a slavish imitation of it, but that it generates what it appears to copy, what it purports to "be." Butler envisions an opening for a strategic maneuver, for an agentless agency:

> It is necessary to learn a double movement: to invoke the category, and hence, provisionally to institute an identity and at the same time to open the category as a site of permanent political contest. *That the term is questionable does not mean that we ought not to use it,* but neither does the necessity to use it mean that we ought not to perpetually interrogate the exclusions by which it proceeds . . . (*Bodies That Matter,* 222)

An iteration at once loyal and disloyal reinscribes the term while evoking the constraints that govern this gesture of inscription.[6] The performative does not represent a radical disloyalty or an outright rebellion against categories of identity, nor does it represent a sort of obedience in bad faith, implying a knowing agent under, above, behind, or otherwise prepositioned outside of the performance itself. It neither subverts nor overthrows, but instead "troubles" apparently immutable identities by making evident their constitutive gesture.

The necessary ambivalence of the performative's destabilizing terms compromises its potential as the theoretical justification for subversive activist strategies. With no "outside" to evoke, the performance of identity can only operate through and never fully against the "questionable terms" of the "inside," and without recourse to a knowing position of truth or authority nothing guarantees that any disloyalty will be detected at all. A disloyal performance necessarily resembles the loyal one that repeats the "sedimented" categories of identity in an uncritical and accepting manner. In short, only a spectator who already believes in the performativity of identity will detect the disloyalty inherent in a performance. There is no radical subversion, only a rearticulation and a redeployment that is at the same time a repetition and perpetuation of the offensive terms targeted for subversion. How effective is the strategy of revelation when it entails a repetition of the very identities deemed injurious in the first place, while relinquishing recourse to a knowing performer who can issue a discreet and reassuring wink at the spectator? How appealing is this "no pain no gain" formulation of performativity when the pain (the reinscription) is a sure thing and the gain (the revelation) tenuous? And what, finally, is there to be gained? Janelle Reinelt has skeptically written of the requisite faith in a postidentity world that underlies theorizations of the performative, an as yet unthinkable world that cannot guarantee that it will be any less oppressive than the one we know and presumably seek to change (101). While Butler's performative is theoretically provocative, it ultimately suggests less how to enact a strategic deconstruction of gender or other subject positions than how difficult such an endeavor might be.

If the performative seems incompatible with the project of a committed author such as Césaire, its import for his dramatic *œuvre* specifically would appear even more questionable. The formulation of identity as performance might at first seem to inform a theater of intervention, and the apparent liberatory promise of the performative has not escaped the attention of theater practitioners. Yet, although she liberally borrows vocabulary and metaphors from the theater, Butler rarely refers to live dramatic performance in its specificity, and her focus on examples of the performative drawn from written texts and film leads Emily Apter to remark the "almost phobic disinterest in theater history and dramatic art" in her work (16). Despite the invocations of performativity that frequently figure in the program notes of performances employing staging practices that Butler once cited as subversive to the patriarchal order, namely drag, on the few occasions when the theorization of performativity mentions the stage it is to oppose performativity to theatrical performance.[7] Butler herself offers a dismissive justification for this exclusion. Writing that the stage of dramatic theater operates through a "modality of appearance" that delineates a clear playing area, a space for illusion and performance, she observes that the exterior to this space is consequently granted a more "real" status, thereby preserving a realm outside the performance inhabited by "real" and undisturbed, apparently *un*performed subjects:

> In the theatre, one can say, "this is just an act," and de-realize the act, make the acting into something quite distinct from what is real. . . . [T]he various conventions which announce that "this is only a play" allow strict lines to be drawn between the performance and life. (*Gender Trouble*, 278)[8]

No matter how subversive the performance within the playing area, it tacitly reinscribes foundational identities of the exterior in the persons of the performer under the character and the spectator outside of the play. A dramatic performance in which the performer freely and knowingly assumes a role therefore represents precisely what the performative is not, and emblematizes the theater's surreptitious reinforcement of an identity's claim to fixity rather than a revelation of identity's constitutive instability. To echo a Butlerian aphorism, the drag queen strutting her stuff on the stage is not nearly as troubling as the one sitting next to you on the bus.[9]

The staging prescribed in Aimé Césaire's *A Tempest,* namely the use of masks to signify racial identity, serves as a telling example of the performative's limited potential to inform or justify the staging strategies of a committed theater. Productions of Shakespeare's *The Tempest* have often dwelt on its colonial overtones, but in *A Tempest* Césaire, a Martiniquais who himself lived and still lives under (neo)colonial rule, explicitly sets the action in terms of the struggle between a colonizing European master and the colonized indigenous slaves.[10] Clearly adapting and not merely translating Shakespeare's text, Césaire adds to the list of *dramatis personae* a few brief but significant specifications of racial identity: Caliban is black, Ariel is mulatto, and both are Prospero's slaves. Indeed, the master/slave dynamic dominates the text, to the expense of the love story between Ferdinand and Miranda and the political intrigue among the Europeans that compete with it in Shakespeare's text. Césaire also adds an additional deity, the Yoruba trickster god Eshu, to those who bless the marriage of the young couple. In its representation of racial identity, the play further deviates from the Shakespearean text when it prescribes cross-race casting through the use of masks. In a brief prologue to the play, a Master of Ceremonies distributes these to the attendant cast in a seemingly arbitrary manner: "Help yourselves . . . You, Prospero? And why not? . . . You, Caliban? I don't see why not. . . . " (9). Césaire specifies that he wrote the play for a *théâtre nègre*, an all-black company; since Caliban, Ariel, and Eshu are the only characters of color, adherence to Césaire's indications would necessitate the cross-race casting of the white Europeans, that is to say, the majority of the roles.

The staging strategies of *A Tempest* promote the political views of its author. Unlike the biologically rooted racial identity celebrated by his contemporaries, most notably in the poems of Léopold Sédar Senghor, Césaire's *négritude* separates racial identity from natural or biological attribution in order to signal its historicity, and consequently its mutability. His use of cross-race casting and masks in *A Tempest* evokes the figurative masks of Frantz Fanon's *Black Skin, White Masks* (1952) and underscores the contingency of the characters' racial identity. Caliban's angry final tirade explicitly links this staging practice to the colonial ideology of race:

> Prospero, tu es un grand illusioniste: / le mensonge, ça te connaît. / Et tu m'as tellement menti, / menti sur le monde, menti sur moi-même, / que tu as fini par m'imposer / une image de moi-même: / Un sous-développé, comme tu dis / un sous-capable, / voilà comment tu m'as obligé à me voir, / et cette image, je la hais! Et elle est fausse!

> (Prospero, you are a great illusionist: deception knows you well. And you have lied to me so much, lied about the world, about myself, that you finally imposed an image on me, an image of myself, an "underdeveloped" you say, an "under achiever," that is how you have made me see myself, and I hate this image! It is false!) (88)

The masks emblematize the repressive identity category into which Caliban has been interpellated, and in which he has misrecognized himself as an inferior. In his final *prise de conscience*, Caliban denounces this image's apparently natural and essential grounding— Prospero's meteorological machinations further betray the human mediation of all that is "natural"—to reveal, to himself, to the other characters, and to the spectators, the history of power relations that generated and perpetuated it to his detriment.

By clearly separating the character's identity from the gesture of its performance, Césaire's desired staging falls squarely in the tradition of Brecht's theater of alienation. Indeed, the use of masks would seem to exemplify the Brechtian *Verfremdungseffekt*, or "alienation effect," which distances the characters' perception of the world around them to reveal what they do not see about the social, economic, and political situation that shapes their identity and determines their life's course. In Césaire's case, the masks serve to reveal race as a historical regime of power relations, and to alienate the characters' assumption that the status quo of race relations on the island is somehow "natural." For the spectator, this split vision discredits the claim to referentiality or "truth" of identities represented by the literal masks. It also betrays the figurative ideological "masks" of identity that Prospero propagates in the dehumanizing discourse he systematically directs at Caliban, revealing it as a rhetoric of power and oppression whose claim to "naturalness" is enforced only by the technological superiority he so jealously guards. The play of masks likewise implicates Gonzalo's no less dehumanizing idealization of the island and its "noble savages."

The revelation of identity's instability through Brechtian alienation enacted in *A Tempest* would seem commensurate with a subversive performativity, and indeed, the performative shares many common tenets with a Brechtian theater. Both displace identity from an autonomous and fixed selfhood onto the gesture of its constitution, and both acknowledge and reveal the constraints that govern this gesture of performance. A crucial difference, however, distinguishes a Brechtian production from a subversive performativity. Brecht's plays frequently suggest an underlying truth about the events represented on the stage, and while his theater alienates the identity and actions of the characters for the spectators' critical assessment, the performers themselves often serve as agents of a truth, of a Marxist truth, about the represented people and events.[11] To qualify as performative, a stage performance would need to take Brecht a step further, displacing not only the performed character but the performer as well to reveal both as the result of a performative gesture. In Butler's words, there would be no "doer behind the deed"; the doer would always be revealed as already the effect of the deed.

As an exemplary Brechtian alienation effect, Césaire's play of masks reveals the contingency of racial attributes, but fails ultimately to reveal the constitutive instability of racial identity itself. By writing his play for a *théâtre nègre* Césaire explicitly establishes a "doer behind the deed" in the person of the performer whose racial identity prefigures and does not participate in the obvious gesture of choice implied in the distribution of the masks in the prologue. If the Master of Ceremonies clearly calls each character into being, drawing attention to this gesture of interpellation (to use Althusser's terminology), the very visible and racially specific performers have themselves already been subjected to a tacit interpellating gesture that is not similarly revealed in the performance. Indeed, for the casting of roles across racial lines to discredit the characters' racial identity, it depends on the previous inscription of the racial boundaries it subsequently transgresses. The alienation of race enacted within the play of masks grants its exterior—the performer behind the mask—the more "real" status of the unperformed, and therefore operates through the "modality of appearance" of Butler's critique. One might argue that Césaire's prescribed staging lodges an oblique critique of all racial identity through the metaphor of these masks, but this critique will always be too late: the masks will already have exacted the spectator's recognition and acceptance of the same racial identities targeted for subversion.

The performative challenges theater to discredit the identities of both theatrical illusion—Butler's "modality of appearance"—and the spectator's "reality," or in terms of Césaire's play, of both the mask and the performer. This has proven difficult to do, and even the most apparently subversive or liberatory performances of identity cannot escape an insidious reinforcement of sanctioned norms.[12] However, the staging prescribed for the closing scene of *Une Tempête* adds a final twist to the play of masks that potentially implicates the racial identities of both the performed character/mask and of the spectator's "reality" in a performative gesture.

Césaire ends his play with a final significant deviation from the Shakespearean text: Prospero chooses to remain on the island at the end of the play instead of returning to Europe with the other Italian nobles. The final scene therefore mirrors the opening, with Prospero the sole master of the island and its indigenous population. The dynamic, however, has changed, and it is a desperate Prospero who closes the play with shrill tirade:

> On jurerait que la jungle veut investir la grotte. Mais je me défendrai ... Je ne laisserai pas périr mon œuvre ...
>
> *Hurlant*
>
> Je défendrai la civilisation!
>
> *Il tire dans toutes les directions.*
>
> Ils en ont pour leur compte ... Comme ça j'ai un bon moment à être tranquille ... Mais fait froid ... C'est drôle, le climat a changé ... Fait froid dans cette île ... Faudrait penser à faire du feu ... Eh bien, Caliban, nous ne sommes que deux sur cette île, plus que toi et moi. Toi et moi! Toi-Moi! Moi-Toi! mais qu'est-ce qu'il fout?

Hurlant

Caliban!

On entend au loin parmi le bruit du ressac et des paillements d'oiseaux les débris du chant de Caliban.

(One would swear that the jungle wants to infest the grotto. But I will defend myself . . . I will not let my life's work perish . . . [*shouting*] I will defend civilization! [*He fires in all directions*] That should take care of them . . . This way I'll have some peace for a while . . . but it's cold . . . it's funny, the climate has changed . . . cold on this island . . . should think about making a fire. . . . well, Caliban, there's just two of us on this island, just you and me. You and me. You-me. Me-you. What the hell is he doing? [*Screaming*] Caliban! [*In the distance is heard, among the sound of the surf and the cheeping birds, the remains of Caliban's song.*]) (92)

The text indicates that Prospero's language in this final scene becomes "impoverished and stereotyped." If Prospero continues to proclaim his role as the defender of civilization it is only by repeating an exhausted racist and racializing discourse. Earlier in this act, Caliban referred to Prospero as a *vieil intoxiqué,* an "old addict," and predicted that Prospero would be too "hooked" on his position as the master to ever return to Europe. The play leaves the spectator with the image of Prospero hopelessly strung out on his whiteness, while his speech degenerates into the babble of a confused pronominal opposition that, in the absence of one of the parties, no longer makes sense. Prospero's final cry represents a failed attempt to interpellate Caliban into the identity categories established in the Prologue, to call him into existence as a savage, as a slave, and as a black man. The lack of response throws the colonial dialectic, and Prospero's identity as the white, civilized master, into crisis.[13]

Significantly, although Caliban effectively refuses to wear the mask of identity that the play so self-consciously imposed upon him in the prologue, the play denies the audience the spectacle of this liberating gesture. In contrast to the very visible imposition of the masks onto already racialized bodies in the prologue, the symmetrical unmasking of the end takes place invisibly in the wings. The body under the mask of race is very deliberately *not* identified with that of the performer who put on the mask in the prologue. Caliban's renunciation of racial identity is therefore double: he refuses to play the racialized role both of the character who is no longer willing to be Prospero's "savage" slave, and also of the racially specific black performer who assumed this role in the prologue. The play leaves the spectator no image of the liberated "unmasked" performer/subject who transcends or otherwise escapes from a racializing and racist discursive regime. As spectators, we cannot see the new Caliban, nor even understand his language, the language taught to him by Prospero, as it decomposes into *débris*. At the play's end the spectator is stuck with the familiar racial identities of the black performer wearing the white mask of Prospero, the emblem of a tired white/black racial binary. Caliban "kicks the habit"; Prospero does not, nor ultimately do the spectators for whom the deracialized subject remains an unimagined, unrealized dream.

Césaire's *mise-en-scène* marks an instance where dramatic performance escapes the insidious "modality of appearance" that Butler decried in her assessment of theater's subversive potential. In its final scene, *A Tempest* discredits racial categories without furnishing a visible "doer behind the deed," a "true" race under the mask of race, a performer whose identity is not implicated in the performance itself. Although the opening of the play might appear to sanction the performers' identities before or under the masks as more "real," the invisible unmasking of the end suggests that the racial identity of the performer, like that of the character, is also constituted in performance. Césaire's language of addiction and this addiction's enactment in the final scene very aptly characterize the constrained iteration of the performative: the spectators might wish to escape the categories of race that have caused so much strife and suffering, but they need racial identities in order to make the world intelligible, they are dependent— *addicted*—to them, and like Prospero, are condemned to iterate them unto exhaustion even when their instability has been revealed and their truthful status questioned.

A Tempest nevertheless does not represent an exemplary revelation of identity's performativity. Butler writes that the goal of a strategic invocation of the performative would be "to avow a set of constraints on the past and the future that mark at once the *limits* of agency and its most *enabling conditions*" (*Bodies That Matter*, 228). Césaire's tactic does indeed avow the constraints that compel the perpetuation of worn-out identities, and depicts their continued iteration as a pathetic and hopeless addiction. *A Tempest,* however, enacts none of the reappropriations or redeployments of the "questionable terms of identity" that represent the performative's constructive, empowering side. Caliban's disappearance does not reaffirm, reinscribe, reappropriate, or otherwise repeat his identity as a black or as a slave, and in his absence, the play does not "provisionally . . . institute identity and at the same time open the category as a site of permanent political contest" (*Bodies That Matter*, 222).

Echoing the conventional reading of this play, one might respond that although *A Tempest* does not represent the liberated Caliban, it evokes a virtual subject, outside of the familiar and oppressive categories of race, and challenges the spectator to imagine what such a subject might be like. In this respect, Césaire's play would resembles Brecht's epic theater, which often poses a dilemma and, without actually furnishing a resolution, nonetheless leads the spectators to conclude that the ideals of a socialist state, if enacted, would solve the problems that plague the lives of the characters: the plights of Mother Courage in *Mother Courage and Her Children* and of Shen-Tê in *The Good Person of Szechwan* are two well-known examples of this. The freed Caliban would also situate Césaire's text in the French intellectual milieu of its time insofar as it evokes an existentialist theater: Caliban resembles Sartre's dramatic heroes when, in an epiphanic moment, he rejects the "mask" of a false consciousness. Like the Orestes of *The Flies,* Caliban makes a conscious decision not to comply with the societal constraints, and though invisible, in the end he both thinks and ultimately acts independently of the epistemological regime that oppresses him. Unlike Brecht, however, there is no previously articulated political solution (a socialist state) waiting in the wings of *A Tempest,* and in contrast to Sartre, Césaire denies the spectators a visible hero with whom they can identify: the same gesture that frees Caliban to act in the world subtracts him from it. If the final scene posits a liberated subject in the not yet intelligible identity of the deracialized subject formerly known as Caliban, this "doer behind the deed" and the "real" it inhabits remain the unrepresentable dream of a postracial utopia, and nothing guarantees or even suggests that this dream will ever be realized. Prospero's exhausted and discredited reality persists in the end, both on the stage and off.

The virtual staging prescribed in *A Tempest* demonstrates the tenuous common ground shared by a dramatic or theatrical performance and the performative. By representing the addictive compulsion to repeat the discredited categories of race, and by making this constraint palpable to the spectators, the final scene of Césaire's play marks an instance where theatrical performance does not represent the reactionary art form to which Butler opposes a subversive performativity. However, one might ask if the imperfect revelation of identity's performativity in this play does not in fact offer a telling illustration of the limits of the performative itself. *A Tempest* tells us that we are stuck with—stuck on—categories of race. As with many addictions, recognizing the problem is an important step, certainly one worth taking; solving it, however, is quite a different story. If Césaire's play generates a heightened awareness that enables the spectator to manage provisionally a dependence on racial identity, it ultimately promises no cure. Nor does the performative, which concedes that the performance of identity is necessarily a reiteration along sanctioned and familiar lines. Césaire's staging and language of addiction ultimately fail to realize a radically subversive performativity, and through this failure emblematize the ambivalence of the agency the performative warrants, on stage or off.

Notes

1. There are now many of these. The ones to which this article will refer include Case (1995), and Reinelt (1994). See also Parker and Sedgwick (1995).

2. *Bodies That Matter: On the Discursive Limits of Sex* (1993) explicitly responds to facile and perhaps overzealous misinterpretations of the agency that the discussion in *Gender Trouble* appears to suggest, and effectively recants the oft-cited passages of *Gender Trouble* that suggest that drag performance radically subverts gender categories. See Butler (*Bodies That Matter*, introduction, *x*).

3. Butler relies heavily on a psychoanalytic paradigm that privileges sexuality and gender roles in identity formation. She also acknowledges, however, the complex intersection of race and other identity categories with her theorization of gender.

4. "Gender is, thus, a construction that regularly conceals its genesis; the tacit collective agreement to perform, produce, and sustain discrete polar genders as cultural fictions is obscured by the credibility of those productions—and the punishments that attend not agreeing to believe in them. . . . The historical possibilities materialized through various corporeal styles are nothing other than those punitively regulated cultural fictions alternately embodied and deflected under duress" (*"Performative Acts,"* 140).

5. On the subject of gender specifically, Butler writes: "Femininity is thus not the product of a choice, but the forcible citation of a norm, one whose complex historicity is indissociable from relations of discipline, regulation, punishment. Indeed, there is no "one" who takes on a gender norm. On the contrary, this citation of the norm is necessary to qualify as a "one," to become viable as a "one," where subject-formation is dependent on the prior operation of legitimating gender norms" (*Bodies That Matter*, 232).

6. The performative's deconstructive underpinnings become evident in this collapse of the loyal/disloyal binary into a constitutive indeterminacy, and Butler's "double movement" recalls Derrida's reading of Plato's *pharmakon*. Some critics have grounded critiques of the performative by locating deconstruction at the root of its refusal of a politically viable subject/agent. Case (1995) worries about the "textualization" of the performative and the concomitant evacuation of the lesbian as bodily practice in Butler's "critical queer," and Bersani (1995) lodges his critique on similar grounds. Reinelt (1994)

also cites Butler's deconstructive tendencies when she opposes performativity to a feminist project. See also Scheie (*"Questionable Terms"*).

7. For further discussion of Butler's ambivalence towards drag, see Scheie (*"Body Trouble"*).

8. Throughout this early article, Butler defines performative acts against the "theatrical" and "dramatic" acts of existentialist (Sartre and de Beauvoir) and phenomenological (Merleau-Ponty) thought.

9. Though *Bodies That Matter* only touches on questions of theater, both its opening and closing discussions insist on the distinction between performativity and performance: "Performativity . . . is not primarily theatrical; indeed, its apparent theatricality is produced to the extent that its historicity remains dissimulated . . . " (12); "performance as bounded 'act' is distinguished from performativity insofar as the latter consists in a reiteration of norms which precede, constrain and exceed that performer and in that sense cannot be taken as the fabrication of the performer's 'will' or 'choice'; further, what is 'performed' works to conceal, if not to disavow, what remains opaque, unconscious, unperformable. The reduction of performativity to performance would be a mistake" (234).

10. Césaire had initially intended only to translate *The Tempest*. He acknowledges the liberties he took with Shakespeare's text: "Le travail terminé, je me suis rendu compte qu'il ne restait plus grand-chose de Shakespeare" (When the work was done, I realized there was not much Shakespeare left.) (Césaire, *"Un poète politique,"* 31).

11. "*True* realism has to do more than just make reality recognizable in the theatre. One has to be able to see through it too. One has to be able to see the *laws* and decide how the processes develop" (*Brecht*, 27, my emphasis). This submission to a deeper, truer "Law" is what led Roland Barthes, in his poststructuralist phase, to distance himself from Brecht after many years of being his staunch apologist in the face of harsh French criticism. See Barthes, 86–93.

12. This becomes particularly evident in Butler's discussion of Jennie Livingston's documentary *Paris is Burning*, which illustrates how an insidious reinscription of the oppressive order inheres in even the most apparently liberatory performance of identity. See Butler (*Bodies That Matter*, chapter 4). Peggy Phelan's critique of "visibility" in *Unmarked: The Politics of Performance*, goes farther, suggesting that recognizable, visible categories of identity are hopelessly tainted with the oppressive symbolic order that enables their representation, and that the invisible and the unrepresented—the "unmarked"—represents a more promising site for subversion.

13. Césaire acknowledges the Hegelian foundation of his play: "[Caliban] est un héros positif exactement comme chez Hegel: c'est l'esclave qui est le plus important, car c'est lui qui fait l'histoire" (Caliban is a positive hero just like in Hegel: It's the slave who is the most important, because it is he who makes history) (Mbom, 91).

Works Cited

Apter, Emily. "Acting Out Orientalism: Sapphic Theatricality in Turn-of-the-Century Paris." *Performance and Cultural Politics.* Ed. Elin Diamond. New York: Routledge, 1996, 15–34.

Austin, J. L. *How to Do Things With Words.* Cambridge: Harvard UP, 1962.

Barthes, Roland. "Diderot, Brecht, Eisenstein." *L'obvie et l'obtus: essais critiques III.* Paris: Seuil, 1982.

Bersani, Leo. *Homos.* Cambridge: Harvard UP, 1995.

Brecht, Bertolt. *The Messingkauf Dialogues.* Trans. John Willett. New York: Methuen, 1965.

Butler, Judith. *Gender Trouble: Feminism and the Subversion of Identity.* New York: Routledge, 1990.

———. "Performative Acts and Gender Constitution: An Essay in Phenomenology and Feminist Theory." *Performing Feminisms: Feminist Critical Theory and Theatre.* Ed. Sue-Ellen Case. Baltimore: Johns Hopkins UP, 1990, 270–282. Original edition, *Theatre Journal* 40, 1988: 519–531.

———. *Bodies That Matter.* New York: Routledge, 1993.

Case, Sue-Ellen. "Performing Lesbian in the Space of Technology: Part I." *Theatre Journal* 47 (1995): 1–18.

Césaire, Aimé. *Une Tempête.* Paris: Seuil, 1969.

———. "Un poète politique: Aimé Césaire." Interview. *Magazine littéraire* 34 (1969): 27–32.

Derrida, Jacques. "La Pharmacie de Platon." *La Dissemination.* Paris: Seuil, 1972.

Dolan, Jill. "Geographies of Learning: Theatre Studies, Performance, and the 'Performative.' " *Theatre Journal* 45 (1993): 417–441.

Fanon, Frantz. *Peau noire, masques blancs.* Paris: Seuil, 1952.

Mbom, Clément. *Le théâtre d'Aimé Césaire.* Paris: Fernand Nathan, 1979.

Parker, Andrew, and Eve Kosofsky Sedgwick, eds. *Performativity and Performance.* New York: Routledge, 1995.

Phelan, Peggy. *Unmarked: The Politics of Performance.* New York: Routledge, 1993.

Reinelt, Janelle. "Staging the Invisible: The Crisis of Visibility in Theatrical Representation." *Text and Performance Quarterly* 14 (1994): 97–107.

Scheie, Timothy. "Body Trouble: Corporeal 'Presence' and Performative Identity in Cixous's and Mnouchkine's *L'Indiade ou l'Inde de leurs rêves.*" *Theater Journal* 46 (1994): 31–34.

———. "Questionable Terms: Shylock, Céline's *L'Eglise*, and the Performative." *Text and Performance Quarterly 17 (1997): 153–169.*

11

"Dark Continents" Collide

Race and Gender in Claire Denis's Chocolat

Dana Strand

Writing about racial and sexual difference in psychoanalysis and cinema, Mary Ann Doane locates the origins of the expression "dark continent," used by Freud to signify female sexuality, in the nineteenth-century colonialist imagination. She argues that Freud's invoking of the dark continent trope, borrowed as it was from Victorian colonialist texts, reveals a complex historical link between the categories of racial difference and sexual difference: "Just as Africa was considered to be the continent without history, European femininity represented a pure presence and timelessness (whose psychical history was held, by Freud, to be largely inaccessible)" (Doane, 212). This merging of two "unknowabilities" posits Otherness as a problem of the limits of knowledge and visibility, defined, it should be noted, in geographical or territorial terms.

Yet, despite the historical articulation of race and gender, social observers and scholars concerned with the dangers of ignoring the mechanisms of oppression operative in each case, have issued repeated warnings (in particular to feminist critics) against conflating the two. In a recent article in the *PMLA*, Gwen Bergner prefaces her critique of Fanon's construction of gender and sexuality in his analysis of racial identity in a colonial context with the following pertinent admonition:

"Although they may emanate from a common construction of otherness in psychoanalytic discourse, racial difference and sexual difference intersect and interact in contextually variable ways that preclude separate or determinist description" (Bergner, 76). To sum up Bergner's warning, then, while it would be simplistic to consider racially based conditions for Othering as interchangeable with gender-based ones (despite the undeniable similarities), it would also be a mistake to assume that the two processes are ever at work independently. As she states, "race and gender are mutually constitutive and reciprocally informing" (Bergner, 85).

In this essay, I propose to examine the complex interplay of race and gender, as a function of visibility, in the colonial and postcolonial settings that form the backdrop for the 1988 French film, *Chocolat*, directed by Claire Denis. Two distinct reasons have prompted me to explore this issue in the film: first, I have been struck by the remarkable disparity in the critical reception of *Chocolat*, ranging from enthusiasm for its effective critique of colonial power and authority (see, for example, Ien Ang's article entitled "Hegemony-in-Trouble" in *Screening Europe*), to condemnation of the film as an illustration of imperialist discourse (here I cite from the syllabus of a Cameroonian who is a professor of French at an American university). Second, since the coherence of both race and gender within psychoanalytic discourse depends upon the specular, cinema seems to be the most logical medium for investigating the intricate play of visibility and invisibility at work in creating these categories. More specifically, as a film structured, even more than most, around the act of looking, *Chocolat* highlights the role of sight in producing difference. Keeping in mind, then, Doane's emphasis on the visual foundations of knowability within the psychoanalytic model she invokes, and Bergner's conclusion that gender and race as categories of Othering operate differently, yet in complexly interdependent ways, I would like to propose an alternative reading of *Chocolat*. My reading will reexamine the dark continent trope from a postcolonial perspective, in order to show that what the film ultimately relegates to "the dark" is white, male European hegemony.

Chocolat begins with the return of a French woman to post-independence Cameroon, where she spent her childhood during the last years of the French colonial presence in sub-Saharan Africa. Raised as the daughter of a colonial administrator in an isolated outpost, France (a name almost too obviously drenched in symbolic meaning) is hoping to discover the Africa of her youthful memories. Clutching her father's journal as her only available guide to this lost colonial space, she crosses the unfamiliar countryside in the back seat of a car driven by a black man who has stopped to give her a lift to the airport. As she travels, her memory is sparked by visual reminders of the past. Presented as a flashback, the action of the majority of the film, which takes place during the waning days of the official French colonial occupation of Africa, is framed by the opening scene and the final one, both set in contemporary Cameroon. Following the paradigmatic outlines of "the colonial family romance" (Hall, 49), the film traces the erosion of trust in the relationship between the young France and the family's physically imposing male servant, Protée, as a consequence of the forbidden sexual attraction between Protée and the girl's beautiful young mother.

This central story develops against the backdrop of a secondary plot line, the unexpected forced landing in the bush of an airplane carrying French passengers. Obliged to remain at the commandant's home until work on a makeshift runway has been completed, the passengers offer a composite portrait of the stereotypical colonizer: blatantly racist and paternalistic, they remain resolutely blind to the rich African cultural traditions that surround them. A coffee planter, whose crass sexual exploitation of an African woman serves as a brutal reflection of his (and his compatriots') economic exploitation of the region, continually ridicules the backwardness of the African people, insulting a local chief who comes to call on the family. Enraged and repulsed by the prospect of a respected indigenous healer treating his ailing wife, a young newlywed chases the African doctor away. Finally, Luc, a young French "hippie," who has joined a crew of African workers hired to build the runway, offends both Europeans and Africans in his efforts to "go native," ungraciously invading the servants' space (to dine and shower) while seizing every opportunity to taunt the sexually frustrated commandant's wife.

The long flashback segment of the film draws to a close following a definitive scene in which Protée, left to watch over Aimée and the child in the commandant's absence, rebukes the European woman's sexual advances. When she retaliates by having him banned from the house, he transfers his sense of betrayal to the child who has until that time been primarily in his charge, thus signalling the gulf of cultural misunderstanding separating them. As the plane bearing the house guests finally departs, marking not only the end of their stay in Cameroon, but symbolically the end of the colonial era, the scene shifts back to the present. After discovering that the man who gave her a lift is actually an African American who shares her feelings of estrangement in Africa, France waits in the terminal while three workers load baggage onto a plane. The film ends with this awkward, enigmatic sequence, as the sound track is gradually taken over by disturbingly loud and repetitive African instrumental music.

Thus summarized, the film appears in many respects to do little more than mimetically reproduce the colonial world view. For example, the characters are allotted the stereotypical roles reserved for Africans and white Europeans under imperial rule: non-Europeans figure in the film primarily as house servants and manual laborers, while Europeans are assigned roles as government officials, missionaries, or plantation owners. Furthermore, the role of Protée, particularly as interpreted by the immensely attractive actor, Isaach de Bankolé, seems to play up the threat to white male subjectivity posed by the black male body. According to Fanon's psychoanalytic paradigm of racial relations, the black male, constructed by the dominant gaze, finds his image objectified by his institutionalized other, the white man, who renders visible his fear of Otherness by stressing the overpresence of skin color as a conveniently accessible sign of excessive sexual power (Fanon, 116). It could be argued that, by devoting extensive footage to the silent, seemingly inscrutable, yet physically imposing Protée, the film encourages the myth of black sexual prowess, itself a manifestation of the sexualization of racism.

Underscoring the effects of gender restrictions and sexual subordination on women, Aimée (whose name translates into English as the female-gendered, passive term 'loved one') is in many ways also the product of the objectifying masculine gaze. Female sexuality in *Chocolat* is in large measure rendered specular, thus excluding the woman character from occupying a place as subject within the film's signifying system. Here, I invoke Laura Mulvey's well-known analysis of visual pleasure in mainstream narrative cinema in order to acknowledge the extent to which the cinematic codes Denis calls upon may function, at some level, to reify the structures of looking that have produced the conventional cinematic representation of women as objects of male desire (See Mulvey, *passim*).[1] The image of Aimée's smoldering sexuality certainly serves as both a forceful and familiar undercurrent running throughout the flashback segments of the film. Her status as "(passive) raw material for the (active) gaze of man" (Mulvey, 38) is nowhere more clearly delineated than in the scene in which the growing antagonism between Protée and Luc erupts into physical violence, as they perform the role of rivals laying claim to the "bearer of male desire."

Denis's filmmaking, then, in many significant ways, works within the codes governing mainstream cinema in its representation of sexual and racial others. Embodying the dominant presence of black men in the film, Protée projects an image that appears designed to evoke simultaneously the fear and desire that Homi Bhabha identifies as the fundamental ambivalence linking the colonial subject to the colonized other (Bhabha, 78). Similarly, the prevailing images of white women in the film (again allied with a single, major character functioning metonymically as a representative of her race, class, and gender) seem to be shaped by the structuring norm of (white) heterosexual masculinity. And finally, it should be noted if only in passing, that black women are all but invisible in the film, no doubt offering proof of Mary Ann Doane's hypothesis that their doubly marginalized position effectively erases them as a meaningful category of cinematic moment (Doane, 231).

The extent to which Denis is staying within the limits of established norms becomes clearer when *Chocolat* is compared to certain experimental films of Marguerite Duras set in colonial times that, through the use of avant-garde cinematographic techniques, constitute a more obvious challenge to sexual and racial stereotypes. Duras has acknowledged that, as a female child growing up in a very poor family in French Indochina, she openly identified with the Vietnamese who were oppressed under French colonial rule. Reflecting this fundamental disavowal of difference, her films continually inhibit the establishment of oppositional categories by substituting visual absence for the scopic regime upon which the legitimacy of patriarchal authority is predicated. In a thoughtful summary of the more radical aspects of Duras's filmmaking, Christine Holmlund writes, "[In Duras's films] sexual and racial/ethnic differences are linked, and Western and Oriental women's voices are privileged. . . . Moreover, because . . . sounds, not images, organize the narrative, it is difficult to use visible difference to legitimate power . . ." (Holmlund, 10).[2]

Denis, on the other hand, underscores the visual, through her almost self-conscious shot composition, her frugal use of dialogue, and above all, her adoption of point-of-view storytelling, creating a recognizable Bildungsroman that relies for its narrativizing force on what the child (and later young adult) sees (or fails to see). Yet, despite the obvious ways in which *Chocolat* seems to reproduce imperialist, paternalistic discourse, I would like to argue that the filmmaker ultimately succeeds in challenging that discourse by introducing potentially destabilizing play into the narrative process. There are several ways in which the film undermines prevailing hegemony, not by proposing a radical dismantling of ideologically tinged structuring codes, but by exposing the shaky foundations of those codes.

First, by underscoring Aimée's contradictory position as both subordinated woman under patriarchy *and* figure of authority under colonial rule, Denis interrogates the functioning of the "dominant gaze"
as it has been analyzed by feminist film theorists. In asserting the need
for a critical model that takes into account the historical role played by
race, class, and gender in determining subjectivity and agency in colonial texts, Jenny Sharpe argues: "The domestic woman is not the
source of female agency nor the passive repository of the domesticated
but exists at the intersection of the two as a precarious and unstable
subjectivity. The contradictions to white femininity are more evident in
a colonial context where the . . . woman, oscillating between a dominant position of race and a subordinate one of gender, has a restricted
access to colonial authority" (Sharpe, 12).

The film, in fact, draws attention to Aimée's oscillating position,
and by extension, the precarious place assigned to the black man
within the racist representational economy. Although the gender restrictions to which Aimée must submit as the wife of a colonial official
in post–World War II Africa are obvious (she is confined to the domestic sphere but appears to have few domestic responsibilities; she is
dependent on her husband and, in his absence, Protée, for physical
protection), it is also clear that she can always fall back on her
unchallenged claim to colonial authority. Following a number of sequences establishing the sexual tension between Aimée and Protée,
signalled by a series of prolonged exchanged glances between the
two, Aimée temporarily withdraws from the potentially dangerous situation by rudely ordering Protée to leave her room and fetch water for
her bath. What follows is a loosely articulated series of shower scenes
offering insights into the film's intelligent treatment of the fundamental
link between seeing, knowing, and power. In the first of these scenes,
Protée fills the cistern and then stands outside the house silently
watching the flow of soapy water that is the only visual marker of
Aimée's otherwise unseen shower. Soon after, Aimée passes by as the
nude Protée is showering behind the house near the servants' quarters.
Acutely aware of the compromising consequences of *having been
seen*, Protée grimaces and bangs his head against the wall. In a complicated reversal of the conventional gendered positions of seeing and
being seen, the female character is able to close herself off from the
look of the (black) male, while he remains susceptible to her controlling gaze.

The debilitating effects for women of being cast in the role of the
bearer of the look have been well documented by feminist critics.
According to Gwen Bergner, for example, "The masculine gaze displaces

the anxiety of lack onto women by objectifying their images, silencing their voices, rendering their sexuality spectacular—in sum excluding them from occupying a place as subject within scopic systems of signification" (Bergner, 79). In an article on masculinity in mainstream cinema, Steve Neale suggests that because the spectatorial look in film is usually implicitly male, "erotic elements involved in the relations between the spectator and the male image have constantly to be repressed and disavowed" (Neale, 15). Citing instances in mainstream films in which the male body is presented as the object of the erotic gaze (e.g., the image of John Travolta's body in *Saturday Night Fever*), Neale argues that in those sequences in which the look is marked as female, the male body is feminized.[3] When, therefore, Protée is forced to submit to the gaze that makes his own sexuality into a spectacle, the results may be even more dramatically harmful, for the black man "may experience the system as additionally destructive to his masculine identity since he is forced to submit to the dismembering gaze that is normatively a male prerogative" (Bergner, 80).

The series of shower scenes in *Chocolat* includes a third sequence that further disrupts the "normative" models as defined under the scopic regime. During one of the extended absences of her husband, Aimée receives a visit from a British friend named Jonathan Boothby. Eager to counter her boredom, Aimée seems ready to accept his harmless sexual advances. Jonathan's credibility as a potential lover, however, is quickly compromised when he is observed taking a shower by a group of black servant women. As they giggle while making derisive comments about this white man's "odd" physical characteristics (for example, he is far too hairy for African tastes), Boothby is transformed for the spectator into an object of curiosity and ridicule. Turning the tables on Western habits of exoticizing the Other, this segment (one of the few in the film that even imagines an African point of view) effectively marginalizes the white European male.

Finally, in a scene that occurs toward the end of the flashback sequence, Luc arrogantly flaunts his freedom to "go native" by using the servants' outdoor shower. Because he is white, his nudity does not leave him vulnerable to the white woman's dominant gaze, but rather constitutes an aggressive challenge to the volatile attraction he intuits between Protée and Aimée. Infuriated by Luc's flagrant exploitation of his social mobility (he can "play at" being black at will, while Protée is obliged to masquerade in the role of "houseboy" as defined by his colonizers), Protée warns him ominously that he has overstepped his bounds. By clearly marking this territory (what he refers to as "la douche des boys"/"the houseboys' shower") as off limits, Protée lays claim to a physical and social space to which he has earned existential squatting rights.

When considered in the light of the disorienting race and gender dynamics called into play in these related segments, the implications of the pivotal scene in which Protée rejects Aimée's advances, become clearer. In discussing the making of the film, Denis herself has acknowledged the central importance of this scene: "I was strongly advised to construct an affair between Protée . . . and the white woman. The producers saw this outcome as good box office. But this would have totally destroyed what the film was about for me, so I resisted the pressure to alter the script. When it came to doing the scene in which Protée resists the possibility of a sexual encounter with the woman I shot it quickly in one take, before anyone could even attempt to suggest an alternative. I know this was a big disappointment for the production company, because they really wanted me to re-shoot the scene and to change it, but Protée's refusal *was the purpose of the film*" (as cited in *Screening Europe*, 67, my emphasis). Denis's own resistance to conventional narrative solutions is a significant clue to the alternative strategies she is proposing. By refusing a sexual relationship with the European woman, Protée resists his own feminization, with all its debilitating consequences. Underscoring the white woman's simultaneous status as passive image of "whiteness" as well as active agent of white power, the scene provides an empowering image of Protée defiantly turning his back on this invitation to have his subjectivity effaced. Courageously returning the gaze, he challenges the structures of power that have sought to neutralize his own looking privileges.[4] At this point in the film, of course, Protée's metonymic relationship with colonial and postcolonial Africa becomes clear. Later, his gesture will find its echo in the rejection "France" encounters when she returns to the home that, in fact, was never hers.

Because cinema is constructed around a series of images, it is commonly understood that all films enjoy a "uniquely optic narrative logic" (Doane, 214). As I stated earlier, the act of looking as a primary concern in *Chocolat*, above and beyond its status as a constitutive element of the medium, is established by the repeated insistence on the motif of seeing and spectatorship. According to film theorist Christian Metz, although cinema appears to be more perceptual than other arts, because of its reliance on visual images, it is in fact decidedly less perceptual, since the perceptions it sets in motion are all ultimately "false," which is to say constructed representations projected on a screen. The spectator, however, is lulled into forgetting the presence of the mediating technology in order to finally identify himself (and I use

the male pronoun as a pointed reminder of Metz's failure to acknowledge gender differences in his analysis) as "pure act of perception"
(Metz, 735). In contrast, when the look of the spectator must pass
through the look of an out-of-frame character, it becomes more difficult
for the spectator in the theater to cling to his belief in his unmediated
visual experience. I would like to suggest that the way in which Denis
manipulates this technique in *Chocolat*, by disrupting the "normal" process of identification as defined by Metz, eventually subverts the authority traditionally accorded the dominant, in this case imperialist, gaze.

A brief description of the camera work in several key scenes will
illustrate my point. The opening sequence of the film, shot from a
distance, shows a black man and boy playing in the ocean. As they
frolic in the water, they eventually run out of the frame. Panning to the
right, the camera picks up a white woman, whose distant form, seated
on a sandy beach, is framed off-center as she watches the two black
figures. The ensuing shot, focusing on the glistening dark skin of the
man and boy, is initially difficult to decipher, since it is taken as an
extreme close-up and at a disorienting angle (reminiscent of the opening shots of Alain Resnais's *Hiroshima mon amour*). Unable to read the
image easily, the spectator is left with an overall impression of the
contrast between light and dark through the juxtaposition of the dark
skin against the white sand. Since the camera has cut from the watching
woman to the man and boy, a technique suggesting the shot is taken
from a character's point of view, the spectator is encouraged to conclude that the viewer, who cannot retain the images in her field of
vision, is incapable of imposing a reading on them. Later, as she rides
along in the car, the rapidly passing countryside also eludes her visual
control. Although she tries to catch at least a glimpse of a familiar
landscape, she (and we) see little more than a jumble of fleeting images.

Throughout the flashback sequences, the spectator continues to be
placed in the position of a tourist, a foreigner with limited understanding
of the host country language or culture. There are several long panning
shots in which characters gradually move out of the frame, leaving the
camera to focus seemingly at random on generic African terrain. Because these shots are usually longer than those typically serving as
informational, establishing shots or providing exotic, local color, and
because the landscapes depicted are often largely undistinguished, they
function as a tugging counterpoint to the narrative line. In fact, such
unintelligible shots do not help establish meaning, but rather shake the
grounds upon which narrative control is normally founded.

Toward the end of the film, following the scene in which Protée
rejects Aimée's advances, there is a series of unconnected shots that

signal a growing lack of cohesion, a sort of hegemonic meltdown. A shot of Protée looking out at the countryside is followed by an image of France's parents sitting inside their house, then one of the child eating alone, and finally the camera cuts to a group of African men praying. The next scene forwarding the narrative proper marks simultaneously the final stage in the breakup of the particular "colonial romance" whose history the film traces and the beginning of the end of the colonial presence in Cameroon. As Protée repairs a generator, France asks him if a nearby pipe is too hot to touch. When he answers by placing his hand on the pipe, she stares in his unwavering eyes, does the same and then immediately draws back with a cry to reveal her severely burned skin. Soon after, when the stranded airplane passengers finally take off from the completed runway, a sober France with a large white bandage wrapped around her injured hand, stands beside her parents silently watching the takeoff.

While these scenes do not overtly interject the point of view of a character who is present, but beyond the scope of the camera, they do serve as a reminder that the film's narrative takes the form of a frame story. In this case, then, the spectator's perspective is mediated and displaced not physically, but rather temporally by the retrospective gaze of the filmmaker's stand-in: the disoriented young woman confronting her guilt through a critical appraisal of her childhood memories. Although the spectator sees the child unconsciously assuming her right to colonial power (she autocratically issues orders to Protée and on one occasion calls him a "sale nègre"/ "dirty nigger"), the camera often betrays the superficial illusion of dominance and control, suggesting the debilitating effects of cultural blindness. Because the camera is unable to offer a coherent image of the African countryside, the spectator becomes aware the colonizers are doomed to failure in imposing meaning on a people and culture that continually prevent them from successfully engaging in Metz's "pure act of perception."

The final scene, in which the three African airport baggage loaders are shown in several inordinately long takes during which the largely immobile camera simply registers from a considerable distance their mundane activities (they are talking, laughing, putting items onto a conveyor belt), ends the film on a decidedly pessimistic note. Unable to produce a coherent picture of colonial Africa, because the European colonizers' assumptions of their own cultural insularity and blind belief in their superiority prevented them from actually *seeing* the continent or its peoples, the filmmaker also fails to achieve a reconciliation with post-independence Cameroon. As the repetitive instrumental music takes over the sound track, the spectator is left with a profound impression of physical and temporal displacement. Although in close proximity, the three Cameroonians and the young European woman are separated in cinematographic terms by successive film frames that seem to stand for an irreparable cultural and historical disconnect prohibiting any conventional narrative conclusion. Rather than completely suppressing the existence of African perspectives and experiences or dismissing their importance, the film concludes with the realization that, at least for the moment, these experiences are inaccessible to the European outsider, France, whose name encourages the spectator to generalize her situation. The film's final message is that Europeans who have failed to come to terms with their colonial past are condemned to view the present-day continent from the margins.

In its unsentimentally detached approach, *Chocolat* breaks with the trend represented by a recent crop of films that nostalgically romanticize the past (for example, Tornatore's conservative idealization of the simple, rural life in *Cinema Paradiso* and Jean-Jacques Annaud's exoticizing portrait of French Indochina in his adaptation of Marguerite Duras's novel, *The Lover*). It is ultimately Denis's politically self-conscious camera that challenges the appeal to timeless differences (of race, class, and gender), furnishing the ideological foundations for the aesthetics that make the films cited above "work" so well. By refusing a nostalgic attachment to those immutable differences, Denis must content herself with telling the story of her own (and her fellow Europeans') failure to achieve (narrative) mastery in a postcolonial world.

Notes

1. While I am of course aware of the cogent critiques that have come in the wake of Mulvey's analysis of the male gaze, as well as Mulvey's own revision of her argument, I believe her general assumption of a fundamental link between heterosexual male desire and the prevailing paradigms for fictional film narrative remains persuasive.

2. Holmlund bases her argument on three of Marguerite Duras's experimental films: *India Song* (1975), *Son nom de Venise dans Calcutta désert* (1976), and *Les mains négatives* (1979). Although citing the progressive strategies deployed in these films, Holmlund nevertheless concedes that Duras does not completely avoid the exotic, essentialist clichés that mark the treatment of sexual and racial difference in mainstream cinema.

3. Neale seems to be implying that feminization precedes the engagement of the look, while my point is that, given the dynamics of the screen, the object of the eroticizing gaze is necessarily placed in a feminized, which is to say, weakened position.

4. While Jean-Paul Sartre speculated about the compromising effects on the white man's privileged vision produced by the transgressive act of the black man looking back, neither he nor Fanon considered the implications of the black man's return of the white woman's imperialist, eroticizing gaze. When the confrontation is displaced from the drama of the white male ego, whose claim to the gaze has been largely uncontested, the "naturalness" of the defining positions and categories is called into question. Once again, I refer the reader to Mary Ann Doane's cogent discussion of the complex relationship between visibility, skin color, and identity at issue in any analysis of the treatment of race and gender in film.

Works Cited

Ang, Ien. "Hegemony-in-Trouble: Nostalgia and the Ideology of the Impossible in European Cinema." *Screening Europe: Image and Identity in Contemporary European Cinema.* Ed. Duncan Petrie. London: British Film Institute, 1992, 21–31.

Bhabha, Homi. "The Other Question: Difference, Discrimination, and the Discourse of Colonialism." *Out There: Marginalization and Contemporary Culture.* Ed. Russell Ferguson, Martin Gever, Trinh T. Minh-ha, Cornel West. New York: New Museum of Contemporary Art, 1990, 71–87.

Bergner, Gwen. "Who Is That Masked Woman? The Role of Gender in Fanon's *Black Skin, White Masks.*" *PMLA* 110 (1995): 75–88.

Doane, Mary Ann. "Dark Continents: Epistemologies of Racial and Sexual Difference in Psychoanalysis and the Cinema." *Femmes Fatales.* New York: Routledge, 1991, 209–248.

Fanon, Franz. *Black Skin, White Masks.* Trans. Charles Lam Markmann. New York: Grove Press, 1967.

Hall, Stuart. "European Cinema on the Verge of a Nervous Breakdown." *Screening Europe: Image and Identity in Contemporary European Cinema.* Ed. Duncan Petrie. London: British Film Institute, 1992, 45–53.

Holmlund, Christine Anne. "Displacing Limits of Difference: Gender, Race, and Colonialism in Edward Said and Homi Bhabha's Theoretical Models and Marguerite Duras's Experimental Films." *Quarterly Review of Film and Video* 13:1–22.

Metz, Christian. "The Imaginary Signifier." *Film Language: A Semiotics of the Cinema.* Trans. Michael Taylor. Oxford: Oxford UP, 1974. Rpt. in *Film Theory and Criticism.* Ed. Gerald Mast, Marshall Cohen, and Leo Braudy. New York: Oxford UP, 1992, 730–745.

Mulvey, Laura. "Visual Pleasure and Narrative Cinema." *Screen* 16. Rpt. in *Film Theory and Criticism.* Ed. Gerald Mast, Marshall Cohen, and Leo Braudy. New York: Oxford UP 1992, 746–757.

Neale, Steve. "Masculinity as Spectacle: Reflections on Men and Mainstream Cinema." *Screen.* November–December 1983: 2–16.

Sharpe, Jenny. *Allegories of Empire: The Figure of Woman in the Colonial Text.* Minneapolis: U of Minnesota P, 1993.

12

Cette enfant blanche de L'Asie

Orientalism, Colonialism, and Métissage
in Marguerite Duras's L'Amant

Jeanne Garane

*Elle aurait parlé de beaucoup de choses, de la géographie des lieux traversés,
de la fin du monde, de la mort. . . . Ces propos n'auraient jamais relevé
d'une connaissance précise du problème abordé. Elle aurait fait des
erreurs—parfois énormes—sur . . . la géographie. . . .*

—Marguerite Duras, Le Camion

*[She might have spoken of many things, of the geography of the areas
crossed, of the end of the world, of death. . . . These words might never
have resulted from a precise knowledge of the problem at hand. She might
have made mistakes—some-times enormous—about . . . geography.]*

The following essay is part of a larger study that examines the links
between the construction of subjectivity and geography in a set of post/
colonial female autographs.[1] This project explores the links between
identity and space for women in the context of colonialism as spatial
appropriation and writing as textual reappropriation, and the ways in
which identity and spatial constructions are grounded in cultural and
political locations of "France" beyond the hexagon. Specifically, I focus

on the figure of the mother in the daughter's text, as she is variously cast as colonizer, colonized, and/or native land. Through metaphors of geography and space, postcolonial autographs investigate the relation of the female self to the mother as origin and generative locus. At the same time, such texts enlist "cartographic"[2] representations to name, map, and/or silence. Drawing on Walter Mignolo's notion of "colonial semiosis," that "conflictive domain of semiotic interactions among members of radically different cultures engaged in a struggle of imposition and appropriation, on the one hand, and of resistance, opposition and adaptation on the other,"[3] I enlarge Said's notion and posit a gendered cartographic that produces a female identity constructed in relation to colonized space. Thus, Said's cartographic—the remapping of (de-) colonized territories in order to reclaim appropriated cultural, linguistic, and literary constructs—becomes gendered when post/colonial women writers cast colonized space as maternal *arrière-pays*.[4] So doing, they link the maternal as the "idealized relation"[5] to the mother, to the (gendered) cartographic as an idealized relation. Colonialism then becomes synonymous with the appropriation of an original/originating space or "mother land" that echoes the daughter's primary expulsion from the mother at birth. As a result, writing reinscribes space as maternal through geographical metaphors, and articulates the constitution of the self over time (the auto-graph) and in space (the carto-graph).

In *The Lover*, the hybridized narrator cartographically constitutes Southern Indochina as the "pays natal" (homeland).[6] It is the place from which she emerges as a writer and the place from which she must be permanently exiled in order to write. While the distance from the mother/land enables the daughter to construct a psychological *arrière-pays* that enables writing, it is at the expense of the native inhabitants, whose objectification and/or erasure have been virtually unquestioned until recently.[7]

∞

"Je n'ai vu s'inscrire de la féminité que par Colette, Marguerite Duras . . . et Jean Genet" (The only inscriptions of femininity that I have seen were by Colette, Marguerite Duras, . . . and Jean Genet), declares Hélène Cixous in *Le Rire de la Méduse*.[8] According to Cixous's definition of *écriture féminine* as revolutionary writing, Duras's texts should constitute "l'espace d'où peut s'élancer une pensée subversive—le mouvement avant-coureur d'une transformation des structures sociales et culturelles ("Rire" 42) (the space that can serve as a springboard for subversive thought, the precursory movement of a transformation of social and cultural structures) ("Laugh," 249). Indeed, "durassian space" has been celebrated for its subversive qualities, where the undermining of the sovereign subject is carried out on such shifting terrains as "la grande plaine de boue et de riz du sud de la Cochinchine, celle des Oiseaux" *(Amant,* 17) (the great plain of mud and rice in southern Cochin China. The Plain of the Birds) (*Lover,* 10). Claude Roy calls this textual landscape "la Durasie," (Durasia)[9] while Marcelle Marini's voyage "au pays de Marguerite" (to the country of Marguerite) produces a map of Duras's territoires of the *féminin* as "un lieu radicalement autre" (a radically other space) (*Territoires,* 62). Following an errant itinerary in search of a textual "passage du plein au vide" (passage from fullness to emptiness),[10] Duras's texts inscribe a theory and practice of writing as "différance," where narrative closure is constantly deferred, and should thereby challenge what Derrida calls the "imperialism of the Logos."[11]

Duras's continual rewriting of her texts—the intertextual nature of much of her *oeuvre*—truly undermines narrative closure. As Madeleine Borgomano writes, "l'intertextualité déplace, dérange le sens prêt à se figer, relance la production, ouvre grand la clôture" (intertextuality displaces, disturbs meaning as it is ready to become fixed, revives writing, opens closure wide).[12] *L'Amant* is certainly no exception to this durassian rule. By rewriting and modifying events, characters, and locations encountered in earlier narratives, *L'Amant* constructs new spaces by rearranging the perimeters of prior texts.

In *Les Lieux de Marguerite Duras,* the writer recounts her mother's "colonization" by French colonial officials in Indochina and Cambodia in the 1930s. She tells Michelle Porte,

> on a vu [la mère] arriver seule, veuve, sans défenseur, complètement isolée et on lui a collé une terre incultivable. Elle l'ignorait complètement, qu'il fallait soudoyer les agents du cadastre pour avoir une terre cultivable. On lui a donné une terre, c'était une terre envahie par l'eau pendant six mois de l'année. Et elle a mis là-dedans vingt ans d'économie. Elle a donc fait construire ce bungalow, elle a semé, elle a repiqué le riz, au bout de trois mois le Pacifique est monté et on a été ruinés. Et elle a failli mourir, elle a déraillé à ce moment-là, elle a fait des crises épileptiformes. Elle a perdu la raison. On a cru qu'elle allait mourir.
>
> (they saw [my mother] arrive alone, a widow, with no defender, completely alone and they stuck her with an unworkable piece of land. She had no idea that she was supposed to bribe the cadastral agents in order to have workable land. She was given a plot, it was

a plot invaded by water six months of the year. And she put twenty years' savings into it. So she had this bungalow built, she sowed, she planted out the rice, after three months the Pacific rose and we were ruined. She almost died, she went crazy at that point, she had epileptic fits. She lost her mind. We thought she was going to die.)[13]

This story is retold in all of the works that draw upon Duras's childhood, and *L'Amant* is no exception. Yet in *L'Amant*, it is greatly condensed:

> Quand je suis sur le bac de Mékong ce jour de la limousine noire, la concession du barrage n'a pas encore été abandonnée par ma mère. (35)

> (When I'm on the Mekong ferry, the day of the black limousine, my mother hasn't yet given up the land by the dike.) (26)

> Ça a été long. Ça a duré sept ans. . . . Et puis enfin l'espoir a été renoncé. Il a été abandonné. Abandonnées aussi les tentatives contre l'océan. . . . La mère est enfin calme, murée. Nous sommes des enfants héroïques, désespérés. (70–71)

> (It lasted all that age, seven years. And then finally hope was given up. Abandoned. Like the struggles against the sea. . . . My mother is quiet at last, mute. We, her children, are heroic, desperate.) (56)

This condensation of what was initially the matter of an entire novel (*Un Barrage contre le Pacifique*), part of a novel (*Le Vice-consul*), as well as a play (*L'Eden cinéma*),[14] opens new perspectives on the effects of the mother's ruin on the family, "ce que nous sommes devenus à partir du spectacle de son désespoir" (69) (what was going to become of us as a result of witnessing her despair) (55). Indeed, the narrator states that this particular text will try yet again to tell a story "qui m'est encore inaccessible, cachée au plus profond de ma chair, aveugle comme un nouveau-né du premier jour" (34) (which I still can't understand however hard I try, which is still beyond my reach, hidden in the very depths of my flesh, blind as a newborn child) (25).

This continued attempt to understand the past by rewriting it creates, as the narrator observes, "silences" (35) rather than explanations. Madeleine Borgomano calls Duras's repeated rewriting of the same story "textual hybridization," a practice that indeed effectively undermines the "imperialism of the Logos," for each subsequent modification prevents any of the texts from congealing into a definitive version. Nevertheless, the question remains: does Duras's textual hybridization challenge the imperialist imposition of Western constructs on non-Western places? Given a critical tradition that recognizes the Durassian text as a space where repressive structures are dislocated and questioned, if never completely overthrown, as Marini points out throughout *Les Territoires du féminin*, it is pertinent to study not only textual hybridity, but also the political implications of the narrator's cultural, and quasi-biological, hybridization. This essay thus examines the ways in which durassian writing as open-ended "différance" is linked in *L'Amant* to the narrator's search for "difference" through a hybridization of cultural and racial identity, even as the process of hybridization described there echoes imperialist theories of miscegenation as "contamination." This double-voiced discourse underscores the narrator's ambiguous position both as anticolonialist and as belonging to the colonizing group. Indeed, while the narrator uses her Chinese lover to undermine her own identity as a white colonist, a move that subsequently threatens the (imaginary) racial identities of other whites in the Indochinese colony, she also "colonizes" him by (textually) transforming him into an Orientalized (m)other. Meanwhile, the mad beggar woman remains an absolute Other who threatens to obliterate the narrator's identity by "contaminating" her with insanity.

The retrospective portrait of the artist as young hybrid that appears in *L'Amant* supplements the more familiar durassian idealization of the mythical "Wandering Jew" as Other. For Duras, "les Juifs sont des gens qui partent et qui en partant, emportent leur pays natal et pour qui celui-ci est plus présent, plus violent que s'ils ne l'avaient jamais quitté" (Jews are people who leave and who, in leaving, take their homeland with them and for whom the homeland is more present, more violent than if they had never left it).[15] Like the narrator of *L'Amant* who declares that she is someone who will "partir de partout" (103) (go away from everywhere) (83), and who celebrates "les départs sur les mers" (departures over the sea) (108) of "les hommes, . . . les juifs, les hommes de la pensée et les purs voyageurs du seul voyage sur la mer," (132) (men . . . Jews, philosophers, and pure travelers for the journey's own sake) (108–109), Duras compares herself to "the Jews," for "everything that in wandering, I took with me, has become even stronger by having been far away, absent."[16] The celebration of absence/errancy figured by the "Wandering Jew" corresponds to the durassian quest to inscribe open-endedness and non-presence in order to liberate the text from a repressive verisimilitude and release it to the imaginary.

Related to this esthetics of absence is Duras's theory of "false memory." In the introduction to *India Song*, Duras celebrates the "deforming," "creative" nature of memory and forgetfulness. "L'oubli," she writes, leaves the text "à la disposition d'autres mémoires que celle de l'auteur: mémoires qui se souviendraient partiellement de n'importe

quelle autre histoire d'amour"[17] (Forgetfulness leaves the text at the
disposal of memories other than those of the author: memories that
would partially remember any other love story). This dialectic of memory
and forgetfulness is emblematic of writing itself as "différance," "cet
oubli de soi, cette extériorisation, le contraire de la mémoire
intériorisante," says Derrida, both "mnémnotéchnique et puissance de
l'oubli" *(Grammatologie,* 39) (that forgetting of the self, that exterior-
ization, the contrary of the interiorizing memory . . . at once
mnemotechnique and the power of forgetting) *(Grammatology,* 24). In
L'Amant, "self-forgetfulness" replaces the figure of the Jew with that of
the hybrid, and (re-) constructs Indochina as the territory of hybridity,
the cartographic *arrière-pays* that serves as a nostalgic backdrop in the
narrator's constitution of her identity as a writer in exile, neither European nor Asian.

Hybridity has been theorized as being synonymous with an indeterminacy and undecideability that can undermine hegemonic structures, since it deconstructs the myths of racial and cultural "purity."[18] In
"Carnal Knowledge and Imperial Power,"[19] Ann Laura Stoler demonstrates that in colonial Indochina, white prestige depended on maintaining these myths intact, while miscegenation, synonymous with degeneracy and "cultural contamination," (72) "represented the paramount
danger to racial purity and cultural identity in all its forms" (78). Myths
of cultural "purity" were not only racist; they were gender and class-
specific as well. Bourgeois European women were crucial to the bol-
stering of white prestige and were charged with maintaining the social
rituals of racial difference. On the other hand, a European proletariat,
and poor white women in particular, be they married, widowed, or
divorced, were seen as the "quintessential 'petit blanc' " for they presented "the dangerous possibility that straitened circumstances would
lead them to prostitution, thereby degrading European prestige at large"
("Carnal," 71) by blurring divisions between colonizer and colonized.

According to Duras, more than any of the white women she knew
in Indochina, her mother was "plus près de n'importe quelle paysanne
vietnamienne" (closer to any Vietnamese peasant woman) (*Lieux,* 56)
not only because she herself was from peasant stock, but more importantly because

> nous étions très très pauvres et qu'elle avait un emploi tout à fait
> parmi les derniers là-bas, voyez—avec les douaniers, les postiers,
> c'étaient les instituteurs des écoles indigènes qui étaient les derniers
> Blancs—,elle était beaucoup plus proche des Vietnamiens, des
> Annamites, que des autres Blancs.

(we were very, very poor and because she had a job that was entirely among the lowest over there, you see—with the customs workers, the postmen, it was the teachers in the native schools who were the lowest Whites—, she was much closer to the Viet-namese, to the Annamese, than to other Whites.) (56)

In *L'Amant*, the mother's hybridity is registered in the way she wears her hair: "ses cheveux sont tirés et serrés dans un chignon de Chinoise" (32) (her hair's drawn back tight into a bun like a Chinese woman's) (23). By joining the ranks of the "natives" the mother's (European) identity is blurred and reduced to a monolithic image: "all of them" have the same "erased" attitude. This erasure is foreshadowed in an earlier passage where the mother's identity is obliterated by madness:

C'était à quelques mois de notre séparation définitive. . . . J'ai regardé ma mère. Je l'ai mal reconnue. Et puis, dans une sorte d'effacement soudain, de chute, brutalement, je ne l'ai plus reconnue du tout. . . . L'épouvante . . . venait de ce qu'elle était assise là même où était assise ma mère lorsque la substitution s'était produite . . . cette identité qui n'était remplaçable par aucune autre avait disparu et que j'étais sans aucun moyen de faire qu'elle revienne. . . . Rien ne se proposait plus pour habiter l'image. Je suis devenue folle en pleine raison. (104–106)

(It was a few months before our final parting. . . . I looked at my mother, I could hardly recognize her. And then, in a kind of sudden vanishing, a sudden fall, I all at once couldn't recognize her at all. . . . My terror . . . came from the fact that she was sitting just where my mother had been sitting when the substitution took place . . . that that identity irreplaceable by any other had disap-peared and I was powerless to make it come back. . . . There was no longer anything there to inhabit her image. I went mad in full possession of my senses.) (85–86)

In the tropics during the colonial period, madness was precisely one of the factors thought to lead to hybridity. In this passage, the erasure of (European) identity and its substitution by an (empty) other echoes the colonialist notion that people who stayed "too long" in the tropics were in grave danger not only of overfatigue and mental breakdown, but "of individual and racial degeneration; of physical breakdown (not just illness); of cultural contamination and neglect of the conventions of supremacy" ("Carnal," 76). In *L'Amant*, the mother's neglect of these conventions is reflected in her "abandonment" of the children. In one passage, the narrator contemplates "cette femme d'une certaine photographie, . . . ma mère" (21) (the woman in another photograph, my mother) (13). While this photo predates the sea wall disaster, the narrator recognizes her mother's subsequent "grand découragement à vivre . . . cette façon, justement, qu'elle avait, tout à coup, de ne plus pouvoir nous laver, de ne plus nous habiller, et parfois même de ne plus nous nourrir" (22) (deep despondency about living . . . the way she'd suddenly be unable to wash us, to dress us, or sometimes even feed us) (14).

In *L'Amant*, the mother's "absences," her "abandonment" of the two younger children allow them greater contact with the local peasants, with local culture, and with the countryside itself. They swim in the "rac," hunt in the forest, and because of their poverty, eat foraged food. In one passage, the narrator sarcastically recollects the family's attempt to assert its "white" privilege when faced with the assimilating power of poverty. Speculating on the reasons for her "destroyed" face the narrator writes,

> On m'a souvent dit que c'était le soleil trop fort pendant toute l'enfance. . . . On me disait aussi que c'était la réflexion dans laquelle la misère plongeait les enfants. Mais non, ce n'est pas ça. Les enfants-vieillards de la faim endémique, oui, mais nous, non, nous n'avions pas faim, nous étions des enfants blancs, nous avions honte, nous vendions nos meubles, mais nous n'avions pas faim, nous avions un boy et nous mangions, parfois, il est vrai, des saloperies, des échassiers, des petits caïmans, mais ces saloperies étaient cuites par un boy et servies par lui et parfois aussi nous les refusions, nous nous permettions ce luxe de ne pas vouloir manger. (13)

> (I've often been told it was because of spending all one's childhood in too strong a sun. . . . I've also been told it was because being poor made us brood. But no, that wasn't it. Children like little old men because of chronic hunger, yes. But us, no, we weren't hungry. We were white children, we were ashamed, we sold our furniture, but we weren't hungry, we had a houseboy and we ate. Sometimes, admittedly, we ate garbage—storks, baby crocodiles—but the garbage was cooked and served by a houseboy, and sometimes we refused it, too, we indulged in the luxury of declining to eat.) (6–7)

Despite these efforts at maintaining a distance from the "natives" by displaying "white privilege," for the narrator and her family, poverty remained "le principal de notre vie" (75) (the ruling principle of our life) (60).

True to the fears of colonial authority, it is indeed "le lien avec la misère" (33) (the link with poverty) (24) that drives the mother to allow her daughter to go out dressed as a child prostitute, an act comparable to the mad "Indian" beggar woman's sale of her daughter for "the symbolic sum of one piastre."[20] The narrator's subsequent encounter

with the Chinese lover constitutes the ultimate infraction of white supremacist conventions in the colonies: sexual contact with a nonwhite,
for "racial degeneracy" was linked to the "sexual transmission of cultural contagions and to the political instability of imperial rule" ("Carnal," 72). Because of poverty, the family can no longer remain racially
and culturally separate from its surroundings; "la misère avait fait
s'écrouler les murs de la famille" (58) (poverty had knocked down the
walls of the family) (45) leaving it open to "outside" influences. The
result is that very "adaptation to local food, language, and dress" as the
source of cultural "contagion and [the] loss of (white) self" ("Carnal,"
78) so threatening to imperial authority.

On the ferry in the middle of the Mékong, the narrator sees herself
as "other" for the first time, "une autre serait vue, au-dehors, mise à la
disposition de tous, mise à la disposition de tous les regards, mise dans
la circulation des villes, des routes, du désir" (19–20) (as another would
be seen, outside myself, available to all, available to all eyes, in circulation for cities, journeys, desire) (13). That she consecrates her alterity
while in the middle of the river underscores her ambiguity. By getting
off of the bus and vacating the seat reserved for white passengers only
(16), she puts herself into "circulation," and enters a cultural flux. Her
gender (she wears a man's hat), her age (her "childish flaws" have been
transformed), and her "race" (the Chinese man is surprised to see a
white girl get off the "native" bus) blur and emphasize her hybridity.

But it is the narrator's affair with the Chinese man that completes the
process of hybridization. As Mireille Caille-Gruber notes, "point
protagoniste, . . . [l'amant] est moyen, passage. Il est miroir de la mutation
de Je et, de façon plus complexe, de Je se regardant devenir Autre dans
le regard de l'amant" (not a protagonist at all, . . . [the lover] is a means,
a way. He mirrors the metamorphosis of "I" and in a more complex
manner, of "I" watching herself become Other in the gaze of the lover)
(112). The narrator's alterity is constituted not only by the lover's gaze,
as Caille-Gruber suggests, but also by his touch. This is one reason why
the relationship between the narrator and her lover is cast in terms of
incest; as the narrator represents her lover as feminized "Other," he also
becomes the miscegenating (m)other whose touch "gives birth" to the
narrator-as-hybrid.

The (m)othering of the man from Cholen begins when the narrator
sets the conditions of the relationship. The Chinese man is "à sa merci"
(46) (at her mercy) (35) as she tells him, "je préférerais que vous ne
m'aimiez pas" (48) (I'd prefer you didn't love me) (37), a statement that
makes the Chinese man "suffer" (37). He is the object of her desire: "il
lui plaît, la chose ne dépendait que d'elle seule" (48) (she was attracted

to him. It depended on her alone) (37). Placed in a position of passivity, the lover is feminized. From object of pleasure (the lover's sexual skill is "comme une profession qu'il aurait" [54] [it's as if it were his profession] [42]), the lover becomes care giver: "Il me douche il me lave, il me rince, il adore, il me farde et il m'habille, il m'adore. Je suis la préférée de sa vie" (79) (He gives me my shower, washes me, rinses me, he adores that, he puts my makeup on and dresses me, he adores me. I'm the darling of his life) (63). At times, "il la lavera sous la douche . . . comme chaque soir elle faisait chez sa mère . . . et puis il la portera mouillée sur le lit" (112) (he'll wash her under the shower . . . as she used to wash herself at home at her mother's . . . and then he'll carry her, still wet, to the bed . . .) (91). Finally, she becomes his child: "J'étais devenue son enfant. C'était avec son enfant qu'il faisait l'amour chaque soir. . . . Il la prend comme il prendrait son enfant" (122–123) (I had become his child. It was with his own child he made love every evening. . . . He takes her as he would his own child) (100–101).

Indeed, as the lover looks at her, she is no longer a "petite blanche," (little white girl) (98), but has become a "jeune fille d'Indochine" (120) (a girl of Indochina) (98). Echoing metropolitan/imperialist theories on the "otherness" of the colonials themselves,[21] the man from Cholen also attributes her difference to the tropical climate, "cette intolérable latitude" (120) (this intolerable latitude) (98) and to adaptation to local customs of eating, bathing, and dressing. According to the lover,

> la croissance de la petite blanche a pâti dans cette chaleur trop forte. . . . Il dit que toutes ces années passées ici . . . ont fait qu'elle est devenue une jeune fille de ce pays de l'Indochine. Qu'elle a la finesse de leurs poignets, leurs cheveux drus dont on dirait qu'ils ont pris pour eux toute la force, longs comme les leurs, et surtout, cette peau, cette peau de tout le corps qui vient de l'eau de la pluie qu'on garde ici pour le bain des femmes, des enfants. Il dit que les femmes de France, à côté de celles-ci, ont la peau du corps dure, presque rêche. Il dit encore que la nourriture pauvre des Tropiques, faite de poissons, de fruits, y est aussi pour quelque chose. Et aussi les cotonnades et les soies dont les vêtements sont faits, toujours larges ces vêtements, qui laissent le corps loin d'eux, libre, nu (120).

> (the growth of the little white girl has been stunted by the excessive heat . . . .He says all the years she's spent here . . . have turned her into a girl of Indochina. That she has the same slender wrists as they, the same thick hair that looks as if it's absorbed all its owner's strength, and it's long like theirs too, and above all there's her skin, all over her body, that comes from the rainwater stored

here for women and children to bathe in. He says that compared with the women here the women in France have hard skins on their bodies, almost rough. He says the low diet of the tropics, mostly fish and fruit, has something to do with it too. Also the cottons and silks the clothes here are made of, and the loose clothes themselves, leaving a space between themselves and the body, leaving it naked, free.) (98–99)

The lover is thus truly a "faire-valoir, producteur pour la partenaire de valeurs et de significations nouvelles" (a foil, producing for his partner new values and meanings) (Caille-Gruber, 112). To be judged "unlike French women" is to be set apart from the colonial society that the narrator disdains. It is to be (purely) a victim of "le grand vampirisme colonial" (*Barrage*, 25) (the blood-sucking proclivities of colonialism) (*Sea Wall*, 19), "la crapulerie de cette engeance blanche de la colonie" (*L'Amant de la Chine du Nord*, 98) (the vileness of that white colonial scum) (89) rather than a perpetrator.

Exclusion from "the Same" of colonial society also allows the narrator to maintain the liberating alterity that she first discovered in the middle of the Mekong. When the mother suspects that her daughter has been sleeping with the man from Cholen, she suddenly begins to worry: "sa fille court le plus grand danger, celui de ne jamais se marier, de ne jamais s'établir dans la société, d'être démunie devant celle-ci, perdue, solitaire (73) (Her daughter's in the direst danger, the danger of never getting married, never having a place in society, of being defenseless against it, lost, alone) (58). Her fears are not unfounded. One day, her daughter's high school classmates will be ordered to no longer speak with her. Unable to marry in the colony, the narrator will remain "in circulation." Like Duras's mythical "wandering Jew," she will always be able to "go away from everywhere" in order to retain an "elsewhere" from which to write. Accordingly, the narrator associates writing with leaving: "Je veux écrire. Déjà je l'ai dit à ma mère: ce que je veux c'est ça, écrire . . . rien d'autre que ça, rien . . . Je serai la première à partir" (31) (what I wanted more than anything else in the world was to write, nothing else but that, nothing . . . I'll be the first to leave) (22).

Despite her rejection of the rules of colonial society, the narrator is unable to transcend the dynamics of power between colonizer and colonized, and becomes a racist hypocrite in her family's presence:

Mes frères ne lui adresseront jamais la parole. C'est comme s'il n'était pas visible pour eux. . . . Nous prenons tous modèle sur le frère aîné face à cet amant. Moi non plus, devant eux, je ne lui parle pas. (65)

(My brothers will never say a word to him, it's as if he were invisible to them ... .We all treat my lover as he does. I myself never speak to him in their presence. (51)

This collaboration places her "du côté de cette société qui a réduit ma mère au désespoir" (69) (on the side of the society which has reduced her to despair) (55). Nevertheless, despite the fact that the mother has been murdered (69) by colonial society the mother herself is not exempt from racist attitudes. In fact, she glorifies "les cultivateurs du Nord" (71) (the farmers in the North of France) (57), comparing her sons to them to the disfavor of the man from Cholen:

> Elle a toujours parlé de la force de ses fils de façon insultante. Pour le dehors, elle ne détaillait pas, elle ne disait pas que le fils aîné était beaucoup plus fort que le second, elle disait qu'il était aussi fort que ses frères, les cultivateurs du Nord. ... Comme son fils ainé, elle dédaignait les faibles. De mon amant de Cholen elle en disait comme le frère aîné. ... C'étaient des mots qui avaient trait aux charognes qu'on trouve dans les déserts. (71–72)

> (She always talked in an insulting way about her sons' strength. For the outside world, she didn't distinguish between them, she didn't say the elder son was much stronger than the younger, she said he was as strong as her brothers, the farmers in the North of France. ... Like her elder son, she looked down on the weak. Of my lover from Cholon she spoke in the same way as my elder brother. ... They were words that had to do with carrion you find in the desert.) (57)

While a victim of colonialism, the mother has also been indoctrinated by its theories of white superiority. Similarly, although the narrator herself condemns colonialism, she cannot help but be "contaminated" by its madness. As Albert Memmi points out in his *Portrait du colonisé précédé du portrait du colonisateur*,[22] even the most politically progressive colonist is recuperated in some way by the dominant order. In "Duras on the Margins," Marie-Paule Ha emphasizes this point: "the power differential between the two condemns the colonizer to live in perpetual contradiction with her/himself. ... No matter how genuine his/her sympathy for the colonized may be, she/he still belongs to the oppressor group and enjoys privileges which accompany his/her position as white master" (303). In *L'Amant*, the narrator's contradictory status lies in the ambiguity of hybridity itself. For while hybridity can indeed undermine hegemonic structures, it can also participate in the politics of oppression. This ambiguity has been fully explored in *Une Tempête*, Aimé Césaire's reinscription of

Shakespeare's *Tempest*. In Césaire's play, Ariel is recast as a "mulatto" slave who vacillates between the desire to please the colonial master (Prospero), and the necessity of siding with the rebel (Caliban).[23]

In *L'Amant*, the complexity of hybridity is further compounded by the fact that the lover himself is a cultural hybrid. Indeed, as he observes the young girl's body, he points out that they have the same roots in the Tropics: "Lui aussi il est né et il a grandi dans cette chaleur. Il se découvre avoir cette parenté-là" (120). (He too was born and grew up in this heat. He discovers this kinship between them) (98). This common "parentage" is thus also their mutual adherence to an oppressor group, since China also has a long history as a colonial power in Southeast Asia. In fact, the man from Cholen is the son of a wealthy financier who made his fortune by building "compartments," cubicles for the Indochinese "natives" to live in. The lover even claims that the cubicles benefit the natives because they are inexpensive, and because the poor like living outside in the street. Thus, despite differences in class and race, the Chinese man is accessible to the narrator precisely because of his own status as not quite/not-white. Having recently returned from Paris, he speaks French. Like the narrator, he is a non-"native" who has grown up in Vietnam. While it is skin color that allows the narrator to negotiate the spaces between white and indigenous culture in the colony, it is wealth that provides a similar, if unequal, mobility to the lover in the form of an automobile.

Conversely, it is the (native) madwoman of Vinh-long, associated in turn with the mad "Indian" beggar woman of Calcutta, who figures the absolute Other. In sharp contrast to her physical relationship with the lover, the narrator dreads contact with the madwoman, lest she herself be "contaminated" with insanity: "Si la femme me touche, même légèrement, de la main, je passerai à mon tour dans un état bien pire que celui de la mort, l'état de la folie" (104) (If the woman touches me, even lightly, with her hand, I too will enter into a state much worse than death, the state of madness) (84).

Unlike the Chinese lover, who mirrors the narrator's hybridized identity, the madwoman represents its erasure. She is the unmanageable "Other who could not be selved," the "subaltern who cannot speak,"[24] but who can only run "en criant dans une langue que je ne connais pas" (103) (shouting in a language I don't understand) (84). Coded in Orientalist terms, she figures the return of the re(op)pressed, an aspect of what Homi Bhabha calls the "unconscious repository of fantasy" that characterizes Orientalist[25] discourse.

Hence the narrator's obsessive multiplication of madwomen to the point where she peoples

> toute la ville de cette mendiante de l'avenue. Toutes les mendiantes des villes, des rizières, celles des pistes qui bordaient le Siam, celles des rives du Mékong, je l'en ai peuplée elle qui m'avait fait peur. (106)

> (the whole town is inhabited by the beggar woman in the road. And all the beggar women of the towns, the rice fields, the tracks bordering Siam, the banks of the Mekong—for me the beggar woman who frightened me is inhabited by them.) (86)

Dehumanized, the madwoman is excluded from human space-time:

> Elle est venue de partout. Elle est toujours arrivée à Calcutta, d'où qu'elle soit venue. Elle a toujours dormi à l'ombre des pommes canneliers de la cour de récréation. Toujours ma mère a été là près d'elle, à lui soigner son pied rongé par les vers, plein de mouches. (106)

> (She comes from everywhere. She always ends up in Calcutta wherever she started out from. She's always slept in the shade of the cinnamon-apple trees in the playground. And always my mother has been there beside her, tending her foot eaten up with maggots and covered with flies.) (86)

Locked in an eternal "fixity," as signaled by the refrain, "she has always . . . " the madwoman also embodies the "disorder, degeneracy, and daemonic repetition that characterizes the ideological construction of otherness" ("The Other," 68). Identified by durassian critics as an archetype whose root lies in a scene Duras witnessed as a child,[26] and by others as a wanderer from the realm of the maternal feminine who figures the disruption of meaning that follows the deconstruction of the sovereign subject, the mad beggar woman is also an Orientalist stereotype.

Just as "the feminine" repeatedly forgets that real women exist,[27] the Orientalist stereotype denies the beggar woman any possibility of development or transformation, so that, as Said puts it, "Oriental absence is replaced by Western presence."[28] While the narrator of L'Amant writes that her life story remains beyond her comprehension, inaccessible and hidden, imperialist structures of dominance "contaminate" her story in spite of her/itself. In this light, "Durasia" is also what Duras called "le lieu sauvage et toujours à explorer de sa propre contradiction" (Parleuses, 236) (the wild place of [her] own contradiction, always ready for exploration) (175).

Notes

1. I excise the "bio" from autobiography and bracket, as does Domna Stanton, the emphasis on the narration of "a life." See Domna C. Stanton, "Autogynography: Is the Subject Different?" in *The Female Autograph: Theory and Practice of Autobiography from the Tenth to the Twentieth Century*, ed. Domna Stanton (Chicago: The U of Chicago P, 1987).

2. In "Yeats and Decolonization," Edward Saïd defines "the cartographic" as "a response to the geographical violence of imperialism" through which virtually every space in the world is explored, charted, and finally brought under control. The "cartographic" counters this violence by seeking out, mapping, inventing, or discovering an uncolonized nature or space that "derives historically and abductively from the deprivations of the present." For Saïd, it is "the primacy of the geographical" that radically distinguishes the imagination of anti-imperialism. Edward Said, "Yeats and Decolonization," in *Nationalism, Colonialism, and Literature,* ed. Seamus Deane, (Minneapolis: U of Minnesota P, 1990) 79.

3. Walter Mignolo, "Colonial Situations, Geographical Discourses, and Territorial Representations: Toward a Diatopical Understanding of Colonial Semiosis," *Dispositio. American Journal of Semiotic and Cultural Studies* XIV, 36–38: (1989) 93. If understood as an element of the domain of colonial discourse as a whole, the cartographic can be used to describe virtually any territorial representation, where, as Mignolo puts it, "spatial boundaries are 'filled' with meaning and memories" (94). Indeed, Mignolo identifies territorial representations such as mapping, naming, and silencing as manifestations of a particular kind of colonial semiosis: "the confrontations of human needs and capacities to carve a space in which memories are inscribed and identities defined" (94).

4. I have used the Antillean search for an *arrière-pays* (hinterland) as the model of a gendered cartographic. See my "Politics of Location in Simone Schwarz-Bart's *Bridge of Beyond,*" *College Literature* 22, 1 (February 1995): 21–36.

5. See Carolyn Burke, "Psychoanalysis and Feminism in France," n.1.

6. Marguerite Duras, *L'Amant* (Paris: Minuit, 1985). In *L'Amant de la Chine du Nord* (Paris: Gallimard, 1991), the narrator refers to herself as "cette enfant blanche de l'Asie" (81) (this white child of Asia) (72). The English translation of *L'Amant* (*The Lover*) is by Barabara Bray (New York: Pantheon Books, 1985). The English translation of *L'Amant de la Chine du Nord* (*The North China Lover*) is by Leigh Hafrey (New York: New Press, 1992).

7. See Suzanne Chester, "Writing the Subject: Exoticism/Eroticism in Marguerite Duras's *The Lover* and *The Sea Wall,*" in *De/Colonizing the Subject: The Politics of Gender in Women's Autobiography*, ed. Sidonie Smith and Julia Watson (Minneapolis: U of Minnesota P, 1992); Marie Paule Ha, "Duras on the Margins," *The Romanic Review* 83, 3 (1994): 299–320; Panivong Norindor, " 'Errances and Memories in Marguerite Duras' Colonial Cities," *Differences* 5, 3 (1993): 52–79.

8. Hélène Cixous, "Le Rire de la Méduse," *L'Arc* 61 (1975): 42. Translated as "The Laugh of the Medusa" by Keith Cohen and Paula Cohen, in *New French Feminisms: An Anthology*, ed. Elaine Marks and Isabelle de Courtivron. Amherst: U of Massachusetts P, 1980, note 3, 248–249.

9. Claude Roy, in Marini, "Une femme sans aveu," *L'Arc* 98 (1985): 7.

10. The expression is from Mireille Caille-Gruber, "Pourquoi n'a-t-on plus peur de Marguerite Duras?" *Littérature* 63 (octobre 1986): 55.

11. Jacques Derrida, *De la Grammatologie* (Paris: Minuit, 1967), 12, translated by Gayatri Chakravorty Spivak as *Of Grammatology* (Baltimore: The Johns Hopkins UP, 1976), 3. Although the publication of *L'Amant de la Chine du Nord* in 1991 is a perfect example of Durassian "différance," it will not be the object of the present study.

12. Madeleine Borgomano, "L'Amant: Une Hypertextualité illimitée," *Revue des sciences humaines* 202 (avril–juin 1986): 73.

13. Marguerite Duras, Michelle Porte, *Les Lieux de Marguerite Duras* (Paris: Minuit, 1977), 59. For other accounts of this episode in interview form, see Leopoldina Pallotta Della Torre, *Marguerite Duras: La Passione sospesa* (Milano: La Tartaruga edizioni, 1989), 11 and ff, and, of course, Marguerite Duras and Xavière Gauthier, *Les Parleuses* (Paris: Minuit, 1974), 135 and ff.

14. *Un Barrage contre le pacifique* (Paris: Gallimard, 1950), *Le Vice-Consul* (Paris: Minuit, 1965), *L'Eden cinéma*, (Paris: Mercure de France, 1977).

15. Marguerite Duras, *Les Yeux verts: Cahiers du cinéma* 312/313 (juin 1980): 221.

16. The interview was originally published in Italian: "Come gli ebrei, tutto quello che, errando, mi sono portato in dietro, è diventato ancora più forte per il fatto stesso di essere stato lontano, assente." Leopoldina Pallotta Della Torre, *Marguerite Duras. La Passione sospesa* (Milano: La Tartaruga edizioni, 1989), 13. Claiming in *Les Parleuses* (translated as *Woman to Woman* by Katherine A. Jensen [Lincoln: U of Nebraska P, 1987]) to have completely repressed her childhood in Southeast Asia, Duras said that after leaving there, "je me trimbalais dans la vie" (I dragged along in life" [*Woman* 98]) saying, "moi, je n'ai pas de pays natal, je reconnais rien ici autour de moi'. Mais le pays où j'ai vécu c'est l'horreur. C'était le colonialisme . . . " (*Parleuses*, 136) (*I* have no native country; I don't recognize anything around me here, but the country where I lived is atrocious. It had colonialism . . .) (98). She goes on to explain the subsequent obsession with the land of her birth as a kind of "return of the repressed." Judging herself fortunate to have never returned to her homeland, Duras declares, "Je suis complètement séparée de mon enfance. Et, dans tous mes livres, elle est là, dans tous mes films, l'enfance est là" (I am completely separated from my childhood. And, in all of my books, it is there, in all of my films, childhood is there) (*Les Yeux verts, Cahiers du cinéma*, 312/313 [Juin 1980]: 199–200).

17. Marguerite Duras, *India Song*, (Paris: Gallimard, 1973), 10.

18. See Françoise Lionnet, *Autobiographical Voices: Race, Gender, Self-Portraiture* (Ithaca and London: Cornell U P, 1989).

19. Ann Laura Stoler, "Carnal Knowledge and Imperial Power: Gender, Race, and Morality in Colonial Asia," in *Gender at the Crossroads of Knowledge: Feminist Anthropology in the Postmodern Era*, ed. Micaela di Leonardo (Berkeley and Los Angeles: U of California P, 1991).

20. In *L'Amant* the madwoman of Vinhlong is associated with the mad "Indian" beggar woman of Calcutta. See Madeleine Borgomano,"L'Histoire de la mendiante indienne. Une cellule génératrice de l'oeuvre de Marguerite Duras," *Poétique* 48 (novembre 1981): 491.

21. According to Ann Stoler, "in metropolitan France, a profusion of medical and sociological tracts pinpointed the colonial as a distinct and degenerate social type, with specific psychological and even physical characteristics. Some of that difference was attributed to the debilitating results of climate and social milieu, from staying in the colonies too long. One tract proclaims, " 'the climate affects him, (sic) his surroundings affect him, and after a certain time, he has become, both physically and morally, a completely different man.' " ("Carnal," 76).

22. Albert Memmi, *Portrait du colonisé précédé du portrait du colonisateur* (Paris: Payot, 1973).

23. See Aimé Césaire, *Une Tempête* (Paris: Seuil, 1969). See also Roberto Fernandez Retamár, "Caliban: Notes Towards a Discussion of Culture in Our America," trans. Lynne Grafola et al., *Massachusetts Review* 15 (Winter–Spring 1979).

24. See Gayatri Chakravorty Spivak, "Can the Subaltern Speak? Speculations on Widow Sacrifice," *Wedge* 7/8 (1985): 119–131.

25. Homi K. Bhabha, "The Other Question: Stereotype, Discrimination and the Discourse of Colonialism." *The Location of Culture* (London and New York: Routledge, 1994), 71.

26. In an interview recorded before the publication of *L'Amant*, Duras remembers,
"Ma mère, une fois, est revenue du marché ayant acheté un enfant . . . une petite de six mois . . . qu'elle n'a gardé que quelques mois et qui est morte. . . . C'est un souvenir très violent . . . toujours très vivant . . . il s'agit d'une mendiante qui passe et qui vend son enfant." (My mother once returned from the market with a child she bought . . . a little six month-old girl . . . that she only kept for a few months and who died. . . . It is a very violent memory . . . always very much alive . . . it was a beggar woman who was passing through and who sold her child). Madeleine Borgomano, "L'Histoire de la mendiante indienne: Une cellule génératrice de l'oeuvre de Marguerite Duras," *Poétique* 48 (novembre 1981): 491.

27. See Anne Herrmann, *The Dialogic and Difference: "An/Other Woman" in Virginia Woolf and Christa Wolf* (New York: Columbia University Press, 1989).

28. Edward Said, *Orientalism* (New York: Vintage Books, 1979), 208.

Works Cited

Bhabha, Homi. "The Other Question: Stereotype, Discrimination, and the Discourse of Colonialism." *The Location of Culture.* London and New York: Routledge: 1994.

Borgomano, Madeleine. "*L'Amant.* Une hypertextualité illimitée." *Revue des sciences humaines* 202 (avril–juin 1986): 67–77.

———. *Duras: Une lecture des fantasmes.* Paris: Cistre-Essais, 1985.

———. "L'Histoire de la mendiante indienne: Une cellule génératrice de l'oeuvre de Marguerite Duras." *Poétique* 48 (novembre 1981): 479–493.

Burke, Carolyn. "Rethinking the Maternal." *The Future of Difference.* Ed. Hester Eisenstein and Alice Jardine. Boston: G.K. Hall, 1980, 3–19.

Caille-Gruber, Mireille. "Pourquoi n'a-t-on plus peur de Marguerite Duras?" *Littérature* 63 (octobre 1986): 104–119.

Capitanio, Sarah J. "Perspectives sur l'écriture durassienne: *L'Amant.*" *Symposium* 41 (Spring 1987): 15–27.

Césaire, Aimé. *Une tempête: D'après La Tempête de Shakespeare: Adaptation pour un théâtre nègre.* Paris: Seuil, 1969.

Chester, Suzanne. "Writing the Subject: Exoticism/Eroticism in Marguerite Duras's *The Lover and the Sea Wall.*" *De/Colonizing the Subject: The Politics of Gender in Women's Autobiography.* Ed. Sidonie Smith and Julia Watson. Minneapolis: U of Minnesota P, 1992.

Cixous, Hélène. "The Laugh of the Medusa." Trans. Keith Cohen and Paula Cohen. *Signs: Journal of Women in Culture and Society* 1, 4 (1976): 875–893.

———. "Le Rire de la Méduse." *L'Arc* 61 (1975): 39–54.

Della Torre, Leopoldina Pallotta. *Marguerite Duras: La Passione sospesa.* Milano: La Tartaruga edizioni, 1989.

Derrida, Jacques. *L'Ecriture et la différence.* Paris: Seuil, 1967.

———. *De la Grammatologie.* Paris: Minuit, 1967.

———. *Of Grammatology.* Trans. Gayatri Chakravorty Spivak. Baltimore and London: The Johns Hopkins U P, 1974.

Duras, Marguerite. *L'Amant.* Paris: Minuit, 1985.

———. *L'Amant de la Chine du Nord.* Paris: Gallimard, 1991.

———. *Un barrage contre le Pacifique.* Paris: Gallimard, 1950.

———. *Le Camion: Suivi de "Entretien avec Michelle Porte."* Paris: Minuit, 1977.

———. *L'Eden Cinéma.* Paris: Mercure de France: 1986.

———. *India Song.* Paris: Gallimard, 1973.

———, and Michelle Porte. *Les lieux de Marguerite Duras.* Paris: Minuit, 1977.

———. *The Lover.* Trans. Barbara Bray. New York: Pantheon, 1985.

———, and Xavière Gauthier. *Les Parleuses.* Paris: Minuit, 1974.

———. *Les Yeux verts: Cahiers du cinéma* 312/313 (juin 1980).

Ha, Marie-Paule. "Duras on the Margins." *The Romanic Review* 83, 3 (1994): 299–320.

Herrmann, Anne. *The Dialogic and Difference: "An/Other Woman" in Virginia Woolf and Christa Wolf.* New York: Columbia U P, 1989.

Hewitt, Leah. *Autobiographical Tightropes: Simone de Beauvoir, Nathalie Sarraute, Marguerite Duras, Monique Wittig, Maryse Condé.* Lincoln and London: U of Nebraska P, 1990.

Lionnet, Françoise. *Autobiographical Voices: Race, Gender, Self-Portraiture.* Ithaca and London: Cornell UP, 1989.

Marini, Marcelle. "L'Autre corps." *Ecrire, dit-elle: Imaginaires de Marguerite Duras.* Ed. Danielle Bajomée, Ralph Heyndels. Bruxelles: Editions de L'Université de Bruxelles, 1985, 21–48.

———. "L'élaboration de la différence sexuelle dans la pratique littéraire de la langue." *Cahiers du grad, Faculté de philosophie, Université Laval à Québec, numéro 1, "Femmes, écriture, philosophie"* (1987): 5–20.

———."Une femme sans aveu." *L'Arc* 98 (1985): 6–15.

———. *Les Territoires du féminin avec Marguerite Duras.* Paris: Minuit, 1977.

Marks, Elaine, and Isabelle de Courtivron, eds. *New French Feminisms: An Anthology.* Amherst: The U of Massachussetts P, 1980.

Memmi, Albert. *Portrait du colonisé.* Paris: Payot, 1973.

Mignolo, Walter. "Colonial Situations, Geographical Discourses, and Territorial Representations: Toward a Diatopical Understanding of Colonial Semiosis." *Dispositio: American Journal of Semiotic and Cultural Studies* XIV, 36–38 (1989): 93–140.

Norindr, Panivong. "'Errances' and Memories in Marguerite Duras' Colonial Cities." *Differences* 5, 3 (1993): 52–79.

Said, Edward W. *Culture and Imperialism.* New York: Alfred A. Knopf, 1993.

———. *Orientalism.* New York: Vintage Books, 1979.

———. "Yeats and Decolonization." *Nationalism, Colonialism, and Literature.* Ed. Seamus Deane. Minneapolis: U of Minnesota P, 1990, 69–95.

Spivak, Gayatri Chakravorty. "Can the Subaltern Speak? Speculations on Widow Sacrifice." *Wedge* 7/8 (1985): 119–131.

———. "French Feminism in an International Frame." *In Other Worlds: Essays in Cultural Politics.* New York and London: Routledge, 1987, 134–153.

———. *The Post-Colonial Critic: Interviews, Strategies, Dialogues.* Ed. Sarah Harasym. New York and London: Routledge, 1990.

———. "The Rani of Sirmur: An Essay in Reading the Archives." *History and Theory: Studies in the Philosophy of History* XXIV, 3 (1985): 247–272.

———. "Three Women's Texts and a Critique of Imperialism." *Race, Writing, and Difference.* Ed. Henry Louis Gates Jr. Chicago: The U of Chicago P, 1986, 262–280.

Stanton, Domna C. "Autogynography: Is the Subject Different?" *The Female Autograph: Theory and Practice of Autobiography from the Tenth to the*

Twentieth Century. Ed. Domna C. Stanton. Chicago and London: The U of Chicago P, 1987, 3–20.

————. "Language and Revolution: The Franco-American Dis-connection." *The Future of Difference*. Ed. Hester Eisenstein and Alice Jardine. Boston: G.K. Hall, 1980, 73–87.

Stoler, Ann Laura. "Carnal Knowledge and Imperial Power: Gender, Race, and Morality in Colonial Asia." *Gender at the Crossroads of Knowledge: Feminist Anthropology in the Postmodern Era*. Ed. Micaela di Leonardo. Berkeley and Los Angeles: U of California P, 1991, 51–101.

————. "Sexual Affronts and Racial Frontiers: European Identities and the Cultural Politics of Exclusion in Colonial Southeast Asia." *Comparative Studies in Society and History* 34, 3 (July 1992): 514–551.

13

African Intellectuals in France

Echoes of Senghor in Ngandu's Memoirs

Janice Spleth

In *Vie et moeurs d'un primitif en Essonne quatre-vingt-onze* (Life and Customs of a Primitive Man in Essonne Ninety-One), Pius Ngandu Nkashama artfully frames his experience as a consultant on African culture to Essonne, France, during the academic year 1981–82. A Zairian teacher, writer, and scholar, he completed a *doctorat d'état* at the University of Strasbourg in 1981 and has been affiliated with universities in Zaire, the Congo, Algeria, France, and the Netherlands. In addition to his substantial literary production—novels, plays, and poetry, he has written extensively on African culture and literature.[1] He classifies this highly selective autobiographical text as a narrative or *récit* and lists it with his fiction. Each chapter pointedly details a single facet of this experience in cross-cultural communication, describing both the author's individual encounters with the French and his professional efforts to insert an African perspective into the schools and cultural events of the community. Often humorous or poignant, this is generally a tale of frustration. The narrator's personal contact with racism and discrimination by and large anticipates the prejudices of the various audiences he attempts to reach, and despite a few memorable successes, he is incapable of countering these stereotypes with a genuine appreciation of Africa. His accounts and reflections are nevertheless provocative in what they show about the relationship between the West and its cultural Others in the postcolonial period.

The author's writing is characterized by abundant, often ironic references to French literature. Musset, Théophile Gauthier, and Rimbaud inspire various chapter titles, and Lamartine, Balzac, Stendhal, and Céline are among those literary figures evoked elsewhere, a stylistic device that is hardly surprising in the work of an academic. Also cited or satirized in various ways are the works of the Senegalese poet and founder of the Negritude movement Léopold Sédar Senghor, who, like Ngandu, was an expatriate in France. Arriving in Paris in 1928, he wrote in part as a response to his own encounter with racial prejudice and French pretensions to cultural superiority.[2] As Senghor became recognized as a major African writer in French, eventually being elected to the French Academy, his works, created originally out of a sense of cultural alienation, became a part of the French literary canon, widely read and taught both in France and in Africa.[3] Ngandu's own remarkable familiarity with Senghor's corpus is readily apparent, not only in this autobiographical work but also in his critical writing on African literature, most obviously *Négritude et poétique: Une lecture de l'oeuvre critique de Léopold Sédar Senghor* (Negritude and Poetics: A Reading of the Critical Work of Léopold Sédar Senghor). My intention in this essay is to focus specifically on the allusions to Senghor's work in *Vie et moeurs* in order to show some of the many ways the younger writer plays on the poetry and ideas of Negritude and to discuss the relationship between the two generations of African intellectuals in France.

THE QUEST MOTIF

Fundamental to Senghor's poetry and implicit in Ngandu's text is the use of the initiate's quest as a structuring device.[4] Traditionally, the initiate—like the questing hero—is taken out of his familiar milieu and made to undergo various trials before eventually being reintegrated into his society with a new identity and new knowledge. In "*Par delà Érôs*" and "*Le retour de l'Enfant prodigue*," two of the major poems in his first collection of poetry, Senghor describes returning to Africa as a rite of passage that allows him to rediscover the culture from which he had been separated by virtue of his education in French schools and his expatriate existence in France. The quest structure dominates the poetry of *Ethiopiques* (1956) and is central to "*Chant de l'initié*" (*Song of the Initiate*), published eventually in *Nocturnes* (1961). In most cases, the ritual culminates in the poet's affirmation of his identity as an African.

The narrator of *Vie et moeurs* also envisions his experience as a quest, but of a different sort. Whereas the alienated poet strives to be reunited with Africa and desires to be reintegrated into his society, Ngandu has spent most of his life on the African continent in the country formerly known as Zaire, and it is rather his ordeals as an African among the French that he transforms into a heroic adventure.[5] To survive, he must, in fact, escape the temptation of assimilation and refuse the integration normally associated with initiation in order to retain an identity distinct from the stereotypes that would reify him. The new insights to be gained stem less from what Europe has to teach than from the clarity of thought that leads to the demystification of the West. In his initial chapter, entitled *"Itinéraires africains: quêtes et conquêtes"* (African itineraries: quests and conquests), he figuratively frames his encounter with France in terms of a classic quest, but one whose locus is Hades itself in the tradition of mythic heroes such as Orpheus, Aeneas, or Dante.[6] Other chapter titles suggest voyages— *"Marcoussis: sur la route des béatitudes"* (Marcoussis: on the road of the beatitudes), *"Allons, marchons, marchons, exilés valeureux"* (March on, valorous exiles), and, in homage to Rimbaud, *"Comme je descendais des fleuves impassibles"* (As I descended impassive rivers)—or carry the notion, albeit ironic, of a sacred experience—*"Dans la basilique des mystères"* (In the basilica of mysteries). One of his earliest chapters, *"L'ascension des Chalmieux"* (Ascent of the Chalmieux), translates an episode in the mountains in mystical terms that have more than a passing resemblance to Senghor's quest poems. The quest motif appears throughout African oral literature, and certainly, other literary models are available besides Senghor's poetry. There are, however, strong parallels to be drawn here between the two writers, and Ngandu's work is enhanced in interesting ways by an intertextual reading.

In a poem celebrating a return to Africa, *"Chant d'ombre"* (Shadow Song), from *"Par delà Érôs"* (Beyond Eros), Senghor describes the figurative conquering of a mountain, which he addresses: "Ta tête noblesse nue de la pierre, ta tête au-dessus des monts, le Lion au-dessus des animaux de l'étable/ Tête debout, qui me perce de ses yeux aigus" (Your head naked nobility of stone, your head above the mounts, the Lion above the animals of the stable/ Head erect, which pierces me with its sharp eyes) (40–41). The lion, the poet's totem animal and a recurring symbol of his African identity, appears also at the end of *"Chant de l'initié,"* again in association with a mountain, but it is in *"Chant d'ombre"* that the poet actually scales the mountain.[7] The object of poet's quest is revealed as both a mountain and a woman that the poet associates with Africa.[8] Ultimately triumphant in his quest, he calls on the shades of his ancestors to bear witness to his victory and the value of his prize.[9]

In "*L'ascension des Chalmieux*," Ngandu analyzes the ceremony that marks the beginning of his project in Essonne, a reception at a *Maison de Culture* outside of Grenoble in which the writer is welcomed to France personally by the French Minister for Cooperation. This interlude in Savoy gives the writer his first exposure to alpine terrain. Coming as it does at the beginning of the text, the experience acts in a very real sense as a rite of passage for the narrator as he prepares for his mission. His interpretation of the events, filled with double entendres and self-deprecating humor, anticipates his narrative, the quest depicted here serving as a microcosm of sorts for his entire experience in Essonne. Juxtaposing excerpts from this chapter with Senghor's poetry brings out additional nuances of the writer's irony as he manages both to convey the notions of importance and privilege he attaches to his task and to deride himself for his expectations, to pay homage to French claims to a superior position in the world and to ridicule them.

Ngandu's mountain is, rather significantly, white and inspires awe, but whereas Senghor's peak resembles the head of a lion, the French mountain clearly outlines the head of a lesser feline, a cat.[10] The contemplation of the mountain leads the writer to the proclamation of a sublime sense of inner harmony,[11] and this epiphany which has, momentarily at least, brought the traveller under its spell, is also couched in terms reminiscent of Senghor's self-discovery.[12] But Senghor's poem is a lyrical celebration of his race and his African origins. What comparable authenticity could the Zairian writer be affirming at the sight of the snow-covered mountains of Savoy?

Confronting the mountain prefigures Ngandu's trials as he combats the rigid curriculum and unbending will of the French academic establishment; in place of the integration normally implied in the initiate's quest, there will be only alienation and failure. The new knowledge that accrues to the writer will consist largely of disillusionment and cynicism about the future of Africa's relationship with France. The mountain, which seemed so compelling at first, is after all "un monstre puissant, qui avale et qui écrase" (a powerful monster that swallows and crushes) (35). As in "*Chant d'ombre*," the mountain is feminized.[13] Perhaps coincidentally, the narrator's supervisor in Essonne will be a woman, an especially cold and unsympathetic figure who could easily be substituted for the mountain as the subject of the preceding passage.

Typically, the explorer and the colonizer—and the Negritude poets—envisioned Africa as female, passive, and ultimately conquerable; Ngandu turns the tables.

Unlike Senghor, Ngandu does not overcome the mountain, but, in this instance, the uncompleted quest may actually be viewed as a triumph for the hero. If he fails to climb the mountain, he also succeeds in not being transformed by it, as he had dreamed he would be, reduced to the frozen stereotypes that would allow him to be subordinated to and assimilated by the dominant culture. This is the essential theme that lies at the heart of his text. The narrator maintains his integrity, whereas the mountain, he tells us at the end of the chapter, stands as a constant symbol to the observer.[14] It is, he tells us later on, partially as a result of his experiences in Essonne that he finds his vocation as a writer: "Non certes comme une revanche, mais une manière de piétiner à mes pieds les illusions de ceux qui se croyaient la puissance de m'écraser et de me réduire en cendres" (Not certainly as a form of revenge, but as a way of trampling under my feet the illusions of those who thought they had the power to crush me and to reduce me to ashes) (179).

Reading Senghor's poem as a possible subtext for Ngandu's chapter intensifies the irony and foregrounds the issues of identity and self-affirmation. The myth-making potential inherent in the quest motif also invites us to see other implications. In many respects, Senghor's questing hero represented not merely the poet himself but an entire generation of African students; the poet of Negritude thus fabricated a myth for his own time, addressing the questions of identity that confronted himself and his peers. By framing his adventure as a similar quest, the author of *Vie et moeurs* speaks for his own generation of postcolonial intellectuals and mythologizes, through the specificities of his personal drama, their courage and frustration. If indeed Ngandu intended for the reader to make the comparison with the poetry of Negritude, as I strongly feel he did, this would further suggest that Ngandu is presenting himself as Senghor's heir. As he evokes his elder throughout the narrative, however, he must also create a distance that allows him to be critical, to express the vital differences that characterize his own experience, and to affirm a separate identity. Thus, in the process of borrowing the paraphernalia of the initiate's quest, Ngandu—in keeping with the general pessimism of his work and his moment in history—has replaced the nobility of the epic with the irreverence of the picaresque and reduced the hero to an anti-hero.

CONFRONTING HAPPY RACES

In translating their personal experiences as expatriates, the two writers have both evoked the awkwardness of their encounters with the French. Each speaks of feeling divided under the gaze of the Other, and both recount their efforts to defend themselves against condescension and scorn. Senghor's image as President of Senegal, member of the French Academy, and spokesman for Francophonie makes it difficult for us to see him as an African student and a foreigner first encountering Paris and the Parisians, but several of his early poems describe his uneasiness. It is in confronting the Other that he comes to feel a need to affirm his own identity as an African and to defend the values of his culture. "*Le totem*" (Totem), for example, addresses the ambiguity of his situation as an outsider trying to be accepted without totally sacrificing his own sense of self: the totem animal, a symbol for the poet's African self, is cherished as a shield against the attitudes of others, the happy or fortunate races who must not be scandalized and to whom he must expose his own vulnerable ego.[15] "*In memoriam,*" the initial poem from his first collection, directly invokes the ancestors and asks their protection against the poet's fear of physical harm. Under the watchcare of the ancestors, he leaves his lodgings to go out among his "frères aux yeux bleus / Aux mains dures" (blue-eyed brothers/With hard hands) (10). Although he depicts the French as his brothers, the qualifiers contain an element of antagonism, even danger.[16] Senghor's memories of Africa offer a defense against the slights of the Western world.

Ngandu, too, must always be on guard against the prejudices of those around him. Like the Senegalese poet, he feels divided inasmuch as he must keep his authentic identity hidden, for all relationships are tainted.[17] Senghor is not explicitly evoked here, but the experiences are depicted in decidedly similar terms. Throughout the text, Ngandu continues to be anxious about the codes of behavior that inform his relationship with the white community. Even on a professional level, the insensitivity of his colleagues and superiors repeatedly imbues his mission with further tensions, and like Senghor, he seeks supernatural support.

Descending one morning to discover an additional impediment to success—the lock on the car door is frozen solid on a day when he has an important meeting—he pleads with the door itself as he articulates his anxiety: "Je t'en prie, ma porte, ma portière. Ouvre-toi. Laisse-toi faire, sois aimable . . . " (I beg you, my door, my car door. Open up. It won't hurt you, be nice) (61). In a style that is closer to poetry than prose, the narrator recounts fears that are similar to Senghor's as each in his own way prepares to face the arrogance of a race that considers

him inferior.[18] Ngandu's decision to frame his distress as a prayer, albeit
to a car door, could easily be an intentional imitation of Senghor whose
characteristic use of the second person form of address as a poetic
device is well established.[19] It is therefore tempting to read these lines
as parody. Ngandu, who is talking about being stereotyped as the
generic African, adopts this typically Senghorian device, thereby con-
forming to the exotic prejudices of the European reader who, like him,
has also read Senghor and expects to see such invocations in African
writing. This irreverent use of stylistic techniques that cannot help but
recall Senghor's work anticipates those passages where Ngandu, in a
similar way, both recalls and revises Senghor's philosophy of Negritude.

Despite the formal similarity, the prayers differ in their outcomes.
The ancestors and totem animal addressed by the poet are, of course,
more sympathetic to his supplications and are ultimately empowering
and enabling, while the inanimate door to which Ngandu directs his
prayers remains closed, thus assuming greater significance as the symbol of a society that is closed to strangers and minds that stereotype
and denigrate. In the end, even the speaker recognizes the futility of
his prayer. These differences, Senghor's victory and Ngandu's failure,
are important, characterizing not merely differences between two tem-
peraments but differences between colonial and postcolonial Africa.
Senghor's experience evolves within the framework of budding nationalism and the prospect of positive political change; Ngandu's reflects
the disappointments of independence, the brutality of Mobutu's oppressive regime, and the injustices of neocolonialism.[20]

In identifying himself as an immigrant, the Zairian writer inserts yet
another element that distinguishes his experience as an African in
France from those of previous generations. The discomfort among the
French created by a growing immigrant population in the postcolonial
period was accompanied by a rising racism in which perceptions of
cultural differences were exacerbated by class prejudice.[21] In trying to
teach black and Beur adolescents in Essonne about Africa, he paradoxically finds himself unable to establish a common ground with these
young people, despite their shared marginalization by the first world,
precisely because of class differences: they deem him to be "trop
embourgeoisé" (too middle-class) (117).

NEGRITUDE AS RACIAL STEREOTYPE

In addition to the new obstacles imposed by the postcolonial period
and the changing attitudes in France toward immigrants from the Third
World, Ngandu's situation as an African in France is rendered more

complex precisely because of Senghor's legacy. In the face of Western claims to cultural superiority, Senghor and his fellow students from Africa and the Caribbean formulated the notion of a collective black personality that became known as Negritude. Because it was framed in response to the colonizer, it expressed itself, in Senghor's writings at least, in terms of sweeping dualities. Emotion was considered an African trait in contrast with European rationalism. The African was viewed as living in harmony with nature; Europeans needed to dominate it, thus their technological advancements, including their engines of war. Religion was deemed an essential part of African life in contrast with French materialism and atheism. In Africa, the sense of community was prized over the individualism that is valued in the West. Because of the canonical status that has been accorded Senghor's work, these tenets would have been familiar to most educated French citizens at the time of Ngandu's visit to Essonne. Thus, in addition to the other racial stereotypes facing him, Ngandu repeatedly confronts the image of the African refracted through Senghor's concept of Negritude. In the main, he responds vehemently to its simplistic assumptions. When his audiences, for example, show a marked preference to restrict their studies of Africa to the works of Negritude writers, Ngandu is visibly frustrated: "Des phrases banales venaient enchaîner sur les littératures orales sur les rhapsodies de la 'négritude' . . . " (Banal sentences would issue forth moving logically from oral literatures to the rhapsodies of "negritude") (100). He effectively makes the point that Negritude, as it is elaborated, assigns a marginal position to the black, defining him in relationship to the white, who occupies not merely the center but virtually all other space on the map that is not specifically marked.[22] At several points in *Vie et moeurs*, Ngandu uses the expression "l'émotion nègre" ("black emotion")—a reference to Senghor's famous or infamous quote: "L'émotion est nègre comme la raison hellène" ("Emotion is black like reason is Greek) (*Liberté I*, 24)—to show how this way of perceiving the world anchors both Senghor's philosophy and poetics.[23] But despite his understanding of Senghor's usage of the term, he rarely employs it in this sense in his narrative, choosing instead to reconstruct it within his reflections on racism.[24] Senghor's vision of black specificity, as he terms it, has become, in the post-independence period, a comfortable category for the European but a confining, distorted image for the African. The philosophy that was once qualified by Sartre as "anti-racist racism" (xl) has itself become a tool in the service of racism.[25]

In numerous ways, Ngandu challenges Senghor's dichotomy, revealing how it misrepresents both Europeans and Africans. Whereas

Senghor sees a fundamental racial and cultural difference opposing "le paysan nègre à l'ingénieur blanc" (the black peasant and the white engineer) (*Liberté I,* 258), the technical superiority accorded to the West by the Senegalese poet in the forties is radically questioned when Ngandu attempts to link Lubumbashi and Essonne by television. In complete contradiction of Senghor's model, everything proceeds smoothly at the African end in spite of French concerns—"vous savez avec ces pays-là, on ne sait jamais!" (you never know with countries like that) (45). It is ultimately the Europeans who are unable to make the necessary technological arrangements, leading Ngandu to meditate on the deficiencies of the communications system in a major developed country. Playing on the stereotypes of Negritude allows the narrator to indulge in what might be termed reverse exoticism as he, the foreign traveller, "discovers" France, occasionally attributing to it a backwardness similar to that imputed to Africa by early European explorers and settlers.

Not only does he find France's technology unreliable, but he also finds its superstitions quaint. The language used to describe the narrator's visit to a small French village cleverly parrots that of the anthropologist intrigued by primitive native rites.[26] Ngandu reminds us that French culture, like African culture, bears traces of the pre-Christian period, although these vestiges are generally assigned to history in the national myth. Furthermore, what is considered "magic" and what is considered "religion" depends to a large extent on where the observer is positioned. Senghor distinguished between the two, saying that "Dans les civilisations traditionnelles—c'est le cas en Afrique noire—, la religion n'est qu'une magie élaborée; elle reste magie" (In traditional civilizations—as in the case of Black Africa—religion is only an elaboration of magic; it remains magic) (268). By qualifying traditional French practice as "magic," Ngandu's anecdote disassociates the notion of "traditional culture" from race in a way that denies the essentialist assumptions of both Senghor and one of Negritude's most prestigious interpreters, Jean-Paul Sartre.[27]

Senghor's affirmation of Africa's communal nature is uncontested by Ngandu, who would like his audience to understand this essential solidarity as a traditional form of defense against the repeated suffering that characterizes African history.[28] Woven throughout the text are many links to Senghor's "Eléments constitutifs d'une civilisation d'inspiration négro-africaine" (Constituent Elements of a Civilization of Black-African Inspiration) (*Liberté I,* 252–286): the importance of the extended family, the role of the dead and the ancestors, and the function of ritual in maintaining the unity of the group. Ngandu, on the other hand, is disturbed by what this harmonious depiction of African society omits, the agony that Africa has endured over the centuries, often at the hands of Europeans. His own vision of African community is sketched against the notion of unity in the face of common misery, a vision he elaborates in his narrative as he goes on to enumerate the offenses committed by Europe against Africa. By revising the idealized image of the bucolic noble savage as it is perpetuated in Negritude, Ngandu once again responds to Senghor.

WHITE HANDS

Senghor, too, occasionally addressed European aggression against Africa, although more effectively in his poetry than in his polemics. Works such as "*Neige sur Paris*" (Snow on Paris) and "*Prière de paix*" (Prayer for Peace) recall the suffering of the colonized and leave no question as to Europe's culpability. Although both poems ultimately end on the theme of forgiveness,[29] the pardon that Senghor bestows on France allows him to continue to address its crimes: to compare, for example, France's humiliation at the hands of the Nazis during the Occupation to Africa's treatment by France, is to question the legitimacy of colonialism in a way that the French could well understand.

Ngandu also finds himself reflecting on the ills that his people have suffered at the hands of the West, but his list complements Senghor's, observing the absence of compensation for the victims of colonization and detailing as well those injustices endured since nationhood.[30] Expressly delineating the circumstances that constitute neocolonialism, in addition to showing how colonialism continues to be rationalized, Ngandu, like Senghor, alludes to the role of the Nazis in World War II,[31] subtly evoking racism as the only explanation for the difference between the world's unceasing efforts to obtain retribution for the occupation and the Holocaust and its patent indifference to what he terms the "crimes" of colonialism.[32] Throughout this chapter he repeats, "Les peuples ne pardonnent jamais" (the people never pardon), when referring to the German war crimes and to the crimes against white colonial settlers in Africa. He implies, by contrast, that Africans have been asked to pardon a great deal, as when he notes derisively: "Et les peuples se sont mis à pardonner" (And the people began to pardon.)[33] Ngandu seems to have Senghor in mind when he writes these lines, listing similar grievances, similarly drawing from World War II, and also raising the issue of forgiveness. But the similarities of style and vocabulary only serve to underscore the differences in tone.[34]

Ngandu continues to challenge Senghor's idealistic premises when, at the end of this chapter detailing Africa's relationship with the former colonial powers, he refers to yet another concept associated with Negritude, the Civilization of the Universal, a vision of a future harmonious state in which all peoples would bring the contributions of their various cultures. The Zairian writer describes the occupation of Kolwezi in 1978 by the Katanga "*gendarmes*," rebels against Mobutu's regime who were, however, welcomed by many dissidents in Shaba province. Because European interests were at stake in this important mining town, the French sent legionnaires to support Mobutu, and Ngandu mourns the many Zairians who died in the ensuing hostilities.[35] As Voltaire's Candide eventually rejected the teachings of his master and the optimism of Leibnitz, Ngandu likewise has little faith in the future envisioned by Senghor, the latter having articulated the theory of Negritude in conjunction with the Teilhardian concept of the Civilization of the Universal and its emphasis on brotherhood and love.[36] In his essay, *Pierre Teilhard de Chardin et la politique africaine* (Pierre Teilhard de Chardin and African politics), Senghor acknowledges his debt to the philosopher in his own efforts "pour définir les valeurs de la Négritude et en faire une contribution à la construction de la Terre: l'édification de la Civilisation de l'Universel" (to define the values of Negritude and to make a contribution with them to the construction of the Earth: the building of the Universal Civilization) (16). Ngandu refers to this idea in his study of Senghor's theories, but with the disclaimer that he does not totally subscribe to the poet's version of Negritude which speaks of "la 'convergence panhumaine' (selon la formule de Teilhard de Chardin)" (the "panhuman convergence") (according to Teilhard de Chardin's formula)) (*Négritude et poétique*, 12). In *Vie et moeurs* Ngandu has already established his position, describing postcolonial politics as incompatible with Teilhard's visions. Reading Zairian current events in juxtaposition with the theme of forgiveness that characterizes Senghor's poetry and with the idealism implied in the Civilization of the Universal has the effect of intensifying the force of Ngandu's indictment of France's current policies in Africa.

REHABILITATING AFRICAN CULTURE

That Senghor's concept of Negritude and his optimistic aspirations toward world harmony are, for the most part, rejected or rectified in

Ngandu's narrative again owes something to the point in history from which each is writing. This distance is further reflected in the ways that the two writers rehabilitate their cultural roots. Affirming the value of African culture is a key element of Senghor's philosophy of Negritude and a recurring theme in his poetry, where he consistently returns to the physical geography of the continent for his imagery and often draws inspiration from African art. Throughout his stay in Essonne, Ngandu similarly strives to familiarize his French audiences with Africa and awaken them to an appreciation of its cultural achievements. One of the final chapters in *Vie et moeurs* deals with an exhibition of Zairian art in Paris organized by Ngandu and his compatriots. His reflections on his experiences are permeated with allusions to poems by Senghor. As in the previous instances, however, these references frequently become the basis for confirming the differences that distinguish the two generations of African writing.

Working with the masks and art objects that pay tribute to the creativity and diversity of his country, Ngandu tries to translate his state of mind: "Du Bas-Congo et du large estuaire vers les clairières des chutes d'Isangila, et des galeries forestières de Dekese. Tout un peuple rassemblé en une route large dans les splendeurs des palmiers qui mènent vers la totalité de l'esprit. La force spirituelle qui crée et qui régénère. Mon fleuve, mon Congo" (From the lower Congo and the large estuary toward the clearings of the falls of Isangila, and the forests of Dekese. A whole people assembled in a broad road in the splendor of palm trees that lead toward the totality of the spirit. The spiritual force that creates and regenerates. My river, my Congo) (172). At this point, he remembers Senghor's poem about the great river, "*Congo*," quoting from its first line, "Pour rythmer ton nom . . . " (To beat out the rhythm of your name . . .) (*Poèmes*, 101), before continuing: "Mais, lui-même, il est déjà le rythme! Un rythme impulsant notre sang sur le cantique de sa gloire!" (But it is already rhythm! A rhythm transmitting the impulse of our blood on the canticle of its glory!). In Senghor's verses, the river is again a feminized Africa who embraces the poet-boatman in sexually charged images.[37] Ngandu's celebration of his country borrows some of the sexual imagery and the ultimate notion of regeneration and rebirth, but continues in its own direction. Using mainly masculine nouns and pronouns in reference to the Congo, he re-appropriates the river and gives Zairian names to the different points of its itinerary. The Congo becomes a source of regional or national solidarity, and he concludes: "Nous avons vu la terre infusée à même nos espérances" (We have seen the earth infused by our hopes) (173). Senghor's poem also ends in images of rebirth and hope: "Mais la pirogue renaîtra par les nénuphars de l'écume / Surnagera la douceur des bambous au matin transparent du monde" (But the pirogue will be reborn amid the water lilies of the foam/The gentleness of bamboos will float in the transparent morning of the world) (*Poèmes*, 103). For both writers, the Congo is an important symbol. For Senghor, it evokes generic Africa in the same way that his concept of Negritude generalizes an African identity; for Ngandu, the river specifically represents home and national affinities.

As he continues to describe the exhibit, Ngandu passes through other territory already marked by Senghor's poetry, and it is difficult not to see allusions. When his colleague Bernard remarks in reference to other masks: "Et je comprends que ces masques aient été interdits aux femmes et aux enfants, tant ils renferment de force" (And I understand that these masks were forbidden to women and children because they enclosed such force) (175), is there a conscious allusion to Senghor's *"Prière aux masques"* (Prayer to the masks)?[38] In that poem, the ancestors are invoked through the masks to come to the aid of their descendants,[39] a theme Ngandu also develops.[40] Moreover, Senghor's adoration before the carved face of the women in *"Masque nègre"* (*Poèmes*, 18) ("Black Mask) (visage fermé à l'éphémère" [face closed to ephemeral things]), appears to be related to Ngandu's ecstatic contemplation of the mythic mother figure, *Mukishi wa pwo*. But Ngandu's depictions of African art, in contrast to Senghor's, almost always return to the theme of suffering that characterizes his own vision of Africa and the Zairian people. This feature appears from the outset with his image of the Congo: "la rivière s'est nourrie des affluents de toutes nos souffrances" (the river was nourished by the tributaries of all of our suffering) (173). The face of *Mukishi wa pwo* is an incarnation of pain: "un visage de femme, tout entière tournée vers la force de la douleur" (a woman's face, completely turned toward the force of pain) (175). Even speculation about the creator of the masks returns to the victimization of the people as he contemplates the role of the artisan transformed by the inhumanity of mass production.[41] While Senghor evokes the glories of a generalized Africa as a reminder of his heritage and a promise of the future, Ngandu's Zairian exhibit is imbued with the pain of the neocolonial present and continued economic exploitation.[42]

CONCLUSION

A reading of Ngandu's work through its relationship with Senghor's highlights a number of areas of convergence: their similar use of the quest motif and the invocation as structuring devices, the common themes of discrimination, race, and violence, and their mutual desire to foster appreciation for African arts and traditions. More importantly, it also reveals differences between the two men and the periods in which they are writing and provides some interesting cultural insights.

The post-independence era has fostered national identities that were considerably less defined when Senghor elaborated his theories of African civilization. In a very real sense, Negritude was intended to speak for the entire continent, not specifically for Senegal. This was the tendency that Frantz Fanon observed early in the movement for independence: inasmuch as colonialism was a continental phenomenon that treated all African cultures as equally inferior, the response of the colonized would necessarily be framed along the same lines.[43] In an era of Pan-Africanism, Senghor fought against the balkanization of Africa and, even after independence, sought coalitions with other countries. If his essays tended to err in the direction of overgeneralization, they nevertheless provided a common theme throughout the French-speaking colonies south of the Sahara in the struggle for autonomy. The inspiration for his poems was drawn not only from the culture of his native Senegal but also from the black experience throughout Africa and the diaspora. Although Negritude poetry developed somewhat later in Zaire, even that nation fostered its own generation of Negritude poets writing about the common characteristics of the black soul.[44]

Ngandu, on the other hand, belongs to the Africa of nation-states and speaks with a specific Zairian heritage in mind. For him, the Congo River is a decidedly national symbol, and in *Vie et moeurs*, he draws on examples of the victimization from his own country to illustrate neocolonial misdeeds. He resents the European powers who support Mobutu, and when he speaks of the intervention of French troops in Africa, he refers explicitly to Kolwezi in Shaba province. The art exhibit he is mounting draws from the unique treasures of Zaire. Even Ngandu's own fiction, in contrast to Senghor's more widely ranging topics, has been termed a "Zairian cyle," in which the writer privileges "le fait historique zaïrois, de la sorte que chaque oeuvre correspond à une période déterminée, qu'elle developpe à travers un événement" (details of Zairian history, in such a way that each work corresponds to a specific period and develops in terms of an event) (Kalonji, 14).

While both writers have explicit political purposes in their literature, these purposes differ importantly. The older articulated the affirmation of African culture that paralleled the movement toward independence. Responding to the assimilationist policy of the French government that saw the African as *tabula rasa*, Senghor attempted to convey the idea that Africa had a culture of its own, that it might well assimilate Western advances but that it would not be assimilated. Ngandu, writing in the postcolonial era, finds the global assertion of African cultural values a feeble weapon to use against the ongoing injustices of racism and neocolonialism. Through their generic nature, the image of Africa and Africans seen through the optic of Negritude has merely confirmed certain Western prejudices and provided additional stereotypes for the African in France to confront. In his mission to introduce African culture into a French community, Negritude, with its inherent idealism, fails to engage the realistic issues of racism, poverty, and suffering. Senghor's optimism anticipates the victory of nationalism; in the disillusionment of the post-independence period, Ngandu is fatalistic.

If Ngandu perceives Senghor's work so negatively, why does he evoke him so consistently? What do these references to Senghor, often marginally introduced and peripheral to the actual narrative, contribute to his purpose in writing? Ultimately, Ngandu is giving an account of his professional experiences as an African intellectual in France and of his efforts to bring African culture to the attention of a French audience. Because his work deals explicitly with questions of race and African culture there is no way that he can avoid the heritage of Senghor and the imprint of Negritude so deeply ingrained not only in the minds of his educated French audience but also in his own view of the world. Despite the efforts of critics such as Marcien Towa and Stanislas Adotevi to diminish the impact of Negritude, Senghor's works are taught widely and often uncritically. Ngandu cannot discuss relationships between Africans and French without confronting Senghor's ghost and, indeed, attempting to vanquish it. He therefore challenges Negritude's place in the contemporary dialogue between France and Zaire, assigning it to its historical moment, recognizing its current limitations, and establishing a certain distance between Senghor's vision and the present. This distance, however, is important. Ngandu's message throughout the text is consistently pessimistic with respect to Africa's future in general and its relationship with Europe in particular, and one of the ways he conveys this sense of hopelessness is by negating not only Senghor's idealistic representation of Africa but also his visions of a harmonious future for that continent within the international community, the Teilhardian notion of civilization, the Universal Banquet to which Africa would contribute on an equal footing with other peoples. Ngandu's enumeration of discrimination, racism, oppression, and exploitation in the present are rendered all the more powerful when juxtaposed with the dreams of the future that Senghor elaborated more than a quarter of a century previously.

Notes

1. For an excellent bibliography of works by and about Ngandu, biographical information, and an overview of his writing, see Kalonji.

2. His experience of this period appears in his first collection of poems, *Chants d'ombre* (1945) and to some extent in his second volume, *Hosties noires* (1948). Most of his early conceptual essays affirming African culture are articulated in *Liberté I: Négritude et humanisme.*

3. On Senghor's tremendous impact on the next literary generation, see V. Y. Mudimbe (36), another Zairian writer.

4. For analyses of Senghor's use of the quest motif, see Lebaud, 41–71 and Spleth, 67–69, 110–16.

5. The Belgian Congo was renamed the Democratic Republic of Congo at independence in 1960, and then Zaire after Mobutu came to power in 1965. With the removal of Mobutu in 1997, it became, again, the Democratic Republic of the Congo. Given that Ngandu was writing during and about the period of Mobutu's regime, I have retained the terms "Zaire" and "Zairian" despite the political transition that occurred during the writing of this essay.

6. "Et lorsqu'un Africain est appelé à violer le sanctuaire, il éprouve comme une angoisse souterraine, qui rappelle bien la traversée du Styx et de l'Achéron. Je pourrais dire, en utilisant la même image mythologique, que mon expérience a été la traversée de l'enfer" (And when an African is called upon to violate the sanctuary, he feels a sort of subterranean anguish, which clearly resembles the crossing of the Styx or the Acheron. Using the same mythological image, I could say that my experience was a voyage to hell) (15). Translations of works by both Ngandu Nkashama and Senghor are mine.

7. See, page 41, the passage that begins: "Voici le Temps et l'Espace . . . "

8. "Tu fus africaine dans ma mémoire ancienne, comme moi comme les neiges de l'Atlas" (You were African in my ancient memory, like me, like the snows of the Atlas Mountains) (41).

9. "Mânes ô Mânes de mes Pères/ Contemplez son front casqué et la candeur de sa bouche" (Shades, oh Shades of my Fathers/ Behold her helmeted brow and the guilelessness of her mouth) (41).

10. "Alors, apparurent, affleurant au-dessus des lianes et culminant dans les nuages, les deux oreilles blanches, puis, la bouche frémissante du chat" (Then appeared, rising above the foliage and culminating in the clouds, two white ears, followed by the quivering mouth of the cat) (30).

11. "Tous les contraires accordés, toutes les contradictions conciliées" (All differences resolved, all contradictions reconciled) (31).

12. See the lines that conclude *"Que m'accompagnent kôras et balafong"* (Let Koras and Balafong Accompany Me), a hymn to the African night: "O ma

Lionne ma Beauté noire, ma Nuit noire ma Noire ma Nue!... Nuit qui fonds
toutes mes contradictions, toutes contradictions dans l'unité première de ta
négritude" (O my Lioness, by Black Beauty, my Black Night my Black Woman
my Naked Woman!... Night that melts away all of my contradictions, all contradictions in the first unity of your negritude) (37).

13. "Elle était là immobile, fascinante, défiante et méprisante à la fois. Et
elle me narguait, elle m'anéantissait" (She was there immobile, fascinating,
defiant and scornful at the same time. And she derided me, she annihilated
me") (37).

14. "Le sentiment de ses limites devant la destinée. Mais également, une
idée qu'il pouvait en triompher, s'il possède suffisamment de foi en lui-même..."
(The awareness of his limits in the face of destiny. But also, an idea that he
could triumph over it, if he possessed enough faith in himself...) (37).

15. See the lines that begin: "Mon animal gardien, il me faut le cacher..."
(I must hide my guardian animal...) (24).

16. In "Que m'accompagnent kôras et balafong," he again describes his
relationship with Europeans in negative terms: "Nuit qui me délivres des raisons
des salons des sophismes, des pirouettes des prétextes, des haines calculées
des carnages humanisés" (Night that delivers me from reasons from salons,
from sophisms, from pirouettes from pretexts, from calculated hatreds, from
humanized carnage) (37).

17. "Cependant, que de comportements ambigus! Tous, faits de
condescendance et de franche supercherie. Une ambiguïté de verbe, qui
finit par corroder la volonté du dialogue..." (In the meantime, what ambiguous behavior! Everything, acts of condescension and of outright trick-
ery. An ambiguity of language that ends up by corroding the intention of
dialogue...) (11).

18. The prayer goes on: "Tu ne comprends pas ma situation. C'est ma
première mission. Si je la rate, ma vie est fichue. Ils ne me feraient plus
confiance.... C'est le pays du Blanc" (You don't understand my situation. It's
my first mission. If I botch it, my life is ruined. They won't trust me anymore....
It's the White Man's country) (61–63).

19. Claire Vander Veken, for instance, writes: "Une lecture globale du
discours politique de Senghor révèle d'emblée l'importance de l'axe 'je'—'tu'
qui le sous-tend et le structure, ainsi que, corrollairement, la portée de
l'apostrophe, qui fonctionne comme élément cristallisateur et révélateur des
sentiments du locuteur envers son allocutaire" (A global reading of Senghor's
political discourse at once reveals the importance of the I-thou axis that underlies and structures it, as well as the significance of apostrophe, which
functions as a crystallizing element capable of revealing the feelings of the
speaker towards the one being addressed) (126).

20. Describing Ngandu's own experience of Mobutu's repressive policies
in Lubumbashi, Kolonji singles out the 1978 crackdown on the university as a
decisive episode for the writer—who denounced it: "C'est le début de ses
démêlés officiels avec le pouvoir politique qui le fait arrêter, torturer et reléguer
dans son village natal, au terme d'une grève à l'université" (This is the begin-

ning of his official difficulties with political power that caused him to be arrested, tortured, and banished to his home village, at the end of a strike at the university) (147). This episode explains in part the morbid state of mind referred to by the writer in *Vie et moeurs*.

21. The dual nature of French racism and its development with regard to the immigrant population is developed at length by Wieviorka: "L'immigré, jusque dans les années soixante-dix, était avant tout un travailleur, généralement venu seul, hébergé dans un foyer ou surexploité par un marchand de sommeil, localisé à proximité de l'emploi, figure ouvrière définie par une position inférieure—la plus basse—dans les rapports de production" (The immigrant, prior to the seventies, was above all a manual laborer, generally arriving alone, staying in a hostel or superexploited by a slumlord, situated near his place of employment, a working-class figure defined by an inferior position— the lowest—in the relations of production) (28). Ngandu illustrates the pervasiveness of this image, mentioning instances in which he is mistaken for a porter or janitor.

22. "Pourquoi nous, on n'a jamais parlé de 'blanchitude:' la pensée et la philosophie, la raison et l'algèbre, la physique et les météorites, les astres et le jour, l'apartheid et le contraceptif, le développement et l'histoire, la paix et la liberté. Et qu'il ne nous resterait peut-être que les lascivités des rites initiatiques, les mystiques des Rastamen, et les vibrations des poésies assonancées" (Why haven't we ever spoken of "blanchitude"; thought and philosophy, reason and algebra, physics and meteorites, stars and day, apartheid and contraceptives, development and history, peace and liberty. And what is left for us except perhaps the lasciviousness of initiatory rites, the mysticism of the Rastamen, and the vibrations of assonant poetry) (100).

23. Several chapters are devoted to this expression in *Négritude et poétique*.

24. "C'est alors que j'ai compris 'l'émotion nègre,' formule qui voudrait dire, dans la situation actuelle, que l'Occidental ne voit le nègre qu'au travers de l'émotion. . . . A la limite, le nègre se trouve ramené à cette émotion, et exige qu'elle le confine à un espace unidimensionnel. En sortir signifie franchir la ligne, signifie faire éclater les cloisons étanches du ghetto historique, signifie s'ériger en une menace potentielle, et donc, un danger à écarter. Le scorpion, la salamandre" (It was then that I understood "black emotion," a formula that meant, in the current situation, that the Occidental sees the black man exclusively through emotion. . . . In extreme cases, the black man finds himself reduced to that emotion, and requires that it confine him to a one-dimensional space. To leave it means crossing the line, bursting through the bulkheads of the historical ghetto, setting oneself up as a potential threat, and therefore, a danger to be averted. The scorpion. The salamander) (9).

25. For another assessment of Negritude as racism, see Towa, 99–108 and Adotevi, 113–121.

26. "J'ai réellement découvert tout un univers de rites et de pratiques magiques, qui survivent avec une force incroyable dans cette France profonde. Non pas des pratiques marginales, mais des faits et des éléments intégrés à la vie, modelant les formes des langages, l'ordonnancement de l'esprit. . . . Je ne

pouvais m'empêcher de rapprocher ces coutumes bruissant de paniques et de menaces sournoises, au monde de mon grand-père au village. Les croyances et les conduites étaient semblables. La même confiance dans les force captives, la même formulation des actes qui se situent au-delà de l'univers du visible" (I really discovered an entire universe of rites and magic practices, that survive with unbelievable force in the heart of France. Not merely marginal practices, but deeds and elements integrated into life, shaping the forms of languages, the ordering the mind . . . I could not prevent myself form comparing these customs, humming with panic and stealthy threats, to the world of my grandfather in the village. The beliefs and behaviors were similar. The same faith in captive forces, the same formulation of acts situated beyond the universe of the visible) (35–36).

27. Sartre, in his preface to Senghor's 1947 anthology of black poetry, similarly contrasts the white and black races, claiming that each relates differently to nature. The former, he tells us, seeks to transform nature through technology; for the latter, "il s'agit bien d'une captation du monde, mais magique, par le silence et le repos" (it is a question of a captation of the world, but magical, by silence and repose) (xxx–xxxi).

28. "Je voulais tant leur dire que la souffrance, dans les villages, est partagée unanimement et uniment par l'ensemble du groupe. Que la naissance et la mort sont assumées collectivement. . . . Que l'enfant appartient en propre à la cellule familiale ou élargie, qu'il trouve son refuge auprès de chaque individu faisant partie de son environnement immédiat. Que les traditions, si primitives soient-elles, n'ont pour finalité précise que de réduire les peines et les misères à des formes concrètes d'une expérience de la vie" (I wanted so much to tell them that suffering, in the villages, is shared unanimously and uniformly by the entire group. That birth and death are assumed collectively. . . . That the child belongs exclusively to the family or extended family unit, that he finds his refuge with each individual belonging to his immediate environment. That traditions, however primitive they may be, have no other end than that of reducing pain and misery to concrete forms of an experience of life) (140).

29. In "Neige sur Paris," where France is referred to figuratively as "white hands," Senghor draws up a list of grievances—imperialism, slavery, insult, humiliation, and the exploitation of the continent's resources—but refuses to nurture resentment (23). In "Prière de paix," a similar recitation of France's sins is followed by forgiveness: "Oui, Seigneur, pardonne à la France qui hait les occupants et m'impose l'occupation si gravement" (Yes, Lord, pardon France who hates the occupiers and imposes occupation so heavily on me) (94).

30. "Nous nous sommes accordés tous pour dire que la colonisation a été un crime contre l'humanité. Mais aucun homme n'a été jugé pour cela. . . . Et les mêmes . . . reviennent sur nos terres, collaborent avec nos dirigeants, participent aux instances de décisions. . . . Et nos peuples applaudissent. Ils ont tout transformé maintenant: le crime a été un bienfait pour nos populations. Il a apporté les écoles et la civilisation. La machine et les billets de banque. Les diplômes et la syphilis. Et les peuples se sont mis à pardonner" (We have

all agreed that colonization was a crime against humanity. But no man was
judged for that. . . . And the same men . . . come back to our lands, collaborate
with our leaders, participate in decisions. . . . And our people applaud. They
have transformed everything now: the crime was a godsend for our populations. It brought schools and civilization. The machine and banknotes. Diplo-
mas and syphilis. And the people began to pardon) (145).

31. "Cette énigme: les nazis pensaient agir au nom du bien de l'humanité.
Sans eux, nous n'aurions pas connu le nucléaire, ni les missiles sol-air-mer. Et
si aujourd'hui, un nazi participe à un gouvernement occidental, qui pourrait
croire à sa conversion" (This enigma: the Nazis thought they were acting in the
name of the good of humanity. Without them, we would not have known
nuclear fission or surface-to-air missiles. And yet if today a Nazi were to
become involved in a Western government, who would be able to believe in
his conversion) (145).

32. The passage quoted above continues: "Je ne voudrais pas prêcher le
racisme. Tous, ils me jetteraient des pierres colossales et m'enseveliraient sous
des tas de roches. Il ne s'agit même pas de racisme. Mais de faire comprendre
que ma conscience des faits est telle." (I would not want to preach racism.
Everyone would throw colossal stones and bury me under a pile of rocks. It
isn't even a question of racism. But of making people understand that my
awareness of the facts is such) (145).

33. See note 30.

34. In demonstrating his reluctance to follow Senghor's lead in pardoning
Europe for its crimes, he joins with other critics of Senghor's generosity. See,
for instance, Marcien Towa, 72.

35. "Je me suis alors rendu compte que la mort nous a été imposée en
permanence. . . . Si des légions étrangères (avons-nous, nous aussi, des légions
étrangères?) peuvent venir chez nous, tirer un petit coup dans des safaris
exotiques et rentrer *at home*, couverts de lauriers, alors notre compte est bon"
(I then realized that death had been continuously imposed on us. . . . If foreign
legions (do we, too, have our foreign legions?) can come to our country, take
a few pot shots on exotic safaris, and return home, covered with laurels, then
we've had it) (148).

36. The reference to *Candide* is explicit, as the passage quoted above
continues: "Bien entendu je peux dépasser ces sentiments primaires. A la
limite je peux les ignorer, les sublimer dans des attitudes généreuses: la
civilisation de l'Universel, par exemple. Nous, peuple magnanime, donateur
des hautes pensées. Légataire universel de l'humanité effondrée. Je peux
considérer que tout est bon, que tout est pour le mieux dans le meilleur des
mondes" (I can of course go beyond these primary feelings. In extreme cases,
I can ignore them, sublimate them in generous attitudes: the Universal Civilization, for example. We are a magnanimous people, donor of high thoughts.
Sole legatee of prostrate humanity. I can consider that everything is for the
best in the best of all worlds) (148–149).

37. Its metaphorical nature is enhanced by references to places in Senegal
that were important to the poet: "Tanns d'enfance tanns de Joal, et ceux de

Dyilôr en Septembre" (Beaches of childhood, beaches of Joal and those of Dyilôr in September) (*Poèmes*, 102).

38. I'm thinking of the line: "Vous gardez ce lieu forclos à tout rire de femme, à tout sourire qui se fane / Vous distillez cet air d'éternité où je respire l'air de mes Pères" (You maintain this place forbidden to women's laughter, to smiles that wither / You distill this air of eternity where I breath the air of my Fathers) (*Poèmes*, 23).

39. "Fixez vos yeux immuables sur vos enfants. . . . Que nous répondions présents à la renaissance du monde" (Fix your immutable eyes on your children . . . That we may answer present at the renaissance of the world) (*Poèmes*, 23).

40. "S'ils ont pu avoir la puissance de réaliser de tels prodiges, qu'en serait-il s'ils pouvaient s'en servir maintenant pour reconstruire un monde nouveau, qui soit le produit de leurs mains?" (If they had the power to accomplish such prodigious feats in the past, what would happen if they were to use it now to reconstruct the new world that would be the product of their hands?) (175).

41. "Mais lorsque ses mains brûlent de soufre et des détresses ignifiées sur les flammes des chalumeaux parce qu'il doit 'produire' à la chaîne des statu-ettes bariolées de couleurs résineuses, de raphia peinturluré, vendues à des touristes boulimiques, alors là, il faut dire que l'univers s'est transformé en une terre de mort." (But when his hands burn from sulfur and from ignified distresses on the flames of the blowtorch because he must "mass-produce" statuettes decorated with bright, resinous colors and painted raffia, sold to bulimic tourists, well then, the universe has been transformed into a land of death) (176).

42. Ngandu thereby affirms in his own historical period the overwhelming importance that Sartre attributes to suffering as part of the black experience in "*Orphée noir*" (xxxiv).

43. "L'intellectuel colonisé qui est parti très loin du côté de la culture occidentale et qui se met en tête de proclamer l'existence d'une culture ne le fait jamais au nom de l'Angola ou du Dahomey. La culture qui est affirmée est la culture africaine" (The colonized intellectual who has gone a long way in the direction of Western culture and who takes it into his head to proclaim the existence of a culture never does it in the name of Angola or Dahomey. The culture that is affirmed is African culture) (Fanon, 159).

44. On Negritude's influence on the development of Zairian poetry, see Kadima-Nzuji (89–101).

Works Cited

Adotevi, Stanislas. *Négritude et négrologues*. Paris: Union Générale d'Editions, 1972.

Fanon, Frantz. *Les damnés de la terre*. Paris: Maspero, 1961.

Kadima-Nzuji, Mukala. *La littérature zaïroise de langue française (1945–1965)*. Paris: ACCT/ Karthala, 1954.

Kalonji, M. T. Zezeze. *Une écriture de la passion chez Pius Ngandu Nkashama.* Paris: Harmattan, 1992.

Lebaud, Geneviève. *Léopold Sédar Senghor ou la poésie du royaume d'enfance.* Dakar: Nouvelles Editions Africaines, 1976.

Mudimbe, V. Y. *L'odeur du Père: Essai sur les limites de la science et de la vie en Afrique Noire.* Paris: Présence Africaine, 1982.

Ngandu Nkashama, Pius. *Négritude et poétique: Une lecture de l'oeuvre critique de Léopold Sédar Senghor.* Paris: Harmattan, 1992.

————. *Vie et moeurs d'un primitif en Essonne quatre-vingt-onze.* Paris: Harmattan, 1987.

Sartre, Jean-Paul. "Orphée noir." *Anthologie de la nouvelle poésie nègre et malgache de langue francaise.* 1948. Ed. Leopold Sédar Senghor. Paris: PUF, 1977, ix–xliv.

Senghor, Léopold Sédar. *Liberté I: Négritude et humanisme.* Paris: Seuil, 1964.

————. *Pierre Teilhard de Chardin et la politique africaine.* Paris: Seuil, 1962.

————. *Poèmes.* Paris: Seuil, 1984.

Spleth, Janice. *Léopold Sédar Senghor.* Twayne's World Authors Series 765. Boston: Hall, 1985.

Towa, Marcien. *Léopold Sédar Senghor: Négritude ou Servitude?* Yaoundé: CLE, 1971.

Vander Veken, Claire. "Analyse de l'axe 'je'—'tu' dans *Que m'accompagnent kôras et balafong.*" *Critical Perspectives on Léopold Sédar Senghor.* Ed. Janice Spleth. Colorado Springs: Three Continents, 1993, 125–137.

Wieviorka, Michel. *La France raciste.* Paris: Seuil, 1992.

14

Interdisciplinarity, Knowledge, and Desire

A Reading of Marcel Griaule's Dieu d'eau

Leslie Rabine

This essay grew out of research on the global circulation of African fashion as both symbolic and economic exchange. Based on field work in Dakar, Senegal, the African American community of Los Angeles, and the Kikuyu area of Kenya, the research studies an informal, decentered transnational network of small-scale designer-producer-vendors. Its subjects are craftspeople from nations and communities that the globalization of capital has placed in economic crisis. Finding creative means to survive economically, the craftspeople actively produce a widely used form of cultural symbolization. Rather than discuss the research itself, however, this essay explores epistemological questions it has raised concerning cultural studies.[1] The field of French cultural studies, and its challenge to the discipline of French literature, has come from deep historical crises in the boundaries that have organized both nations and academic disciplines for the past two centuries. The system of academic disciplines that produced the institution of French literature emerged in a world based on national units. Literature, for instance the French, English, and Russian novels of the nineteenth century, became a celebrated vehicle for the symbolic production of national identities, embodied in national languages. As aesthetic form, literature endowed positive value on national cultures.

In the present age, national boundaries tend to dissolve in global flows of corporate finance, electronic communication, viruses, and travelling people (such as the subjects of my research) seeking political or economic survival. In such a world, forms of symbolic expression that move across national borders and communicate across national languages—such as fashion, but also popular music and video—have decentered the study of literature as the privileged symbolic practice for constructing identities and encoding cultural values. In the humanities, literature has become one of many expressive forms deserving critical analysis. As an effect, the symbolic processes of identity and value formation that literary study had naturalized have themselves become objects of inquiry. This inquiry has in turn thrown into question the methods and tools of the disciplinary critical analysis itself.

For research on the meanings of African fashion, I had to study symbolic practices that were codified neither in printed texts nor in my own subjectivity, but through and by subjects of a culture that my own culture had relegated to the position of Other, and that thus were not readily readable or understandable to me. I therefore had to supplement methods of textual reading with methods of field work, borrowed from social sciences. That double border crossing, learning unfamiliar methods, while also studying people from cultures that my culture has been oppressing, brought me into a strong and multiple sense of doubt. Beginning with my academic identity and identifications, not to mention my abilities, that sense of doubt came to embrace disciplines that developed in and through the process of colonialism, as well as the models of knowledge production that inform them.

The specific object of my research, the cross-cultural study of clothing, only reenforced those doubts. Both method and object of study brought home to me in concrete ways the different critiques of knowledge articulated on the one hand by ethnographers, and on the other by humanists. Ethnographers have shown that the researching subject can have no knowledge of the other that is not already permeated with our own culturally dominant frame of reference. One humanistic critique revolves around a central metaphor of Western knowledge, that of clothing. Clothing figures the false appearance hiding the "naked truth." Knowledge production operates by removing or penetrating that decorative facade to uncover the "bare facts." Whether, as in this traditional model of knowledge, clothing figures the obstacle to truth, or whether, as in the deconstructive critique, it constructs the truth by the act of hiding it, in either case, clothing represents the impossibility of knowledge.

MYTHS OF ORIGIN OF SEXUALITY, KNOWLEDGE, AND CLOTHING

The paradoxically impossible project of trying to gain deep knowledge of a culture by studying the object that represents superficiality and the obstacle to knowledge inevitably led to questions about the structure of knowledge itself. The ethical problems involved in my researching an othered, marginalized culture through a model of knowledge that implies undressing it, and thus violating it, only intensified those questions.

In order to explore them, I will compare this model of knowledge cross-culturally to a West African model of knowledge also figured by clothing, and also, like the Western model, embodied in a myth of origin. The Biblical story of Adam and Eve will be compared to the myth of the origin of clothing and knowledge in the cosmology of the Dogon of Mali as reported in *Dieu d'eau: Entretiens avec Ogotemmêli* (1966) (*Conversations with Ogotemmêli*) (1965) (hereafter DE and CO), the 1948 landmark study by pioneering French ethnographer Marcel Griaule. Griaule's work crystallizes, by its very effort to prove the existence of other complex epistemologies, the impossibility of knowing another model of knowledge from within our own. A discussion of his text and the heated debates it has evoked suggests how epistemological questions raised by the interdisciplinary methods of cultural studies can help us distance ourselves from identity investment in any discipline and its knowledge claims, however valuable. In Adam and Eve's passage from innocence to knowledge, their first knowledge is that of nakedness, and their first conscious act the production of girdles to cover it. They invent clothing to cover the object of their knowledge, and at the same time to try to hide their new knowing state from God. But the product of their first technical invention becomes the sign of their knowledge of nakedness, and by extension, the sign by which God recognizes they have eaten the forbidden fruit. Adam and Eve's use of clothing to hide their knowledge becomes the sign that reveals to God the fact of their knowledge.

This ambiguity of clothing to reveal that which it serves to hide lies at the heart of the Judeo-Christian myth of origin. And since the knowledge Adam and Eve gain is fundamentally that of sexual desire and morality, the ambiguity operates in clothing equally as figure of knowledge and as protector of morality. Clothing functions as a mask or veil which is both the sign of morality and the invitation to immorality. It denies desire, yet solicits desire. For both knowledge and desire, the hiding calls attention to what is hidden. Unveiling or revelation does not reveal that true, hidden object, but destroys knowledge and desire.

Clothing's role of associating knowledge so closely with the body, makes it inseparable from desire. As with the other features in the model of knowledge as an unveiling, this union of scholarly knowledge and erotic desire operates only through ambiguity and denial. Since Plato's *Symposium*, and more determinedly since Descartes's *Discours de la méthode*, Western thought has sought to substitute the eros of the scholarly quest with the sublimated philos of philosophy.[2]

By contrast, Dogon myths of the origin of clothing-as-knowledge, as recounted in Marcel Griaule's *Dieu d'eau*, bring its erotic impulse to the foreground. Published in 1948, the book popularized ethnography in France, revolutionized ethnographic method, had a decisive influence on the study of African art, architecture, and psychology, and established Griaule's unique position in anthropology (Clifford, 55–60; Leclerc, 155–157, 183).

A student of Marcel Mauss and a leading founder of the Musée de l'homme, Griaule began his career by collecting cultural artifacts (cf. *Masques dogons*, 1938), but came to believe that each culture has, underlying its social organization and ritual observances, its own intricate, authentic epistemology. *Dieu d'eau* set him apart from the structural functionalists in Malinowski's school and even the American cultural relativists of the period. In structural functionalism, myth, ritual, and symbolic cultural practices were seen as instruments of an underlying social organization. As a corollary, only an objective outsider could gain knowledge of that organizing structure, inaccessible to those who lived it. Griaule's method reverses this. Since the layers of myth, ritual, custom, and social practice express elements of an underlying epistemological system, only the privileged elders of the group who had passed into possession of its initiatory knowledge had access to it. The anthropologists could gain it only through a similar process of initiation from these insiders. Believing epistemology, rather than social functionalism, to be the foundation of culture, Griaule frequently criticized the ethnocentrism of Western thought and its "esprit cartésien que nous croyons universel" (Cartesian mind that we believe to be universal) (Griaule, *Conseiller de l'union française*, 29).[3]

In an "hommage" to Ogotemmêli, he expressed the wish to "s'excuser pour tous les mépris d'Europe et d'Amérique, pour toutes les ignorances" (DE, 230) (apologize for all the contempt and all the ignorance of Europe and America) (CO, 216). In the course of his career he came to speak and write against the arrogant ignorance of European colonialists:

Lorsqu'ils assument la lourde tâche d'assurer un bonheur conven-
tionnel à des populations qualifiées hâtivement d'attardées sous le
prétexte qu'elles ne possèdent que des techniques rudimentaires,
les Blancs quels qu'ils soient, d'Europe ou d'Amérique, s'ils négligent
la portée pratique d'une manière de penser pleine de nuances et
cheminant par des voies complexes, s'ils n'y cherchent pas le
levain d'une civilisation originale ayant ses valeurs propres, ne font
oeuvre ni de science ni d'humanité.

(When they take upon themselves the onerous task of assuring the
conventional well-being of populations hastily termed backward
on the pretext that they have only the most rudimentary of technology, whites, whether they be European or American, who
neglect the practical implications of a way of thinking full of
nuance and complex pathways, and who do not seek in it the
leaven of an original civilization with its own inherent values,
perform neither scientific nor human work.) (Griaule, *Descente du
troisième verbe*, 81)

Having moved away from his early position as colonial anthropologist, Griaule nevertheless remained in the ambiguous position of any
white ethnographer whether in the age of colonialism or postcolonialism.
V. Y. Mudimbe reproaches him for believing that "the colonial admin-
istration might use [his] science and experience to implement the conversion of the native society" (*The Invention of Africa*, 68).

After leading the French government-sponsored expedition of the
Mission Dakar-Djibouti across France's African colonial empire in 1932,
Griaule increasingly focused on studying the Dogon of what is now
Mali. In 1946, the Dogon elders invited him to spend thirty-three days
in private dialogue with the old wise man Ogotemmêli, learning the
secrets of Dogon initiatory knowledge. *Dieu d'eau* purports to be an
authentic transcription of Ogotemmêli's words, set in a narrative of the
relation between the two men.

The epistemology Ogotemmêli elaborates has clothing as its foundational figure and joins knowledge to desire, but in a way critically
different from the Western model. It unfolds through a complex myth
of the multiple-stage origin of the earth, language, humanity, sexual
relations, all the techniques of human culture, social organization, and
ritual. All these are connected through a web of symbolic "correspondances" or "alliances," which together make up the "système du monde"
(DE, 80) (world-system) (CO, 72).

The origin of symbolization itself, which provides the framework
for the whole structure of connections, happens through the birth of
three successive languages. The first language, or "parole" ("Word")
originates after the God Amma takes the Earth to wife by force, excises

her ant-hill clitoris, brings about her submission, and impregnates her twice, the first time with the disastrous son the Jackal, and the second with the Nommo. The Nommo, twin water genies who "represented perfect union" (CO, 19), created the first language:

> Le Nommo, du haut du ciel, vit sa mère, la Terre, nue et sans parole, ce qui était sans doute la conséquence du premier incident survenu lors des rapports avec le Dieu Amma. Il fallait mettre fin à ce désordre. Le Nommo descendit sur la Terre, apportant des fibres tirées de plantes. . . . Il en sépara dix poignées correspondant à ses dix doigts et en toronna cinq pour les placer devant et cinq pour les placer derrière. . . . Mais le rôle de ce vêtement n'était pas seulement de pudeur. Il présentait au monde terrestre le premier acte d'ordonnance universelle et le signe hélicoïdal qui se projette sur un plan sous forme de ligne brisée serpentante. . . . (DE, 27)

> (The Nommo, looking down from Heaven, saw their mother, the earth, naked and speechless, as a consequence no doubt of the original incident in her relations with the God Amma. It was necessary to put an end to this state of disorder. The Nummo accordingly came down to earth, bringing with them fibres pulled from plants. . . . They took ten bunches of these fibres, corresponding to the number of their ten fingers, and made two strands of them, one for the front and one for behind. . . . But the purpose of this garment was not merely modesty. It manifested on earth the first act in the ordering of the universe, and the revelation of the helicoid sign. . . .) (CO, 19–20)

To be naked, then, is to be without language: "Ainsi vêtue, la Terre avait un langage" (DE, 28) (Thus clothed, the Earth had a language) (CO, 20). Clothing is both language and the symbol of language, with the first clothing constituting not only a sign but the archetype of symbolization itself. It can play this role because it is produced rather than natural, and therefore composed of and resembling many things. Through its multiple identity and associations, it connects things with meanings as well as different meanings among themselves. As archetypal sign, it is both a material thing in itself as signifier and a relation referring to other material things as signified:

> Les fibres, en effet, tombaient en torsades, symbole des tornades, des méandres des torrents, des tourbillons des eaux et des vents, de la marche ondulante des reptiles. Elles rappelaient aussi les spirales à huit tours du soleil pompeur d'humidité. Elles étaient elles-mêmes un cheminement d'eau parce que gorgées des fraîcheurs prises aux plantes célestes. Elles étaient pleines de l'essence du Nommo, elles étaient le Nommo lui-même, en mouvement. . . . (DE, 27)

(For the fibres fell in coils, symbol of tornadoes, of the windings of torrents, of eddies and whirlwinds, of the undulating movement of reptiles. They recall also the eight-fold spirals of the sun, which sucks up moisture. They were themselves a channel of moisture, impregnated as they were with the freshness of the celestial plants.) (CO, 20)

Even at its preliminary stages, this model of knowledge makes explicit those operations that the Western model denies. Knowledge, for which the "Word" serves as vehicle, is not deemed to hide its object but to produce it through its organizing activity. Clothing's role of covering the body can never be separate from and primary to its symbolic functions ("Mais le rôle de ce vêtement n'était pas seulement de pudeur" (DE, 27) (But the role of this garment was not merely modesty) (CO, 20). It can provide modesty only in the sense that its symbolizing activity essentially creates an order among disordered things, thereby giving them meaning and making them accessible to knowledge. The dress/verb through its activity produces the foundational building blocks and connections for the web of symbolic correspondences that will organize all human endeavor.

It can do so because it symbolizes, and at the same time actually is, the materiality of speech itself:

> Mais le Nommo, lorsqu'il parle, émet comme tout être une buée tiède porteuse de verbe, verbe elle-même. Et cette buée sonore, comme toute eau, se meut sur une ligne hélicoïdale. Les torsades du vêtement étaient donc un chemin de prédilection pour la parole que le génie voulait révéler à la Terre. (DE, 27–28)

> (When Nommo speaks, what comes from his mouth is a warm vapour which conveys, and itself constitutes, speech. This vapour, like all water, has sound, dies away in a helicoid line. The coiled fringes of the skirt were therefore the chosen vehicle for the words which the Spirit desired to reveal to the earth.) (CO, 20).

Also explicit is the necessary connection between knowledge and sexuality, emphasized by physical proximity: "Par ces fibres pleines d'eau et de paroles, le Nommo était donc continuellement présent devant le sexe de sa mère" (DE, 28). (In these fibres full of water and words, the Nommo is thus always present *in front of his mother's genitals*) (CO, 20) (Italicized words my addition to translation). As Ogotemmêli will elaborate the "système du monde," it will become more and more clear that the system of symbolic "alliances" includes, symbolizes, and is symbolized by sexual alliances.

But at this early stage, the close physical connection between sex, language, knowledge, and clothing serves to emphasize, again explicitly, their inseparability as objects of desire: "En effet le chacal, fils déçu et décevant de Dieu, désira la posséder [la parole] et mit la main sur les fibres qui la portaient, c'est-à-dire sur le vêtement de sa mère" (DE, 29) (This was because the jackal, the deluded and deceitful son of God, desired to possess speech, and laid hands on the fibres in which language was embodied, that is to say, on his mother's skirt) (CO, 21). She resists his "incest," but ends up defiled by her son. Although the Jackal rapes his mother in part because "il n'y avait pas d'ailleurs d'autre femme à désirer dans le monde" (DE, 29) (There was, it should be explained, no other woman in the world whom he could desire) (CO, 21), in contrast to the Western model of desire/knowledge, his desire explicitly directs itself toward the language/dress. He removes it not to possess the object it covers but to possess the cover itself. "Etre nu" (To be naked), as Ogotemmêli explains later, is not only to be "sans parole" (speechless), but also to be undesirable (DE, 91 [CO, 82]).

His myth also makes explicit another denied element of the Adam and Eve myth. In both accounts of the origin of knowledge/desire/clothing, the woman receives the blame for the Fall and must pay by succumbing to the domination of man. But where the biblical narrative is constructed to make the woman seem responsible, Ogotemmêli's discourse reveals the mechanisms of male supremacist ideology that motivate her Fall. First, while the biblical tale traces male supremacy back to a mythic origin of feminine evil, Ogotemmêli's story traces it back to an act of masculine violence: "[F]inalement elle dut s'avouer vaincue. Ainsi étaient préfigurées les luttes équilibrées des hommes et des femmes qui se terminent pourtant par la victoire masculine" (DE, 29) ([I]n the end she had to admit defeat. This prefigured the even-handed struggles between men and women, which, however, always end in the victory of the male) (CO, 21). Second, the act of telling the story reperforms the original injustice, for although the narrative makes it clear that the Jackal's incest is also a rape, neither Ogotemmêli nor Griaule as narrator recognizes it as such. And neither recognizes the injustice in the fact that although Earth resists as strenuously as she can, she has still "devenue impure" (become impure), and so her state is "incompatible avec le règne de Dieu" who "se détourna de cette épouse" (incompatible with the reign of God (who) turned away from this wife) (my translation).

A significant difference between the two models of knowledge/desire does result, however, from this different treatment of the origins of feminine submission and impurity. In Ogotemmêli's story, the Nommo seeks to redeem and repurify its mother, and by the same token to invent a second language/dress for her since the first one has been stolen. The two language/dresses carry two distinct types of knowledge. The "crude" dress of plant fibers carries divine, oracular knowledge: "L'inceste . . . donna d'abord la parole au Chacal, ce qui devait lui permettre, pour l'éternité, de révéler aux devins à venir les desseins de Dieu" (DE, 29) (The incestuous act . . . endowed the jackal with the gift of speech so that ever afterwards he was able to reveal to diviners the designs of God) (CO, 21).

The second language/dress constitutes practical, human knowledge, including that of technology. In order to redeem and regenerate the Earth, as well as to give instruction to newly created humanity, the Nommo, of whom there are now eight, redescend into their mother's vagina and womb. The seventh, most perfect and also symbol of sexual union, receives "la connaissance parfaite d'un verbe . . . plus clair que le premier, non plus, comme le premier, réservé à quelques-uns, mais destiné à l'ensemble des hommes" (DE, 34) (the perfect knowledge of a Word . . . clearer than the first and not, like the first, reserved for particular recipients, but destined for all mankind) (CO, 27). Working from within to transform his mother's sexual organ, he merges his mouth with the mouth of her vagina, and invents the second language/knowledge as weaving:

> [L]e Septième génie expectora quatre-vingts fils de coton qu'il répartit entre ses dents supérieures utilisées comme celles d'un peigne de métier à tisser. . . . Il fit de même avec les dents inférieures. . . . En ouvrant et refermant ses machoires, le génie imprimait à la chaîne les mouvements que lui imposent les lices du métier . . . et la bande se formait hors de la bouche, dans le souffle de la deuxième parole révélée.
>
> En effet, le génie parlait. . . . Il octroyait son verbe au travers d'une technique, afin qu'il fût à la portée des hommes. Il montrait ainsi l'identité des gestes matériels et des forces spirituelles ou plutôt la nécessité de leur coopération. Le génie déclamait et ses paroles . . . étaient tissées dans les fils et faisaient corps avec la bande. Elles étaient le tissu lui-même et le tissu était le verbe. Et c'est pourquoi étoffe se dit *soy*, qui signifie "c'est la parole." (DE, 35)
>
> ([T]he seventh ancestor spat out eighty threads of cotton; these he distributed between his upper teeth which acted as the teeth of a weaver's reed. . . . He did the same with the lower teeth. . . . By opening and shutting his jaws the Spirit caused the threads of the warp to make the movements required in weaving . . . and the web

[strip] took shape from his mouth in the breath of the second
revealed Word.

For the Spirit was speaking while the work proceeded. . . . [H]e
imparted his Word by means of a technical process, so that all men
could understand. By so doing he showed the identity of material
actions and spiritual forces, or rather the need for their cooperation. The words that the Spirit uttered . . . were woven in the threads,
and formed one body with the cloth. They were the cloth, and the
cloth was the Word. That is why woven material is called soy,
which means "It is the spoken word.") (CO, 27–28; words in
brackets my addition)

This second language binds even closer together and more explicitly sexual desire, knowledge, and clothing. Throughout West Africa,
variations on strip weaving provide the foundation for traditional
clothing. The narrow, portable looms, of a required width and holding a required number of threads in the warp, produce strips the
whole length of a fifty-meter field. Strip weaving provides the foundation for Malian *bogolan* or mud cloth, and also includes the Ashante
kente of Ghana, as well as the *séru râbbal* of Senegal. As Ogotemmêli
says, the work of the weavers repeats and also symbolizes the words
and acts of the originating genie. Technically more refined than the
plant fiber dress, woven cloth is a higher language, and as such it is
not just a "cache-sexe" (DE, 149) (genital cover [literally "hide-sex"]),
but the transformed feminine sexual organ itself.

Like the dress of plant fibers, weaving (both the act and the cloth)
attains this foundational status because of its power to connect things
and meanings at multiple levels. Weaving is itself the art of connecting.
So where the plant fiber dress becomes the symbol of symbolization,
weaving symbolizes, and even produces, the system of equivalences
among language, sexuality, technologies, material culture, and rituals
that make up the "système du monde." The "va-et-vient" (coming and
going) of the "navette universelle" (universal shuttle) weaves them all
together (DE, 120 [CO, 107]).

The other techniques, especially architecture and agriculture, are
forms of weaving:

La culture étant un tissage, le champ est comme une couverture à
huit bandes. . . . Or le tissage étant une parole, fixant la parole dans
le tissu par le va-et-vient de la navette sur la chaîne, la culture, par
le mouvement de va-et-vient du paysan sur les parcelles, fait pénétrer
le verbe des ancêtres, c'est-à-dire l'humidité, dans la terre travaillée,
fait reculer l'impureté de la terre. . . . (DE, 86)

(Cultivation thus being a form of weaving, a field is like a blanket made of eight strips. . . . Moreover, weaving is a form of speech, which is imparted to the fabric by the to-and-fro movement of the shuttle on the warp; and in the same way the to-and-fro movement of the peasant on his plot imparts the Word of the ancestors, that is to say, moisture, to the ground on which he works, and thus rids the earth of impurity. . . .) (CO, 77).

In the Adam and Eve story, knowledge also results in agriculture but in a different way. Like Eve's need to submit to her husband, Adam's need to toil in agriculture by the sweat of his brow is a punishment for the sin of stealing knowledge. By contrast, the work of agriculture in Ogotemmêli's myth is a new kind of knowledge that redeems humanity from the first violent theft and repurifies the Earth. While the model of knowledge that grows out of the Judeo-Christian tradition retains that mark of aggression as an unveiling or penetration, the model of knowledge as weaving repeats the purifying redemption from violent penetration.

Since its spiritual teaching is fused with the material technique, one learns by doing. Knowledge is not figured as mastering a resisting object, but as absorbing "l'héritage des hommes et que les tisserands transmettaient de génération en génération, aux claquements de la navette et au bruit aigre de la poulie du métier dite 'grincement de la parole' " (DE, 37) (. . . the heritage of mankind and which the weavers transmitted from generation to generation to the accompaniment of the clapping of the shuttle and the creaking of the block, which they call the "creaking of the Word") (CO, 29. Words in parentheses my translation). In Descente du troisième verbe (1996) (Descent of the Third Verb), Griaule, like Jomo Kenyatta in Facing Mount Kenya a few years before him, uses this more relaxed and integrated form of learning to criticize Western methods of instruction where knowledge is gained through punishing hardship and difficulty. Yet the Dogon model resembles its Western counterpart in the striking sense that knowledge as a sexual act carries with it the assumption of woman as the figure of knowledge and man as its agent.

This gendered structure of knowledge becomes even more apparent in the invention of the third "parole complète et claire des temps modernes" (DE, 74) (Word, complete and clear, of the new age [of modern times]) (CO, 65. Words in parentheses my translation), which incorporates weaving and sexuality in the form of metaphor. Through an act of weaving/talking/teaching, the Nommo creates the drum: "Et frapper le tambour est aussi tisser" (DE, 73) (Beating the drum is also a form of weaving)

(CO, 65). The ear, which receives the sound of the drum, figures both the male and the female sexual organs (DE, 149–150).

CRITIQUES OF DIEU D'EAU

The cosmology laid out in *Dieu d'eau* seems to present an alternative, uncannily parallel epistemology that denaturalizes and also implicitly critiques Western structures of knowledge. Yet the text that initially seemed to solve the problems of Western knowledge turned out to raise a whole new series of problems.

Mainstream, more positivist anthropologists had always been suspicious of Griaule's data on cosmology and initiatory knowledge in *Dieu d'eau* and its sequel *Le Renard pâle* (*The Pale Fox*). In the 1980s, Dutch anthropologist Walter E. A. van Beek did a restudy of the Dogon and was unable to replicate the findings of these two books. The publication of his critique, "Dogon Restudied: A Field Evaluation of the Work of Marcel Griaule" (1991), is accompanied by responses from seven noted anthropologists and scholars of Dogon culture, who debate the issues of ethnographic writing, researcher-informant relations, and the nature of initiatory knowledge and its secrets. They defend Griaule or concur with van Beek in varying degrees.

Griaule's claim to have transcribed without interpretation the voice of Ogotemmêli is well established. But who really speaks in this text? To what extent did Griaule's very presence over a long period influence the invention of a "traditional" knowledge? To what extent did Ogotemmêli tailor his dissertation to the ears of a white man? On the other hand, was van Beek unable to replicate the findings because only a few initiates had access to them, and those who did chose not to initiate him? All of these questions point to different ways that ethnographic knowledge founders when it attempts to unveil the truth of another culture.

Van Beek's own answer to them is implied in his conclusions. Assuring us that the work of *Dieu d'eau* and *Le Renard pâle* "is definitely not an individual fraud" ("Dogon Restudied," 155), he characterizes it as follows: "It is the product of a complex interaction between a strong-willed researcher, a colonial situation, an intelligent and creative body of informants, and a culture with a courtesy bias and a strong tendency to incorporate foreign elements" (157). But one could ask what field interview situation with what informants from what cultures this would not describe? As writings in feminist ethnography have argued, field interview data is always the result of a complex interaction between researcher and informant, rather than an "objective" finding (See Behar and Gordon; and Wolf). It brings to bear, as I have found, their personal intimacy and interpersonal chemistry, but also the relation between the unequal social positions they occupy, including the whole history of colonial and postcolonial relations that haunts the room with the two conversants.

Van Beek's conclusion raises even more questions: "[C]laiming to write ethnography, [Griaule] offered anthropology a glimpse into the highly intriguing territory between fact and fiction, the realm of created cultures, European as well as African. At the rim of the science of man, he embarked upon a veritable journey into the realm of intercultural fiction" (158). Van Beek's recourse to the field of literature in order to protect ethnography as a purely positive science of fact connects Griaule's work to issues of interdisciplinarity in its relation to desire and knowledge. In the recent "postmodern turn" in anthropology, ethnographers and literary critics alike argue that the literariness of ethnographic writing—and of the informants' speech itself—has always created a blurred, unstable, porous boundary between ethnography and fiction (See Behar and Gordon; and Clifford and Marcus).

Trying to preserve that imaginary boundary, van Beek's own disciplinary desire is at work in his strange claim that *Dieu d'eau* constitutes an "intercultural *fiction*." It is significant that as an ethnographer, he did not see the possibility that Ogotemmêli's account, especially if it possesses his own creativity, constitutes rather an insider's *ethnography* of Dogon culture. In her essay on Ruth Benedict, Barbara Babcock states that as early as the 1930s, Benedict argued in her writing on Pueblo myth "that myths are 'a native comment on native life,' " and considered the old storytellers' "textualizations of their culture as valid, as important, as the constructions of Pueblo life" by the ethnographer (Babcock, 118, 120).

If Ogotemmêli's myths constitute a "created culture," they also constitute, like an ethnography, an *interpretation* of Dogon culture as a coherent whole. They are based on long observation of daily life, material practice, custom, and ritual. They serve not to depict but to explain all levels of communal existence, and to organize them in an intelligible structure.

Seen in this light, *Dieu d'eau* could be approached less as an "intercultural fiction" than as an "intercultural knowledge," especially since the foregoing analysis has implied the necessarily fictional aspect shading any model of knowledge. As an intercultural knowledge, the text of *Dieu d'eau*, jointly produced by Griaule and Ogotemmêli, illustrates the impossibility of knowing another epistemological structure, as other, from within one's own. Through the interactions of Griaule and

Ogotemmêli, their respective structures necessarily become, depending on one's point of view, either hopelessly contaminated with each other, or intricately woven together in a fabric more than the sum of its threads. In the following analysis, I tease out five of the threads in order to draw some conclusions about interdisciplinary boundaries, desire, and knowledge.

A COMPOSITE, INTERCULTURAL MODEL OF KNOWLEDGE

(1) Griaule's desire to find an Other knowledge places him in a contradiction. He conceives of it, in spite of his criticisms of Western thought, according to the Western model of a hidden object, that must be "unveiled" or whose hiding place must be "penetrated." At one point, Griaule interjects his long-held belief that the key to Dogon institutions had been guarded in "enigmas" and "mysteries." These lay in "un haut-lieu central" (central point) that "apparaissait tantôt comme un roc impénétrable, tantôt comme un brouillard sans consistance. . . . Ogotemmêli avait accompli le miracle de *dévoiler* ce centre prestigieux auquel tout se rattachait" (DE, 158. Emphasis added) (appeared at times like an inaccessible rock, at times like an insubstantial mist. . . . Ogotemmêli had performed the miracle of unveiling this famous central point to which everything was linked) (CO, 148). Griaule's reflection intervenes precisely at the point that Ogotemmêli fits into the system Dogon beliefs and taboos on femininity, clitoral excision, and menstrual blood.

Feminist psychoanalytic critics have analyzed the phallocentric mixture of knowledge and sexual desire epitomized in the structure of the enigma through readings of Freud's "Femininity." He theorizes femininity as a "riddle" (Freud, 100) which, he claims, can be solved only by male scholars. Hélène Cixous, Luce Irigaray, and Teresa de Lauretis, among others, have argued that Freud's theory of the feminine enigma allegorizes a foundational structure of Western thought and subjectivity. In this structure, to solve the riddle of woman is to unveil the central truth of being. The phallocentric foundations of Griaule's and Ogotemmêli's epistemologies are structurally very different from each other, but enable their intertwining in the text.

(2) Ogotemmêli obliges Griaule's desire for a hidden object of knowledge by staging its unveiling with deliberate, exaggerated drama. Ogotemmêli builds up the suspense with long delays, pauses, silences, and hesitations, all necessary, according to him, to guard "les conversations entre hommes mûrs" from "l'inconcevable curiosité des femmes" (DE, 21) (conversations between men of mature years (from) the un-

conscionable curiosity of women) (CO, 13). He supplies Griaule's quest to penetrate the enigma as feminine object with all the male homosocial trappings necessary.

Yet, at the same time, Ogotemmêli makes it clear that in his epistemology the veil does not hide a preexisting object of knowledge, but rather produces its object. He explains this when he talks about how modern clothing, as a constant reliving of its mythic origin, fuses desire and knowledge:

> "Le pagne est serré," dit-il, "pour qu'on ne voie pas le sexe de la femme. Mais il donne à tous l'envie de voir ce qui est dessous. C'est à cause de la parole que le Nommo a mise dans le tissu. Cette parole est le secret de chaque femme et c'est cela qui attire l'homme. Il faut qu'une femme ait des parties secrètes pour qu'on les désire. Une femme qui se promènerait nue au marché, personne ne courrait derrière elle. . . ." (DE, 91)

> ("The loin-cloth is tight," he said, "(so that one does not see) the woman's sex, but it stimulates a desire to see what is underneath. This is because of the Word, which the Nommo put into the fabric. That word is every woman's secret, and is what attracts the man. A woman must have secret parts to inspire desire. If she went about in the market with nothing on, no one would run after her. . . .") (CO, 82. Words in parentheses my translation.)

The very resemblance of Ogotemmêli's theory to Judeo-Christian desire/knowledge turns the latter inside out by foregrounding the causal mechanisms that it denies. The enigma is not an essence inherent to woman as Other. Rather, clothing confers it upon her as it makes her into a cultural subject.

In explaining the mechanism of desire as a cultural product, Ogotemmêli explains the mechanism of knowledge as well. Griaule does not seem to recognize that Ogotemmêli's theory of sexual desire describes the very knowledge of the "haut-lieu" (central point) Griaule seeks from him. It is not the content of the mysteries in the "centre prestigieux" (famous central point) that makes them into valuable knowledge, but rather the secretiveness itself. As with any initiatory knowledge, its value lies in the fact that only the initiates know it.

(3) In addition to dismantling the Western model of knowledge as unveiling an enigma, even as he plays upon it, Ogotemmêli also offers Griaule an alternative model of knowledge, embodied in weaving. By joining spiritual and material forces in the process of instruction, weaving explicitly critiques, as we have seen, knowledge as aggressive sexual conquest.

(4) Yet in another layer of contradiction, Griaule, as we have also seen, accepts this knowledge and this critique, and even uses it to criticize Cartesian thought.

(5) The final possible contradiction concerns not Griaule, as he is caught between two cultures, but Ogotemmêli. Both the initiatory knowledge and the model of practical instruction, as Ogotemmêli presents them to Griaule, are necessarily traditional forms of knowledge. They must, as Ogotemmêli says, be inherited from the ancestral spirits and passed from generation to generation in order to count as knowledge. Yet, according to van Beek and many of his respondents, the "système du monde" that Ogotemmêli articulates is, at least in some part, his own creation. Mary Douglas, one of the respondents, says: "Who can read *Dieu d'eau* and not recognize it for the individual ratiocinations of a brilliant, thoughtful Dogon conversing with an eager, unsophisticated museum curator?" (van Beek, 161).[4]

Yet this contradiction may be only apparent, the product of another Cartesian misunderstanding. Theorists of traditional African art, such as Abdou Sylla (1988), and of traditional oral literature, such as Isidore Okpewho (1992), argue that artistic practice based on inheriting and transmitting traditional stories or art objects does not preclude creative originality. They break down the dichotomy between a Western individual creativity and an African transmission from generation to generation. They also show that African artists can conceive their originality in terms not recognizable to Cartesian individualism.

As with cross-cultural conceptions of art and literature, so with cross-cultural practices of ethnographic knowledge. Could the old, blind Dogon wise man, through his years of meditation, have received his information from the "Word" of spirits and therefore be said to have "inherited" rather than "created" it? In a culture that structures knowledge as reception rather than as aggressive possession of an object, this is possible. Yet a Cartesian or Hegelian frame of reference makes it difficult for us to conceive.

All the above contradictions illustrate various ways in which the search for other models of knowledge leads to the impossibility of knowing them as detached objects. Rather than unearthing an unmediated object hidden in the depths, what van Beek calls "fact" as opposed to fiction, Griaule found complex webs of mediation. One was the network of symbolic correspondences organized by the "Word" and its "world-system." The other was the intense relation between himself and Ogotemmêli that itself produced his findings. Without such an intense relation, Ogotemmêli would not have revealed to him the secret knowledge, but the two men could not have developed such a relation without Ogotemmêli having gained Western knowledge from Griaule through years of working with him and his ethnographic team. Griaule found, in many ways, the means of symbolic mediation itself, of which he himself was an integral part.

THE PLEASURES AND ANXIETIES OF INTERDISCIPLINARY RESEARCH

From my own point of view, finding through *Dieu d'eau* this role of clothing in the production of knowledge in some ways assuaged and in some ways intensified my many worries about a research project on the global circulation of African fashion. Did the subject matter of fashion still appear too superficial, and did my field work still reproduce too sharply the oppressor/oppressed relations of postcolonialism? Further textual readings of Griaule's field work account in relation to my novice attempt deepened without resolving these questions.

In keeping with the contradictions of the *Dieu d'eau*, when Ogotemmêli adds his concluding correspondences to his system, Griaule says: "Il n'était pas possible de pénétrer plus à fond cette pensée millénaire" (DE, 218) (It was not possible to penetrate more deeply this millennial thought). Griaule here speaks in terms of a hidden depth, when Ogotemmêli is emphasizing the development of a thought system as a surface infinitely extending its correspondences. He is showing how the ancestors determined that the system would be fulfilled through commercial exchange as a way to continually produce equality between people and so re-balance the "système du monde." In his account, commercial exchange in Dogon culture also weaves all the elements and levels of the system into more intricate connection because the "Word" is activated by the human exchangers who, like weavers and wearers of clothing, revivify the actions of the first ancestors.

Exchange as human communication thus integrates on many levels the network of correspondences:

> "La parole est pour tous. Pour cela il faut échanger, donner et recevoir. . . .
>
> Le Nommo a dit que lorsqu'on offre des cauris pour acheter une marchandise, le vendeur meurt s'il refuse. C'était pour obliger à échanger. De même que la bande d'étoffe s'allonge pendant le tissage, de même que la culture s'étend sous le fer du paysan, de même les cauris doivent circuler.

Les cauris portent en eux-mêmes la force de cette loi et cette force agit sur celle des marchandises comme sur celle de l'homme. . . . Leur force entre dans celle de l'homme et augmente son désir de commerce." (DE, 218)

("The Word is for all. Therefore it is necessary to exchange—to give and to receive. . . .

The Nummo said that, when someone offers cowries for goods, the vendor dies if he refuses them. That was to compel him to exchange. Just as the strip of stuff gets longer and longer in the process of weaving, and cultivation spreads under the tool of the cultivator, so cowries ought to circulate.

The force of this law is inherent in the cowries themselves, and it acts equally on the goods and on man. . . . Their force enters into him and stimulates his desire to trade") (CO, 204–205)

Through this analogy with weaving, the archetypical form of transmitting knowledge, Ogotemmêli makes commercial exchange into a form of knowledge transmission, especially by endowing it with the same kind of desire cloth possesses. (Cloth is the first and archetypical object of exchange.) Knowledge, inseparable from desire, becomes inseparable from interpersonal economic exchange. There is thus no hidden object of knowledge because the object of knowledge always changes, renews, and expands as exchanges between people add new correspondences. Neither does there exist, consequently, culture seized as empirical fact separate from a "created culture" since the exchangers are perpetually creating culture. The "système du monde" never stops producing new connections. Says Ogotemmêli: "Il y a entre les hommes un échange continu, un mouvement incessant de flux invisibles. Et il est necéssaire qu'il en soit ainsi pour que dure l'ordre universel" (DE, 148) (A perpetual exchange goes on between men, an unceasing movement of invisible currents. And this must be so if the universal order is to endure) (CO, 137).

The Dogon marketplace of Ogotemmêli's account, so aesthetically and ethically satisfying, bears a striking lack of resemblance to the marketplace of today's economic "world-system" (Hopkins, Wallerstein et al. 1996) in whose shadow African fashion is exchanged. This world-system seems rather the nightmare inversion of Ogotemmêli's "universal order," precariously teetering in imbalance: imbalance between powerful corporations and the struggling microenterprises of third world craftspeople, between well-off consumers in so-called developed nations and producer-vendors deprived of necessities in so-called developing nations, between the wasteful, polluting overproduction of mass-consumer commodities and the toxic dumping in Third World countries it produces.

Needless to say, in my study of African fashion circulation, North American researcher and African informants occupy unequal locations within this un-balance, and the exchanges between them partake of and contribute to this contemporary cosmology in manifold and ambiguous ways. But these exchanges have become part by necessity of the study that attempts to trace, through the informal commerce circuits of African fashion, the interpersonal symbolic "correspondences" that produce today's "world-system." The very informality of the circuits among exchangers of African fashion, their very marginality to circuits of corporate capitalism provide both insights into otherwise unrecognized imbalances in today's world and also glimpses of a possible alternative balance.

Notes

1. For essays on this research, see Rabine 1997a; Rabine 1997b; Rabine 1998, and the in-progress book manuscript *The Global Suitcase: African Fashion in Transnational Circuit.*

2. In *Subjects of Desire* (1975), Judith Butler discusses the problem of desire and philosophy in the works of Hegel and post-Hegelian philosophers.

3. Unless otherwise indicated in parentheses after the translated quotation, translations are mine.

4. In an earlier piece (If the Dogon . . . , 1967), Douglas voices no such views but rather takes *Dieu d'eau* at face value as the foundation upon which to build an argument about the difference between French and English ethnographic method.

Works Cited

Babcock, Barbara A. "'Not in the Absolute Singular': Rereading Ruth Benedict." *Women Writing Culture.* Ed. Ruth Behar and Deborah Gordon. Berkeley, Los Angeles, London: U of California P: 1995, 104–130.

Behar, Ruth, and Deborah Gordon, eds. *Women Writing Culture.* Berkeley, Los Angeles, London: U of California P, 1995.

Butler, Judith P. *Subjects of Desire: Hegelian Reflections in Twentieth-Century France.* New York: Columbia UP, 1987.

Cixous, Hélène. *La jeune née.* Paris: 10/18, 1975.

Clifford, James. *The Predicament of Culture: Twentieth-Century Ethnography, Literature, and Art.* Cambridge: Harvard UP, 1988.

Clifford, James, and George E. Marcus, eds. *Writing Culture: The Poetics and Politics of Ethnography.* Berkeley: U of California P, 1986.

de Lauretis, Teresa. "Desire in Narrative." *Alice Doesn't: Feminism, Semiotics, Cinema.* Bloomington: Indiana UP, 1984.

Douglas, Mary. "If the Dogon. . . ." *Cahiers d'études africaines* 28 (1967): 659–672.

Freud, Sigmund. "Femininity." *New Introductory Lectures on Psychoanalysis.* Translated by James Strachey. New York: Norton 1965 (originally 1933), 99–119.

Griaule, Marcel. *Marcel Griaule, Conseiller de l'union française.* Paris: Nouvelles Editions latines, 1957.

———. *Masques dogons.* Paris: Institut d'ethnologie, 1963 (originally 1938).

———. *Conversations with Ogotemmêli.* Translated by R.Butler and A. Richards. London: Oxford UP, 1965.

———. *Descente du troisième verbe.* Paris: Fata Morgana, 1996 (originally 1947).

———. *Dieu d'eau: Entretiens avec Ogotemmêli.* Paris: Fayard, 1966 (originally 1948).

Griaule, Marcel, and Germaine Dieterlen. *Le Renard Pâle.* Vol. I. Paris: Institut d'Ethnologie, 1965.

Hopkins, Terence K., Immanuel Wallerstein et al. eds. *The Age of Transition: Trajectory of the World-System, 1945–2025.* London: Zed Books, 1996.

Irigaray, Luce. "La Tache aveugle d'un vieux rêve de symétrie." *Speculum de l'autre femme.* Paris: Editions de Minuit: 1974, 9–164.

Kenyatta, Jomo. *Facing Mount Kenya.* Nairobi: Kenway, 1987 (originally 1938).

Leclerc, Gérard. *Anthropologie et colonialisme.* Paris: Fayard, 1972.

Mudimbe, V. Y. *The Invention of Africa: Gnosis, Philosophy, and the Order of Knowledge.* Bloomington: Indiana UP, 1988.

Okpewho, Isidore. *African Oral Literature: Backgrounds, Character, and Continuity.* Bloomington: Indiana UP, 1992.

Rabine, Leslie W. "Dressing up in Dakar." *Esprit Créateur* 37 (1997):84–108.

———. "Not a Mere Ornament: Tradition, Modernity, and Colonialism in Kenyan and Western Clothing." *Fashion Theory: Journal of Dress, Body, and Culture* 1(1997):145–168.

———. "Scraps of Culture: African Style in the African American Community of Los Angeles." *Borders, Exiles, and Diasporas.* Ed. Elazar Barkan and Marie-Denise Shelton. Stanford: Stanford UP, 1998.

Sylla, Abdou. *Création et imitation dans l'art africain traditionnel: Éléments d'esthétique.* Dakar: IFAN, 1998.

van Beek, Walter E. A. "Dogon Restudied: A Field Evaluation of the Work of Marcel Griaule." *Current Anthropology* 32 (1991):139–167.

Wolf, Diane L., ed. *Feminist Dilemmas in Fieldwork.* Boulder: Westview Press, 1996.

15

Political Geography of Literature

On Khatibi's "Professional Traveller"

Réda Bensmaïa

One of the recurrent features in Abdelkébir Khatibi's[1] work is his insistence on pointing out the *gap* that exists for Maghrebian writers between the languages they *speak* and the language in which they *write*. In a previous study on *Amour Bilingue*, my aim was to bring to light some of the stakes involved in approaching language as "*bi-langue*," as bi-language,[2] as Khatibi does. In this essay, I would like to show that it is the particular "geopolitical" position occupied by the "*bi-langue*," or bi-langual, writer that conditions his or her specific treatment of history whenever it is conceived as the history of a *people*, a "real" *individual*, or a "fictional" *character*. If Khatibi's work does not really include any "fiction"—with the notable exception, however, of *Un été à Stockholm*—if it is continually divided between various literary regimes (poetry, essay, autobiography), then, some logical conclusions must be drawn: the *bi-langual* writer—who is, for Khatibi, simultaneously a "professional traveller"—is a writer who, living between two languages, two borders, and therefore between different temporalities, can no longer belong to *one* history, *one* people, *one* country, but who belongs instead to a new time-space, which, though it is the product of an artistic creation, cannot be reduced to pure "fiction" or "myth."

My examination of several of Khatibi's texts is meant to show how they are inscribed in an attempt to problematize, and thereby redefine, the traditional borders of national, cultural, and ethnic *belonging* in the wake of a most compelling political reality: the emergence of what some contemporary sociologists call "global ethnoscapes," in other words, those "transnational" spaces of identity that take up an increasingly important place in the politics of old nation-states. My working hypothesis will thus be that Khatibi's concept of the "professional traveller" might possibly mirror the changes that have occurred in the cultural and political life of Third World intellectuals during the past twenty-five years.

We have long been accustomed to thinking (about) literature in ethnic, national, and of course, linguistic terms. Even today, being a teacher in a French department generally entails reciting the names and displaying the works of the "great" French or "Francophone" writers. Very often, teaching a course on francophone literature still involves "smuggling in" a certain number of works that, though written in French, are not French. Now, what seems important to me in Khatibi's work, is that it radically challenges this type of cleavage. As a matter of fact, the criteria that were used to carve out literary nationalities are no longer operative in his work. If writing in French links a writer to a linguistic "community," it does not necessarily subject him or her to an ethnic or national community. It is this insight that has enabled Khatibi to formulate some of the destabilizing questions raised in "Nationalisme et internationalisme littéraires:"

> Quelle est la patrie d'un écrivain? Est-ce uniquement sa langue, l'hospitalité de sa langue d'écriture, qu'elle soit natale ou extra-natale? Est-ce l'unité idéelle entre un terroir, une langue et une identité culturelle d'esprit et du corps? Est-ce la mosaïque d'un exil et d'une transposition universelle?
>
> (Which is the writer's homeland? Is it only his or her language, the hospitality of the language in which he or she writes, whether it be native or non-native? Is it the conceptual unity between a native soil, a language, and an identity of mind and body shaped by the cultivation of that soil? Is it the mosaic of an exile and a universal transposition?) (Khatibi, "Nationalisme," 206)

For Kathibi, the writer's "homeland" does not refer to a given land, native soil, or culture, but rather, as evidenced by the context from which this quote was taken, to a *circulation*—indeed a migration—between lands, languages, and cultures. But what becomes of the "nation," then? Does the writer even have a Nation? Here too Khatibi's response is very clear and incisive. In *Francophonie et idiomes littéraires*, a text that has not yet received the attention it deserves,[3] he states: "On dit souvent que la nation de l'écrivain est la langue. Y aurait-t-il donc, au delà des variétés idiomatiques de la francophonie, une nation littéraire, ou plutôt, une trans-nation qui serait le coeur même de la francophonie?" (It is often said that language is the writer's nation. Could there possibly be, beyond the linguistic diversity of the francophone world, a literary nation or, rather, a *trans-nation* that would be the very heart of the francophone world?) (Khatibi, *Francophonie*).

Khatibi's recourse, or return to the idea of (the) nation could have been operative had the idea of nation itself not become pluralized and problematic. But as he points out, "Toute nation est, en son principe, une pluralité, une mosaïque de cultures, sinon une pluralité de langues et de généalogies fondatrices, soit par le texte, soit par le récit vocal, ou les deux à la fois" (Every nation is fundamentally plural, it is a mosaic of cultures, if not a plurality of languages and of genealogies founded either through the text or the oral narrative, or through both at the same time) (Khatibi, "Nationalisme," 209). So the question must be raised anew, for as Khatibi carefully explains, the "plurality" at issue here "is never in a relation of real equality," but rather "in a relation of hierarchy and dissymmetry" (209):

> En son principe, la fonction de l'Etat est de gérer—avec pertinence ou sans—cette dissymétrie dont il est un principe paradoxal. Bien. *Mais qu'est-ce qu'une nation littéraire?* On peut rêver à une nation littéraire qui respecterait la pluralité et l'art de la dissymétrie. Une nation dont chaque composante aurait son lieu d'émission et de réception dans le langage comme une force active et affirmative dans l'ensemble de la nation et de *l'internation*.
>
> Mais vous imaginez que le respect de cette pluralité est plutôt discret, fragmentaire, *sinon absent.* Ce respect appartient à *l'utopie d'une cité idéale*, une cosmopolis.
>
> (In its very principle, the function of the state is to manage—judiciously or not—this dissymmetry, of which the state itself is a paradoxical principle. Fine. *But what is a literary nation?* We can dream of a literary nation that would respect plurality and the art of dissymmetry, a nation in which each component had language as its place of production and reception like an active and affirmative force within the whole nation and *internation*.
>
> But you can well imagine that respect for this plurality is rather restrained and fragmentary, *if not absent.* Respect for plurality belongs to *the utopia of an ideal city*, a cosmopolis.) (Khatibi, "Nationalisme," 209)

If I find this passage worth quoting at length, it is because it high-lights the kind of impossibilities and contradictions Khatibi patiently uncovered before putting forward his own positions on the questions of homeland, nation, culture, and national identities. As vividly illus-trated here, Khatibi is fully aware of some of the theoretical and political dead ends convulsing the contemporary world when he starts reflecting on the notion of the "professional foreigner." In fact, the concept is being developed at a time in history, in our history, when the "defensive"—or more accurately perhaps "reactive"—principle of the Nation—a timorous nation in search of its one and indivisible identity—can no longer play the role and function still assigned to it not so long ago. Faced with the convulsions that are shaking the Maghreb and the larger Europe—I'll get back to this point shortly; faced with the globalization of trade and modern technologies, the writer must devise new tactics to address questions of language or ethnicity; develop a new position on problems of identity (his own, as well as that of his readership); and adopt a strategy that is no longer defensive, but flexible and active, "adapted," Khatibi says, "to a double principle: *respect for linguistic diversity* and *"pluralized" (multipolar) universality. Gone is the illusion of a center, of an ethnocenter*, seen as the generating principle of a French civilization integrated around a territory, a State and an ideology" (Khatibi, *Francophonie*, emphasis is mine). But having gone that far, questions still remain open and have to be raised again:

> [Q]u'est-ce que l'exotisme? La nation et l'internation littéraire? Le cosmopolitanisme? Ecrire? Ecrire sur l'étranger? L'étrangère? Le se-cret à partager? Lui? Elle? Le tout-étranger? Que faites-vous de la francophonie? De la littérature maghrébine? Belge? Canadienne? Suisse? Où se trouve le continent noir? La négritude? Où se trouvent sur cette planète les Français-Français?

> (What is exoticism? The literary nation and internation? What about cosmopolitanism? Writing? Writing about the foreigner, male and female? The secret to be shared? Him? Her? The all-foreign? What do you do with the francophone world? With Magrebian literature? Belgian? Canadian? Swiss? Where is the black continent? Négritude? Where are the French-French on this planet?) (Khatibi, *Francophonie*)

Whichever way the problem is looked at, what confronts us is an extraordinary disintegration of the idea of "center" as well as a mixture of languages, peoples, and identities. The difficulty in locating a "cen-ter"—or an "ethno-center" even—makes the recourse to the classical concepts of race, culture, and nation completely obsolete and ineffec-tive. People, nation, public, language, foreigner, border—these are all concepts that no longer function without further ado. On the contrary, everything seems to indicate that they must be revised, or that other concepts must be created in order to account for a radically new situation. We are no longer dealing with "peoples," or even with distinct "minorities," but with diasporas—the francophone diaspora(s), as some put it. The formula is attractive because it seems to bring a solution to the problem raised here. But we should be wary of latching on to it too fast: when referring to Maghrebians, for instance, the term "diaspora" takes on quite a different political and philosophical meaning than the one it has in "Jewish diaspora." In the second case, the central idea is that of the presence, in a "foreign" land, of a people from elsewhere who create, in exile, an extraterritorial and cultural community.[4] In the first, by contrast, diaspora becomes transnational rather than national and "non seulement parce qu'elle joue entre plusieurs états nationaux, ce qui se produit aussi pour les immigrations anciennes, mais que la référence ethnicitaire n'est plus nationale" (not only because it plays out among several national states, which also occurred with former immigrations, but because *the ethnic reference is no longer national*) (Galissot, 122).

In the Maghreb, there are Moroccans, Algerians, and Tunisians, but also Arabs, Berbers, Tuaregs, and M'zabites; but in Europe, there will be "Maghrebians," just as there were "North Africans" in France yesterday, and just as there are men and women who call themselves "Maghrebians of France" or "Beurs" today in order to mark out a double distance: a distance with respect to French nationalism or racism, but also a distance with respect to the nationalisms of the Maghrebian states—which return the feeling by playing the card of Islamic fundamentalism or Arabic Islamism.[5] René Galissot's comments on these developments are particularly relevant for the point I'm trying to make:

> L'identification comme "maghrébins" n'est pas seulement un refus d'allégeance au nationalisme d'état, mais aussi échappée à l'assignation identitaire d'Arabes et plus encore de Musulmans, et par là la marque de détachement des normes communautaires par l'ostentation d'une identité nouvelle, l'invention d'une culture en diaspora,
>
> (To identify oneself as a "Maghrebian" is not only to refuse to pledge allegiance to state nationalism, but also to contravene the attribution of an Arab identity, and even more so, of a Muslim identity. Through and beyond that, it is also a sign of distanciation from community norms by the ostentation of a new identity, the invention of a new diaspora culture.) (Galissot, 122)

These remarks bring us back to Khatibi's notion of "cultural pluralism," a pluralism that can now be better situated historically, sociologically, and politically, and indeed characterized as a "radical questioning of any type of *genealogical identification*":[6] what used to hold together nationality and citizenship, race and culture, people or local community and specific individual identity has disintegrated. We are no longer dealing with this or that "ethnic group," but with "*métis culturels*," cultural hybrids. In France, for many years the same population has been labelled in turn, as "Kabyles," "Arabs," "North Africans," and now as "Moslems." Today, however, it has become obvious, as Galissot puts it, that:

> [C]es identités ne sont que des identifications inscrites dans un champ idéologique d'altercation, assignées mais aussi revendiquées, stigmatisées et emblématiques. Elles discriminent dans la plus grande proximité de précarité et d'exclusion sociale. C'est pour être dans la même misère économique et culturelle, que s'affrontent les bandes qui cognent au nom du nationalisme et de la race sur ceux qui exhibent leur différence, en jouant de l'ethnicité sur le mode racial.
>
> ([T]hese identities are only identifications inscribed within an ideological field of altercation, [that they are] assigned but also claimed, stigmatized and emblematic. They function as discriminating signs where precarity and social exclusion co-exist in close proximity. Those who use ethnicity on the racial mode and beat up, in the name of nationalism and race, those who flaunt their difference, do so because they suffer the same cultural and economic poverty.) (Galissot, 125)

Galissot notes elsewhere in the same text that today, there are no longer "dangerous classes," but "dangerous ethnic groups," gangs, young people, workers, and intellectuals, who are dangerous because of a difference attributed to another "origin." These dangerous ethnic groups are precisely the "cultural hybrids" mentioned above, the "mixed" populations—Maghrebians, *Beurs*—who can no longer be isolated in ghettoes and who are increasingly, and more and more openly, exhibiting signs of identity so as to better mark out their radical distancing from the dominant French symbolic system and from the nationalisms of their countries of origin. But another change must also be noted. Whereas in the nineteenth century, these "hybrids" could only be found in the intelligentsia—that is, in a minority culture of outcasts, Jews, and socialists—today, they comprise millions of people who have broken with national stereotypes and characteristics traditionally associated with a given community.

As pointed out by anthropologist Arjun Appadurai, the "land-scape" of group identities—what he calls a "global ethnoscape"—has completely changed in today's world. One thing is certain: these group identities are no longer the familiar anthropological "objects" to which classical anthropology and sociology had accustomed us. As groups, they no longer exhibit the characteristics that made them entities firmly attached to a well-defined territory and/or to a homogeneous culture. What we are witnessing more and more today is a generalized process of "deterritorialization," evidenced by the transnational movements of large corporations and financial markets of course, but also by the movements of ethnic groups, cults, and political and religious formations. But this deterritorialization obviously does not stop there, it also involves the displacement of entire populations from one country to another. Deterritorialization provides cheap labor to rich societies while impoverishing the countries from which such labor is uprooted and as such it has affected Hindus and Sikhs in India, Palestinians in Israel, Ukrainians in Russia, Maghrebians or Africans in France, Belgium, and increasingly Spain and Italy, and, recently, a new wave of Haitians and Cubans in the United States. It has led to the creation of "pockets" of internal resistance against "imperialism," and to its counterpart, the "fundamentalist" or "nation-alist" reaction in these populations' countries of origin.

In the area of communications, the "globalization" discussed above has played a determining role in the emergence of planetary communications systems in both advertising and television, with the creation of multinational corporations in Europe, Japan, and the United States, and, not too long ago, such famous megamergers as those of Time and Warner, or more recently, of Viacom and Paramount.[7]

The transition from the "international" to the "global" has occurred so rapidly that it has masked a phenomenon that has not failed to attract the attention of theoreticians of economic geography and communications. I have already referred to Appadurai's work, and would like to briefly discuss Armand Mattelart's analysis now. In an article entitled "Comment résister à la colonisation des esprits?" Mattelart demonstrates that what we are witnessing today is not so much a simple "massification," as a contradiction between two logics—the logic of globalization and that of a generalized demassification. One of the consequences of this phenomenon is the creation of "transnational segments," that is, large groupings of individuals sharing, *beyond their national borders,* the same conditions of outlook, the same systems of values, priorities, tastes, and norms, in short, similar "sociocultural mentalities." In this sense, "globalization and localization" become two facets of the same phenomenon, as Mattelart also points out:

> Depuis le début des années 80, la dynamique de la globalisation a déclenché un autre mouvement antagoniste, la revanche des cultures singulières. La tension entre, d'une part, la pluralité des cultures, et, d'autre part, les forces centrifuges de l'universalisme marchand a révélé la complexité des réactions contre l'émergence d'un marché planétaire.

> (Since the beginning of the 1980s, the dynamic of globalization has sparked an antagonistic movement—the revenge of singular cultures. The tension between the plurality of cultures, on the one hand, and the centrifugal forces of market universalism, on the other, have revealed the complexity of reactions against the emergence of a global market.) (Mattelart, *Le Monde diplomatique*)

As the "world-system" was unfolding, linking various societies with products and networks operating on the "global" scale, culture itself was experiencing the impact of transnationalization. Meanwhile, civil societies were opposing their own responses to the project of reorganizing social life by drawing from local cultural traditions, with new methods of communication speeding up the process. As we know, these responses have sometimes taken "the form of resistance, reversals, parodies, adaptations and reappropriations," and sometimes "une très forte nostalgie des différences et des mécanismes de différenciation. Partout, on assiste à un retour aux cultures particulières, à la tradition, au territoire, aux valeurs singulières, [ou] à une renaissance des nationalismes et des fondamentalismes" (of a very strong nostalgia for differences and mechanisms of differentiation. We are witnessing a widespread return to specific cultures, to tradition, territory and singular values, [or] to a rebirth of nationalism and fundamentalism) (Mattelard, *Le Monde diplomatique*).

This convoluted "dialectic" has led nongovernmental organizations (the "Greens" and the Associations for the Rights of Man, Woman and Democracy) to the project of creating what Mattelart calls a "third space," a space "qui viendrait s'intercaler entre les logiques inter-marchés et les logiques inter-étatiques, médiatisant le pragmatisme marchand et la Realpolitik du prince" (that would insert itself between intermarket logics and interstate logics, and thereby serve as a mediation between market pragmatism and the *Realpolitik* of the prince).

It seems to me that it is in such an international and/or global sociopolitical context that we must understand Khatibi's reflections in his essays on the Maghreb and the Gulf War and in his "novel" *Un été à Stockholm.* When he coins the concept of the "professional traveller" Khatibi reveals a clear understanding of these changes and upheavals, and particularly of the impact of internationalization on the cultural sector—new markets for the large film studios, international travel agencies, television, and, recently, the new information superhighways— as well as on the "formation" of these new ethnoscapes: while American families from Key West are relocated to the mainland to make way for Cuban refugees; Algerians pirate French television using dish antennas; the Beurs become intoxicated with American rap music; and young African Americans are initiated into Algerian raï music. In that context, it is particularly significant to see Khatibi raise the following questions:

> Pourquoi établir une distinction entre *littérature* et *paralittérature?* Parce que la paralittérature n'est pas soutenue par un secret et une force d'écriture. C'est une reproduction monumentale (pastiches, imitations, parodies, simulations), reproduction déterminée par le marché du livre, la circulation médiatique, l'échange commercial. La paralittérature est cette circulation entropique des mots dans une économie d'objets interchangeables. Economie où l'écriture n'a plus de lieu propre.

> (Why is it necessary to make a distinction between *literature* and *paraliterature?* Because paraliterature is not supported by a secret or a force of writing. It is a monumental reproduction (pastiches, imitations, parodies, simulations) determined by the market for books, media circulation, and trade. Paraliterature is this entropic circulation of words in an economy of interchangeable objects. *An economy in which writing no longer has its proper place.*)
> ("Nationalisme," 211; emphasis is mine)

I believe that it is this sort of *disappropriation* of a "proper place" for the nomadic *écriture* of the Maghrebian writer that perhaps best explains the need to introduce the paradoxical "figure" of the "professional traveller" as well as the means and goals attached to it. Let me say a few words about the means first. They include, for a start—and in an effort to open up to plurality and differences—a new relation to language, languages, and to writing, which Khatibi calls the "laws of hospitality in language:"

> Si l'écriture est exploration de l'inconnu et quel qu'il soit (natal ou extra-natal, naturel et surnaturel, culturel, interculturel et transculturel), si écrire, c'est donner forme à la force de vie, de mort et de survie, il convient d'accueillir l'autre (écrivant, parlant, aimant) dans sa capacité de parcourir les différences (de sexe, de langue, de culture, d'imaginaire).

(If writing is the exploration of the unknown, whatever it may be—
native or non-native, natural or supernatural, cultural, intercultural
or transcultural—if the purpose of writing is to give shape to the
forces of life, death, and survival, it is appropriate to welcome the
Other [writing, speaking, loving] for his or her ability to traverse
differences [of gender, language, culture and imaginary].)
("Nationalisme," 206)

But these means also involve a new relation to identity (ethnic *and*
cultural). For Khatibi identity no longer refers to an onto-logic of the
"One," the "I," or even the "We," but either to a paradoxical logic of
the "Third Term"—similar to Roland Barthes's logic of the "*Neutre*,"[8] or
Michel Serres's logic of the "*Tiers-Instruit*"[9]—or to a relational logic, a
logic in which relations takes precedence over binary oppositions:

> Oui, un étranger est toujours étranger pour l'autre, mais ENTRE
> EUX, il y a le TOUT-AUTRE, le TROISIEME TERME, la RELATION
> qui les maintient dans leur singularité qui est d'une manière ou
> d'une autre, INTRADUISIBLE.

> (Yes, a foreigner is always foreign for the Other, but BETWEEN
> THEM, there is the COMPLETELY-OTHER, the THIRD TERM, the
> RELATION that maintains them in their singularity which is, in one
> way or another, UNTRANSLATABLE.) ("Nationalisme," 204)

These comments bring us closer to understanding what may have
determined the creation of the main character in *Un été à Stockholm*.
I am referring to Gérard Namir, who is, as you might have guessed, a
professional *translator*, but also a character created around three cultural traits, as Khatibi explains:

> En arabe et en berbère, Namir signifie: tigre, panthère. Le référent
> berbère renvoie à la légende de Hammou ou Namir, connue surtout
> au Maroc. Conte où l'on voit le jeune héros, amoureux d'une fée
> angélique qu'il rendit enceinte, la poursuivre entre ciel et terre. On
> connaît le nom de Namir sous d'autres appellations: "Agnaou"
> (Guinée) qui veut dire en fait "L'HOMME AU LANGUAGE
> ININTELLIGIBLE autrement dit *l'étranger*.

> (In Arabic and Berber, Namir means tiger or panther. The Berber
> referent alludes to the legend of Hammou or Namir, a legend best
> known in Morocco. In this tale, the young hero falls in love with
> an angelic fairy, makes her pregnant, then pursues her between
> heaven and earth. Namir is also known by other names: in Guinea
> he is called Agnaou, which actually means "THE MAN WHO SPEAKS
> UNINTELLIGIBLY"—in other words, the foreigner.) (Khatibi, *Un été
> à Stockholm*, 9–10)

And also:

> Je fixai des yeux cet horizon, sa mobilité. Je le fis, je crois, avec
> un grand calme. Dois-je attribuer ce calme à mon métier? Ne suis-
> je pas un voyageur professionnel qui veut traverser les frontières
> avec une souplesse d'esprit? Souplesse qui ne m'est pas toujours
> accordée à chaque changement de climat, de pays, de langue, et,
> comment dire, à chaque croisement de regards et de paroles.

> (I stared at the horizon, at its mobility. I believe I did so with
> great calm. Should I attribute this calm to my profession? Am I
> not a professional traveller who wants to cross borders with an
> openness of mind? An openness which is not always granted to
> me with each change of climate, country, language and, how
> shall I describe it, with each exchange of looks and words.) (*Un
> été à Stockholm*, 9–10)

Leaving. Going out. Letting oneself be seduced. Becoming several
people, becoming someone else (with the others), becoming, braving the
outside world, branching off elsewhere, forming a rhizome with others,
discovering oneself as a foreigner, forging a new identity. These are
some of the peculiarities, some of the forms of alterity and exposure
encountered by the "professional traveller," who must be a "simultaneous" translator, because he knows there is no learning without exposure, without encounter with the Other, and without loss too. He will
never have to know *in advance* who he is, where he is, where he comes
from, where he is going, where he will have to pass through. All this
is of little importance to him because what he desires above all is to
expose himself (to the Other), to expose himself to his own peculiarities
and to the foreigners that are within him. What he wants is to become
(the Other, a foreigner, a foreigner more foreign than the foreigner); in
a word, to become (with the others, not like the others). Doing away
with gregariousness, such is his work, his passion, and his secret:

> Je pensai un moment à mon travail. Une vie, toute une partie de
> ma vie à voyager! Comment revenir auprès de moi? Me recentrer
> sans perdre mes points d'équilibre? Je conçois ma naissance au
> monde en une vitesse qui me sépare de plus en plus de mon passé
> en le voilant, me détachant de ma ville natale et de ses racines
> grégaires, presque immobiles au bord d'une large place océanique.
> Ah! Mûrir sans succomber à cette distance.

> (I thought for a while about my work. A life, a large part of my
> life spent travelling! How will I return to myself? How will I recenter
> myself without losing my points of reference? I envision my birth
> in the world with a swiftness that separates me more and more

from my past, that veils my past, pulling me away from my home town and its gregarious roots, almost immobile along the edge of an oceanic spot. Ah, to mature without succumbing to this distance.) (10)

Finally, what will be the *goals*? Because his goal is to "liberate thought from the imaginary" and to free "the imaginary from thought," because the final end of his writing is to record "dissidence" as a "desire to consolidate the life force as a work of art and to explore the unknown in language" (211), the new francophone writer will have to go a step further by transforming himself into a "professional foreigner," that is, into a writer only engaged in writing as an "exercise in cosmopolitan alterity able to traverse differences" (211). And in this sense, the writer is a *"parèdre"* (acolyte) of the philosopher whom Michel Serres speaks about in *Le Tiers-Instruit*: for the "professional foreigner," who has no "method" at his disposal and doesn't search for any, aimless exile remains the only sojourn, the only white page. He neither makes his way nor travels by following a map that would repeat a space already explored; he has chosen to wander. It is true that wandering carries the risk of making errors and losing one's way. But this is the necessary price to pay if one wants the chance to touch the men and women who form the new cultural space he hovers in, a global ethnoscape that has sprung up—as a "third space"—on the ruins of the community-based world of yesteryear and of identity- based nationalism. For the "professional foreigner," or to use Victor Segalen's term, for the *"exote"* (exiled person) Khatibi is, what matters is not the assimilation of other people's mores, races, and nations, but rather "the durability of the pleasure of feeling the Diverse [and, I would add, sharing, and making it felt]." The Other is the *unassimilable* that we must learn to preserve, to protect against a global market whose "logic" is to assimilate the Other. As a bi-langual writer, the "professional traveller," like Hermes, the god of translators, is among those messengers who:

> appartiennent [toujours] à deux mondes parce qu'ils les mettent en communication, tel Hermès, le dieu des traducteurs, volant d'un rivage à l'autre, mais que l'on peut aussi trouver sur terre ou en mer, îles ou chemins; ces tierces places . . . du projet plus intellectuel, savant ou culturel, et d'éthique tolérante, de la tierce instruction, milieu harmonique, fille entre deux rives, de la culture scientifique et du savoir tiré des humanités, de l'érudition experte et du récit artiste, du recueilli et de l'inventé, ensemble conjugués parce qu'en

réalité ne se peut séparer l'unique raison de la science universelle et de la souffrance singulière.

(belong [always] to two worlds because they bring these worlds into contact, flying from one shore to the other, but who can also be found on land or sea, on islands or roads; these *tierces places* (third places) . . . of the more intellectual, scholarly or cultural project, with its tolerant ethics, of *tierce instruction,* an harmonic space, daughter between two shores of scientific culture and knowledge drawn from the humanities, of expert erudition and artistic narration, of transmission and invention, brought together because the unique reason for both universal science and human suffering cannot, in reality, be parted.) (Serres, 245–46)

—Translated by Karen Tucker

Notes

1. This essay was written for the International Colloquium organized by Hédi Bouraoui, Yvette Bénayoun-Szchmidt, and Najib Rédouane at York University on "The passage of French through Moroccan literary, cultural and artistic signs," Toronto, April 20–23, 1994. Thanks to Karen Tucker for translating it into English.

2. See Bensmaïa, "Traduire ou blanchir la langue."

3. The booklet *Francophonie et idiomes littéraires* was published by Al Kalam in Rabat, Morocco, following the general assembly of French-speaking communities on December 11–13, 1989, in Paris. No page numbers are provided in this small volume.

4. See René Galissot, "Pluralisme culturel en Europe."

5. See Galissot, 122.

6. In French: "la mise en cause de toute identification généalogique."

7. On that subject, see Mattelart's "Comment résister à la colonisation des esprits?"—("How Can the Colonization of Minds Be Resisted?").

8. See Barthes, "Les Allégories linguistiques," 127–128.

9. See Serres, "Naissance du tiers," 26–27.

Works Cited

Appadurai, Arjun. "Global Ethnoscapes, Notes and Queries for a Transnational Anthropology." *Recapturing Anthropology: Working in the Present.* ed., Richard Fox. Santa Fé, New Mexico: School of American Research Press, 1991.

Barthes, Roland. *Roland Barthes par Roland Barthes.* Paris: Seuil, 1975.

Bensmaïa, Réda. " 'Traduire' ou 'Blanchir' la langue: *Amour Bilingue* d'Abdelkébir Khatibi." *Imaginaires de l'autre, Khatibi et la mémoire littéraire.* Paris: L'Harmattan, 1987, 133–160.

Galissot, René. "Pluralisme culturel en Europe: Identités nationales et identité européenne. De l'intellectuel métis au métissage culturel de masses." *Information sur les sciences sociales* 31, 11 (1992): 117–127.

Khatibi, Abdelkébir. "Nationalisme et internationalisme littéraires." *Figures de l'étranger dans la littérature française.* Paris: Denoël, 1987: 203-214.

———. *Francophonie et idiomes littéraires.* Rabat, Morocco: Al Kalam, 1989.

———. *Un été à Stockholm.* Paris: Flammarion, 1990.

Mattelart Armand. "Comment résister à la colonisation des esprits?" *Le Monde diplomatique,* Avril 1994.

Serres, Michel. *Le Tiers-Instruit.* Paris: François Bourin, 1991.

Contributors

RÉDA BENSMAÏA is Professor of French and Francophone Literature in the French Studies Department and in the Department of Comparative Literature at Brown University. He has published numerous articles on French and Francophone Literature as well as on film theory and contemporary philosophy. He is the author of *The Barthes Effect: Introduction to the Reflective Text*, *The Years of Passage*, and *Alger ou la maladie de la mémoire*, as well as the editor of two volumes on Gilles Deleuze. He is now working on a book entitled Nation of Writers dealing with contemporary North African writers.

ROSS CHAMBERS is the Marvin Felheim Distinguished University Professor of French and Comparative Literature at the University of Michigan, Ann Arbor. His publications include *Story and Situation: Narrative Seduction and the Power of Fiction* and *Room for Maneuver: Reading (the) Oppositional (in) Narrative*.

MICHÈLE DRUON is Professor of French in the Department of Foreign Languages and Literatures at California State University, Fullerton. With primary research interests in the ethics of representation in contemporary critical theory and postmodern thought, she has also published several articles on Marguerite Duras and the problematics of "the deconstruction of the subject."

JEANNE GARANE is Assistant Professor of French at the University of South Carolina, Columbia. She has published on Simone Schwartz-Bart and Maryse Condé.

CILAS KEMEDJIO is Assistant Professor of Francophone Studies in the Department of Modern Languages at the University of Rochester. His publications include essays on Edouard Glissant, Maryse Condé, Mongo Beti, Michel Foucault, Carribean, and African Literatures. His book on

La malédiction de la théorie: Les littératures africaines et antillaises face à l'hégémonie de la théorie is forthcoming.

LAWRENCE D. KRITZMAN is Ted and Helen Geisel Third Century Professor of French and Comparative Literature at Dartmouth College. He is the editor of *Auschwitz and After: Race, Culture and the Jewish Question in France* and the English translation of Pierre Nora's *Realms of Memory: The Construction of the French Past.*

MARIE-PIERRE LE HIR is the Elizabeth M. and William C. Treuhaft Associate Professor of French and Comparative Literature and chair of the department of Modern Languages and Literatures at Case Western Reserve University. A specialist in nineteenth-century literature and culture, she is the author of *Le romantisme aux enchères*, a study of French romantic drama. She is currently working on a book on the discipline of French in the United States.

FRANÇOISE LIONNET teaches French at the University of California at Los Angeles. She is the author of *Autobiographical Voices: Race, Gender, Self-Portraiture* and *Postcolonial Representations: Women, Literature, Identity.* She is also the co-editor of volumes 82 and 83 of *Yale French Studies* on "Post/Colonial Conditions: Exiles, Migrations, Nomadisms" and a special issue of *Signs* on "Postcolonial, Emergent, and Indigenous Feminisms."

JEAN E. PEDERSEN is Associate Professor of History in the Humanities Department at the Eastman School of Music in Rochester, New York. Her book-in-progress, "Legislating the Family: Republican Politics and Culture in France, 1870–1920," explores the intersections between feminist activism, social theater, and republican politics in debates over divorce, paternity suits, abortion, and birth control in the first half of the Third Republic. Her publications include an essay on the relation of Durkheim's social theories to Victorian morality and another dealing with paternity suits and citizenship in France and its colonies.

LESLIE W. RABINE teaches French and African literature and culture at the University of California at Irvine. Her publications includes *Reading the Romantic Heroine: Text, History, Ideology, Feminism, Socialism, and French Romanticism* and *Rebel Daughters: Women and the French Revolution,* as well as numerous articles on Western and African fashion.

Mireille Rosello teaches in the Department of French and Italian and the Comparative Literary Studies Program at Northwestern University. She has recently published *Declining the Stereotype: Ethnicity and Representation in French Cultures* and *Infiltrating Cultures: Power and Identity in Women's Writing*. She is currently working on a book on hospitality, generosity, and their perversions.

Timothy Scheie is an assistant professor of French at the Eastman School of Music in Rochester, New York where he teaches humanities courses and conducts research on performance theory and contemporary theater practice.

Janice Spleth is professor of French and African Literature at the West Virginia University. In 1977–78 she served as a Fullbright Lecturer at the national University of Zaire. In addition to having published numerous articles on African literature, she is the author of *Léopold Sédar Senghor* and *Critical Perspectives on Léopold Sédar Senghor*.

Dana Strand is Professor of French in the Department of Romance Languages at Carleton College in Minnesota. She has published articles on postmodern fiction and a book-length study of the short stories of Colette. Her research interests include theories of gender and representation, film and culture, and postcolonial studies.

Alawa Toumi, originally from Kabylie, Algeria, teaches French and Francophone Studies at Franklin and Marshall College. He has published several articles, including "Le cas Kateb Yacine," and "A la recherche de Kateb Yacine." He is also the author of a play entitled *Madah-Sartre: Le kidnapping, jugement et convers(a/t)ion de Jean-Paul Sartre et de Simone de Beauvoir mise en scène par les islamistes du GIA,"* a rewriting of Peter Weiss's *Marat-Sade*. Published by Marsa Editions, the play has been performed in Paris.

Index

Emotion, 260
Ethics: of consumption, 93; egalitarian, 111; of the ephemeral, 6, 81–98; impartiality in, 7; of knowledge, 103–118; postmodern, 103–118
Ethiopiques (Senghor), 254–257
Ethnography, 105, 149, 276
Exceptionalism, 21
Exoticism, 298
Experience: daily, 135; as expatriates, 253–268; expressions of, 18; island, 155; lived, 7, 9n5, 124, 127–128; ordinary, 130; representations of, 147; social, 18; of social conditions, 136; subjective, 9n5, 124; truth of, 126

Fanon, Frantz, 180, 211, 221, 224, 232n4, 266
Farabé, 5, 72, 73, 74, 75, 76, 77
Fashion. *See* Clothing
Felman, Shoshana, 168, 171
Feminist: theory, 15; views of *Nana* (Zola), 43; writing, 148
Fernandez Retamar, Roberto, 179
Film: avant-garde, 225; camera work in, 229–231; *Chocolat* (Denis), 147, 221–232; function of visibility in, 221–232; *The Lover* (Duras), 233–246; reliance of visual image, 228; spectatorial male look in, 227
Finkielkraut, Alain, 12
Fiske, John, 125
Forbes, Jill, 29, 96
Foucault, Michel, 21, 24, 25, 29, 43, 109, 207
France: African intellectuals in, 253–268; assimilation and, 12; colonial suspicion of, 163; cultural identity in, 12; cultural locations of, 233; cultural superiority in, 254, 256, 258–259, 260; *Declaration of the Rights of Man* and, 12, 13; disillusionment in, 11; expatriates in, 253–268; *fraternité* in, 12; idea of nation in, 11–14; identity crisis

in, 19–21; migration in, 22; myth of national unity and, 3; political locations of, 233; racism in, 8n3, 270n21; relations to colonial past, 147; relations with Africa, 256; singularity of, 3, 17; universalism in, 12, 13
Frankfurt School, 125
Freadman, Anne, 52, 57, 65
French: class status and, 15, 51; creolization of, 72; discipline in United States, 3, 13, 15–23, 52, 100n21, 143; domain of knowledge of, 2; elitism and, 15, 100n21; multiple cultures of, 51; nationhood, 11–14; in North Africa, 69–78; as origin of theorical approaches, 3; redefining, 2; relation to cultural studies, 4; republicanism, 51; universalism, 12, 13
French cultural studies: in American universities, 2, 3, 13, 15–23, 52, 100n21, 143; anthropological model, 16; autonomy in, 16; canonical poetry and, 83–86; canonical texts in, 43–44; commercialization of, 81–83; cultural stereotypes and, 16, 17; defining, 29, 44n1, 44n2; discrete truths in, 3; ethno-cultural model, 3, 22–23; intuitive approach, 16; language-culture nexus of, 4, 5, 49–66; language pedagogy in, 4; memorialist model, 3, 19–21; politics and, 86–92; rap music and, 81–98; in relation to cultural studies, 4; semiotic model, 3, 18; under siege, 24–25; socio-epistemic model, 3, 19; as "strange attractor," 6, 95–98; study of daily life and, 15, 16, 17; traditionalism in, 16
Frow, John, 126, 127, 129, 130, 134, 139n13, 139n14, 140n19
Fundamentalism, 302

Identity *(continued)*
20; national, 2, 11–14, 20, 23,
29, 34, 40, 181, 205, 266, 275–
276; oppressive categories of, 207;
performative, 146, 205–206, 207,
209, 215; positional, 112; postdiscursive notion of, 146; racial,
146, 147, 148, 205, 206, 210,
211, 212, 213, 214, 215, 217,
221, 237; reaffirming, 148; recasting,
207; relational, 112; social, 123;
spaces of, 144, 296; theatrical
performance and, 146; totalized,
23; transnational, 150, 296
Ile de France. *See* Mauritius
Images: African, 264; of colonial
power, 151*n6;* cultural, 179;
hybrid, 175; monolithic, 239;
objectified, 227; refracted, 151*n6;*
sexual, 264; visual, 228; of
"whiteness," 228; of women, 225,
227
Impartiality, 111; utilitarian model of,
112
India, 155, 157, 163, 174, 175
Indochina, 233–246
Injustice, 110, 112
"In memoriam" (Senghor), 258
Interaction: cultural, 64; cultural
circumstance and, 52; genre of,
54; nature of, 59; pragmatics of,
64; presupposition and, 56, 57–
58; semiotic, 234; social, 50, 51,
52, 58, 64, 66; success of, 58
Interdisciplinary studies, 2, 4
Intertextuality, 148; meaning and, 235
Irigaray, Luce, 288

James, C. L. R., 180
Jardine, Lisa, 179
Justice, 13; cognitive, 105, 106, 117,
118; democratic conception of,
117; knowledge and, 106;
possibility of, 106; representational, 107–110, 111, 112; search
for, 110; social, 107; universal
distribution of, 117

Kelly, Michael, 29, 96
Kemedijio, Cilas, 145, 146, 151*n2,*
185–204
Kenyatta, Jomo, 285
Khatibi, Abdélkébir, 71, 144, 150,
295–307
King Daddy Yod, 9*n4*
Knowledge: construction of, 106;
cultural, 104; de-neutralization of,
7, 109, 110; disciplinary division
of, 4; ethnographic, 290; first,
277; as form of governmentality,
109; gendered structure of, 285;
geographical, 156; historico-
cultural, 156; ideological, 109;
impossibility of, 277; intercultural,
149, 287, 288–291; justice and,
106; limits of, 221; linguistic, 53;
local framework, 9*n5*, 104;
objectified, 7; object of, 292;
origin of, 277–286; postmodern
model, 108; practical mode of,
130; pragmatic, 52, 53, 64;
production of, 108, 109, 133,
140*n23,* 149, 156, 276, 281, 291;
of reality, 110; reconsidering, 2;
recycling, 21; redefining, 95; as
sexual conquest, 289; sexuality
and, 281; sociology of, 44*n1;*
structure of, 277; time and, 6, 97;
traditional, 6, 286, 290; transmission of, 292; as unveiling, 278;
unwritten, 192; will to, 124
Kourouma, Ahmadou, 172
Kritzman, Lawrence D., 2, 3, 8, 11–19

"La Belle Dorothée" (Baudelaire), 156,
165–166, 171–172, 174
Lacan, Jacques, 15, 24, 151*n4*
LaCapra, Dominick, 153
La débâcle (Zola), 34, 35, 38
La Kahina, 70, 78*n5*
La Misère du Monde, 135, 136
Lamming, Georges, 179, 180
Lang, Jack, 88, 89
Language: acquisition, 15, 82; of
addiction, 215, 217; ambiguous,

Other, The *(continued)*
of, 148; power over, 108;
productive encounters with, 150;
recognition of, 107; representation
of, 106, 110; right to difference
of, 117; speaking about, 7, 105,
106; speaking for, 7, 23, 103,
105, 106, 116, 117; speaking to,
116; underrepresentation of, 110,
111; valorization of difference of,
105; voice of, 118*n1*, 168
Ozouf, Mona, 21

Paglia, Camille, 24–25
Paraliterature, 303
"Par delà Érôs" (Senghor), 255
Parker, Andrew, 42
Paternalism, 223, 225
Patriarchy, 32, 206, 207, 209, 225,
226
Patrimony: cultural, 15
Pedersen, Jean E., 2, 3–4
Performativity: agency of, 206;
ambivalence of, 209; autonomy
and, 207; destabilization of agency
and, 207; gender and, 207;
identity and, 207, 209, 215; of
racial identity, 205–206; space for,
210; subversive, 206, 212;
textualization of, 217*n6*; theatrical,
146; theorization of, 206
Petrey, Sandy, 6, 9*n4*
Phelan, Peggy, 218*n12*
Pichois, Claude, 174
Poetry: colonial cartographies in,
163–164; Creole culture and,
153–181; cultural studies and,
83–86, 145; gender and, 166,
168; local dialect in, 171;
multiplicity of voices in, 157;
nationalism and, 144, 154;
postcolonial criticism and, 144;
quest motif in, 254–257; rap
music and, 99*n7*, 99*n8;*
rhetorical textures in, 179;
urban, 94, 199; vernacular
language in, 154

"Police" (song), 86, 91, 100*n10*
Politics: of centralization, 51; of
difference, 103, 107, 114,
119*n13;* emancipatory, 180;
French cultural studies and, 86–
92; hegemonic, 127–128;
imperial, 30, 34, 42; literature
and, 88; of locality, 171; municipal, 188; of old nation-states, 296;
of oppression, 148, 244; redefining, 95; of representation, 7, 107,
108; sexual, 30–33
popular, The, 7–8
Portuges, Catherine, 147
Positivism, 20
Postcolonialism, 3, 44*n2*, 233–246
Power: acquisition of, 109; balances of,
151*n2;* centralized, 12; colonial,
145, 222; cultural, 19, 154;
depotentiation of, 116; distribution of, 185, 186, 189; institutionalized, 19, 97; intellectual,
136; interpersonal relations and,
62; in language, 109; legitimating,
225; mediators, 19; political, 189;
of poverty, 240; redistribution of,
145; relations of, 2, 19, 108, 109,
114, 115, 208, 212; representational, 115; rhetorical, 116; sexual,
224; sites of, 191; social systems
and, 19; of spoken word, 145;
structures, 146; symbolic, 139*n17*
Prarond, Ernest, 155, 181*n3*
Presupposition: cultural, 55–59;
generic, 56, 57, 58; propositional,
56, 57, 58; sensitivity to, 55, 56,
57, 59; situational, 55; status of,
56
"Prière aux masques" (Senghor), 265
"Prière de paix" (Senghor), 262
Production: of agency, 168; cognitive,
109; cultural, 93, 111, 118*n9,*
127, 130; of cultural criticism,
104–105; elimination of, 189,
190; of French literature, 164;
informal modes of, 186; of
knowledge, 108, 109, 133,